A NEW KEY

Modern Belgian Art from the Simon Collection

EDITED BY JEFFERY HOWE

McMullen Museum of Art, Boston College

Distributed by the University of Chicago Press

This publication is issued in conjunction with the exhibition *A New Key: Modern Belgian Art from the Simon Collection*, organized by the Charles S. and Isabella V. McMullen Museum of Art, Boston College.

McMullen Museum of Art, Boston College
February 10– July 22, 2007

Curated by Jeffery Howe, *A New Key* was organized by the McMullen Museum of Art, Boston College. The exhibition has been underwritten by Boston College with major support from **SV Life Sciences** and the **Patrons of the McMullen Museum**. This exhibition is also supported by an indemnity from the Federal Council on the Arts and the Humanities.

Library of Congress Control Number: 2006937006 ISBN: 1-892850-12-5

Distributed by the University of Chicago Press

Exhibition Coordination: Naomi Blumberg, Diana Larsen, Gilles Marquenie
Copyediting: Naomi Blumberg
Design: John McCoy

Cover: James Ensor, *From Laughter to Tears*, 1908, oil on canvas, 50.5 x 100 cm
Endpapers: (front) Paul Delvaux, *The Riddle*, 1946, oil on panel, 90 x 120 cm; (back) Emile Claus, *The Mower*, 1905, oil on canvas, 90.5 x 117.5 cm

Contents

Director's Foreword

After attending the opening of our exhibition *Fernand Khnopff: Inner Visions and Landscapes* in Fall 2004, Joan and Eugene Hill, patrons of the Museum's Director's Circle, sent a catalogue to their London friends Henry and Françoise Simon. The Hills then arranged for the Simons, who had been collecting modern Belgian art for over thirty years, to visit the McMullen on their next trip to New England. Professor Jeffery Howe of our Fine Arts Department, an expert on Belgian art, had organized our *Khnopff* exhibition. He and I met with the Simons on their visit, by the end of which all were eager to pursue a scholarly exhibition based on works from their collection.

Scholars recognize the Simon Collection, housed in London and France, as the finest assemblage of modern Belgian art outside Belgium. In 2003-2004, a different and larger selection of works from this collection, which included contemporary abstract art, was shown at the Musée d'Ixelles in Brussels and the Singer Museum in Laren (Netherlands). In 2005-2006, the exhibition traveled to four museums in Japan, the Fuchu Art Museum, Shimonoseki City Art Museum, Sakura City Museum of Art, and the Akita Senshu Museum of Art, under the patronage of the Embassy of the Kingdom of Belgium. The fifty-three works that Howe has chosen for *A New Key* tell the story of Belgian Modernism through six themes, ranging from landscape to interiors and from the impact of the Great War to the carnivalesque. While canonical modernist scholarship centers on Paris, Berlin, Moscow, and New York, this exhibition challenges that canon to reveal how the history of modern art looks different when viewed from the vantage point of the "marginal" center of Belgium; hence the title of the exhibition, *A New Key.*

To pursue this line of inquiry, we gathered a group of professors from the faculty who specialize in the art and culture of northern Europe of the late nineteenth and early twentieth centuries. Their voices determined the selection of works and generated new questions for the exhibition to address. Each of the contributors to the catalogue from various disciplines, Professors Claude Cernuschi (art history), Sura Levine (art history, Hampshire College), Katherine Nahum (art history), John J. Michalczyk (film), and Susan A. Michalczyk (Romance languages and literatures), chose works from the collection around which to chart a new avenue of research for his or her essay. We owe them an enormous debt. In addition, our colleagues Sebastian Bonaiuto and John Houchin revived little-known Belgian music and theatrical productions, respectively, to accompany this exhibition.

Special thanks are due Patrick Derom and Gilles Marquenie of Brussels for their crucial roles in organizing the exhibition. We are grateful also to the Embassy of Belgium in Washington, especially to His Excellency Dominique Struye de Swielande, Ambassador of Belgium in the United States, and to the Consulate of Belgium in New York, especially the Honorables Renilde Loeckx-Drozdiak and Geneviève Verbeek, and Linda Edwards for guidance and support.

The curator's knowledge of the field and wise judgment have informed every aspect of the project; Professor Howe and the museum staff worked tirelessly to achieve this distinguished exhibition and catalogue. Others from across the University have given generously of their time and expertise at various stages. In particular, Diana Larsen designed the exhibition to enhance the themes developed. Naomi Blumberg shouldered the editing and production of the catalogue and exhibition materials and took part in the exhibition's overall organization. In designing this book, exhibition materials, and website John McCoy has captured the aesthetic of Belgian book design from the beginning of the last century. We are also grateful to Rosanne Pellegrini for publicity, and to the members of our Advancement office, especially Catherine Concannon and Mary Lou Crane, who aided our funding efforts.

Such an ambitious project could not have been attempted were it not for the generosity of the McMullen Family and the administration of Boston College. We especially thank president William P. Leahy, S.J., provost Cutberto Garza, vice-provost Patricia DeLeeuw, and dean of arts and sciences Joseph Quinn. Major support was provided by SV Life Sciences and the Patrons of the McMullen Museum, chaired by C. Michael Daley. The Newton College Class of 1956, led by Patricia Dowling, made additional contributions to the exhibition. This exhibition was also supported by an indemnity from the Federal Council on the Arts and the Humanities.

Finally, we wish to thank Henry and Françoise Simon. Their enthusiasm for Belgian modern art, their fine eyes and their unfailing support of scholarly inquiry inspired a new vision of Belgian Modernism. This book celebrates and, we hope, preserves their contribution to an understanding of Modernism in its broadest sense.

Nancy Netzer
Director and Professor of Art History

Preface and Historical Outline

Jeffery Howe

The exhibition, A New Key, Modern Belgian Art from the Simon Collection, provides a rich sampling of the extraordinary accomplishments of Belgian artists in the period 1890-1940. This was the era that defined modernism, and Belgium was touched by artistic breakthroughs and cataclysmic historic upheavals. The works of art in this exhibition tell the story of artistic vision, doubt, and perseverance. Rather than present a chronological sequence of these paintings, it is more revealing to group them into six themes, incorporating the questions of meaning and identity that haunted these artists: (1) Looking Outward: Landscape and Village Scenes, (2) Work and Labor, (3) The View from Within: Interiors and Still life, (4) The Human Dimension: the Figure, (5) The Impact of the First World War, (6) The Fantastic and Carnivalesque.

These themes will be further discussed in my essay, "A New Key: Modernism and National Identity in Belgian Art." Other essays in this catalogue will probe these dimensions of Belgian art. Claude Cernuschi illuminates the parallels between George Minne's works to Freudian psychology, Katherine Nahum in "Ensor's Parrot" investigates the fantastic imagery of the painter from Ostend. The historical origins and relevance of carnival is also explored by Susan A. Michalczyk. John J. Michalczyk discusses the impact of the First World War. The making of this collection is the subject of an essay by Sura Levine.

It should be noted that this collection does not represent a complete survey of modern Belgian art; the works in this exhibition reflect choices made by the collector, and represent a personal view and opportunities in the market. Many of the most important Symbolist artists of the late nineteenth century are not represented. Most significantly for the early twentieth century, this exhibition does not include examples of abstraction and constructivism in the period 1915-40.[1] Despite these gaps, however, the richness of Belgian art in this period is abundantly clear.

This exhibition and catalogue seek to understand Belgium as a place and idea, rooted in history and geography, where issues of political identity and linguistic identity have been particularly challenging. Place names in Belgium can be confusing, as anyone who has driven there can attest. Mons and Bergen are the same town, as are Tournai and Doornik, depending upon whether you are coming from the French or Flemish speaking regions. In the east, where German is also a nationally recognized language, the same city may be referred to as Liège, Luik or Lüttich. In this essay, places will be referred to by local terms, except when there are long-standing English variants. For instance, Ypres is so well known to English speakers, that it would be confusing to call it Ieper, and Bruges is more familiar than Brugge.

Preface and Historical Outline

Historical Overview

The Low Lands enter recorded history at the time of the Roman empire, when Julius Caesar described the Belgae as the bravest (or wildest) of the Celts.[2] Essential lines were already being drawn in those early years. The Germanic, or Frankish population, was separated from the Romanized Celts by a great forest, the Silva Carbonaria, which extended from the Rhine to the North Sea. The Romanized Celts were called "[...] the Wala (old German wealh, foreigner or Celt, as in Welsh), and their language waals, hence the Walloons. This early boundary serves as the basis for the linguistic and cultural division of twentieth century Belgium."[3]

After the breakup of the Carolingian empire in the ninth century, the regions of Flanders and Brabant were ruled by competing dynasties of Counts. Castles were built in Ghent and Antwerp to resist the Vikings, and consolidate local power. The first Count of Flanders was Baldwin I "Iron Arm" (d. 879). With no dominant central authority, cities became the centers for regional identity and developed strong traditions of independence. Manufacturing and trade, particularly of cloth, developed early, and the cities of Ypres, Bruges, and Ghent were among the leading cities of Europe, larger than Paris or London. Guild halls and town halls are more important than palaces in medieval Belgium, as is clearly reflected in the architecture. The region became a buffer zone between the more powerful kingdoms of France and Germany and was occasionally hotly contested, with the participation of English forces. Somewhat greater stability came in the late fourteenth century, when Flanders was joined to Burgundy; this is often identified as the high point of the influence of trading cities, such as Bruges, and coincided with the rise of Flemish painting in artists such as Jan van Eyck, Rogier van der Weyden, and Hans Memling.

The history of Belgium can be confusing, since so many historical events have had an impact on this region. This brief timeline is provided to give the reader an outline of major developments and historical context:

1302 The Battle of the Golden Spurs, Courtrai (Kortrijk). In this critical battle, French aristocratic knights were defeated by Flemish foot soldiers. Flanders remained independent of France, and an increase in the rights of the guilds and middle classes followed. In modern times, this event was seen as a milestone in the struggle for independence of the Flemish speaking population.

1348-49 The Black Death. The Bubonic plague and other plagues recurred several times in the 14th century. Estimates suggest that Flanders lost one-sixth to one-quarter of its population in 1349.[4]

1384-1482 The Burgundian Period.

1384 Flanders and Burgundy were united by Duke Philip the Bold.

1430 Duke Philip the Good (who ruled 1419-67) united Brabant with his other territories.

1467-1477 Charles the Bold ruled; after his death, his daughter Mary inherited the throne. When she married Maximilian of Austria, Belgium fell under Hapsburg control.

1482-1555 The Netherlands were under the control of Holy Roman Emperors. Maximilian of Austria was the first Hapsburg ruler of Belgium; he was succeeded by Charles V, King of Spain, another Hapsburg.

1555-1585 Revolt of the Netherlands. Philip II of Spain ruled the region; his reign was characterized by violent repression of reformation protestants and independent cities. Pieter Bruegel reflected this violence in *The Massacre of the Innocents*. Protestant Holland became a separate republic, while the area that will become Belgium remained under Spanish control.

1568-73 The Duke of Alva was sent to crush the rebellion, causing great suffering in Brussels, Ghent, and Antwerp.

1579-1713 Spanish Netherlands. During this period of Spanish control, Belgium was Catholic, relatively peaceful, and somewhat independent. Pieter Paul Rubens was the major artistic figure.

1713-1794 Austrian Rule.

1794-1814 French Rule—The French rule Belgium as a consequence of the French Revolution, which continues through the Napoleonic era.

1815-1831 The United Kingdom of the Netherlands. After the fall of Napoleon, Belgium was united with the Netherlands to keep it from either French, German, or English control.

1830 Revolt against the Dutch, leading to Belgian independence. Cultural and religious differences separated the Dutch and Belgians; revolution broke out in 1830, and independence was achieved in1831. Leopold of Saxe-Coburg-Gotha, a German prince and an uncle of Britain's Queen Victoria, became King Leopold I.

1870	Franco-Prussian war—Belgian neutrality was respected.
1886	Widespread labor strikes.
1914-18	World War I; Belgium was the first country to be invaded in August 1914. Only a small sliver of the country remained unoccupied until the end of the war.
1939-45	World War II; Belgium was occupied between May 1940 and September 1944.

Notes

1. Frederik Leen, Anne Adriaens-Pannier, and Gisèle Ollinger-Zinque. *L'Avant-garde en Belgique 1917-1929*, catalogue of exhibition (Brussels: Musée d'Art moderne, 1992).
2. "Gaul is divided in three parts, one of which is inhabited by the Belgians. [...] Of all the Gauls the Belgians are the bravest, because they live farthest removed from civilization and human refinement, because merchants do not often visit them and bring those things which tend to weaken the spirit, and because the Germans, who live across the Rhine, are quite close and the Belgians continually fight with them." Julius Caesar, quoted by Bernard A. Cook, *Belgium, A History* (New York: Peter Lang, 2004) 1.
3. Cook, *Belgium, A History* 3.
4. David Nicholas, *Medieval Flanders* (London and New York: Longman, 1992) 266.

Pauvre Belgique: Collecting Practices and Belgian Art in and Outside of Belgium

Sura Levine

BELGIAN ART OF THE MODERN PERIOD REMAINS, IN A VERY REAL SENSE, a great unknown beyond the borders of its homeland. Posters of the paintings of René Magritte might adorn many college dormitory walls or the front covers of best-selling theoretical texts,[1] yet few in this country would be able to name more than a small handful of artists who hail from Belgium. Even an unsystematic survey would demonstrate that, aside from Magritte (1898-1967), James Ensor (1860-1949), Constantin Meunier (1831-1905), Alfred Stevens (1823-1906), and Paul Delvaux (1897-1994), nineteenth- and twentieth-century Belgian art is often absent from public collections in this country. There are many reasons for this lack, not the least of which have to do with the history of collection practices in this country and abroad, the biases and emphases made in the art market and within the academy, the size of Belgium and the relationships between Belgium and other countries, and, finally, the primacy of other artistic centers, especially Paris and New York, over such smaller cities as Brussels.[2]

During the turn-of-the-century period and well into the twentieth century, Paris indeed was the largest and most active artistic center in Europe, and, following World War II, New York took the place of the French capital when Abstract Expressionism reached its pinnacle of popularity.[3] Brussels and Belgian art nonetheless were crucial to the development of modernism as it was produced in Europe. In both Paris and Brussels, a number of independent exhibiting societies formed, especially in the last quarter of the nineteenth century. Artists from all over Europe and the United States eagerly hoped to participate in these independent groups.

Almost simultaneously with the more famous Impressionist exhibitions in Paris, Brussels boasted several important exhibiting societies, including the Realist-based Société Libre des Beaux-Arts, which held its first exhibition in 1868. This group, which included such artists as Constantin Meunier, based its exhibition policies not on a jury system, but instead, on a combination of shared aesthetic and political practices. Such extra-Salon activity paved the way for many other independent exhibition societies, especially during the final twenty years of the nineteenth century.

Brussels' position as a cultural center supportive of revolutionary artists and thinkers was uncontested especially in the second half of the nineteenth century. From the early years of the new country's existence, the capital city witnessed the residencies of such notables as the French poet and art critic Charles Baudelaire, Karl Marx, and the French artists Gustave Courbet and Auguste Rodin.[4] In rapid succession, groups that specialized in Impressionism, Neo-Impressionism, Symbolism, and the decorative arts developed in each of the major Belgian cities during the turn-of-the-century period. Of greatest importance among these groups, was Les XX (The Twenty), which organized ten exhibitions between 1884 and 1893.[5] This group's "anarchist" mission was to present the newest art by, ideally, twenty Belgian member artists and an equal number of invited guests from Belgium and abroad. From the beginning, membership was dominated by but not limited to Belgian born artists. Among its founding members was James Ensor (**nos. 23-24, 46-47**), an artist who already was considered the most important proponent of an idiosyncratic Impressionism and proto-Expressionism infused by Belgian subjects. Another founding member was Fernand Khnopff (1858-1921), who eventually became Belgium's most famous Symbolist painter (fig. 1), and Théo van Rysselberghe (1861-1926), a close friend of and advisor to the impresario of Les XX, the lawyer Octave Maus. Van Rysselberghe was initially an Impressionist painter, but from the mid-1880s forward became a masterful painter of portraits and landscapes in the pointillist technique.[6] In 1889, membership was extended to Georges Lemmen (1865-1916), a painter of intimate portraits and scenes (**nos. 30-31**), and to the Symbolist sculptor George Minne (1866-1941) in 1891 (**nos. 27-28**). And, Constantin Meunier (**nos. 17-18**), an artist who since the late 1870s had turned to industrial subjects, was invited to join the group, but chose instead to remain independent. He nonetheless was very supportive of and exhibited with the group in 1885, 1887, 1889, and 1892.

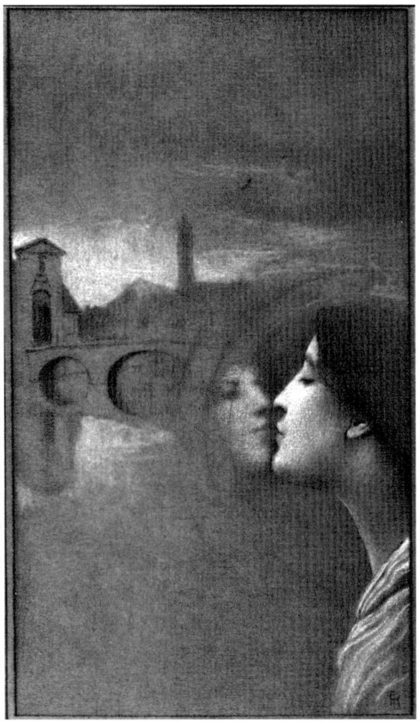

1. Fernand Khnopff, *Avec Grégoire Le Roy. Mon coeur pleure d'autrefois (My Heart Weeps for Other Days)*, 1889. Black pencil, white chalk, and colored pencils on blue-gray paper, 23.5 x 14.5 cm. Hearn Family Trust.

Full-member invitations were also provided to the foreign artists Pericles Pantazis, Dario de Regoyos, Paul Signac, Auguste Rodin, and Jan Toorop. Many other foreign artists were invited to show with the group during its ten-year existence and at the Libre Esthétique, the larger exhibiting group that succeeded Les XX in 1894. A subgroup of the Belgian Les XX's artists quickly adopted and further developed the innovations of French artists Georges Seurat and Paul Signac, following their important first exhibition of pointillist works in 1886 at Les XX. A fine example of Van Rysselberghe's pointillism in portraiture is the large *Portrait of Claire Demolder* (1902) in the present exhibition (**no. 29**).[7]

The large number of works by nineteenth- and twentieth-century French artists in American public collections has been due mostly to the largesse of such collectors as Louisine Havemeyer, Paul Mellon, Duncan Philips, Claribel and Etta Cone, Bertha and Potter Palmer, and Iris and B. Gerald Cantor, who purchased many of their works and brought them to the United States between the end of the nineteenth century and the end of the twentieth.[8] Outside of the major metropolitan areas in this country is the wonderful eponymous collection of predominantly French art at the Sterling and Francine Clark Art Institute in Williamstown, MA. This collection is notable among the short list provided above in that it includes important examples of Belgian art, including Théo van Rysselberghe and Alfred Stevens.[9]

A second, and equally important reason has to do with the history of collecting and its impact on what becomes privileged as a result in art historical texts. Standard art historical surveys published in this country necessarily concentrate on the already-famous artists of history in order to create a coherent timeline of artistic production throughout history. As a result, such texts often include only scant mention of Belgian art if such artists are mentioned at all.[10]

There has been no analogous concerted effort to acquire a cross-section of Belgian art in this country. Indeed, if one looks at the catalogues of the major museums in this country, it is difficult to find examples of Belgian art before 1900.[11] Happily, however, there are some very important exceptions to this lack. Throughout the twentieth century, curators at the Art Institute of Chicago have looked toward Belgium; this institution has amassed a collection of the sculptures of Constantin Meunier as well as important works by Georges Lemmen, Fernand Khnopff, Magritte, and Delvaux.[12] Among Meunier's statues in this collection, this institution purchased the life-sized cast of the *Hammersmith* (1886) following its inclusion in a traveling retrospective of the artist's work in the United States in 1913.[13]

The Menil Collection in Houston also acquired a large number of Magritte paintings during the middle of the twentieth century in its quest to compile an important collection of Surrealist and contemporary art. This organization has been inexhaustible since then in lending their Magritte paintings and works on paper to

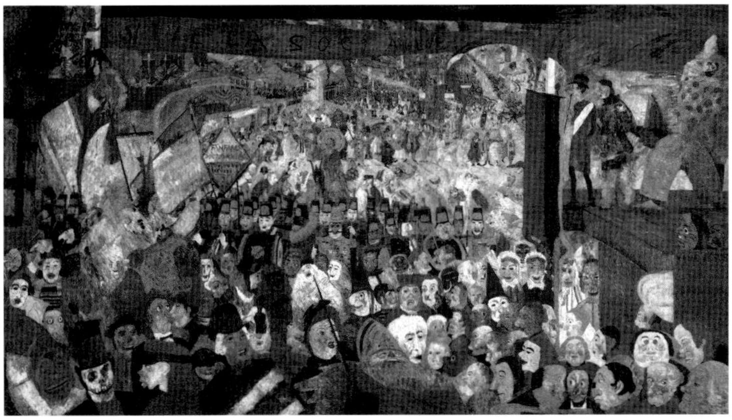

2. James Ensor, *The Entrance of Christ into Brussels in 1889*, 1888. Oil on canvas, 252.2 x 430.5 cm. J. Paul Getty Museum, Los Angeles. © 2006 Artists Rights Society (ARS), New York/SABAM, Brussels

exhibitions here and abroad including, most recently, to the Magritte retrospective organized in 1998 by the Royal Museums of Fine Arts of Belgium.

The J. Paul Getty Museum in Los Angeles acquired the single most important painting by James Ensor, *The Entrance of Christ into Brussels in 1889* (1888, fig. 2), in 1987 following a huge outcry by the Belgian populace.[14] The Getty has continued to acquire works by Belgian artists in the past two decades, including Fernand Khnopff's *Portrait of Jeanne Kéfer* (1885), Constantin Meunier's *Head of Christ* (1900), and George Minne's *Adolescent* (c. 1891) to complement its first purchase.[15]

A number of other museums own smaller collections of works by Belgian artists. The Kimbell Art Museum in Fort Worth, Texas owns Ensor's masterful painting *Skeletons Warming Themselves* (1889), and the Museum of Fine Arts in Springfield, MA owns Van Rysselberghe's *Portrait of Anna Boch* (c. 1893), a founding member of Les XX. The Philadelphia Museum of Art purchased Léon Frédéric's polyptych of *The Four Seasons* (1894), Ensor's *Self-Portrait with Masks* (1937), and Magritte's *Six Elements* (1929) to broaden its holdings in art of the nineteenth and twentieth centuries. The Detroit Institute of Art owns several works by Meunier and Ensor, as well as Minne's *Man with a Watersack* (1897) and Léon Spilliaert's *Self Portrait* from 1903. The Guggenheim Museum has acquired two of Magritte's paintings: *Voice of Space* (1931) and *Empire of Light* (1953-54),[16] as well as Paul Delvaux's *The Break of Day* (*L'Aurore*) of 1937. The Museum of Modern Art similarly owns works by Magritte and Delvaux, and the Museum of Fine Arts in Boston owns Ensor's *Still Life with Fish and Seashells* (1923).

It should be clear even from this brief and hardly thorough survey of Belgian art in American museum collections that certain artists have become canonical figures. The Belgian artists listed above continue to be avidly collected here. As additional turn-of-the-century works become available through auction, private sale, and gifts, museums here will, no doubt, continue to enrich their collections with examples of their oeuvres. Even if the major works of Belgian art have found their way into American museums, such collections are dwarfed in depth by artists of the same generations hailing from other countries.

By contrast, European museums have supported Belgian artists to a much greater extent. The Musée d'Orsay, the Albertinum in Dresden, the Ny Carlsberg Glyptotek in Copenhagen, and the Folkwang Museum in Hagen, Germany, in particular, have acquired huge collections of Belgian turn-of-the-century art.[17] Each of these collections boasts many examples of painting and/or sculpture by turn-of-the-century Belgian artists, including Meunier, Henry van de Velde, Lemmen, Van Rysselberghe, Khnopff, Ensor, and the bulk of each of these collections was formed in the final years of the nineteenth century while the artists were still alive.[18]

Belgian museums have been particularly adamant in foregrounding its artistic patrimony. Whether in the royal museums in the major cities or in communal museums outside of the urban centers, it is possible to see the full spectrum of Belgian art. The works were often purchased when they were first exhibited and many of these museums have continued to purchase objects since then. Similarly, private collectors from the period and since have amassed major collections, some of which subsequently have come to public institutions. Of particular note in this context is the collection of Octave Maus, who, during his years of administering Les XX and the Libre Esthétique, had developed an exceptional collection of art created between 1880 and 1914. This collection is now housed in the Musée Communal in Ixelles. And, known especially for its abstract art, the Goldschmidt collection came to the Royal Museum of Fine Arts in Brussels in the 1990s.

Similarly, Belgium's turn-of-the-century art has been avidly collected both in Belgium and abroad. Among the private collections of Belgian art housed outside of Belgium is the Hearn Family Trust in New York, which, among other late nineteenth-century works, has acquired an extraordinary collection of paintings and drawings by Khnopff (fig. 1), Léon Frédéric, and Xavier Mellery. This collection was developed during the early 1980s through purchases made at auction and through several dealers in Belgium and abroad. The administrators of this Trust continue to deepen their nineteenth-century collection. More recently, the Hearn Family Trust has acquired works by Belgian landscape painters, especially the School of Tervuren and paintings and drawings by Belgian realist painters.

The Simons began purchasing nineteenth- and twentieth-century Belgian art in the 1970s. Their collection is distinguished from these other private collections in its focus on several different schools of painting, and, to a lesser extent, sculpture. The collection also diverges from the Hearn Family Trust in that the Simons have collected across the linguistic divide of Belgium. The Simon Collection has been built around several crucial periods and artistic vocabularies in Belgian art. It begins with artists associated with Brussels-based exhibition groups, like Les XX and the Libre Esthétique (Ensor, Meunier, Minne, Van Rysselberghe, Lemmen, William Degouve de Nuncques, and Rik Wouters). The collection then contains a marvelous cross-section of artists associated with the artists' colony at Sint-Martens-Latem (Saint-Martins-Laethem) near the city of Ghent and with Expressionism in Belgium (Minne, Claus, Frits van den Berghe, Leon de Smet, Constant Permeke, Albert Saverys, Gustave de Smet, Gustave van de Woestyne, Floris Jespers, and Valerius de Saedeleer). With Magritte and Delvaux, the Belgian contribution to Sur-

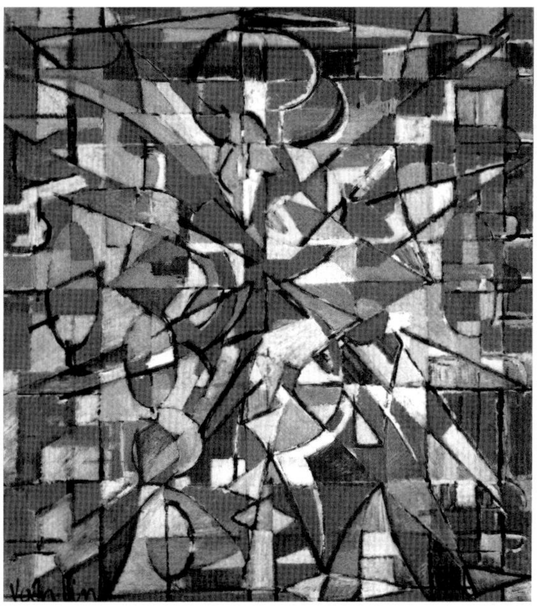

3. Louis van Lint, *Fun Fair*, c. 1951. Oil on canvas, 130 x 81 cm. Simon Collection.

realism is evidenced. Finally, and in the part of the collection not on display here, the Simons have collected many paintings from the *Jeune Peinture Belge* and CoBrA (Louis van Lint, Anne Bonnet, Luc Peire, Pierre Alechinsky, and Joseph Lacasse).[19] The Simon Collection, in its entirety, begins chronologically with James Ensors's *Still Life with Fish and Shellfish* of 1895 (**no. 23**) and ends with abstract works from the 1970s by such artists as Louis van Lint (fig. 3), Anne Bonnet, and Pierre Alechinsky. How this collection came into being and how it is different from other collections outside of Belgium are the subjects of the remainder of this essay.

An engineer by training, Henry Simon came to art collecting seemingly precipitously while he and his family were living in Belgium in the mid-1970s. At the time, an architect friend suggested he think about acquiring a work of contemporary art for the entryway of their newly constructed home in the Tervuren neighborhood of Brussels. Through this contact, Henry Simon purchased with his first wife the first of many works by van Lint in the middle of the 1970s. He explained:

> We were building a home in the suburbs of Brussels at the time and there was a young architect who came and said "the entrance hall is all white with the beige marble floor, it needs a bit of color." And he said there's an artist I know named van Lint and, if you want, we should go and see him. In those days, I hardly spoke French, so I couldn't communicate with him and then I bought a painting from him. And then I got interested in auctions. I went to various auctions and bought mainly abstract paintings because the figurative paintings were out of reach for me financially.[20]

Van Lint was a founder of the *Jeune Peinture Belge* (Young Belgian Painting), a post-War group of abstract artists who organized themselves into a loose conglomerate beginning in 1945. His work might be characterized as comprising either a lyrical or geometrical abstraction.

The artists of the Young Belgian Painting movement were not tied together by a style or common subject matter, yet their works were based in the exploration of plastic and abstract forms often rendered with the charged, bright colors associated with Expressionist art. Soon after purchasing his first Van Lint painting, Simon quickly expanded into other artists associated with this group, including Gaston Bertrand, Anne Bonnet, and Luc Peire. In addition, Simon collected paintings by other post-War groups, including CoBrA. Pierre Alechinsky is the most famous of Belgium's CoBrA artists.[21] While these works fall outside the scope of the present exhibition, it should be noted that the Simons have collected as deeply in the post-War period as they have in the art from the 1880s to the 1930s.

Henry Simon turned his attention to figural paintings, and, in particular, to the Belgian Expressionist painters in 1985 and, soon thereafter, to turn-of-the-century artists. Since that time, he and his wife, Françoise, have put together an abundant collection of paintings and sculptures from the period between the turn-of-the-century and 1930. His first purchase of an Expressionist work was Gustave de Smet's *Accordion Player* of 1926 (**no. 35**). This part of the collection was assembled only after the Simons left Brussels in 1977.

Having already created a large collection of abstract art, the Simons realized that they could develop a more coherent whole if they concentrated on Belgian art rather than spreading their collection across geographic borders.

> But then later I pretty much decided to concentrate. We'd both been to many countries, to the States and China and Japan, and I saw a lot of nice things I could have bought for a reasonable price, but I didn't want to because concentration allows you to see the relationship between the different painters, they all influence each other and the certain influences of the country and the history of the country has on the painting. You get all [of] that if you concentrate.[22]

The Brussels art dealer, Patrick Derom, who has assisted the Simons in building their collection, offers a personal insight in the remarks that follow this essay.

The figural works in the Simon Collection, the subject of the current exhibition, present the infusion and eventual rejection of French-influenced painting in Belgium. The works of Emile Claus and Adrien-Joseph Heymans, in particular, demonstrate an art that is based on the direct observation of nature rendered in harmonious tones. This quasi-Impressionist work is distinctively Belgian in that the Flemish countryside, life in the villages, fishing for eels at night, and other typically Belgian subjects are the inspiration. In 1904, Claus created the *Vie et Lumière* exhibiting group with George Morren, Adrien-Joseph Heymans (**nos. 5** and **19**), William Degouve de Nuncques (**no. 11**), and others, to foreground an Impressionist art that focused on the specific light and feel of the Flemish countryside.[23]

The largest group of figurative artists in the Simon Collection was associated with the artist colony in and around the village of Sint-Martens-Latem, on the banks of the Leie (Lys) River from c.1895 to the 1930s. This small village and its neighbors became an important locale for Flemish-language artists, including Claus. Within a matter of months, a second group of artists arrived in the area and, by the second decade of the twentieth century, rejected Claus's light-filled canvases. Rendered with heavy outlines, the subjects of the works of such Expressionists as Permeke (**nos. 16, 21, 22**), Frits van den Berghe, and Gustave de Smet, are often contained in large fields of charged, unmodulated, and anti-naturalistic colors. Although there are examples of early Belgian Expressionism in the Simon Collection, here, as was the case historically, many of the most important works of the Expressionists date to the years following World War I.[24] Mr. Simon explains:

> I like a painting that tells a story and I like paintings that tell several stories even better, depending on whether you look at it on a Monday morning or a Sunday afternoon. That's why I like the Frits van den Berghe so much. Because I can look at it again and again, and each time it tells me a different story.[25]

The Simons have not acquired objects simply because some object might fit into the collection or would fill a hole in works they own already by a given artist. Underlying each purchase is an aesthetic judgment, based, at this point, on many years of looking at Belgian art together. What underlies their collection is a complex grouping of similarities and complementarities. In the dining room of their former home in London, Claus's and Heymans's luminist paintings were paired with Van Rysselberghe's and Ensor's imagery, while, through the doorway, it was possible to see example of Belgian Expressionism, as well as works by George Minne and Constantin Meunier. Similar kinds of juxtapositions and oppositions were found throughout their home.

Bringing the Simon Collection to the United States will indeed have important ramifications over time. The Simon Collection provides a fine reintroduction to Belgian art. It also serves as an important place to examine and study the crucial contributions that Belgian artists have made to the history of modern art.[26] Having such a collection exhibited publicly allows for a reassessment of turn-of-the-century art as well as of figural art of the first half of the twentieth century. This collection thus is an important example of how, through the choice of objects to collect, an individual might transform our understanding of a particular period in art. Our understanding of the history of Modern art cannot help but be deepened by including the artists shown here.

Notes

1 The cover of Michel Foucault's *This is Not a Pipe* (Berkeley: University of Calilfornia Press, 1982) was illustrated by Magritte's justifiably famous painting *The Use of Words I* (or *Ceci n'est pas une pipe*) of 1928-29. This painting is now at the Los Angeles County Museum of Art. The cover of John Berger's now classic *Ways of Seeing* (London and New York: Penguin, 1972) reproduced Magritte's *The Key of Dreams* (1936).

2 Brussels' population in the middle of the nineteenth century was roughly 150,000, whereas Paris was almost ten times more densely populated.

3 In his text on post-World War II art and abstraction in the United States, Serge Guilbaut has argued persuasively that, for a variety of reasons that entailed both economics and politics, New York became and remains, to a great extent, the cultural capital of the world. See his *How New York Stole the Idea of Modern Art* (Chicago: University of Chicago Press, 1985).

4 See my "L'Art et l'engagement social," *Bruxelles, carrefour de cultures*, ed. Robert Hoozee (Antwerp: Fonds Mercator, 2000) 159-167.

5 See *Les XX, Catalogue des dix expositions* (Brussels: Centre internationale pour l'étude du XIXe siècle, 1981).

6 Les XX has been the subject of exhibitions and monographs too numerous to note here. Its history is recounted in Madeleine Octave Maus, *Trente Années de lutte pour l'art,* (Brussels: Lebeer Hossman, 1980). At present, the Musées Royaux des Beaux-

Arts de Belgique in Brussels, which houses the Les XX archives in their Archives de l'art contemporain, is in the process of creating an online archive of XX material.

7 Several portraits by Van Rysselberghe are among the holdings of museums in this country. They include the *Portrait of Anna Boch in Her Studio* (c. 1893) in the Museum of Fine Arts in Springfield, MA, and the *Portrait of Madame Monnom* of 1900 at the Sterling and Francine Clark Art Institute in Williamstown, MA.

8 Mrs. Havemeyer was a close friend of the American expatriate Impressionist painter Mary Cassatt and, following the artist's advice, began to amass a huge collection of French Impressionist imagery. This collection formed a central portion of the Metropolitan Museum of Art's extraordinarily rich holdings in French Impressionist art. In 1993, the Met celebrated the Havemeyer collection in an exhibition *Splendid Legacy: The Havemeyer Collection* (New York: Metropolitan Museum, 1993). Paul Mellon, a founding benefactor and trustee of the National Gallery, donated some 1,000 works to the national museum. Duncan Philips' collection in Washington, DC, the first museum dedicated to modern art, opened its doors in 1921. The impressionist and post-impressionist collection of the Cone sisters is a cornerstone of the holdings at the Baltimore Museum of Art. Bertha and Potter Palmer's collection of French art, including Georges Seurat's *Grande Jatte* (1884-86), came to the Art Institute of Chicago a century ago.

9 The Clark's collection includes the impressive portrait of the book publisher and mother-in-law of the artist, the Veuve Monnom of 1900, as well as a fine collection of his drawings. In addition, the Clarks collected Alfred Stevens and a Belgian student of Jacques-Louis David, François-Joseph Navez.

10 The second edition of Marilyn Stokstad's *Art History* (Upper Saddle River, NJ: Pearson Prentice Hall, 2005) and the new edition of *Janson's History of Art* (7th edition, Upper Saddle River, NJ: Prentice Hall, 2006) are cases in point. The writers of both of these volumes have gone to great lengths to be more inclusive than were earlier art history survey books, yet they do not include Belgian examples from the fields of Impressionism, Symbolism, Neo-Impressionism, Luminism, Expressionism, Surrealism, or contemporary abstract art outside of Ensor, Magritte, and Victor Horta.

11 The Metropolitan Museum of Art in New York owns Ensor's *The Banquet of the Starved* (1915) as well as Alfred Stevens's painting *In the Studio* of 1888. The National Gallery in Washington, DC owns no major work by a nineteenth-century Belgian artist even if its collections include a number of prints and drawings by artists such as Ensor.

12 This collection includes Lemmen's *Portrait of the Artist's Sister* (1891), a Khnopff drawing of *The Veil* (c. 1887), Ensor's *Still Life with Fish and Shells* (1898), Magritte's *The Eye* (c. 1932-33) and *Time Transfixed*, and Delvaux's paintings *The Awakening of the Forest* (1939) and *The Village of the Mermaids* (1942).

13 During his lifetime and in the decades following his death in 1905, Meunier was one of the most famous of nineteenth-century artists from Belgium. The 1913 traveling retrospective was reported at length in the American media. For this artist's impact on American artists and reviews of the exhibition, see Melissa Dabakis, *Visualizing Labor in American Sculpture: Monuments, Manliness, and the Work Ethic, 1880-1935* (Cambridge and New York: Cambridge University Press, 1999).

14 Over the years, reporters for the *New York Times* have reported regularly on the Getty's collection and, almost invariably, they single out this crucial acquisition. Art critic Michael Brenson made the case for the importance of this one work to the Getty's collection in his article "How One Work Colors an Entire Museum" (*New York Times*, February 3, 1991, H31).

15 Ensor's painting was purchased in 1987. Two years later, the Getty acquired a related drawing, *Christ Entering the City of Jerusalem*, a preparatory study for a monumental drawing of the same subject, now housed in the Museum voor Schone Kunsten in Ghent. For analyses and illustrations of this painting, see Patricia G. Berman, *James Ensor. Christ's Entry in Brussels in 1889*, (Los Angeles: The J. Paul Getty Museum, 2002) and Susan M. Canning, "*La Foule et le boulevard*: James Ensor and the Street Politic of Everyday Life," *Belgium: The Golden Decades, 1880-1914*, ed. Jane Block (New York: Peter Lang, 1997) 41-64.

16 Numerous versions exist of this latter, including those in the collections of the Museum of Modern Art and the Royal Museum of Fine Arts, Brussels.

17 A fair percentage of the collection of the Musée d'Orsay hails from the nineteenth-century French contemporary art museum, the Musée du Luxembourg. Works by Belgian artists were acquired by the Luxembourg Museum when they were shown at the official salons and a number of the Belgian artists, especially Meunier, received awards at these exhibitions. Osthaus's collection, in many ways, is an homage to Belgian art; the building was designed by the Belgian architect, painter, designer, Henry van de Velde. Among the jewels of this museum's collection is a version of Minne's *Fountain of Kneeling Youths* (1898).

18 The Albertinum collection contains more than forty sculptures and drawings by Constantin Meunier, thanks to Georg Treu, staff member of that institution during the 1890s. Carl Jacobsen, the founding director of the Ny Carlsberg Glyptotek, was an avid collector of Belgian art, and especially of Meunier's art. In the course of a decade, he had purchased for the Museum some fifty sculptures. Both museums also contain documentary archives about the development of their collections.

19 CoBrA was an acronym for Copenhagen, Brussels, and Amsterdam, the cities from which the participating artists hailed, was founded in Paris in 1948 and continued into the 1950s. Inspired by a Marxist politics, these artists, including the poet Christian Dotrement, and the visual artists Constant, Asger Jorn, Karel Appel, and Alechinsky, CoBrA artists drew much of their inspiration from the art of children and from primitive art forms.

20 Interview with the author, conducted in London on March 22, 2006.

21 Formed under the guidance of the influential Belgian art critic, Robert L. Delevoy, the short-lived *Jeune Peinture Belge* was a crucial post-War artistic phenomenon in Belgium. In addition to van Lint, the group included among its adherents the painters Jean Milo, Gaston Bertrand, Pol Bury, and Pierre Alechinsky, which latter soon became a leader of CoBrA. For histories of these movements, see Robert L. Delevoy, *La Jeune Peinture belge* (Brussels: Editions Formes, 1946); Eleanor Flomenhaft, *The Roots and Development of Cobra Art* (Hempstead, New York: Fine Arts Museum of Long Island, 1985); and Willemijn Stokvis, *Cobra: An International Movement in Art after the Second World War* (New York: Rizzoli, 1988).

22 Interview with the author, conducted in London on March 22, 2006.

23 Serge Goyens de Heusch, "Impressionism, Neo-Impressionism and Luminism," *Impressionism to Symbolism: The Belgian Avant-Garde, 1880-1900*, eds. Mary Anne Stevens and Robert Hoozee (London: Royal Academy, 1994) 35-9.

24 The most comprehensive survey of Belgian Expressionism is Piet Boyens's *Flemish Art. Symbolism to Expressionism at Sint-Martens-Latem* (Tielt: Lannoo, 1992).

25 Interview with the author, conducted in London on March 22, 2006.

26 American audiences have been introduced to Belgian art on several occasions already. During the 1930s, there were a number of exhibitions of Belgian modernism in New York. Most recently the Belgian contribution to art was seen in the *Belgian Art, 1880-1914* at the Brooklyn Museum in 1980.

The Simon Collection—a Personal Perspective

Patrick Derom

It was quite by chance that Henry Simon came into contact with Belgian art. In 1968, his career as a telecommunications engineer brought him to Belgium, and it was through his architect that he met the abstract painter Louis van Lint, one of the cofounders of *Jeune Peinture Belge*. This marked the start of a voyage of discovery through almost one hundred years of Belgian art, from the end of the nineteenth century to the 1970s.

Nine years later, Henry left Belgium and moved on to live and work in Monaco, New York, and London. It might have been expected that these travels would direct his interest as a collector toward more popular movements such as French Impressionism or American Pop Art. As it turned out, nothing could be further from the truth. His years in Belgium aroused an interest, which later blossomed into a true passion, although there was no reason to suspect then that he would devote himself exclusively to Belgian art. Paradoxically enough, Henry Simon acquired the most important works in his collection after his time in Belgium, principally in the past twenty years.

The determination with which this "foreign" collector concentrated on art that was at the time not much in demand is evidence of his open mind and perhaps even of a certain contrariness. After all, it went completely against the dominance of French art on the international art market and in the majority of international collections.

We also become acquainted with the personality of the man behind the collection through his choice of works. It becomes very clear that his great preference is for Expressionism, and especially for the work of Frits van den Berghe. It was never Simon's intention to create a collection that provided a complete survey of the history of modern Belgian art. Or, to put it in his own words, "my choices will always be determined by personal taste and my financial resources." The only additional influence we can discern—discreet but by no means negligible—is that of Françoise, his wife. Their extraordinary collection has been shown in Belgium, the Netherlands, Japan, and now Boston.

This text is excerpted from Patrick Derom's forward to the exhibition catalogue by Piet Boyens, Masterpieces of Modern Belgian Art, The Simon Collection *(Brussels: Musée d'Ixelles, 2003) 5.*

A New Key: Modernism and National Identity in Belgian Art

Jeffery Howe

In 1902, a great exhibition of Flemish "primitives" was held in Bruges, including works by Jan van Eyck, Hans Memling, Gerard David, and Pieter Bruegel. It was a landmark in the rediscovery of fifteenth- and sixteenth-century painting for a generation of historians.[1] The Bruges exhibit was a defining moment in the assertion of a cultural identity specific to the lowlands, one equal to the Italian Renaissance. The relationship between art and history is fascinating, but seldom clear-cut, due to controversies over authenticity, interpretation, and the relationship between art and society. Although the interpretation of art is subjective, it often seems equally impossible to separate historical facts from ideology and national myths. Because of its particularly complicated history, a clear understanding of Belgium's identity often seems to elude our grasp. In the absence of more secure institutions or traditions, art has been made to carry heavy freight in histories of Belgium. The Belgian contribution to the development of modernism, and the relationship of this art to the developing Belgian national identity, is the subject of this essay. Works from the Simon Collection will be used to illuminate major points whenever possible and will try to illuminate the past and suggest future lines of inquiry. The section headings generally follow those of the McMullen Museum exhibition.

The nation known as Belgium is relatively recent, born of a revolution against the Dutch in 1830. However, the regions of Flanders and Wallonia have a much longer history, with antecedents dating back at least two thousand years. In 1899, the historian Henri Pirenne stressed that modern Belgium was a continuation of the ancient Netherlands, rejecting the popular criticism that Belgium was merely an artificial creation born of political expedience.[2] Unity was hard won, however, since neither Flanders nor Wallonia had been allowed to develop without interference. Edmond Picard, the socialist lawyer, author, and one of the founders of the journal *l'Art Moderne*, insisted that a defining characteristic of the "Belgian soul" was persistence in the face of adversity.[3] As Chantal Kestaloot has observed: "Though one may write a history of the Walloons, one should not really speak of the history of Wallonia—not in the way that one speaks of the history of France—because, between 843 and 1793, the Walloons never possessed a common fatherland."[4] In the face of frequently changing political entities, the artistic tradition was sometimes claimed to provide a common bond. The Belgian art historian Max Rooses wrote in 1914: "Belgium is a geographical expression which in the course of the centuries has often changed its meaning. It is more to its art than to anything else that this country owes its real moral homogeneity."[5] The visual arts were expected to transcend linguistic and political barriers. In actuality, however, the interpretation of these works has also often been shaped by political concerns.

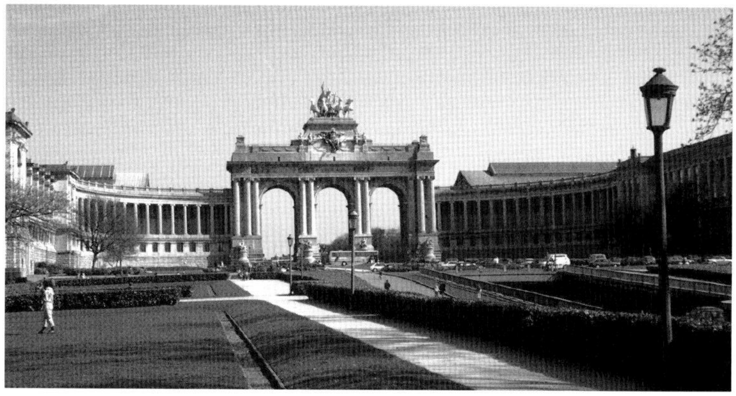

1. Charles Girault: Cinquantenaire arch, Brussels, 1905. Photo by author.

Linguistic divisions were already present in the division of the territory after the death of Charlemagne. Language has been a continuing problem for Belgian identity, since the unity of language and culture which was assumed to be manifest in a *Volksgeist* seemed likely to pull the Flemish and French speaking peoples apart.[6] It was hoped that the idea of Belgium would transcend these linguistic divisions. When Belgium became independent in 1831, the dominant language was French, but even the Francophone culture was said to possess an "ethnic-mythical core" which was Flemish. Charles de Coster's novel *The Legend of Tyl Ulenspiegl* (1867) can be seen as a prime example of this movement to define Belgium "as a Flemish country with French as its language."[7] De Coster himself was born in Munich, of a Walloon father and Flemish mother. The hero of his novel, Tyl Ulenspiegl, was a prankster from Damme (a village near Bruges) who resisted the Spanish occupation.

The identification of Belgium with Flemish culture was encouraged by the prestige of earlier Flemish painting, and by the great Symbolist writers Maurice Maeterlinck and Emile Verhaeren, Flemings who wrote in French.[8] This optimistic vision ignored real problems in the equality of the two groups, since the Francophone group achieved economic and political superiority, with the Flemish movement assuming increasing importance by 1890.[9] Tensions were exacerbated by the war years 1914-18, but in the 1920s the Flemings won the struggle to have Flemish be the language of the University of Ghent. Post-WWII compromises have led to the present Federal system, which is still evolving.

National identity was a major issue in many countries during the nineteenth century, and particularly relevant for the newly independent Belgium. Nationalism was deeply rooted in Romanticism, and many painters focused on themes from Belgian history. Gustave Wappers (1807-1874) became famous for his enormous painting of an *Episode During the*

Belgian Revolution of 1830 (1834, Royal Museums of Fine Arts of Belgium, Brussels), which commemorated Belgian resistance to the Dutch during the struggle for independence. Wappers's rather theatrical reenactment of a moment of revolutionary fervor is one of the largest of the new wave of national history paintings. It joins Eugène Delacroix's painting of *Liberty Leading the People* (1830, Louvre) and Francois Rude's sculpture on the face of the Arc de Triomphe in Paris, *The Departure of the Volunteers of 1793* (1833), as a major Romantic work.[10]

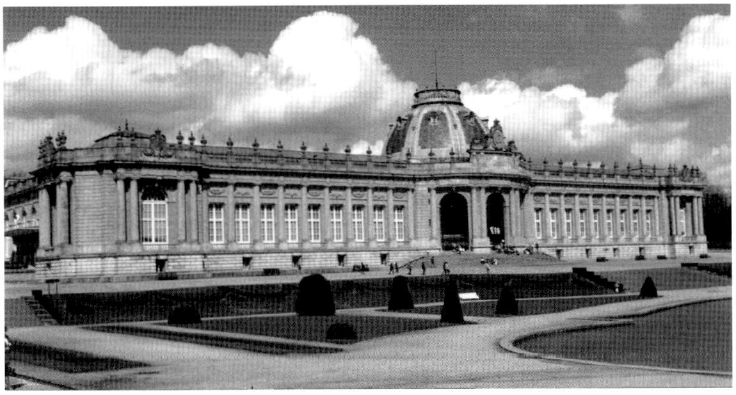

2. Charles Girault: Royal Museum of African Art, Tervuren, 1910. Photo by author.

Historical recreations were prevalent in mid-nineteenth-century Belgian art. Painters such as Henri Leys and Henri de Braekeleer portrayed scenes of sixteenth- and seventeenth-century history with nearly photographic realism. The taste for such staged recreations waned by the end of the century, although historical consciousness was still strong in other themes, including landscape and village scenes.

Architecture is often used to reinforce or create a connection to historical traditions. In Belgian architecture of the nineteenth and early twentieth centuries, Classical and French revival styles dominated for official buildings. To celebrate the seventy-fifth anniversary of Belgian Independence in 1905, Leopold II commissioned Charles Girault, architect of the Petit Palais (1900), to design a large triumphal arch for the Cinquantenaire Park in Brussels (fig. 1). This arch would connect the 1879-80 Palaces of the Cinquantenaire, originally built by the architect Gédéon Bordiau for the fiftieth anniversary of the nation of Belgium. The massiveness of the arch, measuring 148 feet high and 197 feet wide, recalls the triumphal arches of ancient Rome, as well as those built by Napoleon. One may suspect that Leopold II wanted to associate his reign with the Imperial aspects of those earlier periods as much as with their high culture. The goal of the architecture here is not to embody a national Belgian style, but to bring Belgium into parity with other European capitals.

In the colonial era of the nineteenth century, nearly every European country felt it had to control a foreign colony in order to compete economically. One of Leopold II's most controversial moves was his acquisition of the large colony in the Congo. First purchased with his own funds, the territory was exploited for its natural resources and became the property of the state in the twentieth century. In addition to other sources of money taken from the Congo, many works of art and ethnographic objects were removed. To house them, a museum was constructed in Tervuren by Charles Girault (fig. 2). This building was commissioned by Leopold II and inaugurated by King Albert in 1910. The style is

French Baroque and particularly reminiscent of buildings for Louis XIV, such as the Grand Trianon at Versailles. Classicism, in its various forms, was the international language of power when it came to official architecture of the nineteenth and early twentieth centuries. Colonialism was the most direct expression of power politics, so the style was a perfect match. The French Baroque style exuded the confidence, even arrogance, of imperial power.

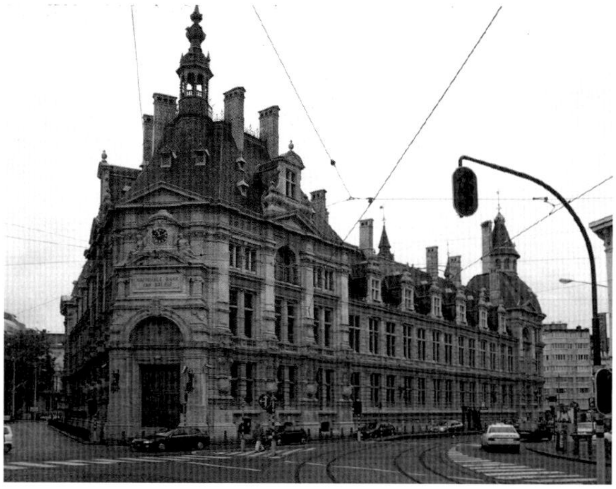

3. Henri Beyaert: National Bank, Antwerp, 1872-79. Photo by author.

The synthesis of French and Flemish traditions that was thought to be key to Belgian identity was asserted in buildings which looked back to earlier Flemish architecture as well as French styles. Eclecticism prevailed in the National Bank in Antwerp of 1872-79 (fig. 3), which combines aspects of a French Renaissance chateau with French Baroque end pavilions and a variety of Flemish forms. In its combination of styles, it almost exemplifies the history of Belgium. Max Rooses praised it as a synthesis of "a sixteenth century French palace with Flemish turrets of various periods, in a splendid *ensemble*."[11] It was designed by Henri Beyaert (1823-1894) and is an early example of "total design," in that the architect designed the interiors and many of the furnishings for the building. French architectural forms within this building can be explained by the great prestige of the French Ecole des Beaux-Arts in the nineteenth century and also perhaps by the Romantic longing for a return to the glories of the Burgundian years in Belgium, when the French and Flemish cultures were united.

A more consistent example of the Flemish Revival is the town hall of Schaerbeek, one of the communes of Brussels, which was designed by Jules-Jacques Van Ysendyck (1836-1901). The Schaerbeek town hall (fig. 4) strongly resembles earlier Flemish town halls, especially that of Audenarde, with its rich detailing, prominent central tower and stepped gables.

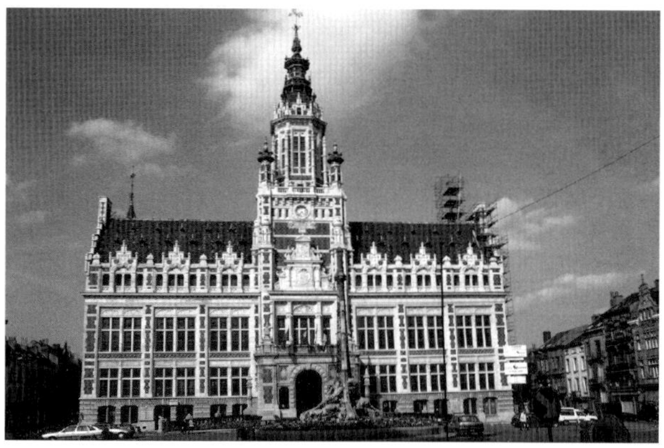

4. Jules-Jacques Van Ysendyck: Town Hall, Schaerbeek, 1884-87. Photo by author.

By the late nineteenth century, there was a growing desire for a new style of art and architecture to embody the aspirations and achievements of the day. Prosperity and a rising middle class empowered a new generation of patrons and consumers of art. To signal the break with the past, this style was called simply the "new art." *Art Nouveau* was a style that had the confidence to abandon the crutch of historicism, and to turn to nature for its inspiration. The modern world was embraced in the new technologies of steel and electricity, which were prominently featured in Art Nouveau architecture. There was also an important psychological dimension to the style, as the sensuous and artistic interiors reflected the sensibility and even emotions of the architect and/or client.[12] Belgium was one of the birthplaces of Art Nouveau, and Brussels in particular is rich with architectural examples.

Victor Horta was its leading proponent; his Tassel House in Brussels (1893) was the first example of Art Nouveau in architecture, and his Maison du Peuple in Brussels (1895; demolished) was a landmark building. One of the most individualistic of Art Nouveau houses is that built for the painter Léonard de Saint-Cyr in Brussels by Gustave Strauven (1878-1919) in 1903 (fig. 5). The house is tall and narrow, even more so than most Belgian urban townhouses. It is adorned with florid, even delirious, wrought iron work, culminating in a dramatic abstract crown. Strauven had worked for Victor Horta, but surpassed him with this eccentric design. The individualism shown here may be seen as typically Belgian; even the Baroque palaces on the Grand' Place in Brussels do not share a common style, but each asserts its own character, unlike the carefully orchestrated unity of French Baroque ensembles.

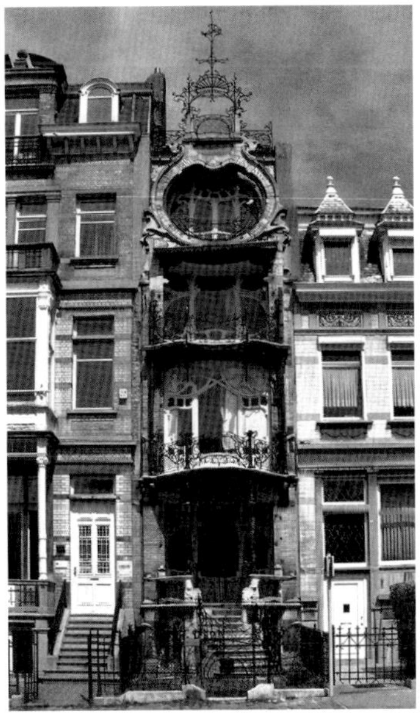

5. Gustave Strauven: House for the painter Saint-Cyr, Square Ambiorix, Brussels, 1903. Photo by author.

Looking Outward – Landscape and Village Scenes

Landscape became part of the national iconography, and the painting of Belgian sites strengthened national consciousness.[13] The landscape itself evoked historical associations, from the fields of Waterloo to the site of the Battle of the Golden Spurs. The medieval cities of Bruges and Ghent, and even the small villages of the countryside, were also natural memorials to the past.

Although landscape was considered a lesser genre in the hierarchy established by the French Academy in the seventeenth and eighteenth centuries, it became a major focus during the Romantic era. The relationship of humans to nature was reconsidered, and the exploration of the variety of landscape became increasingly important, as a reflection of personal experience and the historical context. The Romantic legacy included an emphasis on nature as a restorative for the spirit and as an index of national identity. Landscape reinforced a sense of national identity in every country.

In Belgium this was particularly resonant, in a region where the land has endured, despite the many dramatic political upheavals.

Until the twentieth century, Flanders was essentially rural, except for seaports (Antwerp, Bruges, Ostend); Wallonia was comprised of agricultural areas (the Ardennes), but was also the most industrialized region in Europe, with coal mines and factories dominating the area around Charleroi. Belgium became one of the most densely populated regions of Europe, and because of this the landscape is essentially constructed. After centuries of land reclamation and cultivation, there is little virgin nature—nearly all has been shaped by human activity.[14] While this is true in much of Europe, the small scale of Belgium intensified the human alteration of the land. This is seen most dramatically in the polders, large areas of land reclaimed from the sea. Landscape painting in Belgium is a portrait of the relationship between humans and nature. The tone is closer to the picturesque depictions of England by John Constable than to the sublime cataclysms of J.M.W. Turner. Moreover, the widespread predilection for Realism also discouraged melodrama.

The popularity of landscape painting is clearly related to the impact of industrialization. Nature became more important as it was increasingly threatened by modernization; there was a sense of preciousness in the face of encroaching factories. The Romantic idealization of nature was partly a denial of the negative impact of industrialization. Such art appealed to the new middle class; landscape could be appreciated by anyone, even those without the classical learning required to appreciate history painting. Undercurrents of political and social meaning have been detected in French Impressionism; Robert Herbert revealed layers of significance in Claude Monet's *Grainstacks*, and Paul Tucker has illuminated unsuspected meanings in Monet's *Poplars* series.[15]

The concept of nature itself was evolving during the nineteenth century. Some asserted that, after Darwin, nature should replace the Bible as the reference for rules to live by and the basis of moral principles.[16] Yet, for many, the Romantic (and ultimately medieval) ideology that nature reflects God's gifts and was a sort of visible testament, endured. This persisted even in scenes of Realism. These factors encouraged a blossoming of landscape painting in the late nineteenth and early twentieth centuries, most notably in artists' colonies, where artists retreated to escape the congestion and distractions of city life and to live closer to nature. By stepping away from the city, they could see it more clearly and offer alternative visions.

Artists' Colonies

The artists' colony at Laethem-Saint-Martin (Sint-Martens-Latem) was centered on a cluster of tiny picturesque villages, including Bachte-Maria-Leerne and Deurle on the banks of the river Leie (Lys) near Ghent.[17] Laethem-Saint-

Martin had a population of only fourteen hundred in the late nineteenth century, but was quite hospitable, with thirty inns and easy access to Ghent.

One of the oldest cities in Belgium, Ghent was torn by modern social tensions at the turn of the century. Ghent had been the historic center of independence struggles since the late Middle Ages and was the birthplace of the Belgian Worker's Party (Parti Ouvrier Belge) in the late nineteenth century. The city was also a vibrant intellectual and artistic center and the birthplace of the writers Maurice Maeterlinck and Karel van de Woestyne, the architect Victor Horta, and visual artists George Minne, Gustave van de Woestyne, and Valerius de Saedeleer. As part of the emerging avant-garde, Minne and De Saedeleer were inspired by anti-bourgeois ideals.[18] The search for a simpler life in the country was one response to their discontent.

Cities had come under increasingly harsh criticism for the emphasis on materialism, and the negative effects on physical and mental health in crowded urban environment.[19] Rejecting the life in urban centers, artists began to gather at Laethem-Saint-Martin. One of the main attractions was the engaging personality of Albijn (also known as Binus) van den Abeele (1835-1918). Van den Abeele had been a town clerk and burgomaster and, with no formal artistic training, began painting scenes of the Flemish landscape about 1875.[20] Van den Abeele found escape from modern strife in nature, which for him also provided a link to the divine:

> I am more of a dreamer, someone who would prefer to see and judge everything in a poetic and artistic way. Every day I am aware that I am in no way suited to joining the masses with their materialist tendencies. My spirit is lifted by thinking of God, or by one look at unspoiled nature, [...] and this makes me happy.[21]

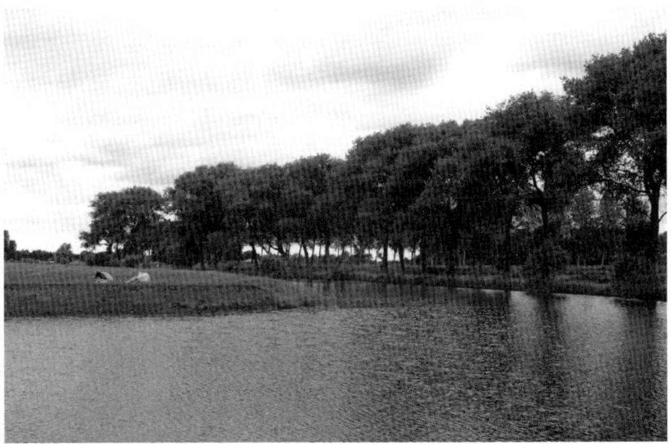

6. The Leie (Lys) River, near Laethem-Saint-Martin. Photo by author.

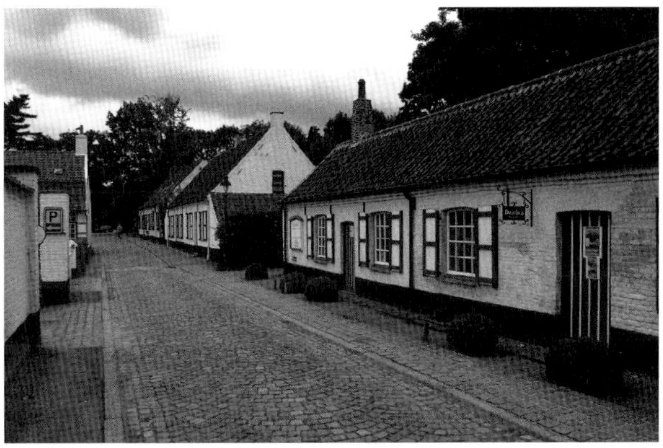

7. Deurle, near Laethem-Saint-Martin. Photo by author.

His friendship with artists from Ghent attracted them to this quiet and beautiful region beside the Leie river. Piet Boyens has observed that it was the tranquility and freedom of rural life that appealed most to the artists who moved there, even more than the picturesque qualities of the village (figs 6-7).[22]

The first generation of artists at Laethem-Saint-Martin, notably Valerius de Saedeleer who arrived in 1898, George Minne who came in 1899, and Gustave van de Woestyne who arrived in 1900, were more spiritually inclined and closer to the Symbolist movement than the group who assembled there in subsequent years.[23] Gustave van de Woestyne moved to the country, partly for health reasons. He became quite religious and painted traditional Catholic themes, including an altarpiece of *Our Lady offers the Rosary to St. Dominic* for the church of Laethem-Saint-Martin (1900), given as a gift to the village (fig. 8). An important exhibition of so-called Flemish Primitive art in Bruges in 1902 had a major impact on the Flemish artists. This exhibition reintroduced them to the works of Van Eyck and Memling, and both the style and religious themes had a major impact on them. At this point in his career, Van de Woestyne rejected the temptations of modernism in favor of a starkly archaic style. With its solid gold haloes and flattened space, this deliberately archaic work also resembles Italian Quattrocento altarpieces. The adoption of an archaic style suggests both the deep religious faith of the artist and also his cosmopolitanism. The Catholic church was supportive of Flemish nationalism, but also loyal to Rome.[24] In 1905, Van de Woestyne briefly entered a Benedictine monastery at Louvain, but left after two months to return to painting in Laethem-Saint-Martin.[25]

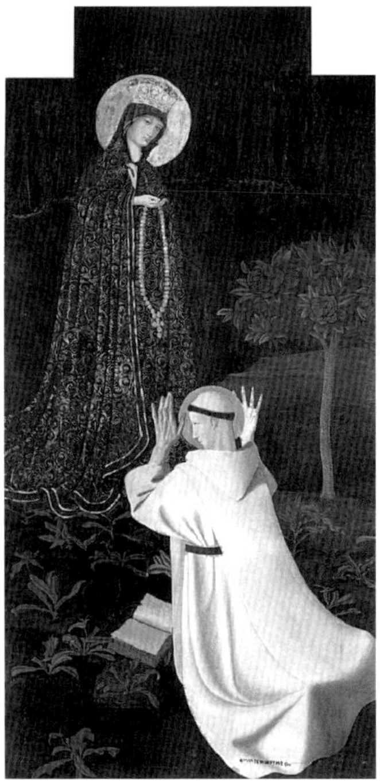

8. Gustave van de Woestyne: *Our Lady Offers the Rosary to St. Dominic*, 285 x 140 cm., 1905. Church of St. Martinus, Laethem-Saint-Martin.

A return to primitive simplicity and even religiosity was a radical rejection of bourgeois values. Paradoxically, modernism often involves a strong anti-modern component, as part of the rejection of the dominant culture of the time. Increasingly, the critical discourse of modernism has embraced this notion of resistance to modern life as an integral part of the development of the avant-garde.[26] As a friend once put it, "the more modern we are, the more medieval we get."

A second group of artists, including Gustave de Smet, Frits van den Berghe, and Constant Permeke, settled in Laethem-Saint-Martin a few years later. Unlike the first group, they led a more bohemian existence and embraced experimental styles. For both groups, the colony at Laethem-Saint-Martin offered the opportunity for retreat from the world, and also collaboration and participation in a shared artistic venture. Artists could meditate on nature, as well as spiritual and artistic issues in the peacefulness of the village, yet also have convenient access to the city of Ghent or Brussels. Paintings made here reflect an emphasis on local traditions and an idealized vision of rural life. In this regard, the Belgian artists' colony has much in common with others formed in Europe at this time. Notable examples include Pont-Aven in Brittany in the 1880s and 1890s, led by Paul Gauguin; Worpswede in Germany, where Paula Modersohn-Becker was the leading figure after 1897; and the Scandinavian artists' colony at Skagen on the Danish coast in the 1880s through the early 1900s.

To get closer to nature was one of the primary goals for those who settled in these artistic colonies. Modern landscape painting strongly reflects the personality of the artists and their response to nature, as well as their concept of artistic style. Earlier Naturalist artists such as Guillaume Vogels (1836-1896) and Hippolyte Boulenger (1827-1874) employed blended though visible brushstrokes and somewhat muted colors to create art based on realist observation. They exemplify Emile Zola's dictum in a salon review of 1866 that: "The definition of a work of art cannot be other than this; a work of art is a part of the universe viewed through a temperament."[27] The emphasis on personal interpretation helped pave the way for Impressionism.

Emile Claus created his own version of Impressionism using more abstract, visible, autonomous touches which are signifiers of individuality, authenticity, and spontaneity.[28] His use of brighter color distinguished him from the earlier Belgian landscape artists. The impact of Impressionism in Belgium was noted by Emile Verhaeren: "From now on, light is in control of every painting, determining the appearance and the shape and structure of each object, by turns gnawing away at it, changing its shape, exaggerating its structure. Light creates colour, then breaks it up into an infinite variety of separate shades."[29] Part of the appeal of Impressionism and especially Neo-Impressionism was that the techniques for representing light and color were thought to be fundamentally scientific and, thus, transcended national borders. Nevertheless, Claus's art embodies one aspect of the Belgian national ideal. His subjects are rooted in Flemish life, though the style is French. Claus spent winters in Paris between 1888 and 1890, reinforcing his ties to the new style.[30]

In the mid-1880s, Claus moved to the rural village of Astene, on the Leie river near Ghent. A former hunting lodge known locally as 't Rattenkasteel (the Rat Castle) became his house and studio and, after remodeling, was rechristened Zonneschijn (Sunshine).[31] It became a magnet for artists who shared his devotion to painting sunlit scenes.

The passion that artists such as Claus, George Morren, and A.-J. Heymans showed for capturing light and color led them to be called Luminists, a term meant to distinguish them from French Impressionists and used only in Belgium.[32] It should not be confused with the earlier movement in American art also called Luminism. Building on a Realist foundation, Belgian Luminism represented a combination of Impressionism and Neo-Impressionism.

The Realist aspect of Claus's style is exemplified by the 1890 painting *Woman Reading* (**no. 1**). While marvelously sensitive to the atmosphere of light, the painting does not yet show the luminous color that would characterize his art after his winter stays in Paris, during 1889-1892. The image of a woman reading in nature combines motifs of intellect and sensitivity to nature, or sense and sensibility, and was popular from the earliest days of Romanticism. One can compare it to George Stubbs's painting of a *Lady Reading in a Wooded Park* (1768-70, private collection) or Joseph Wright of Derby's *Sir Brooke Boothby* (1781, Tate Britain, London).

Emile Claus's painting *Marguerites (Daisies,* 1897, **no. 2**), a scene of a flower-filled field and household labor, shows influence from the Impressionism of Claude Monet and Camille Pissarro, but with a more intimate connection to domestic life. In this picture, the humble wild daisies flood the foreground, while in the background the daily work of laundry goes on, with clothes being hung to dry in the sun. In Claus's paintings, figures are seldom dissolved by the light and color, as they are in Monet's contemporaneous works of late Impressionism. Nature and rural life are idealized as counterpoints to the chaos of modernism and urbanism.

In 1904, Claus and Adrien-Joseph Heymans became the leaders of an artistic group called *Vie et Lumière* (Life and Light); the title of the group perfectly described their aims. A retrospective exhibition of French Impressionism and Post-Impressionism held by the *Libre Esthétique* in Brussels in 1904 was the immediate impetus to their luminist group.[33]

Rodolphe Wytsman's shimmering painting of the *Pond at Linkebeek* (1894, **no. 4**) also shows the constructed and domestic side of nature in Belgium. Painted just outside Brussels, not far from the medieval ruins of the castle at Beersel, the artist depicts a quiet rural setting. There is a characteristic row of polled (heavily pruned) willows beside the bank of a small pond and a white house with red-tiled roof in the background. A carefully planted avenue of poplars blocks the distance and encloses the scene. Quiet symmetry in the reflections in the water provide a further sense of harmony and a dialogue between nature and culture. The mirror of nature echoes the Symbolist fascination with structure and vision.[34]

Such a quiet rural landscape might seem like a throwback to the Romanticism of Constable, and it does resemble Romantic *Stimmungsmalerei*, or "mood paintings," which were created to evoke emotion.[35] However, the framing and composition are more typical of Modern art. The silvery reflections in the surface of the water remind one of the importance of water in the history and culture of Belgium. The land above seems almost insubstantial, as if the reality of earthly life and the nation of Belgium were only a mirage.

French and Belgian Impressionism was in a sense born from the painting of water, and water continued to be a major subject for modernist painters who found the shimmering surfaces and broken reflections to be a perfect analog for the flux of life and time and the contingency of vision.

The gossamer delicacy of mist and water are seen in Théo van Rysselberghe's painting of *Veere in the Morning Mist* of 1906 (**no. 6**). Veere is a Dutch village on the coast near Middleburg and a favorite locale for painters (fig. 9). It had once been a thriving commercial center, but had lost its major trade business by the nineteenth century. This work

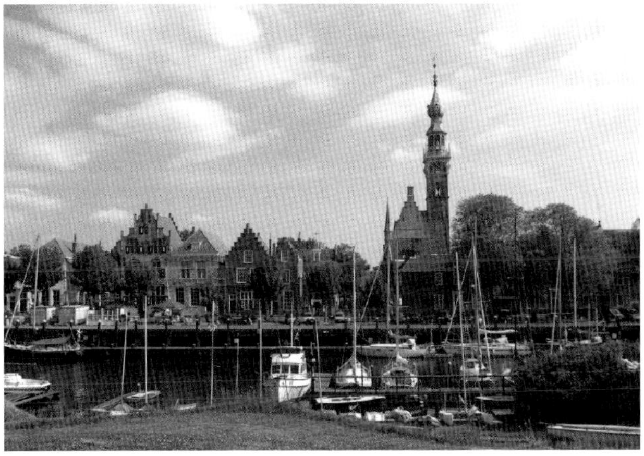

9. Veere, Netherlands, 2006. Photo by author.

compares very favorably to Claude Monet's paintings of London in 1904. Van Rysselberghe was the leading Belgian exponent of Neo-Impressionism, as seen in his *Portrait of Claire Demolder* (**no. 29**, discussed below). Neo-Impressionism came early to Belgium: Georges Seurat exhibited his *Sunday Afternoon at La Grande Jatte* at the exhibition of Les Vingt in 1887. Van Rysselberghe and Georges Lemmen were early adopters of the style.

The emotional and spiritual response to landscape had been emphasized by Symbolist artists in the late nineteenth century. Although most well known for paintings of *femme fatales* and mysterious images of mythic scenes, the Symbolists maintained as their chief principle the goal to "objectify the subjective." Even the "*obermystiker*," or chief mystic of Brussels, Fernand Khnopff, painted small landscapes of sites important to his life throughout his career.[36] Symbolist artists allowed their feelings to shape their landscape paintings, which at times resembled dreamscapes, or in the term of Gerard Manley Hopkins, "inscapes." This was particularly true of William Degouve de Nuncques.

William Degouve de Nuncques (1867-1935) was born in the Ardennes region, the son of an aristocratic family. It was said of his work that: "Whereas the Impressionists saw objects illuminated from the *outside*, Degouve saw them from the *inside*."[37] Degouve de Nuncques's Symbolist paintings at the turn of the century evoke a sense of quiet mystery through his use of eerie and magical light effects. Degouve de Nuncques had strong literary connections to the Symbolist poet Emile Verhaeren, and he designed the sets for at least one of Maurice Maeterlinck's plays. One of his paintings, *The House of Mystery,* or *The Pink House* (1892), was inspired by Edgar Allan Poe's Gothic tale "The Fall of the House of Usher." Degouve de Nuncques's landscapes begin with an impression from nature, but subtly transform natural settings to elicit emotion and mystery.

After 1900, Degouve de Nuncques moved away from Symbolism toward more realistic, if idealized, images. The painting *Le Caillou-qui-bique* (1909, **no. 11**) shows a small village of red-roofed houses nestled between carefully tended fields and rows of poplars. This hamlet, near Roisin and the French border, is named for a precariously balanced rock formation. Emile Verhaeren lived in this village for the last fifteen years of his life.

The heritage of the Symbolist movement was very strong in the first generation of artists who worked at Laethem-Saint-Martin, and especially so in Valerius de Saedeleer (fig. 10). His work shows the influence of Pieter Bruegel, but also the formal patterns of *Japonisme*, and the French *Nabis,* mystical artists who followed the example of Gauguin

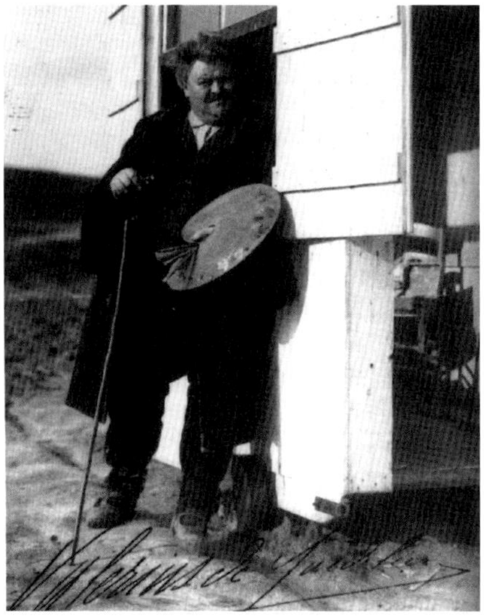

10. Valerius de Saedeleer outside his portable studio at Tieghem, 1913.

at the artists' colony at Pont-Aven.[38] The Nabis had been featured at an exhibition at La Libre Esthétique in Brussels in 1908. The Nabis extended Gauguin's precepts to develop a style of abstraction built on flattened areas of color and strongly outlined forms.

The tranquility of the natural setting and the spiritual influence of George Minne led to an artistic rebirth and religious conversion in 1904 for De Saedeleer: "I discovered the Leie, my soul and my conscience: Flemish mysticism and the ancient faith I should never have abandoned."[39] His ideal was a quiet life, free of distractions. His earlier work featured close up views of interiors, including a triptych depicting the interior of his house titled *In My House* (private collection), with three close views of the rooms of his house. He seems to use the interior spaces of the house to serve as analogs to the life and emotions of the artist, his "inner world." This equivalency was implicit in much Symbolist literature and painting and even had antecedents in Baroque medical books, where the body was metaphorically depicted as a house.[40] After 1904, there is more nearly infinite space in De Saedeleer's canvases, as in his view of *The Leie on a Gray Day* (1904, Collection Stadsbestuur, Aalst). The expansive view of deep space continued in his art and is exemplified in the background of his *Old Orchard in Winter* (1925, **no. 12**). Returning to Belgium after the war, De Saedeleer moved to the hilly landscape of Etikhove in south Flanders. His admiration for Pieter Bruegel was more pronounced than ever. The interlace of the trees against the setting sun is distinctly reminiscent of Bruegel's *Hunters in the Snow* (1565, Vienna, Kunsthistorisches Museum), or the snowy *Census in Bethlehem* (c. 1566, Brussels, Royal Museums of Fine Arts).

The intricate patterns of nature's growth fascinated De Saedeleer. He noted that "It often happened that I would study a simple pear tree for weeks on end in order to unravel the tangle of intertwined branches, to clearly see the capricious pattern of the delicate twigs and understand the purpose and meaning of this wondrous sight."[41] Contemporary naturalists now recognize in the complexity of tree branching the properties of fractal geometry, characterized by replication and self-similarity.[42] These qualities are exquisitely depicted in paintings like De Saedeleer's *Old Orchard in Winter*. Although he predates the discovery of the mathematics of this pattern, the artist's intuition led him to a visual study of the phenomena.

Albert Saverys's painting of a *View of the Leie* (1918, **no. 10**) shows a characteristic scene in Flanders along the Leie River (the Lys in French), near Laethem-Saint-Martin. The bony branches of the trees indicate the winter season, and the pulsing colors suggest an early sunset. The technique owes something to the divisionist technique of Neo-

Impressionism, but the linear agitation of the trees and the brick-like blocks of color suggest the works of Piet Mondrian when he was at the stage between Impressionism and Cubism, c. 1909. His *Red Tree* of 1908 (Gemeentemuseum, The Hague) has similar knobby and gnarled branches flattened into an angular pattern on the surface of the canvas. Mondrian exhibited several of his paintings, including a *Windmill* and a *Tree* in Brussels in 1909 at the circle *Doe Stil Voort* ("Moving on quietly").[43]

After 1908, there was a general reaction away from Luminism and Impressionism toward Expressionism. The Belgian Expressionists fall into two groups: the first is very closely tied to Symbolist aesthetics and includes Léon Spilliaert, Gustave van de Woestyne, and Valerius de Saedeleer. These artists seek to combine a greater degree of abstraction, with a return to Flemish roots. The second group is more international in focus, influenced by German Expressionism, Cubism, and African art. This group includes Gust de Smet, Constant Permeke, and Frits van den Berghe.

Even in the context of the strongly individual artists who flourished in Belgium in the early twentieth century, Léon Spilliaert is remarkable for his originality. Spilliaert (1881-1946) was born in Ostend and shared with his fellow Ostend native, James Ensor, a powerful visual imagination, a taste for literature, and solitude. Spilliaert had met Emile Verhaeren in Paris in 1904, using an introduction from the Belgian publisher Deman, for whom Spilliaert had worked for two years.[44] They established a long-lasting relationship, which was only ended with Verhaeren's death in 1916.

Never quite fitting into any group, Spilliaert expressed ambivalence about his work in a letter of 1900:

> Never make painting from imagination, Symbolism, mysticism, etc., etc., all that is a distraction, a sickness: everything I have done up to now, I would like to destroy it all, destroy it all. Oh! if I were only rid of my uneasy, feverish character, if life did not hold me in its grip. I would go to some part of the countryside, go to copy everything stupidly, or with complete simplicity, everything my eyes saw, neither taking away, or adding anything. That's what life is, that is the truth of painting.[45]

Although Spilliaert expressed his profound distrust of imagination, it is clearly his strongest feature.

In the years immediately preceding World War I, Spilliaert created some stunning works of abstraction, using vibrant color and tensions between flat patterns and deep space to create powerful images. The French author Jollivet-Castellot, who met Spilliaert in 1909, wrote of his art in 1912:

> His art communicates, above all, the vertigo of the infinite. When he paints a seascape, it is as if, there in front of you, is the endless ocean with its mysterious waves, the monotonous beach and a sky which becomes one with the sea in the distance. When he represents the sea-wall or the quay, their lines stretch until they are lost in empty distance... No limits, no milestones, no premature stopping places. Horizons flee, plunging through space, creating a dream of thought and hopes.[46]

Spilliaert's *Wharf With Fisherman Seated On a Mooring Post* of 1909 (**no. 7**) shows a dreamlike space with an exaggerated perspective, as the lines of the wharf recede dramatically, isolating the tiny figure of the fisherman in the distance. The picture plane seems tilted, though, so that the wharf seems to rise upward as much as it recedes. The ambiguity of space creates a mesmerizing effect. Although the painting is completely rooted in the natural scene, the stylization makes it very abstract.

His *Park in Autumn* (1925, **no. 8**) emphasizes the lyrical rhythms of nature. As with Gustave van de Woestyne and Albert Saverys, Spilliaert was fascinated by the complex linear pattern of tree branches, and the tension between surface pattern and the illusion of depth.

Gustave de Smet (1877-1943; also known as Gust de Smet) and others celebrate the modern world with links to cosmopolitan abstraction, especially the German Expressionists. De Smet studied from 1889 to 1896 at the Royal Academy of Fine Arts in Ghent. Along with Frits van den Berghe, he was part of the second school of artists at Laethem-Saint-Martin. When World War I broke out, he fled Ghent with his wife and son to the Netherlands. This period of exile brought him closer to foreign styles, such as Cubism and German Expressionism.[47] His painting of *Horses in an Orchard* (1920, **no. 14**) resembles certain works of the German Expressionist Franz Marc. The fusion of animal, house, and trees into a faceted cubistic landscape suggests the unity of nature and spirit that infused modern abstract art.

The crystalline geometry of the painting hints at a deeper unity in nature than can be found in Impressionism, which breaks up the natural forms with light. The variety of surfaces and light effects found in Emile Claus's Impressionist pictures is de-emphasized in favor of a less organic structure. De Smet almost seems to be following the prescription of Wilhelm Worringer, who called for a transcendental form in his book *Abstraction and Empathy* (1908):

> Thus all transcendental art sets out with the aim of de-organicising the organic, i.e. of translating the mutable and conditional into values of unconditional necessity. But such a necessity man is able to feel only in the great world beyond the living, in the world of the inorganic. This led him to rigid lines, to inert crystalline form. He translated everything living into the language of these imperishable and unconditional values. For these abstract forms, liberated from all finiteness, are the only ones, and the highest, in which man can find rest from the confusion of the world picture.[48]

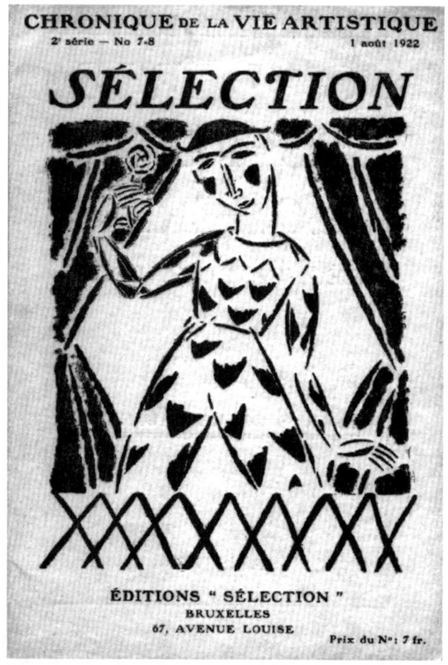

11. Gustave de Smet: cover for *Sélection*, 1922. Photo courtesy of Gallery Patrick Derom, Brussels.

De Smet discovered this new approach while working in the Netherlands during the war, achieving his breakthrough to Expressionism in 1916. Color and form became more abstract and were used as signs to convey mental and emotional states rather than simple visual perceptions.

Belgian Expressionism is more contemplative and less filled with torment than the art of the German Expressionists. Their characteristic inner anxieties, doubt, and ambivalence are lacking here.[49] The Cubist influence prevails, leading to a more measured analysis of form and tempering the outpouring of emotion. Perhaps to accommodate that analysis, color is more restrained as well. The other side of the Expressionist coin, the faith in utopian solutions, is also absent. Instead, the artist escaped to the village and countryside in search of a modest and achievable form of purity.

Gust de Smet had returned to Belgium after the war, and continued to live and work in the region around the Leie river. Gust was a key figure among the artists supported by the Sélection gallery in Brussels, and his work was strongly promoted by Paul-Gustave Van Hecke, the gallery owner. De Smet's design for the cover of the *Sélection* magazine (fig. 11), leading organ of the Belgian avant-garde, was used for several years. The harlequin figure clearly signals an admiration for the works of Picasso, in subject and in its simplified synthetic cubist style it is like a painted collage.

Having finally achieved a new level of economic stability through exhibitions and sales, Gust de Smet commis-

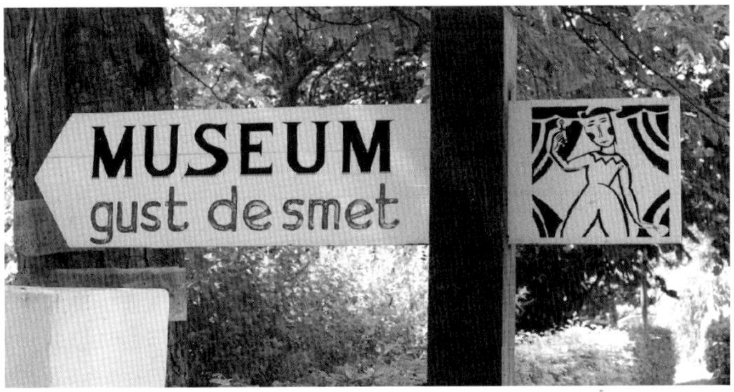

12. Museum Gustave de Smet, Deurle. Photo by author.

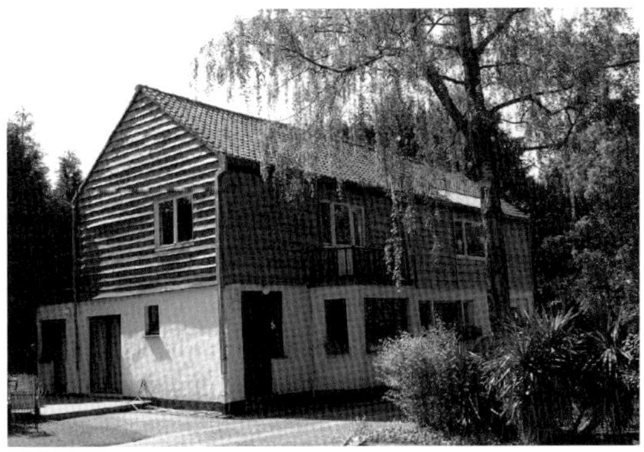

13. Museum Gustave de Smet, Deurle. Photo by author.

sioned the building of a large villa in Deurle in 1929.[50] The world-wide financial depression which began later that year forced him, however, to sell the villa in 1935 and move to a smaller and simpler house, which is now used as a museum to his art (figs. 12-13). The harmony of music and art is reflected in De Smet's studio at Deurle; a piano shares the space with his easel, both beside the stove for comfort.

The village was a sign of personal identity, as well as regional and national identity. "Local color" is not just a phrase. The small town reflects security and permanence as a symbol of the root unit of society, as much as the nuclear family. Village scenes had a particular resonance in Belgium, reflecting a nostalgia for the Middle Ages, when local cities

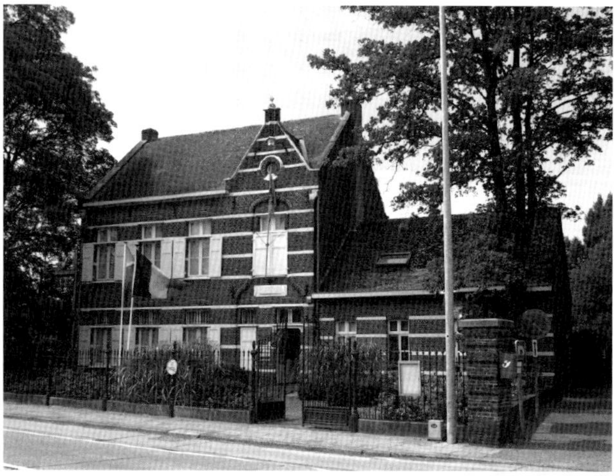

14. Jakob Smits Museum, Mol. Photo by author.

were a source of freedom, resisting distant rulers. De Smet's *View at Laethem-Saint-Martin* of 1936 (**no. 15**) depicts the artist's colony in colors as rich as stained glass.

Attachment to the landscape and village was particularly strong in the art and career of Jakob Smits (1855-1928). Born in Rotterdam, he studied art in Brussels (1873-1876), Munich (1878-1880), and Vienna and Rome (1880). In 1888 he settled in the Kempen region of Belgium, in the small village of Achterbos near Mol. He became a Belgian citizen in 1902. His profound attachment to the local community was evident during WWI, when Smits ceased painting to devote himself to the "Committee for Assistance and Providing Food for the Canton of Mol." After the war he resumed painting, but his health began to fail in 1923, bringing his career to an end.

Smits's earliest work was influenced by Impressionism, but after 1900 his style was closer to Symbolism and Expressionism. He is particularly known for his religious paintings, scenes of village life, and images of the aftermath of the war. In *The Village* (1920, **no. 13**), a group of villagers in the foreground are sheltered by the clustered houses and village church. The town is the foundation of their security, and the embracing group of buildings gives a visual analog to that sense of shelter. Smits's style features a crusty, almost frozen, frothy brushstroke, as is also found in the late works of Monet. Smits is highly regarded in Belgium, and in 1977 the former vicarage of the village of Mol/Sluis was turned into a museum of his art (fig. 14).

Smits was attracted to the integrity and spiritual values that he found in village life. Folk culture became a primary subject for him, and the focus of historical and preservation studies in the culture at large. The second half of the nineteenth century saw the first organized preservation movements for architecture. Preservation was an essential tool in the shaping of national myths. In Belgium, the Grand' Place was restored under the leadership of Charles Buls, mayor of Brussels. Preservation was seen as a means not only to preserve the relics of the past, but also to validate the sense of a tradition. Decisions about what to preserve are never neutral; after all, in America it was the monuments of the Yankee founding fathers which were preserved, not the residences of immigrants.[51]

Folk culture received increasing attention in Europe in the late nineteenth and early twentieth centuries, partly as a response to modernization and partly as a source of national identity.[52] Rural life was attractive to artists not just for its picturesque value, but because the rural landscape seemed to offer a glimpse of the deeper national identity. Open air museums were created to preserve elements of folk culture and allow people to interact with relics and re-creations of the past.[53] This signaled a new recognition of the importance of material culture and also nationalistic awareness. In Belgium, the open air museum of Bokrijk, near Hasselt, was founded in 1953. Examples of vernacular architecture were moved to the site at Bokrijk, including farm structures from all over Belgium, and even a small section of a Flemish town.

Such open air museums can serve as a symbol of resistance to aristocratic dominance. Peasant life can be seen as pleasantly nostalgic and conservative, but also can be interpreted as the foundation of fundamental revolution, as in the French Revolution, or even earlier, the battle of the Golden Spurs. In Belgium, bucolic rural scenes of Flemish village life were also viewed as the counterpart to Walloon industrial cities, with conservative Catholic values opposing modernist socialism. This division became more polarized after WWII.[54] Only recently have abandoned industrial sites become museums, as at the site of Grand Hornu near Charleroi in Wallonia.

The new attention to folk culture and vernacular architecture was part of a revaluation of peasant life, which was believed to embody positive values of simplicity and honesty and to reflect a direct tie to the land. Peasant life was increasingly valued in literature as well, from Maurice Maeterlinck's *Le Trésor des Humbles* (*The Treasure of the Humble*, 1896) and Emile Verhaeren's three-part trilogy of poetry evoking the relationship between the city and rural life: *Les Campagnes Hallucinatoires* (*The Hallucinatory Countryside*, 1893), *Les Villes Tentaculaires* (*The Tentacular Cities,* 1895), and *Les Aubes* (*The Dawns,* 1898). These represented a rejection of the neurasthenia of Joris-Karl Huysmans's famous Symbolist novel, *À Rebours* (*Against Nature*, 1884), and Georges Rodenbach's melancholy and morbid *Bruges-la-Morte* (*Bruges the Dead*, 1892). While valuing the psychological acuity of Huysmans and Rodenbach, the new authors found a more positive outlook on nature. This was furthered by Karel van de Woestyne (1878-1929), brother of the painter Gustave. He was the leading poet associated with the *Van Nu en Straks* ("From Now On") group in the 1890s, and he led the artistic circle *Open Wegen* ("Open Roads") in Laethem-Saint-Martin in 1902-1913. His writing analyzed the struggle between intellect and nature. His novella, *De Boer Die Sterft* (*A Farmer Dies*, 1918), was highly regarded.

Tales of peasant life were favored in the teens and twenties because they seemed apolitical, focusing on issues of local identity, piety, and character—Felix Timmermans's 1916 novel *Pallieter,* set in the town of Lier, is an important example.[55] However, they could be read either as offering tacit support for the activist Flemish political agenda, or as a rejection of politics. Flemish and Walloon folk songs played similar roles as cultural symbols.

Constant Permeke (1886-1952) lived in Ostend when he was young, then studied at the academies in Bruges and Ghent. In 1909 he joined Frits van den Berghe and others at the artists' colony of Laethem-Saint-Martin. Permeke fought in the defense of Antwerp in 1914 and was seriously wounded. He was sent to England to recover, where he spent the rest of the war years. In 1929 he moved to the village of Jabbeke, between Bruges and the coast, and built a house and studio called *De Vier Winden* ("The Four Winds"), which is now a museum of his art. During WWII, Permeke remained in occupied Belgium, but was unable to obtain painting materials, and so concentrated on drawing. After the war he was appointed as Director of the National Higher Institute of Fine Arts and of the Royal Academy of Fine Arts in Antwerp.

The image of the horseman might seem very old-fashioned, but it also has an iconic role in modernism. The Expressionists Franz Marc, Paul Klee, and Wassily Kandinsky named their group The Blue Rider, after all. Even Futurists, such as Umberto Boccioni, included powerful horses in their avant-garde art as well. Horses still played important roles even in the mechanized environment of the First World War. The horse was a symbol of nature and power, as well as the human relationship with nature and culture. It was an emblem of a pre-industrial era that was vanishing. Permeke's painting of *The Village Rider* (1936, **no. 16**) is thus simultaneously modern and traditional. His fusion of traditional imagery and modernism will also be seen in *The Fisherman*, discussed further below.

Work and Labor

In the second half of the nineteenth century, Belgium became one of the most industrialized and one of the wealthiest nations in the world. Living standards for the working classes were poor, however, and there were violent labor actions in the 1880s and 1890s. While in some ways the political situation was more liberal than in other countries—freedom of the press and freedom of association were protected—until 1893, voting rights were severely limited. Even in 1893, the new universal male suffrage was qualified by a system which gave more votes to property holders. The labor movement was rooted in a long democratic struggle: the record of workers challenging aristocrats and the bourgeoisie extends back to the weavers of medieval Ghent and the Battle of the Golden Spurs. The Belgian Worker's Party (*Parti Ouvrier Belge*, or P.O.B.) was founded in 1885 and won wide support from intellectuals and artists with its program which stressed evolution over revolution.[56] Origins of the party can be traced to cooperative associations, such as a worker's cooperative bakery founded in Ghent in 1881. The leaders of the Belgian Worker's Party sought out the participation of writers, artists, and architects. The Workers' Centers (Maisons du Peuple), which were founded in the major cities, included provisions for artistic events to bring culture to the working classes. Many Belgian artists lent their support to these efforts, even if their personal politics remained more conservative.

Labor was one of the most important social and artistic issues in the late nineteenth century. Modernism was predicated on the depiction of contemporary life, and the worker was emblematic of the impact of industrialization. From the Realist movement onward, avant-garde artists were drawn to radical labor politics. Gustave Courbet's pivotal painting *The Stonebreakers* was shown in Brussels at the Salon of 1851, and workers were increasingly represented in painting and sculpture in subsequent decades. Jules Destrée noted that "The Worker entered into Art and was recognized as the equal of the ancient gods."[57] The painter Jakob Smits declared in 1921 that "I like the workers, for they are honest and honourable and their hearts are in the right place. People think that money means power, a good education, etc. They forget that it is a question of sensitivity and nobility of the soul... A working man is a man of high moral standing."[58]

Belgian avant-garde artists and socialists shared the belief that art was both a collective expression of the people and also a personal statement of the individual. Although art had historically been the province of the wealthy, they believed that the social benefits of art should be shared by all. This belief reinforced the new interest in commercial art and decorative arts. It was hoped that art could become a part of ordinary life. Designers, even if producing luxury goods, considered their works as models that would elevate the standards of mass production. Architecture was even more directly linked to society.

The Section d'Art of the Maison du Peuple was founded to establish alliances with leading artists and to bring art to the workers. The directors of the Section d'Art included the writers Emile Verhaeren and Edmond Picard, the artist Fernand Khnopff, and the critic Octave Maus, secretary for the group of artists known as Les XX. They were not required to belong to the Belgian Worker's Party, or even to agree with its program.[59] The Section d'Art organized lectures, musical evenings, and exhibitions. Inspired by British experiments such as the Working Man's College in London, where John Ruskin and Dante Gabriel Rossetti had taught, the Section d'Art even included slide lectures on Flemish painting by the Symbolist artist Fernand Khnopff.

In 1895, the directors of the Belgian Worker's Party chose Victor Horta as the architect for a new home for the Maison du Peuple.[60] Horta's Art Nouveau masterpiece, the Maison du Peuple (House of the People, or Worker's Center) in Brussels, was the most striking demonstration of the paradoxical connections between Modern art and socialism in Belgium. Built on a very irregular site, the building included a café, a cooperative bakery, with a butcher and other shops on the ground floor, and a lecture hall and theater which held fifteen hundred people on the second floor. This new style of architecture was thought to be a fitting complement to the reforms sought by the Belgian Worker's Party. The program for the building was practical and stressed functionality. Spaces were open and uncluttered. The industrial strength of Belgium was reflected in the exposed iron and steel columns and girders. The innovative use of industrial materials was one of Art Nouveau's chief contributions to the development of later modernist architecture. The destruction of Horta's Maison du Peuple in 1965-66 was a tragic loss.

There were many other workers' centers in Belgium, some of which survive. Although not all were built in the Art Nouveau style, this was the style most widely identified with the movement. The Worker's Center in Antwerp

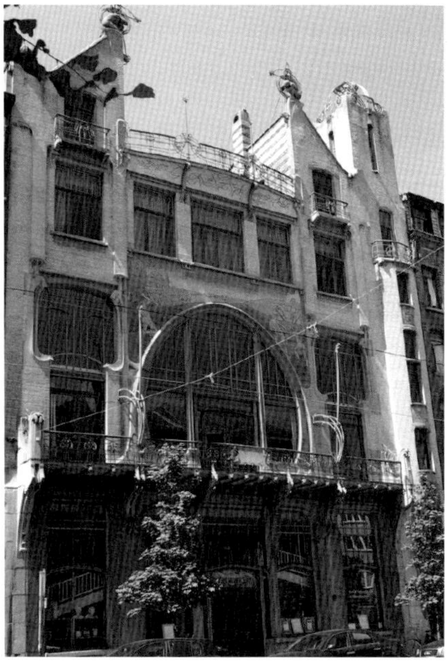

15. Emile Van Averbeke and J. Van Asperen: Liberaal Volkshuis "Help u zelve," Antwerp, 1898. Photo by author.

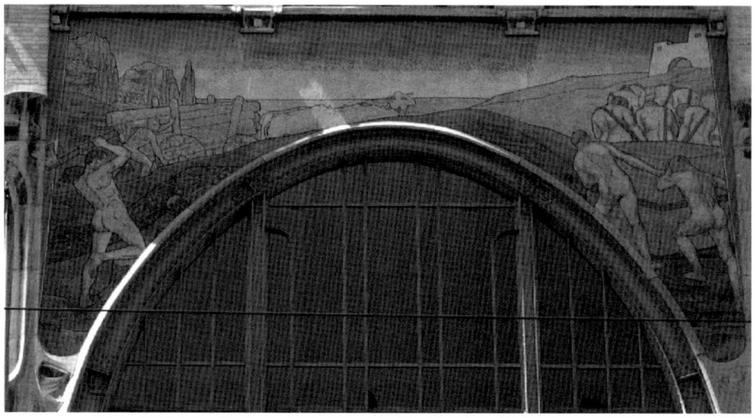

16. Emile Van Averbeke and J. Van Asperen: Liberaal Volkshuis "Help u zelve," Antwerp, 1898, detail. Photo by author.

(40 Volkstraat), the Liberaal Volkshuis, was designed by Emile Van Averbeke and J. Van Asperen (fig. 15). It bears the motto on its facade: "Help u zelve" (Help yourselves) and a mosaic of workers around the Art Nouveau curved central window (fig. 16).[61]

Workers were the primary focus of Constantin Meunier (1831-1905), the most important sculptor in Belgium of the late nineteenth century.[62] Meunier was trained as both a painter and sculptor, working primarily in painting until 1880. Through the 1870s, most of his works were religious paintings. After about 1885, he concentrated on creating realist sculptures of workers in Belgium, especially coal miners. His images of miners were inspired by the scenes of misery in the Borinage area near Charleroi, which had had such a powerful effect on Vincent van Gogh when he briefly served as a minister in that region in the late 1870s. In 1889, Van Gogh praised Meunier's works: "... a man who is very much my superior, Meunier, has painted the 'Sclôneuses' of the Borinage and the shift going to the pits, and the factories, their red roofs and their black chimneys against a delicate gray sky—all things that I have dreamed of doing, feeling that it had not been done and that it ought to be painted."[63]

Although Van Gogh's fame has since eclipsed that of the Belgian artist, Meunier's realist images are very highly regarded. From 1887-1894, Meunier served as director of the Louvain (Leuven) Academy of Fine Arts.

Meunier's large scale sculptures show laborers who are often heroically powerful, as in *The Stevedore* of 1885, which has become a symbol for the city of Antwerp. Sometimes they are worn-out and exhausted, depicted as martyrs to labor. One sculpture in the Royal Museums of Art in Brussels, titled *The Fire Damp*, shows a dead miner with his mother bending over his nude body. Were it not for the miner's lamp and helmet beside the body, one might mistake the subject for a Pieta, with Mary bending over the body of the dead Christ.

During his lifetime Meunier was perhaps the leading rival to Auguste Rodin as a sculptor. There is a museum dedicated to him in Brussels at 59 rue de l'Abbaye, his former house and studio, located just off the Avenue Louise. The two sculptures by Meunier included in this exhibition juxtapose images of two kinds of labor: modern industrial production in *The Rolling Mill Worker* (1900, **no. 17**), which depicts a modern ironworker, and traditional rural occupation in *The Woodcutter* (1898, **no. 18**). These are powerful figures of labor in the modern world, exemplifying industrial and agricultural strength.

Traditional rural labor is also the subject of Emile Claus's work *The Mower* (1897, **no. 20**), which parallels the harmony of this labor with the rhythm of the seasons. This work follows Camille Pissarro and Jules Bastien-Lepage in the depiction of farm labor in glowing sunlight. Celebrating the environment was integral to the development of Belgian Luminism.

In 1891, Henry van de Velde gave a lecture at Les XX titled "On the Peasant in Painting," in which he called for the emulation of Camille Pissarro's more naturalistic portrayals of peasants, where the environment is included, rather than the heroic images of J.F. Millet, where a single figure might fill the canvas. As an Arts and Crafts designer who was soon to be a leader of the Art Nouveau movement, Van de Velde was committed to a nostalgic idealization of the simple life of the peasant.[64]

Belgium is bound to the sea by trade and fishing, and toil at sea has provided numerous subjects for artists. Fishing is a traditional occupation in coastal Belgium, pursued with many variations. Adrien-Joseph Heymans's painting of *Eel Catchers* (c. 1893, **no. 19**) shows fishermen working at night by lamplight to catch nocturnal feeding eels through the ice. With Emile Claus, Heymans was a leader of the Vie et Lumière group in the Laethem-Saint-Martin region. This work has a delicate brushstroke which is nearly Neo-Impressionist with its small divided touches. The luminosity of sky and snow prevails, even though the fishermen are using lanterns to attract the catch.

Constant Permeke's *Harvesters Sleeping in the Sun* (1917, **no. 21**) recalls images of Pieter Bruegel, although with a tighter focus on the large forms of the sleeping workers. It was painted in 1917 in Devonshire, England. Permeke had been wounded in the war and was evacuated to England to recuperate. During this period of exile, he developed a more abstract, modernist style. This picture is flooded with the warm light of mid-day, when the workers take their rest.

The sailor shown in Constant Permeke's *Fisherman in Ostend* (1923, **no. 22**) shows a much larger, more simplified figure, and a more somber palette. The heroic half-length figure dominates the canvas. The monochromatic color range recalls the early Analytic Cubism of Picasso and Braque. The powerful figure of the sailor is part of the tradition of strong images of laborers in modern Belgian art.

Permeke's work not only shows the impact of early Cubism and Expressionism, but also goes back to their sources. The fisherman's triangular chiseled nose and angular jaw strongly resembles African masks and sculpture. African art played a complex role in Belgian art, beginning with the late nineteenth century. King Leopold II's exploition of the Belgian Congo, a tragic episode in world history, brought him great wealth, and his regime sought to expand the market of Congolese products in Europe.[65] Artists were even given free ivory in the 1890s to encourage them to use this material in sculptures. In 1908, the Congo Free State was transferred from Leopold's private control to the Belgian government, as the colony of the Belgian Congo. Except for the precocious example of James Ensor, who introduced African masks in his paintings as early as the 1880s, it was not until the twentieth century that artists began to be influenced by African art, particularly masks. The most famous example is Picasso, but Henri Matisse, André Derain, and Maurice Vlaminck were also among the first major artists to collect African art, beginning around 1906. The German Expressionists Ernst Ludwig Kirchner and Emil Nolde began intensive study of African Art around 1910-11.[66] The Belgian artists Permeke, Gustave de Smet, and Frits van den Berghe began to collect African sculpture after 1920.[67] Underscoring the tie between modernism and African art, the Brussels journal *Variétés* featured a mask on the cover

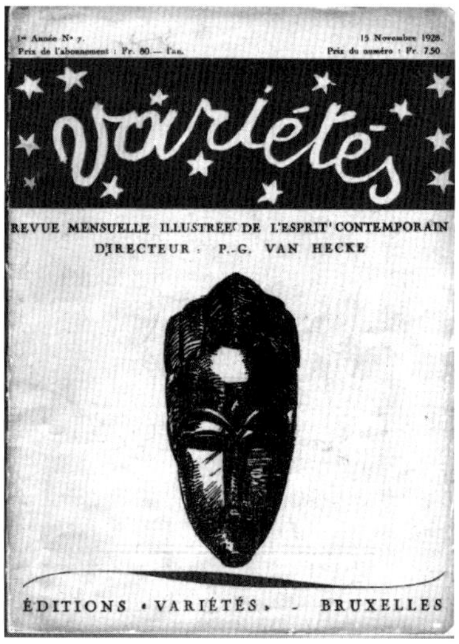

17. Cover to *Variétés*, featuring African Mask, 1928.

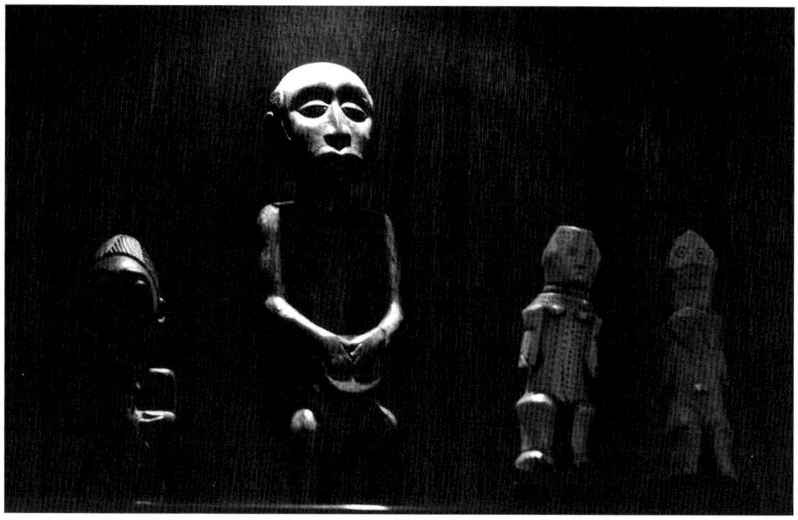

18. African Sculpture in Permeke's collection, Jabbeke. Photo by author.

in 1928 (fig. 17). Examples of Permeke's collection can still be seen in his house, which is now a museum (fig. 18). Although the Congo was no longer the private domain of Leopold, the colonial enterprise was still going strong. As partial reparation for the economic damage Belgium suffered during World War I, Belgium was awarded Rwanda, part of the former German East Africa.

Modernist artists were attracted to African and other so-called "primitive" art forms not only for their formal qualities, but also for the mystique of an idealized life closer to nature. The art came from places untainted by western civilization, and thus offered a new alternative to the academic tradition. The simplified abstract style seemed to evoke an essential quality more powerful than photographic realism. Permeke's ponderous figures clearly owe something to Giotto as well as African art.[68] To more fully express their response to the modern world, avant-garde artists sought alternative forms of visual expression in other cultures, which would allow them to establish a distance between themselves and European bourgeois culture.

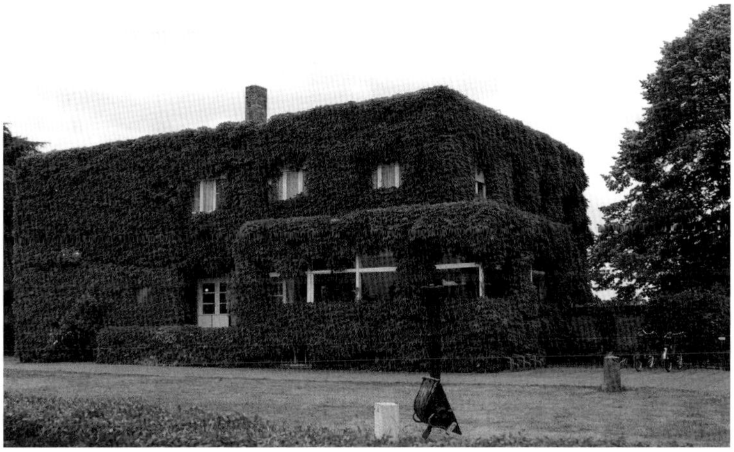

19. *De Vier Winden* (The Four Winds), Constant Permeke house, built in 1929, Jabbeke, now a museum. Photo by author.

The paradox of Permeke's Primitivist style is highlighted by *De Vier Winden* ("The Four Winds"), the ultramodern house he built in Jabbeke in 1929 (fig. 19). This flat-roofed, anti-traditional house (now covered with ivy) was inspired by the latest examples of the International Style, which celebrated technology and modern life.

The View from Within: Interiors and Still life

Where landscape painting reflected the dialogue between the artist and the external world, painting interiors and still lifes focused on the domestic sphere and often the artist's own environment. Indeed, the art of living, including an emphasis on food and cuisine, is an integral part of the cultural heritage of Belgium.

Although the French academy, which was established in the seventeenth century, relegated still life painting to a very minor position, Flemish and Dutch painters ignored the academy's hierarchy and created major works in this field. Still life painting first emerged in the mid-sixteenth century in the works of Pieter Aertsen, a Dutch artist who lived in Antwerp for thirty years. Aertsen combined religious scenes with sumptuous still life compositions in a novel way. In Aertsen's works, the still life subject typically dominates the foreground, while the religious scene is relatively small and in the background. This is a kind of "inverted" perspective related to Mannerist art and is extremely sophisticated in the ambiguity regarding which subject is primary in the painting.[69]

The symbolic meaning of Baroque still life paintings has been much discussed. They clearly stem from the tradition of including realistic details in religious paintings, such as those of Jan van Eyck and Robert Campin. Pieter Aertsen's "inverted still lifes" are clearly religious in content. There is strong evidence that many still lifes were painted to include "disguised symbolism" representing the transience of mortal life. Some paintings include skulls or other symbols of death, obvious symbols which were combined with beautiful flowers and fruits, sometimes with flies on them. Soap bubbles were also used as parallel symbols. Flowers and fruits are notoriously short-lived, and emblem books of the period include them as symbols of *vanitas*, the theme of the brevity of life. (Emblem books are compilations of symbolic images and moralizing texts which were popular in the sixteenth and seventeenth centuries. They often provide an invaluable key to the symbolism of the period.) One of the basic qualities of disguised symbols, however, is that they can also be seen as ordinary objects. Some art historians have downplayed the significance of *vanitas* symbolism in still life painting, arguing that the works are fundamentally descriptive.[70] However, while these works were almost certainly created to be beautiful paintings and to celebrate the bounty and seasons of life, that is not inconsistent with a secondary layer of more somber metaphysical meaning. The role of *vanitas* symbolism is surely stronger in some paintings than others. While it can be tempting to look for symbolism in every detail of a painting, a sensible balance must be found. As one art historian observed, "Cheese was rarely consumed on an allegorical level in the seventeenth century."[71]

The same might be said of fish and vegetables, which figure in two wonderful still-life paintings by James Ensor in the Simon Collection. The *Still Life with Fish and Shellfish* (1895, **no. 23**) and the *Still life with Vegetables and Lamp* (1908, **no. 24**) are luminous images of the bounty of the sea and land. There is nothing ostentatious about these still lifes, however; they are not at all like the Baroque excess of *pronkstilleven*, the showy displays of food and costly goblets and silver created by artists such as Willem Kalf or Jan Davidsz. de Heem in the seventeenth century. These are more humble, yet rich in their restrained elegance. Katherine Nahum offers stimulating insights into these paintings in her essay on "Ensor's Parrot" in this volume.

Still-life paintings are about life and also death; the term for "still life" in French is *Nature morte*. The still-life painting freezes the harvest of life in a perpetual image of perfection and balance. The sustenance of fish and fruit is removed from practical life, but made permanently accessible for the delectation of the viewer. The visual pleasure here is created by Ensor's color and brushstroke as much as it is by the inherent beauty of the objects; the painterly style reminds us that we are looking at a work of art. There is no attempt to trick the eye into believing that these objects are in fact real, in the manner of illusionist or *trompe-l'oeil* painting. They are celebrations of the act of painting and creative vision.

Léon de Smet's sunlit painting *The Table* (1910, **no. 25**) is an image of domestic pleasure and aesthetic simplicity. De Smet (1881–1966) was the younger brother of Gust de Smet, and also a painter. The artistic interior shown here reveals the influence of the Arts and Crafts movement and Art Nouveau, particularly evident in the modern bentwood furniture. Art and life merge in the Arts and Crafts movement. The domestic sphere of daily activities is displayed before a backdrop of nature in bloom. Inside and outside are juxtaposed, with the window mullions revealing a glimpse of the garden outside while the tablecloth repeats the geometry of the window in a two-dimensional pattern. The table itself becomes a still-life object in the hushed interior. The small sculpture at the rear is George Minne's *Man with a Water Sack* (1897), which belonged to De Smet. It appears in contemporaneous photographs of the De Smet family in their home. The artist's technique shows the tightly controlled yet luminous brushwork of Neo-Impressionism.

The return to a simpler mode of life, such as the rural life of Laethem-Saint-Martin, was associated with a rejection of bourgeois values. The idealized cottage life found its visual form in the sleek Art Nouveau designs of the furniture. Amy Ogata has noted that Belgian Art Nouveau interior design suggested a rustic simplicity, in contrast to French Art Nouveau, which sought to revive a more ornate neo-Rococo style.[72]

The *Still Life with Two Shells* (1926, **no. 26**) by Jean Brusselmans (1884-1953) in this exhibition is a focused study of objects on a tabletop. It shows a more somber palette, and almost collage-like approach to the composition that resembles the Synthetic Cubism of Picasso. Objects are outlined with thick brushstrokes, and the flattened silhouettes of the shells and vases seem to be collaged onto the canvas. There is no attempt to render the illusion of depth, and the flattened forms appear to float on the surface of the canvas. The harmonies of shape and form, of nature (the shells and flower) and culture (the vases and fan), form a series of visual rhymes. The abstract focus and emphasis on structure in the stil-life subject recalls the works of the Italian artist Giorgio Morandi. The viewer focuses on the outline, and perhaps the essence, of the shells and vases.

Brusselmans, as his name suggests, was born in the Belgium capital and entered the Académie Royale des Beaux-Arts in 1897. He shared a studio with the artist Rik Wouters in 1907 and developed friendships with other young avant-garde artists. He joined Constant Permeke, Léon Spilliaert, Edgard Tytgat, and Wouters in a notable group show at the Galerie George Giroux; his first one-person show was in Antwerp in 1921. Through the 1920s, he exhibited frequently at the gallery Le Centaure, and he also became a member of the artistic group Kunst van Heden (Contemporary Art) in Antwerp.

The Figure

Although the human figure was the basis for academic study, it was by no means outmoded in the early modern period. The human form is one of the richest subjects and has long been the focus of struggle for meaning and control in the modern world. In recent years, the body has not only served as the subject for artists, but also as the medium in the field of "body art." Figure painting lends itself to many purposes. It can either reflect a conservative tradition and a return to order, or provide the basis for transgressive images. The figure can be used to reintroduce a mythic dimension in art or serve as a motif for experiments in style. From conservative leanings to the avant-garde, we can see all of these in the Simon Collection paintings.

Théo van Rysselberghe's *Portrait of Claire Demolder* (1902, **no. 29**) presents a fascinating image of a strongly independent woman. Claire Demolder (1870-1944) was the daughter of Félicien Rops, and wife of Eugène Demolder, writer and poet. Her mother was Léontine Duluc, sister of Aurélie Duluc, who also shared a household with Rops in Paris. Her mother and aunt were talented dressmakers, for whom Rops made dress designs.[73] Claire's husband was a leading figure in the *Jeune Belgique* movement at the end of the nineteenth century. Demolder's adventurous side is suggested by his writing one of the first accounts of travel by automobile, *L'Espagne en auto* (1906).

Van Rysselberghe's portrait captures the confidence and intelligence of Claire Demolder. She leans forward in her chair, her gaze interrogating the viewer, while her body language portrays both thoughtfulness and mobility. The pointillism of the Neo-Impressionist style enhances the color and further conveys modernity and energy.

Georges Lemmen (1865-1916) was a child prodigy, who first exhibited at age ten. In the mid-1880s, he participated in the group L'Essor, exhibiting works which were highly detailed and similar in style to that of the Symbolist artist Fernand Khnopff. In 1888, he joined the exhibition group Les XX and quickly adopted the Neo-Impressionist style of the French artist Georges Seurat. By 1900, however, he dropped the pure pointillist technique for a less demanding and more realist approach, as seen in *Little Pierre* (c. 1901, **no. 30**). The prominent sunflowers reflect his long involvement with the decorative arts movement and strong influence from the English Aesthetic Movement.[74] The pairing of child and sunflower recalls earlier Romantic paintings which showed the beauty and growth of children by depicting them with burgeoning sunflowers, such as Philip Otto Runge's portrait of the *Hülsenbeck Children* (Hamburg, Kunsthalle, 1805-06). Vincent van Gogh's famous sunflower paintings of 1888 underscored the importance of the sunflower as a symbol of art and nature.

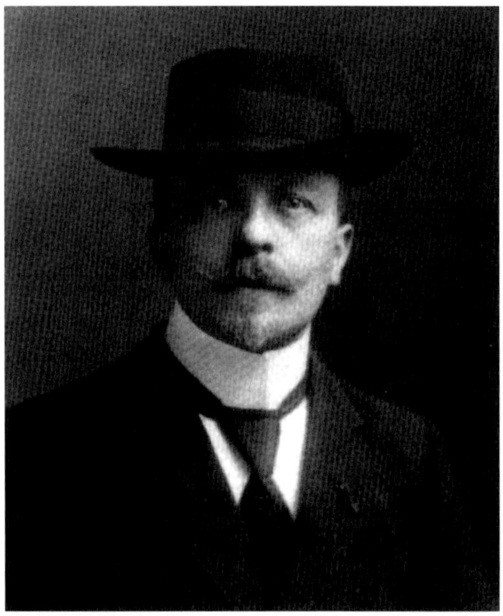

20. George Minne, 1911.

Lemmen's lush *Nude* (1908, **no. 31**) presents a model surrounded by flowers and fruits, painted in rich glowing colors. The image of fecundity parallels some of the Symbolist images of nature and fertility painted by Léon Frédéric in the late nineteenth century and Peter Paul Rubens in the Baroque era. It is both modern and slightly old-fashioned at the same time. Like the French artist Pierre-Auguste Renoir, Lemmen returns to a luxuriant classicism.

One of the most important sculptors of this period was George Minne (1866-1941). Minne, also well known for his drawings and prints, was deeply influenced by the Symbolist literature of Grégoire Le Roy, Maurice Maeterlinck, and Emile Verhaeren. He created illustrations and designs for many of their books of poetry. His style is archaic, and his sculpture is usually characterized by a Gothic slenderness, giving an almost ethereal quality to his figures.

The essay in this volume by Claude Cernuschi, "Freudian Themes in the Symbolist Art of George Minne," explores the deeper meaning of Minne's figures, including the oak carving known as the *Kneeling Pair,* or *Adam and Eve* (1889, **no. 27**).

A plaster variant of Minne's most well-known work, *The Fountain with Kneeling Youths,* was first exhibited at La Libre Esthétique in Brussels in 1899. The final form was commissioned in 1905 and completed in 1906.[75] Bronze copies are found in Ghent and Brussels (fig. 21). The sculpture consists of five identical adolescent male nudes, kneeling around a fountain with their arms crossed over their chests. The eurythmic repetition of a single figure echoes Khnopff's duplicated images of his sister in *Memories* (1889, Royal Museums of Fine Arts of Belgium, Brussels) and also parallels Auguste Rodin's method of combining several casts of a single figure to make a group composition. Rodin's group of the *Three Shades* over *The Gates of Hell* is the most obvious example. The repetition of the forms removes the work from any possible naturalistic setting, and the tripled ritualistic pose creates a sense of mystery.

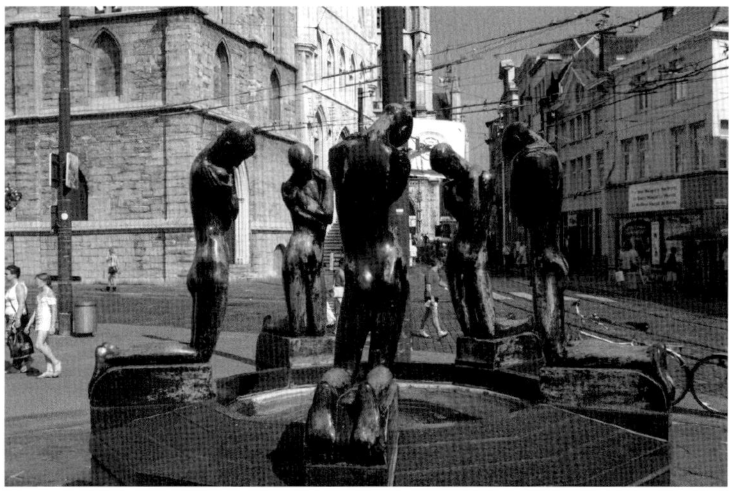

21. George Minne: *The Fountain of Kneeling Youths*, Ghent. Photo by author.

The fountain is a quiet and enigmatic work; Minne's art was often compared to Maeterlinck's dream-like and suggestive Symbolist poetry. Even the subject is not clearly articulated, although it must be based on the myth of Narcissus, the beautiful Greek youth who fell in love with his own mirrored reflection in the water. Unable to tear himself away from the image of his beloved, Narcissus eventually died. Mystics of the late nineteenth century revived older traditions which viewed Narcissus' love of his own image to be an allegory of the desire for self-knowledge and the concurrent peril of becoming trapped by the attractiveness of matter, which could snare the soul on an earthly plane. Minne's religious faith led him to emphasize the spiritual aspect of his figures.

Minne was extremely productive before 1900 but attained his greatest fame after that. His work became somewhat repetitive, a problem he attempted to address by studying anatomy and working from live models in 1910-12.[76] During the First World War he was limited to drawing, but created a large body of works depicting highly expressive religious subjects and themes of motherhood.

Rik Wouters (1882-1916) is one of the most engaging artists of what has been called Brabant Fauvism. He was born in Mechelen and studied sculpture and painting. Early on, he worked in an Impressionist style, but influenced by Cézanne, whom he discovered in Paris in 1912, he moved to a more abstract style. His color was clearly influenced by Matisse and also the German Expressionists, but his paintings generally have a calm serenity which is foreign to the German artists. The French Fauves, including Henri Matisse, were featured in an early exhibit at La Libre Esthétique in Brussels in 1906. His favorite model was his wife, Nel.

Wouters's *Woman with Gray Gloves* (1911, **no. 32**), set in a quiet interior, portrays a moment of daily life in the modern world, resembling similar earlier pictures by James Ensor. The woman in the corner of the bourgeois room is caught between interior and exterior, being inside, but still wearing her hat and gloves. Wouters's talented career was cut short by his early death in 1916 in the Netherlands. He had been mobilized into the Belgian army in 1914, and after the fall of Antwerp, he had been interned by the Dutch, but was released due to ill health.

Jos Albert (1886-1981) was born in Brussels, where he lived almost all of his life. His first art studies were at the Academy of Saint-Josse-ten-Noode, located in a suburb of Brussels. Often described as a Fauvist, his paintings clearly show the influence of Matisse and the French school, but they are calmer than the works of the "Wild Beasts." The stability and gravity of Cézanne also inspired him. The French Fauves were first shown in Brussels in 1913 at the Galerie Giroux.[77] Albert spent the war years in Brussels, but after the armistice spent three months in Paris, renewing contact with French art.[78]

In his *Portrait of the Artist's wife in a Scottish Shawl* (1918, **no. 33**), the reflected colors of the greenery and the vibrant tones of the shawl elevate this work beyond simple realism, and give a more musical effect. The pursuit of "color music," building on the psychological effect of synaesthesia, where one sense evokes another, was a major focus of Symbolist art and a key factor in the development of modernist abstraction.[79]

In 1861, Charles Baudelaire used the music of Wagner as an example of how meaning was expressed in the world and in art:

> For what would be really surprising would be if sound were incapable of suggesting colour, colours incapable of evoking a melody, and sound and colour incapable of translating ideas; for things have

> always expressed themselves through reciprocal analogy, since the day God decreed the world a complex and indivisible whole.[80]

Paul Gauguin reinforced the parallel of music and art: "Color which, like music, is a matter of vibrations, reaches what is most general and therefore most undefinable in nature: its inner power..."[81] Shortly before the war, the Belgian Symbolist Jean Delville inspired Alexander Scriabin to delve deeply into these parallels. Scriabin premiered his symphony *Prometheus: A Poem of Fire* in 1915 accompanied by an electric color organ.[82]

After the groundbreaking innovations of Belgian Symbolist art and Art Nouveau, it is something of a paradox that, although many aspects of modernism were available in Belgium, the new directions of Modern art had little direct impact in Belgium until after the First World War. This delayed effect, often remarked upon, cannot be entirely explained by the interruption of the First World War.

Les XX and La Libre Esthétique began a tradition of exhibiting cutting edge works by international artists, which continued into the early twentieth century. The controversial works of Matisse and other "Fauves" were shown at La Libre Esthétique in 1906. Mondrian's works were exhibited in Brussels.[83] Futurism was also known early in Belgium. Umberto Boccioni's paintings were shown with those of Carlo Carrà, Luigi Russolo, and Gino Severini in the first Futurist show in Paris, at the Galerie Bernheim-Jeune in 1912. The exhibition then traveled to London, Berlin, and it was shown at the Galérie Giroux in Brussels in May-June 1912. George Giroux also showed German Expressionists, including Franz Marc, in 1913.[84] James Ensor had been a fundamental influence on the young German painters. He was visited by Emil Nolde in 1911, and later by Erich Heckel, and his works were frequently exhibited in Germany before the war. The publication *The Blue Rider Almanach* was also available in Belgium, making accessible the abstract art of Kandinsky, Klee, and Franz Marc.

Some Belgian artists participated in these European movements early on: Jules Schmalzigaug and Joseph Lacasse showed the influence of Futurism as well as Cubism. Georges Vantongerloo provided direct contact with the Dutch artists of De Stijl. The abstract currents of Russian Constructivism and Suprematism were exhibited at the gallery Van Diemen in 1922 and were studied by the artists Victor Servranckx and Marcel Baugniet.[85] Frits van den Berghe and Gustave van de Woestyne found interesting parallels to their concerns in the *Neue Sachlichkeit* style of Christian Schad and other German artists.

The cross currents of Belgian modernism offer many undiscovered rewards for European and American audiences. The art and architecture in Belgium in the 1920s is of very high quality. In addition to outstanding examples of elegant art deco architecture, several first-rate planned communities, both English-style garden cities and international style communities, were built. Le Logis (fig. 22) and Floréal were two exceptional garden cities built in the suburb of

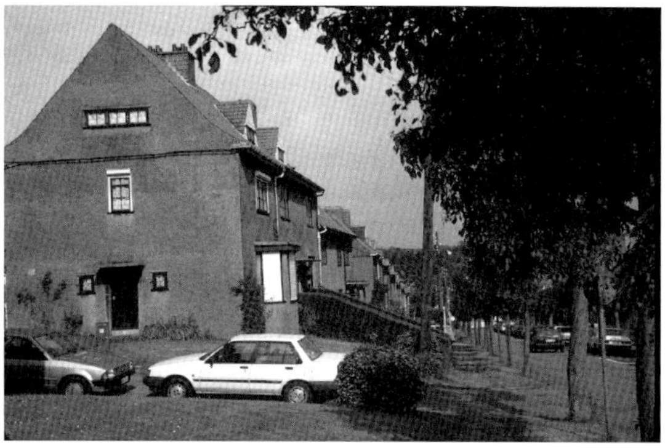

22. Louis van der Swaelmen, et al: Le Logis, Garden City, Watermael-Boitsfort (Brussels), 1920-27. Photo by author.

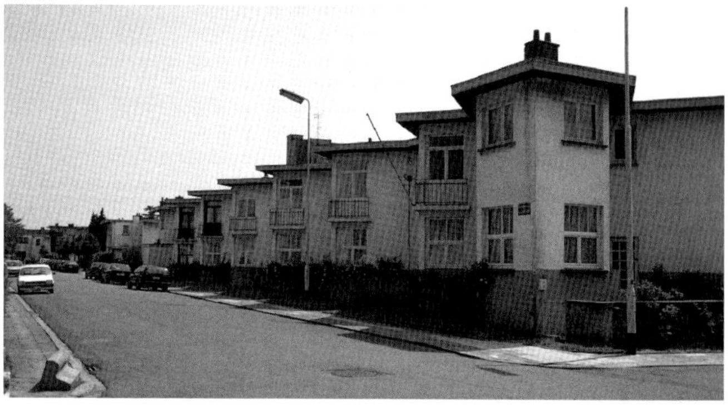

23. Victor Bourgeois and Louis van der Swaelmen: Cité Moderne, Brussels, 1922-24. Photo by author.

Watermael-Boitsfort (1920-27) by the architect Louis van der Swaelmen. Victor Bourgeois and Van der Swaelmen also built the Cité Moderne settlement in Brussels in 1922-24 (fig. 23).

The Cité Moderne project in particular featured flat roofs and pure white facades, with faceted angular facades which echo Cubist and Expressionist painting. The taste for avant-garde architecture was shared by many artists, as we have seen in Constant Permeke's house *De Vier Winden* ("The Four Winds"; fig. 19). Also noteworthy in this era is the house built by Le Corbusier for the painter René Guiette in Antwerp (fig. 24), and the house for Oscar Jespers by Victor Bourgeois of 1928 in Brussels. These modernist houses stood out dramatically against the earlier revivalist architecture that dominated Belgium. The abstract forms and flat roofs also challenged Art Nouveau, which had been the pre-eminent avant-garde style before 1914. The florid ornament of Art Nouveau has been abandoned in favor of a sleek, chaste style which was intended to celebrate technology, efficiency, and sober clarity. The style that had symbolized youth itself was now seen as old-fashioned.

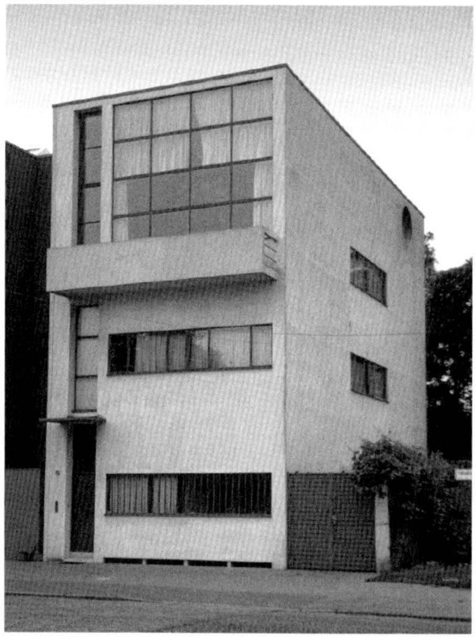

24. Le Corbusier: House for the painter René Guiette, Antwerp, 1926. Photo by author.

In a different setting, the tension between generations is also starkly depicted in Gustave van de Woestyne's painting of *Two Women* (1926, **no. 34**). The two figures are seated in rhyming postures, with the sensual nude torso of the young woman contrasted with the pinched figure of the scowling old woman, who is sheathed in a tight black dress. The repetition of poses reminds one of the eurhythmic compositions of George Minne and the similar composition in Paul Delvaux's painting

The Conversation (1944, **no. 52**). The old woman is shriveled, and even darkened in color, while the nubile young woman is luminous. She has a serious, even melancholy expression, however, suggesting that she is only too aware of the fleeting quality of youth. The tradition of *vanitas* painting is centuries old in the lowlands. The contrast of youth and age, of sexuality and the constrictions of society and age, are very stark here.

There is nothing primitive in this painting, either in subject or technique. The pale background is embossed with the pattern of handmade lace, which was a traditional occupation for women in Belgium. The artist may have actually pressed lace into the wet paint to establish the pattern. The lace background references the interior sphere occupied by these women and may also denote their occupation. Amy Ogata quotes a 1902 study on lace making by the Ministry of Industry and Work, in which the author Pierre Verhaegen asserts that lace making contributes to the moral preservation of young Belgian women, in that it "secures a woman to her home: later it reunites girls with their mothers and therefore protects them from harmful external contacts, and maintains among them a spirit of family."[86] The cottage industry was seen as a force to preserve national and family traditions.

The juxtaposition of the older clothed woman and nude young woman also raises the possibility of a connection to the brothel scenes painted by Pieter de Hooch and others during the seventeenth century, however. The tone of the picture seems to argue against the interpretation that this is a scene of illicit sexual commerce, but the precedent of Félicien Rops, who portrayed an older Madame presenting her latest employee to a client in *My Daughter, M. Cabanel* (1880s), and similar pictures by Frits van den Berghe (*Presentation of the Young Girl*, 1931, private collection) at least suggest that possibility.

Both *The Accordion Player* (1926, **no. 38**) and *The Young Captain* (1927, **no. 39**) by Gust de Smet show happy couples, radiant in domestic bliss. The style is lightly abstract, with bright areas of flat color. *The Accordion Player* in particular has a flattened, collage-like quality which recalls the Synthetic Cubism of Picasso in the teens and twenties and is also reminiscent of Fernand Léger. The accordion is a folk instrument frequently depicted by Picasso. Issue 4 in the first year of *Variétés* (1928) was largely an accordion special, with an article by Pierre Mac Orlan titled "Accordions," and many illustrations of works of art that include this instrument, by artists such as Van den Berghe, De Smet, and Osip Zadkine.[87] The accordion was invented in 1829 and became very popular in Paris in the 1880s in the style of music known as *Bal-musette*. The genre flourished in the 1920s, 1930s and 1940s, when jazz and tango influences revitalized the style. De Smet's *The Accordion Player* brings this musical form into the private sphere and reinforces the happy mood of the picture.

The couple in *The Young Captain* are dressed in matching sailor suits and pose beside a harbor, depicting the joy of life. Such images of domestic bliss were hard won after his depression over the death of his son during the war.

(See the discussion below of Frits van den Berghe's *Obsession III*, 1919, which portrays De Smet in the grip of this deep depression.)

Couples were also frequently the subject of paintings by Edgard Tytgat (1879-1957). In particular, the figure of a nude woman often appeared as Tytgat's muse. This role is explicit in a 1926 painting, *The Inspiration of the Artist* (Kortrijk [Courtrai], private collection). In this work, the white-haired artist confronts a blank canvas, but he is rescued from artist's block by the appearance of a nude woman seated on a cloud, accompanied by flying putti. Love and desire are both the subject and motivating force of his art.

The Interrupted Walk of 1936 (**no. 40**) shows the same artist (undoubtedly a self-portrait) in the countryside above a farm and paddock, holding a mandolin behind his back. A woman who has almost entirely removed her clothes, which lie on the ground behind her, stands before him as he scratches his chin. A certain innocence and ambiguity are present even in this image of potential disruption and desire. Is she the artist's model, and is he contemplating a revision of Edouard Manet's *Luncheon on the Grass* (Musée d'Orsay, 1863)? He holds a musical instrument rather than a paintbrush, so this may be a more general meditation on the role of desire in art. A realist reading of the scene would suggest that he has either stumbled upon this woman, interrupting his walk, or that they have interrupted their walk together to make love out of doors. The question remains open.

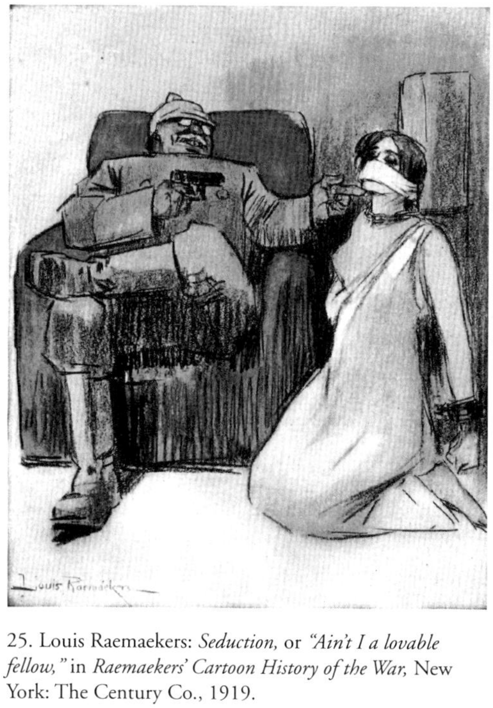

25. Louis Raemaekers: *Seduction,* or *"Ain't I a lovable fellow,"* in *Raemaekers' Cartoon History of the War,* New York: The Century Co., 1919.

The Impact of the First World War

Again and again in the history of Belgium, geography has shaped destiny, from Julius Caesar to Napoleon. Belgium was created as a neutral state to deny excess power to France or Germany. The neutrality of Belgium had been respected in the Franco-Prussian war of 1870, and Belgians counted on this again in 1914. However, on 4 August 1914, German forces invaded Belgium en route to attack France. The German high command counted on quick victory, using the Belgian transport system, in order to preserve their economy and to avoid a simultaneous two-front war. Meeting unexpected resistance, this quick victory did not happen, and the resulting four years of war transformed Europe and history.

The invasion of Belgium was delayed by resistance at Liége and Antwerp, and the German army was stalled by the Belgians flooding the fields near Nieuwkerk. However, most of Belgium fell, and Laethem-Saint-Martin was occupied on 12 October 1914. One consequence of the occupation was that artists were forbidden to paint out of doors.[88] The fear of spies eventually waned, however. By November of 1914, two million (out of a total population of 7.5 million) Belgians had fled the country; 600,000 stayed in exile until war's end.[89]

Occupied Belgium was depicted in art and propaganda images as a victim of brutality, with the invasion often portrayed in sexual terms of plunder and conquering. Such gender images and the feminization of conquered peoples is common in times of war.[90] The "Rape of Belgium" was a wide-spread image; this metaphor for vulnerability was effective as a plea for sympathy, even though it emphasizes the weakness of the victim (fig. 25).[91]

Although there were a few instances where the common humanity of the soldiers on both sides was acknowledged, particularly early in the war, the overwhelming majority of journalistic representations were intensely partisan propaganda images. The now famous "Christmas Truce" of December 1914 (fig. 26), a spontaneous cessation of hostilities in the trenches which was widely reported in the press, was not repeated and the episode was soon nearly forgotten.[92] The ambiguities of war were lost in the patriotic fervor. John Michalczyk's essay in this volume, "Occupied Belgium: The Art of War," highlights the struggle to represent these cataclysmic events.

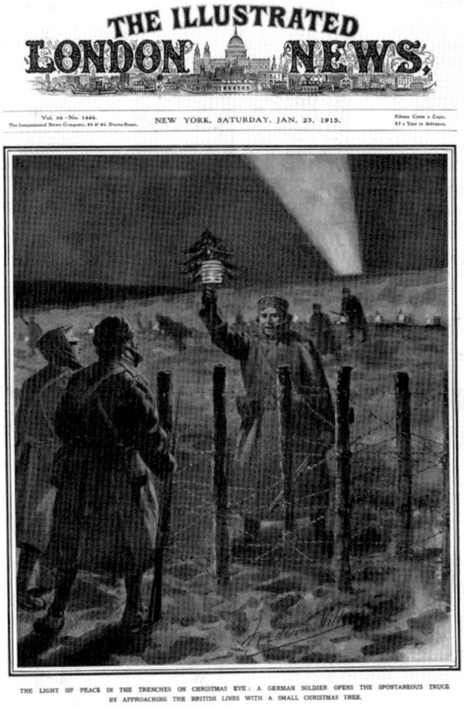

26. The Christmas Truce, Dec. 25, 1914. *The Illustrated London News* (New York), Saturday, Jan. 23, 1915. Author's collection.

Surprisingly, a Belgian artist who witnessed the invasion of his country captured some of that ambiguity. The first days of the occupation of Belgium were recorded in a drawing in 1914 (**no. 43**) by Edgard Tytgat, which he turned into a painting in 1918 (**no. 42**). *The First Invaders of Watermael* depicts an eerily calm scene where the first German soldiers appear in the square of a suburb of Brussels. Two are on horseback, while another steals apples from a tree. Belgian citizens—perhaps Tytgat and his wife?—watch from a balcony above. People go about their normal business, and the tram still runs. The color is light and tone almost droll, including a Bruegel-like motif of one soldier exposed in an outdoor toilet. The terror of invasion is defused through the almost Impressionistic approach, which must be a form of denial of the unacceptable reality. The calm tone contrasts strongly with the intense propagandistic images of the invasion published in England and France.

All Belgian artists were affected by the war, whether they stayed in Belgium or fled the country. Some served in the military forces: Constant Permeke, who was wounded near Antwerp and recovered in London; Rik Wouters; and Léon Spilliaert, who was mobilized as a member of the civil guard, but released from service. George Minne had three sons serving in the war. Also affected were Gustave de Smet, who lost his son, and Jakob Smits, who abandoned painting to aid his fellow villagers during the occupation.

Artists who stayed in Belgium spent the war years in various locations: Jakob Smits stayed in Achterbos, a tiny village near Mol, not far from the Dutch border. Brussels sheltered the Symbolist Fernand Khnopff, Georges Lemmen (d. 1916), Jos Albert, and the young artists Paul Delvaux and René Magritte. James Ensor and Léon Spilliaert were in Ostend, although Spilliaert moved in 1917 to Sint-Agatha-Berchem near Brussels. Jean Brusselmans lived in Oudergem, also on the outskirts of Brussels, during the war.

The war drove many artists from Belgium. Some escaped to the neutral Netherlands, which eventually put up an electrified fence to preserve their border and neutrality. William Degouve de Nuncques lived in Blaricum, near Amsterdam. Gustave de Smet lived together with Frits van den Berghe variously in Amsterdam, Blaricum, and Laren. Rik Wouters (d. 1916) was mobilized, captured, and interned at Zeist (near Utrecht) in the Netherlands in 1914; in 1915 he was sent to Amsterdam. The Futurist Jules Schmalzigaug (not included in our exhibition) committed suicide in 1917 in Amsterdam.

Many Belgians sought refuge in England. Jean Delville, Léon de Smet, Edgard Tytgat, and Emile Claus lived in London during the war. Claus was never happy in England, however. He returned to Belgium in early 1919 after the armistice, but his joyous Impressionist style was now seen as outdated.[93] Constant Permeke was mobilized early in the war, and seriously wounded in battle near Antwerp. Evacuated first to London, he was sent to Devonshire to recover from his wounds. Private benefactors, particularly Gwendolen and Margaret Davies, helped some artists to live in Wales for the duration, among them Valerius de Saedeleer, George Minne, and Gustave van de Woestyne (who had first lived in London).[94]

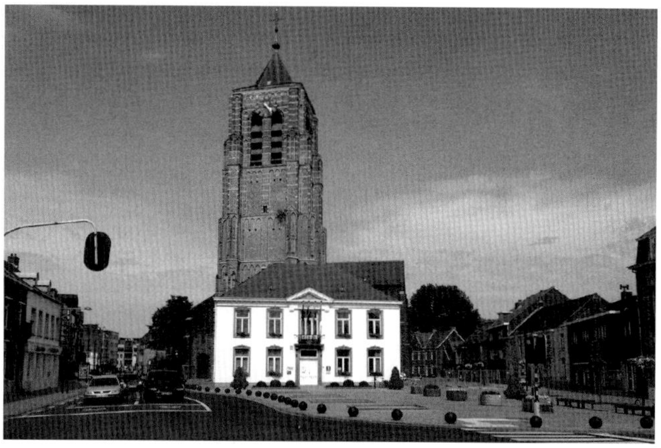

27. City Hall and Church, Mol, Belgium, 2006. Photo by author.

Peace returned with the armistice on 11 November 1918. The celebrations in the rural Flemish town of Mol were commemorated by Jakob Smits, who shows an understated gathering of the townspeople near the city hall and historic church tower in his picture *The Armistice* (1919, **no. 41**). The tower and town hall remain much the same today (fig. 27). Several Belgian flags hang in the foreground, but the overwhelming mood is stillness and reflection rather than an exuberant celebration of triumph.

In the aftermath of the First World War, many cities in Belgium were faced with massive reconstruction projects.

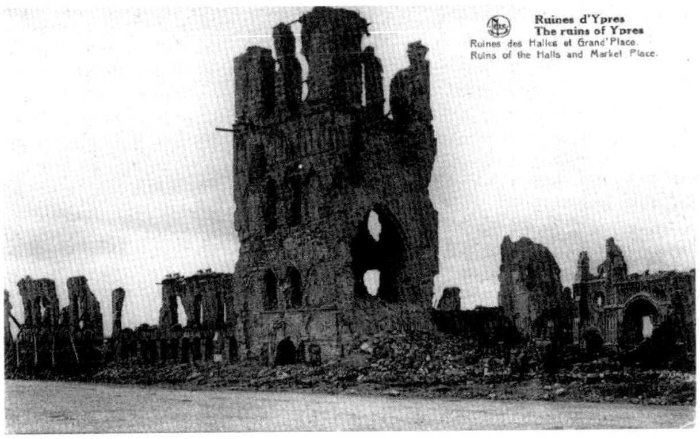

28. Ypres in Ruins, WWI postcard. Author's collection.

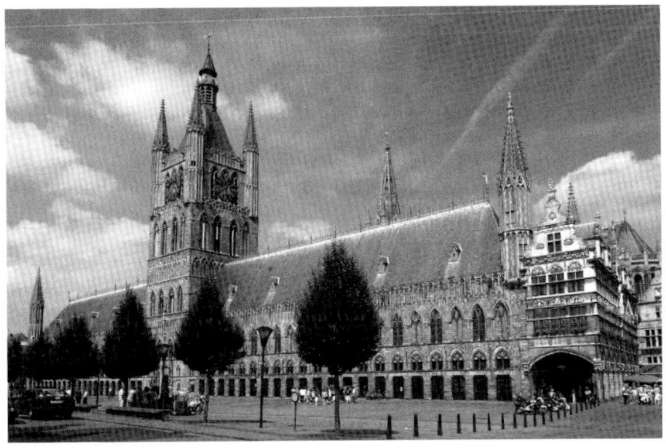

29. Cloth Hall, Ypres reconstructed. Photo by author.

Many of the most beautiful and historic Belgian cities lay in ruins. Ypres and Diksmuide were virtually destroyed. The destruction of Ypres, which once rivaled Bruges as an early commercial center, presented an almost apocalyptic vision which exerted a strange fascination on at least one observer in 1915:

> On Saturday... I took advantage of the temporary calm, and had another look around Ypres. It is really a wonderful sight—weird, grotesque, and desolate of course—but most interesting. I expect the place will be flooded with sight-seers and tourists after the war, and they will be amazed by what they see. The ancient ruins of Pompeii and such places will be simply out of it.[95]

Although the architecture of destroyed cities such as Ypres and Louvain was rebuilt as nearly identical replicas of the original structures, in some of the greatest works of restoration ever accomplished, the continuity with tradition was severed (figs. 28-29). Traditional images and myths that had served as metaphors were now inadequate to express the new reality which had so violently emerged.

The restoration of these medieval buildings is remarkable, but did not come without controversy. The Brussels architect Eugène Dhuicque (1877-1955) was in charge of the Belgian commission that documented artistic losses during the war. Appointed hastily in 1915, he witnessed the destruction of Ypres and took part in debates over the reconstruction after the war, suggesting that it might be better to leave the ruins as a memorial to the war:

> On the morning after the armistice the ruins of the hall and of the cathedral of Ypres, expressed the unshakable resistance of an entire race with more eloquence and relief than any description could possibly give. [...] Certainly no one more than I, who have had the sad privilege of beholding day after day the progressive ruining of these illustrious monuments, regrets their tragic fate. But do they not still belong to history? Are yesterday's events less important than those of years ago? What entitles us to erase their traces?[96]

In the end, the decision was made to rebuild Ypres and other destroyed cities. Belgium regained much of its economic strength by 1925,[97] but rebuilding the cities took many more years.

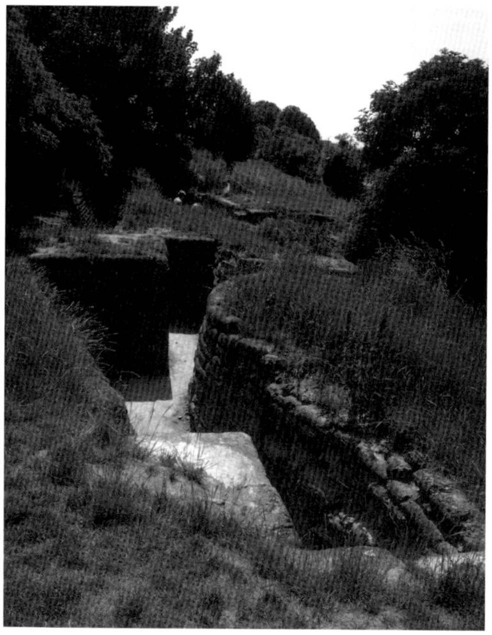

30. Dodengang (Boyau de Morte; Trench of Death), portion of World War I trench, near Dijksmuide. Photo by author.

A museum to the First World War was created in the rebuilt Cloth Hall. Redesigned in 1998 and now renamed the In Flanders Fields Museum, this institution hosted a remarkable exhibition in 2006. Titled *Innocent Landscape*, it examines the provocative thesis that the ghostly reconstructions are a hoax, denying the reality of the war, while only the landscape remains innocent. All the works of humanity are complicit in the tragedy of the war.

The late medieval theme of the "Dance of Death" was insufficient to communicate the horrors of mechanized mass slaughter that characterized trench warfare. The intricate zig-zagging trenches, which extended from the North Sea to Switzerland, were a kind of grim utilitarian architecture. They provided shelter, although the name of one preserved stretch near Dijksmude reveals its true nature: the *Dodengang*, or *Boyau de Morte* (Trench of Death; fig. 30).

In the midst of a war that brought technology to new heights, soldiers were reduced to seeking shelter in holes in the ground in this flat land. The architecture of the trenches, which conjured up atavistic echoes of womb and tomb, was resolutely horizontal as the trenches snaked past the vertical Gothic cathedrals.

The inadequacy of traditional imagery for expressing the disruptions of the war is seen in the rather odd stained glass windows that were created for a memorial near the trenches of Diksmuide and Ypres (fig. 31). Beside the ruins of a church that was destroyed in the war, a small memorial chapel was built in 1925, designed by the architect van Elsland. An unlikely local war hero is memorialized in this chapel: a Belgian Franciscan monk, P. Martial Lekeux, who returned from Cairo to join the army. He became an artillery officer and set up his observation post in the ruined church of Oud Stuyvekenskerke.[98] In the ancient medium of Gothic churches, the stained glass depicts the priest/soldier praying in the ruins of the church in his military uniform with a statuette of the Madonna in front of him and beside him a several hundred pound shell which miraculously lodged in the wall without exploding.

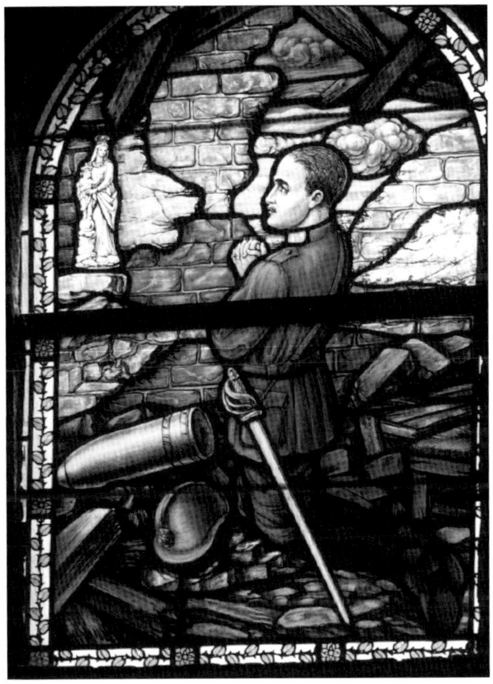

31. Stained glass window of Franciscan Artillery Officer, chapel of Oud Stuyvekenskerke, or Onze Lieve Vrouw Hoekje, 1925.

Another window shows the battlefield seen from the trench, with exploding shells painted in purples and greens against the muddy landscape, while other windows show the traditional military saints, St. George and St. Martial. The artist tried to avoid expressionist distortions and has portrayed the scenes in a sincere and straightforward manner. The poignancy of this little Gothic style chapel and its modern glass leaves one with two impressions: one, an overwhelming sense of the impossibility of symbolizing the disasters of war through language or visual images, and the other, a recognition of the deep need for serenity, faith, and continuity represented by the forms of traditional architecture and art.

By the spring of 1915, the Brussels art market resumed somewhat, but was obviously hampered by the lack of communication with the outside world, the closure of Belgian press, and the absence of many artists and patrons, all of which stifled creativity.[99] Andre de Ridder, along with Gust de Smet and Frits van den Berghe, founded an association of modern Belgian artists called *Open Wegen* ("Open Roads"—a somewhat ironic title, considering the occupation of Belgium by the Germans at the time). In the spring of 1917, several Flemish artists in Brussels founded a group called *Doe Stil Voort* ("Moving on quietly"; the same title had been used for a different group led by Karel van de Woestyne in 1902-1913).[100] They organized an exhibition of modern Belgian art in Amsterdam in the spring of 1918 and a Summer Exhibition in Brussels, with the assistance of the *Raad van Vlaanderen* (Council of Flanders). Other groups began to organize in Antwerp, such as *Le Cénacle* and Paul van Ostaijen's *Bond zonder gezegeld papier* (*Alliance sans papier scellé*, or Association without Stamped Papers).[101] During the occupation, Brussels artists used to meet in the cabarets "Le Compas" and "Le Diable au Corps." Among them was the young playwright Michel de Ghelderode.[102]

In the aftermath of the war, grief and mourning pervaded European culture. This was especially true in Belgium, where many suffered personal losses, as well as the death of cultural figures such as Emile Verhaeren in 1916. In addition to the deaths of Belgian soldiers and civilians, the damage to the national pride and self-image was devastating. The very idea of Belgium as a nation had been severely tested. The German occupiers encouraged this self-doubt with a propaganda policy of *Flamenpolitik* (Flemish politics), a German strategy intended to encourage Flemish dissatisfaction with the national union, with the hope that Flanders would unite with Germany. This policy was clumsily executed and not well received. Although the German occupiers granted the Flemings one of their most cherished desires, creating the first Flemish speaking university at Ghent in 1916, the opening of the university unfortunately corresponded with the first mass deportations of Flemish workers to Germany to support the war effort.[103] The *Flamenpolitik* propaganda effort was matched by a much less significant, and even more inept, *Wallonenpolitik*.

Although the 1920s are primarily known as the "Jazz Age," this was an era of deep grief.[104] Mourning, as opposed to Melancholia, or depression, allows a person or a nation to move beyond the loss.[105] Memorials necessarily looked backward, but could also be created with a modernist sensibility. Time was required for artists to find a new expressive language; historical distance, even if brief, was necessary.[106]

The First World War was a crucible of modernism, as Modris Eksteins, Kenneth Silver, Jay Winter, and Stephen Schloesser have noted.[107] Modernist responses that emerged after the war ranged from a conservative recall to order, to often spiritually motivated styles of non-objective abstraction, as well as the rejection of reason expressed in Dada and Surrealism, and the raw emotional power of Expressionism. Although few major works were produced by Belgian artists during the war, it was nevertheless a crucial time of development for many.

The ironies and dislocations of the war were the cradle of the modernist art movements of Dada and Surrealism. The experience of sudden shocks and surprise that typified the war, such as gas attacks and submarine warfare, became part of the aesthetic of both movements.[108] The French Surrealist André Breton, who had served in a hospital for shell shock victims during the war, articulated the principle of "convulsive beauty," a vision so startling that it changed one's sense of reality, and which he made a primary principle of Surrealism. The therapeutic function of art became a kind of shock therapy.

Belgium began to re-engage with the international avant-garde in the 1920s, especially in Brussels. Many of the fundamental institutions that had fostered Modern art had to be rebuilt, however, notably galleries and journals. The leading art galleries in Belgium not only sold works of art, but served to promote their artists in many ways. The galleries also served as centers of community for artists. Of the new galleries founded in Brussels after the war, the following were among the most significant:

- Centre d'Art, established in 1919 by Victor Bourgeois and Aimé Declerq;
- Sélection, A Studio for Contemporary Art, opened by P.-G. Van Hecke in 1921;
- Le Centaure, opened by Walter Schwarzenberg in 1921; this gallery gave René Magritte his first one-person show in 1927, exhibiting 61 of his works;
- Gallery Giroux, run by George Giroux between 1918-1957;
- the Manteau Gallery;
- Le Cabinet Maldoror was founded by Geert van Bruane in 1923, and named for the famous proto-surrealist novel by Isidore Ducasse, the so-called Comte de Lautréamont, *Les Chants du Maldoror*. Its opening exhibit included works by René Magritte. Michel de Ghelderode was in charge of contracts and arranging the rooms.[109]

Other galleries included La Viérge Poupine, opened by Geert van Bruaene and Camille Goemans in 1926; L'Époque, another gallery run by P.-G. Van Hecke; Les Compagnons de l'Art, founded by Luc and Paul Haesaerts in 1937; the Galerie Dietrich (Walter Schwarzenberg, 1941); and the Galerie Lou Cosyn (Cosyn and Camille Goemans, 1942.)

The Modern art journal had emerged the late nineteenth century, when independent magazines played a leading role in promoting the new art. *La Jeune Belgique* (Brussels, 1881-97), *l'Art Moderne* (Brussels, 1881-1914), and *Van Nu en Straks* (Antwerp and Brussels, 1893-94; 1896-1901) were especially important. In the post-War era, many galleries published small art journals intended to promote the new art, including *Le Centaure* (fig. 32) and *Sélection*. The tension between the classical call to order and the passion for raucous new discoveries is clear in these contrasting covers (figs. 32, 33). Other

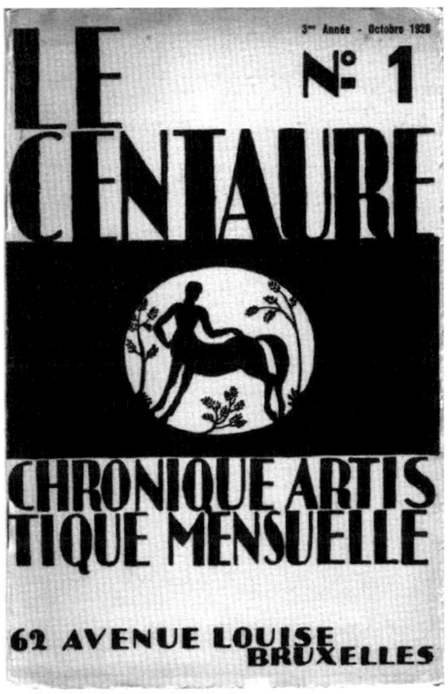

32. *Le Centaure*, 1928. Photo courtesy of Gallery Patrick Derom, Brussels.

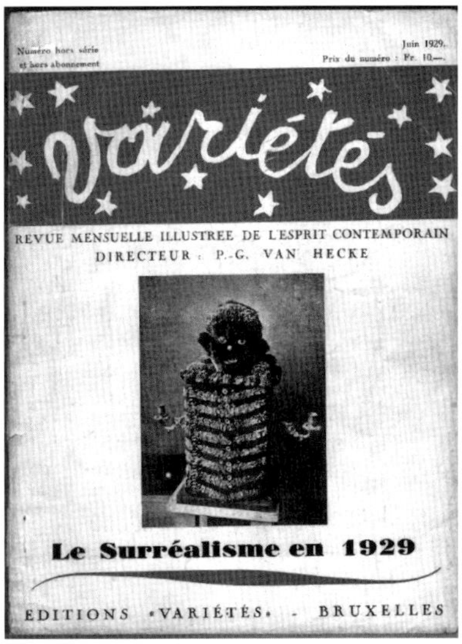

33. *Variétés*, 1929. Photo courtesy of Gallery Patrick Derom, Brussels.

important journals included the Surrealist journal *Variétés* (Brussels, P.-G. Van Hecke, founder, 1928; fig. 33); the Constructivist journal *7 Arts* (Brussels, 1927-); and the Surrealist journal *L'Invention Collective* (Brussels, 1940, which featured Magritte and others).[110] Many of these were short lived, but some, such as *Le Centaure* (1926-30), *Sélection* (1920-27), and *Les Cahiers de Sélection* (1928-33) ran for years. *Variétés* published writings by Sigmund Freud, André Breton, and Louis Aragon, as well as the critical reviews of P.-G. Van Hecke.

In August of 1925, André Breton and Paul Eluard visited Brussels to make contact with the young artists there, attracted by the presence of new artists and this efflorescence of modernist journals. Since late 1924, Paul Nougé, Camille Goemans, Marcel Lecomte, Paul Hooreman, and André Souris had collaborated on an avant-garde review called *Correspondence.*[111] René Magritte and E.L.T. Mesens (1903-1971) published the first and only issue of the Dada-inspired journal *Oesophage* in March of that year. In the summer of 1926, they published two issues of *Marie*, also a Dada journal, which included works by Picabia, Arp, Man Ray, Marcel Lecomte, and Paul van Ostaijen.

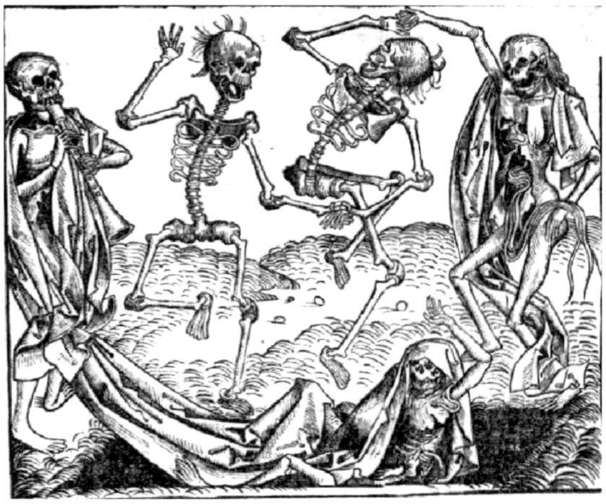

34. Michael Wolgemut, *Dance of Death*, woodcut, 1493.

The Fantastic and Carnivalesque

One of the distinctive features of art produced in this region since the Middle Ages is the extraordinary power of the artists' visual imagination. From Hieronymus Bosch and Pieter Bruegel to James Ensor, Fernand Khnopff, and René Magritte, Belgian artists have exceled at creating astonishing visions.

For James Ensor (1860-1949), art was a means to provoke shock as well as to offer a glimpse into a strange world of beauty. Music was an important part of this world and particularly close to Ensor's heart. He often remarked that he should have devoted his life to music. Even his macabre trio entitled *From Laughter to Tears* (1908, **no. 46**) seems to evoke a song. The "danse macabre" was a theme rooted in the Middle Ages, where the Dance of Death served as a call to reflect on the vanity and transience of life. Michael Wolgemut's *Dance of Death*, a woodcut from 1493, is a typical example (fig. 34). Ensor brings that tradition up to date. Death calls the tune in many similar images; we all dance to the music of death, whether we know it or not.

Ensor was immersed in the fantastic world of carnival and imagination from his earliest youth. His parents owned a shop which sold masks, souvenirs, and curiosities to tourists in Ostend; his Aunt Mimi owned a similar shop in Blankenberghe. Ensor reveled in this environment and often spoke of its lasting impact on him. The house Ensor lived in from 1916 until his death, above his uncle's shell shop, is now a museum in Ostend (fig. 35).

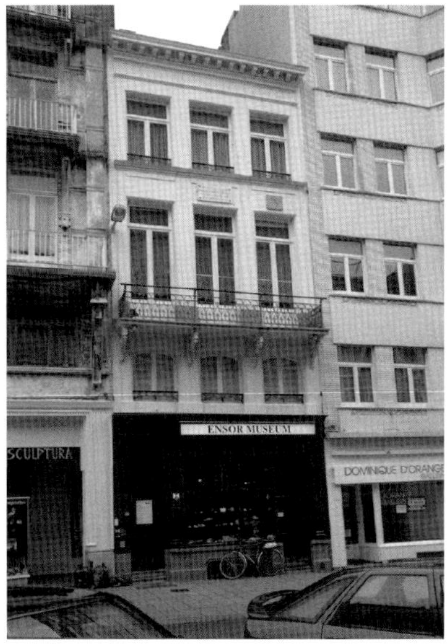

35. Ensor Museum, Ostend. Photo by author.

Morbid thoughts of his own death haunted Ensor. Several times he portrayed himself as a skeleton. Ensor feared an early death; in a letter of 1886 he wrote:

> I'm twenty-six years old... I am not happy. Ideas of survival haunt me. Perishable pictorial material upsets me; I dread the fragility of painting. Poor painting exposed to the crimes of the restorer, to insufficiency, to the slander of reproductions. Yes, I want to speak for a long time yet to the men of tomorrow. I want to survive and I think of solid copper plates, of unalterable inks, of easy reproductions, of faithful printing, and I am adopting etching as a means of expression.[112]

Ensor's extensive activity as an artist seems to be at least partly motivated by his desire for immortality.

Early setbacks left Ensor bitter and resentful of many of his contemporaries; in about 1915 he wrote:

> My unceasing investigations, today crowned with glory, aroused the enmity of my snail-like followers, continually passed on the road... Thirty years ago, long before Vuillard, Bonnard, van Gogh, and the luminists [Neo-Impressionists], I pointed the way to all the modern discoveries, all the influence of light and freeing of vision. A vision that was sensitive and clear, not understood by the French impressionists, who remained superficial daubers suffused with traditional recipes. Manet and Monet certainly reveal some sensations—and how obtuse! But their uniform effort hardly foreshadows decisive discoveries... Narrow minds demand old beginnings, identical continuations. The painter must repeat his little works, and all else is condemned... Yes, before me the painter did not heed his vision.[113]

Ensor's most famous picture, *The Entry of Christ into Brussels in 1889* of 1888, is now in the J. Paul Getty Museum in Los Angeles; Ensor had kept it with him his whole life. *The Entry of Christ into Brussels* shows a satirical view of the second coming of Christ. A controversial painting, it was listed in the catalogue for the 1889 exhibition of Les XX, but was not shown. In fact, it was not shown publicly until 1929.[114]

The Entry of Christ into Brussels is a very large painting, in bright, sometimes garish colors, painted in a deliberately crude style. Ensor aggressively challenged the rules of perspective as well as good taste in this picture. Most of the figures are shown wearing masks that cannot be distinguished from their true faces and perhaps cannot be removed. Ensor reasoned that if Christ were to return to earth, modern commercial and political interests would certainly try to co-opt the event. Although Christ is honored with a parade where he enters Brussels on the back of a donkey, just as he entered Jerusalem on Palm Sunday, he is almost lost in the crowd. The mayor of Brussels (at upper right, with the cane and sash) seems to be trying to use the event for his advantage. Ensor identified with the martyred Christ, and he used his own features for the face of Christ. In its free use of color and space and brushwork to enhance the psychological impact, Ensor's work paved the way for Expressionism in the twentieth century. His status among German artists was very high; Emil Nolde visited him in 1911, and during the war, Erich Heckel and other artists serving at the front kept in contact with him and vouched for his character when he was jailed for drawing a caricature of Kaiser Wilhelm as a vulture.[115] Ensor and Rik Wouters were featured in a joint exhibition in Berlin in Herwarth Walden's gallery, Der Sturm, in September 1912.

The fantastic vision of Ensor and his musical inclinations are shown in *The Fantastic Ballet* (1918, **no. 47**). This was related to many earlier pictures Ensor had made of comic figures such as the clown Pierrot, but includes clergymen, military figures, and members of the bourgeoisie as players in his sardonic assemblage. The coarse satire reveals his love of the caricatures of Goya and the English satirical cartoons of Thomas Rowlandson. Like them, Ensor caustically portrays modern life as an empty performance, wherein all is acting and falseness. The comedy and costumes mask his pain, while the humor provides a safe cushion for the viewer.

Manet and the Impressionists participated in creating a mode of experience in modern life, the observation of life as if it were a spectacle. Distance and irony dominate the paintings of these *flâneurs*. Ensor was not capable of such distance, and his cruel caricatures reveal his rage as well as his humor.

Carnival provided one of the most colorful spectacles in modern life, and Ensor grew up in the center of carnival celebrations, above stores that sold carnival masks. Mikhail Bakhtin's seminal essay on Rabelais and the subversive role of carnival in early modern culture underscored the revolutionary aspect of the liberties of carnival. As Michael Holquist notes:

> Bakhtin's carnival, surely the most productive concept in this book, is not only not an impediment to revolutionary change, it is revolution itself. Carnival must not be confused with mere holiday or, least of all, with self-serving festivals fostered by governments, secular or theocratic. The sanction for carnival derives ultimately not from a calendar prescribed by church or state, but from a force that preexists priests and kings and to whose superior power they are actually deferring when they appear to be licensing carnival.[116]

Carnival and images of the world turned upside down reflect deep seated human urges to resist authority, but also a cry for social justice and a new unity. While life can be seen as merely a spectacle, suborned by commercial and political interests, the origins of carnival take one back to a spiritual focus.

Ensor's paintings *From Laughter to Tears* (1908, **no. 46**) and *The Fantastic Ballet* (1918, **no. 47**) are based on carnival imagery. These paintings are much more fully explored by Katherine Nahum in her essay "Ensor's Parrot" and by Susan A. Michalczyk in "'Laughter Liberates Us from Fear'—The Place of Carnival in Our Lives."

Frits van den Berghe and Belgian Expressionism

The dominant narrative of Modernism in the twentieth century has not dealt well with regional or hybrid varieties of modern expression. The canonical group of modernist works still centers on Paris, Berlin, Moscow, and New York.[117] To focus only on these does not do justice to local traditions, which often produced significant works of art, deeply rooted in their cultural context. Belgian art between the wars challenges that canon; it can be compared to the art of US regionalists, as well as local developments in Scandinavia, Poland, Germany, and Italy. The history of Modern art looks quite different when viewed from the vantage point of these more "marginal" centers.

The attempt to negotiate and discover an authentic identity was a major factor in the development of Belgian Expressionism. The connection to international styles has been noted, as well as the connection to the tradition of early Flemish painting. The legacy of nineteenth-century Symbolism was particularly influential, reflected in an aesthetic that highlighted subjectivity and an emotional, even mystical, affinity with nature. Links to Romanticism and Realism are also seen in the quest for authenticity and truth, which motivated these artists.

Expressionism built on the introspective aspects of Impressionism and Symbolism to stress the interior world of the artist. Belgium can rightly claim to be one of the major sources of modern Expressionism, with James Ensor's *Entry of Christ into Brussels* in 1888 arguably launching the entire movement. Ensor was an inspiration for Emil Nolde and the other artists of Die Brücke in Germany. Expressionism in Belgium also reshaped the legacy of the Symbolist movement.[118] Laethem-Saint-Martin, where Constant Permeke, Gustave de Smet, and Frits van den Berghe worked together, was one of the later centers of this evolution.

Frits (Fredericus Henricus) van den Berghe (1883-1939) was born in Ghent, and came to Laethem-Saint-Martin as part of the second wave of avant-garde artists to settle there, arriving in 1904. He had studied at the Academy of Fine Arts in Ghent from 1898 until 1903 and taught there in 1908. His life was unsettled in the years before the war. He had married, but began a torrid affair with the actress Stella van de Wiele in 1909, estranging him from his family. In 1914 he went to New York for six months, but Stella was not able to enter the country, and he soon returned to Belgium.[119]

When war broke out, he fled to neutral Amsterdam with Gust de Smet and De Smet's wife. He lived a difficult life there, but discovered Cubism.[120] He was also able to see Piet Mondrian's 1911 painting *Evolution* in a private collection in Blaricum, which furthered his turn toward abstraction.[121] In September 1917, he returned to occupied Belgium and accepted a provisional position as bureau chief in the Ministry of Flemish Arts and Letters in Brussels. After the armistice, he faced some problems for having worked for this ministry, including being stripped of his (by then largely honorary) position teaching in the academy at Ghent.[122] He again took temporary refuge in the Netherlands. De Smet introduced him to Expressionism, and he subscribed to the German periodical *Das Kunstblatt,* which contained woodcuts by Emil Nolde and other notable artists.

The painting *Obsession III* (1919, **no. 44**) depicts Van den Berghe's close friend, the painter Gust de Smet, whose only child, Firmin, had been killed at age twenty in September 1918 in a railway accident in the Netherlands. He was on his way to enlist.[123] His death left De Smet shattered. The strong color and flattened planes of the space owe much to German Expressionism, and the distorted space may reflect the influence of German Expressionist film, such as *The Cabinet of Dr. Caligari* (1919), where the distorted stage sets are used to create an unsettled mood in the mind of the viewer and serve as an analog for mental disturbance.[124]

The hot colors, the flat planes, and distorted space of *Obsession III* show that Van den Berghe was exploring the techniques of Expressionism, where the physical and emotional engagement with the material aspects of the work of art is as important as the subject.[125] Academic standards of perfection are also discarded.

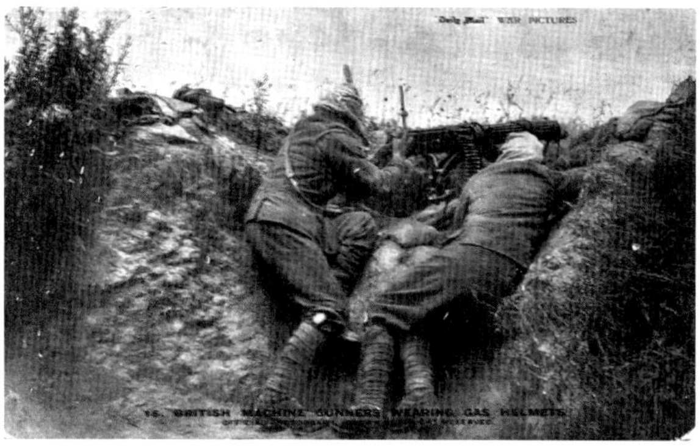

36. British Gunners in trench warfare; WWI era postcard. Author's collection.

The Last Gunner (1929, **no. 45**) explores other avenues of composition and the application of paint. The disarticulated, almost decaying figure of a WWI soldier dominates the foreground of a canvas filled with a flat background of hot orange. Above and around this figure hovers an outline of another figure, perhaps a ghost, or another aspect of the soldier. *The Last Gunner* is embedded in this flattened background just as the real soldiers were flattened into the mud of Flanders (fig. 36). The crusty impasto in the body of the soldier may owe something to the *frottage* technique of Max Ernst, whose works were shown in a major exhibition in Brussels in 1927.

One of Van den Berghe's most intriguing images is *The Geographic Man* of 1927 (**no. 49**). The large, hulking golem-like figure wears a coat of many colors, which contains collage-like images of a nude woman, some houses, a fish, a deer, an owl, a tree, and clouds. A man's life is shaped by geography, his local environment, as well as foreign adventures. He is a "hollow man," but he contains multitudes, at least in memory. The mysterious images which accompany him do not suggest a narrative, but are juxtaposed in a manner that seems almost like free association. The use of this technique links Van den Berghe to the Surrealists, who prized the new poetry of unexpected meetings of imagery that sprang from the unconscious. The random imagery was a visual equivalent to the free association method used by Freudian analysis to uncover unconscious motivations, and a parallel to automatism in verbal and graphic techniques. This work is thus a bridge between Expressionism and Surrealism.

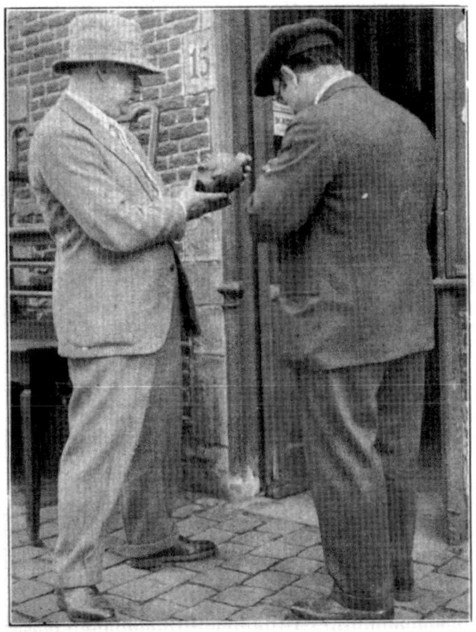

37. Frits van den Berghe and P.-G. van Hecke examining African sculpture, photo in *Variétés*. Photo courtesy of Gallery Patrick Derom, Brussels.

The crude features of the figure in this painting show the influence of African sculpture; Van den Berghe shared this interest in non-Western art with many of his colleagues. This was an early form of globalism, and Belgian artists entered into a dialogue with African art as part of an attempt to redefine the nature of modern Belgium in a colonial era. Van den Berghe's collection of African artifacts is now in the Royal Museum of African Art in Tervuren.[126]

The disparate images enclosed in the Geographic Man's figure resist interpretation. Are they a collection of memories, or souvenirs of past experiences? The juxtaposed images could almost be projected on the figure, in the manner of a cinematic collage. The simultaneous presentation of these different places (and perhaps times) links Van den Berghe to Futurist art and theory.[127] The Futurist goal was to "break open the object and enclose the environment in it."[128] In this case the form of the man encapsulates the environment.

The various images relate to the basic elements of water, earth, and air. This seems to parallel the classical theory of humors and the relationship between the zodiac and man as a microcosm of the universe, which developed in the late Middle Ages.[129] The microcosm of the human body was linked through cosmic relationships to the macrocosm of the universe. Each part of the body was associated with astrological signs. These are depicted in many manuscripts, including the *Très Riches Heures of Jean, Duc de Berry* by the Limbourg Brothers (before 1416; Musée Condé, Chantilly). In this astrological image, the signs of the zodiac are superimposed on the body part over which they are supposed to have influence. The symbolic figure is thus encrusted with crabs, archers, twins, and lions, etc.

The benighted figure in *The Geographic Man* contains simple images, which may reflect a simple mind, an image of innocence or even folly. In 1926, he painted an image of a simple villager, titled *The Idiot by the Pond* (Ghent, Museum voor Schone Kunsten). Van den Berghe's interest in mental states may have coincided with a Dadaist rejection of rationality as defined by the bourgeois world. There have been many Belgian evocations of the vainglory of the world, going back at least to the publication of Erasmus' *In Praise of Folly* (1509, printed 1511). One particularly striking image is found in a map which may have been printed in Antwerp. In this image, the map of the world replaces the face of a fool, who wears the traditional fool's cap, with tassels and bells, as if a globe has been substituted for the head. The world-wide dominance of folly is signified by this precociously Surreal image. Van den Berghe provides an important link between Expressionism and Surrealism; René Magritte acknowledged Van den Berghe as a significant influence.[130]

The bridge between Expressionism and Surrealism may also be seen in Van den Berghe's painting *The Riverbanks* of 1926 (**no. 48**). This large canvas can actually be hard to read at first glance; the plane of the picture is tilted up so that the space is flattened and distorted. It depicts five romantic couples on the banks of a narrow river in Flanders. A woman steers a small boat toward the bottom of the scene, and the prow of a second boat is just emerging under the arch of a bridge at the background. The carefree scene resembles Edgard Tytgat's *Memory of a Sunday* (1926; Museum Dhondt-Dhaenens, Deurle) in subject, but the style is more Expressionistically distorted. There are clear echoes of Georges Seurat's *Sunday Afternoon on the Island of La Grande Jatte* (1886; Art Institute of Chicago) in both of these works. Even more than Seurat, however, Van den Berghe's work is more conceptual than visual; he sought to evoke his interior world as much as the world around him. This could be considered, in part, a legacy of the Symbolist movement. Van den Berghe wrote in 1927:

> The world of the imagination, the world of illusions and hallucinations, the lyrical universe of the poet, the abstract world of the thinker—are they less meaningful, less valuable than the world of physical phenomena? Everything down here is life, in whatever form, and the artist is free to choose his subject from this. Dreams are every bit as much a reality as any other form of life, a reality that is just as clear, just as valuable, in short, just as real as the reality of the waking condition.[131]

Although this echoes Symbolist statements which praised dreams, Van den Berghe equally foreshadows Surrealist aesthetics.

The mysterious picture *Corridors (Gangen)* of 1927 (**no. 35**) is an Expressionist evocation of an interior world filled with erotic tension, where the shadows and tilted space echo the atmosphere of German Expressionist films. In the foreground, a man enters a dream-like maze of corridors, encountering scantily clad and nude women. A woman dressed in a short undergarment and black stockings confronts him. Her empty coat stands beside a headless man in a blue suit, who stands before a black hole in the ground. A snake wriggles off in the background, near a nude female torso, suggesting menace as well as mystery. The man seems perplexed by this labyrinth of conscious and unconscious desires. His startled reaction and nearly headless body suggest his lack of comprehension, as if all rational thought has been cut away. A handprint on the wall at left may be an attempt to mark a path through these corridors, like the thread used by Theseus in the labyrinth of the minotaur. The mysterious theater of this encounter in Van den Berghe's *Corridors* has powerful mythic overtones.

The man seems out of place in this sophisticated milieu which is more mysterious than the cabarets and brothels of Toulouse-Lautrec. The atmosphere is closer to the *Neue Sachlichkeit* elegance of Christian Schad's *Portrait of Comte St-Genois d'Anneaucourt* of 1927 (Centre Pompidou, Musée national d'art moderne, Paris). Schad depicts the suave world of decadent sensuality of Weimar Germany, which was also recreated in the 1972 film *Cabaret*.

In 1924-25, Van den Berghe executed a series of watercolor and gouache drawings of erotic scenes of men and women together. *The Mirror* (**no. 36**) shows a nude woman rising up from the lap of a well-dressed gentleman to kiss her reflection in the mirror. The narcissism of the woman and the self-satisfied leer of the man create a satirical commentary on the relationship of the sexes. Since he is clothed and she nude, the sexual tension may recall his passionate affair with Stella van de Wiele before the war, which caused such upheaval in his life. Unlike William Holman Hunt's Pre-Raphaelite painting of an illicit union, *The Awakening Conscience* (1853, Tate Gallery, London), which has a similar composition, this woman does not rise to return to a moral life, but to a greater self-absorption.

The back of this work has a portrait of Van den Berghe's friend and patron, René de Clercq, sketched on it. Van den Berghe stayed with de Clercq in the Netherlands during the First World War and was aware of his many extramarital affairs. The atmosphere of decadence in *The Mirror* may be partly related to this experience.[132]

The anonymous figures may also suggest a brothel scene, and as such, it recalls the even more caustic caricatures of the German artist Otto Dix, whose *Memory of the Mirrored Halls of Brussels* (fig. 38) presents a recollection of his wartime experiences. Mirrors were a common feature of the erotic décor in brothels, since they double the image of voluptuousness and add a flavor of voyeurism. The use of the mirror in both works suggests the traditional role of art as a mirror held up to nature, and also as an image of the insubstantiality of the these elusive and fleeting moments of pleasure, whether in the context of war or in the 1920s business world.

The rawness of sexuality in brothel scenes was a staple of avant-garde art. We see this in the monotypes of Edgar Degas in the 1870s and 1880s, which related to literature by Emile Zola and Guy de Maupassant, and in the paintings of Henri de Toulouse-Lautrec, which he made while actually living in a brothel in Montmartre in the 1890s.[133] Pablo Picasso's *Les Demoiselles d'Avignon* (1907, Museum of Modern Art, New York) was the ultimate fusion of avant-garde art and the psycho-sexual drama of the brothel.[134] German Expressionism emphasized the raw power of primitive sexuality

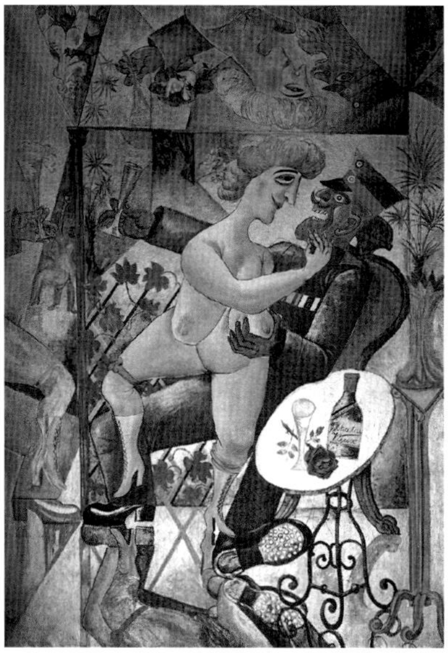

38. Otto Dix: *Memory of the Mirrored Halls of Brussels*, 1920. Centre Pompidou, Musée national d'art moderne, Paris. © 2006 Artists Rights Society (ARS), New York/VG Bild-Kunst, Bonn

in many paintings, especially those by Ernst Ludwig Kirchner.[135] The Surrealists of the 1920s and 1930s focused on sexuality for its shock value and its links to the unconscious. Freudian psychological theory bolstered their obsessive interest.[136] The narcissism of the woman drawn to her mirror reflection reveals a further connection to Freudian psychoanalysis, which declared women particularly prone to narcissistic tendencies.[137]

The heated enigma of the sexes is suggested also in the 1931 picture *Filles d'eau douce* (**no. 37**). The flesh of the three nude women here actually glows with an incandescent light which suffuses the canvas. In the early 1930s, Van den Berghe continued to experiment with richly textured brushstrokes. His exploration of natural themes grew from his interest in psychoanalysis, science, and mythology.[138] A major retrospective exhibition of the work of James Ensor in 1929 at the Palais de Beaux-Arts in Brussels may have encouraged him in the use of bright color.

After the stock market crash in 1929, Van den Berghe supplemented his income by working as an illustrator, including for the political journal *Vooruit* published by the Ghent Worker's House of the same name. Van den Berghe's illustrations during the 1930s have inspired current Belgian comic book and graphic novel illustrators.

Ill-matched couples have been a frequent subject theme in northern art since the fifteenth century; Lucas Cranach painted some outstanding examples. Floris Jespers brings this theme up to date with his *Marriage of Convenience* of 1927 (**no. 50**). The style is abstract, even Surreal, with a touch of Futurism. An elegant couple in evening dress stands before us, the dark-skinned man holding his top hat, and the woman in white stands headless. A silhouette of a head appears on the man's shirt front, while other African style sculptures appear on the floor and in the background. The woman's fan seems to leave a trail of repeated after-images, like the chronophotographs admired by the Futurists. The hem of her dress trails diamonds, and the man wears a diamond in his lapel. Is this *Marriage of Convenience* a commentary on the colonial union of Belgium and the Congo? Their Jazz Age costumes and the modernist imagery juxtaposed with African sculpture reminds one that the roots of postwar modernism are linked to Primitivism, in the visual arts and in the rhythms of jazz.

Floris Jespers (1889-1965) was born in Antwerp and studied painting with Frans Courtens at the Antwerp National Higher Institute of Fine Arts. He was also a skilled musician and played the violincello in a music hall in Antwerp during the war. His older brother, Oscar Jespers (1887-1970), was a talented sculptor. Floris and his brother

Oscar were associated with the Antwerp based Kring Moderne Kunst (Modern Art Circle), which sought contacts with international Futurists and the Dutch artists of De Stijl in 1919.[139] Under the leadership of Jozef Peeters and Paul van Ostaijen, this group organized a series of three meetings of a Congrés d'Art Moderne in Antwerp and Bruges, which, like an artistic League of Nations, invited representatives of various modernist trends from Belgium and the Netherlands.

Surrealism and René Magritte (1898-1967)

Surrealism, which was inspired by the psychoanalytic theories of Sigmund Freud and the French psychologists J.M. Charcot and Pierre Janet, flourished in Belgium. Given the emphasis on visionary art in the Symbolist and Expressionist movements, not to mention the delirious precedent of earlier artists such as Pieter Bruegel and Hieronymus Bosch, Belgian artists were quite at home in this new world of dreamlike and shocking images.

Surrealism began as a literary movement, and André Breton emerged as its leading spokesman. Breton published the Surrealist Manifesto in 1924, in which he defined Surrealism as "pure psychic automatism," which was meant to express "the actual functioning of thought... exempt from any aesthetic or moral concern."[140] In the same manifesto Breton called for the integration of dreams with reality: "I believe in the future resolution of these two states, dream and reality, which are seemingly so contradictory, into a kind of absolute reality, a surreality, if one may so speak."[141] Dreams were not a substitute for reality in the Surrealist movement, but contributed to the revolutionary reform of society by presenting an alternate form of consciousness, a guidepost for a new utopia of liberated instincts. The Surrealists vowed to fight, through their art and aesthetic gestures, for the total freedom of thought and the liberation of instinct.

The most important Belgian Surrealist was René Magritte (1898-1967). His relationship with the French Surrealists was complicated by his representational style, which resisted the French emphasis on automatism in technique, and by his desire to remain independent from the dictatorial Breton. Breton first met Magritte in 1925, when he journeyed to Belgium to obtain his signature for a petition protesting the French war with Morocco.[142] Magritte had by that time gained a local reputation as an experimental artist and had participated in Belgian avant-garde literary reviews. In September 1927, Magritte and his wife Georgette moved to Paris, where they were in frequent contact with the French Surrealists. By mid-1928, Breton had acquired four paintings by Magritte.[143] In December 1929, Magritte was featured in the final issue of the Surrealist journal *La Révolution surréaliste*. Just as the issue appeared, however, Magritte and Breton quarreled. The disagreement was over a crucifix that Georgette, who was a devout Catholic, wore while visiting Breton's apartment. Breton ordered Georgette to remove it, and she refused. The Magrittes departed, and Breton excommunicated them from the Surrealist group. Paris became even less hospitable when the gallery that had supported

Magritte declared bankruptcy in February, due in part to the world-wide financial crash. In July 1930, Magritte moved back to Brussels.

Despite the rift, Breton used one of Magritte's designs for the cover of his 1934 book *Que est-ce que le Surréalisme?* and maintained occasional contact thereafter. Regardless of the attraction of Paris as a center of art, it was clear that Belgian Surrealism was to develop as an independent entity and would not be a colony of the French movement. As with all Belgian art, Belgian Surrealism was shaped by history and drew strength from the traditions of Flemish art.

Magritte could not escape the historical events that overtook Belgium in the twentieth century. He was born in Wallonia, in Lessines near Charleroi. When he was ten years old, his family moved to the nearby village of Châtelet. His education was interrupted by the invasion of German forces in 1914; his family lived only about thirty miles from the front lines. In 1915, his family moved to Brussels, where he studied at the Academy of Fine Arts. His first commissioned work was a poster for a bouillon product in 1918, featuring a child emulating a soldier. Magritte was drafted in 1921 and spent almost a year in the military. The experience of the war and his own military service may have had a greater effect on his art than is often recognized.

When the Nazis invaded Belgium in May of 1940, Magritte fled to Carcassonne in France, fearing arrest. This was not an unrealistic fear, given the Nazi attitude toward Surrealism and "degenerate" art. Several of Magritte's friends were interned during the war. Carcassone had been populated with many French intellectuals and writers, but although he was a Francophone, Magritte did not feel that he fit into the French culture. Magritte wrote of his disenchantment to his friend Marcel Mariën, who was in a German prisoner of war camp:

> Actual contact is rather disillusioning: one has the very distinct impression of being in the presence of "men of letters" preoccupied above all with their petty literary affairs. I'm not bringing back favourable impressions of France. No question, I am indeed a man of the North, and it's no doubt because of this that I haven't been very responsive to "the French mind."[144]

Magritte returned to Brussels after only a few months in France. He spent the duration of the war in Belgium and worked for the Resistance.[145]

Sexuality and Desire

Although the Surrealists considered themselves "troubadours of love," the contradictions in the Surrealist attitude toward women are evident in a 1929 photomontage of portraits of the leading Surrealists surrounding Magritte's painting of *La femme cachée* (fig. 39). This painting depicts a rebus of a woman inscribed between a text reading: "I do not see the [nude woman] hidden in the forest." The elusive ideal of woman is depicted, and perhaps unwittingly, a willful refusal to see the woman is also suggested. Breton is at the top center of the portraits; Magritte's photograph is at the right, level with the bottom line of text. Magritte praised the power of eroticism many times, and he was completely devoted to his wife, Georgette.

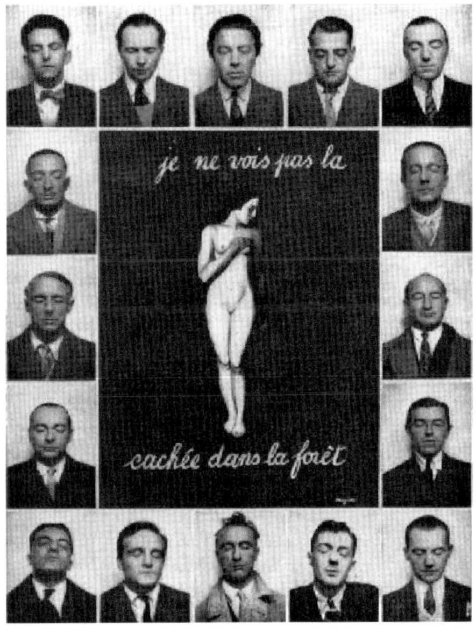

39. René Magritte: *La femme cachée (The Hidden Woman)*, Photomontage in *La Révolution Surréaliste*, no. 12, 1929.

The great tragedy of Magritte's early life was the death by suicide of his mother, which occurred when he was only ten years old when the family moved to Châtelet. This event haunted him throughout his life. Many of his images of distant or inaccessible women can be linked to this traumatic loss. The cover of *Variétés* in 1929 (fig. 40) reproduces a drawing of the shrouded heads of *The Lovers* (1928, oil painting, private collection). The uncanny image of blocked communication reveals his fascination for hidden and secret forms. His skill as an artist is revealed in the way that he transforms a personal tragedy into powerfully resonant images of universal significance.

The enigmatic picture, *Dialogue Raveled by the Wind* (1928, **no. 53**), presents three headless and legless torsos of nude women, grouped together as if in conversation. They almost seem like a condensed version of the classical group of the Three Graces. They have no mouths to speak, nor ears to hear, so the conversation must be taking place on a different plane of reality. The headless woman was a staple of Surrealist imagery, used for shock value and to create an image of uncanny beauty.[146] They are like fragments of classical statuary, but made of living flesh. The eroticism of the figures is undercut by their awkward fragmentariness; they look disturbingly like trussed chickens, or like mannequins waiting to display new fashions.

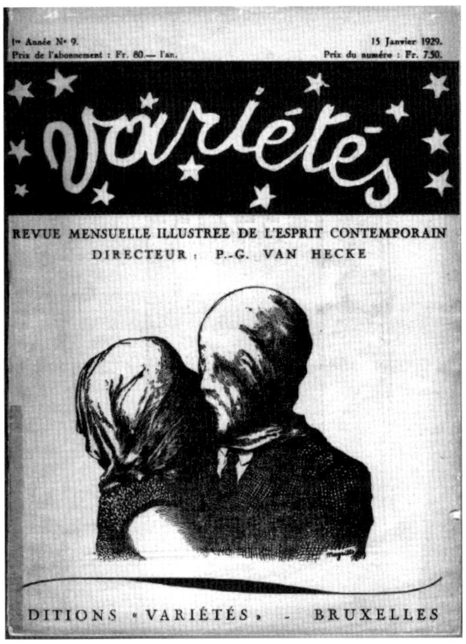

40. René Magritte: cover for *Variétés*, 1929. Photo courtesy of Gallery Patrick Derom, Brussels.

The title of this picture, *Dialogue Raveled by the Wind,* is suggestive and enigmatic, but certainly loses something in the translation. Raveled is an ambiguous and unfamiliar word in English, in any event. The original French title is *Dialogue dénoué par le vent*, where *dénoué* has the sense of a conclusion, or something finally happening (as in *dénoument*). Magritte was very clear that his titles were to be taken as another kind of poetry: "Titles of works are not explanations and the paintings

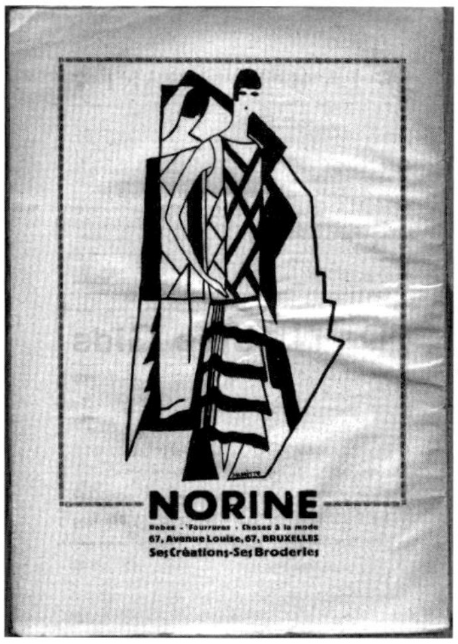

41. René Magritte: advertisement for fashions by Norine, published in *Sélection*, October, 1925. Photo courtesy of Gallery Patrick Derom, Brussels.

are not illustrations of the titles. The relationship between the title and the tableau is poetic, that is to say the relationship only retains certain characteristics habitually ignored by consciousness, but which is at times present on the occasion of extraordinary events which reason has not yet come to elucidate."[147]

No matter how fanciful his visions, however, Magritte was always engaged with the real world. He earned a considerable portion of his income from advertising during the 1920s and 1930s. Many of these were for the fashion shop owned by Norine, the wife of P.-G. Van Hecke, the art dealer and editor (fig. 41).

Many of Magritte's Surrealist innovations made their first public appearance in these advertisements.[148] A 1926 advertisement for automobiles perches the car on planks balanced on balusters, partially screened by cut-out wooden curtains from a theatrical set (fig. 42).

One distinct difference between the Belgian Surrealists and their counterparts in France was the Belgians' consistent interest in music.[149] Although Magritte downplayed his musical knowledge, his friend Louis Scutenaire listed Magritte's favorite composers as: "Brahms, Bach, Ravel, Lalo, Duparc, Churchill, Sibelius, Fauré, Debussy, Satie, Chopin, Smetana and a hundred others."[150] Music played many roles for the Belgian avant-garde, including shocking the bourgeoisie. The artistic circle of Paul Nougé, Camille Goemans and Lecomte, which published the review *Correspondance*, invited the composer André Souris to join them, and they organized concerts which included the Belgian national anthem played backwards on a mechanical organ. Souris also composed the music for *Une page de Clarisse Juranville*, for which Nougé rewrote the text of a popular school book. Music was used to subvert bourgeois expectations, as Nougé noted in his "Conférence de Charleroi."[151] Stressing the romance of crime and social transgression, the Belgian Surrealist journal *Variétés* published "Crime distingué" (fig. 43), which set the text of Tristan Tzara to music by E.L.T. Mesens.

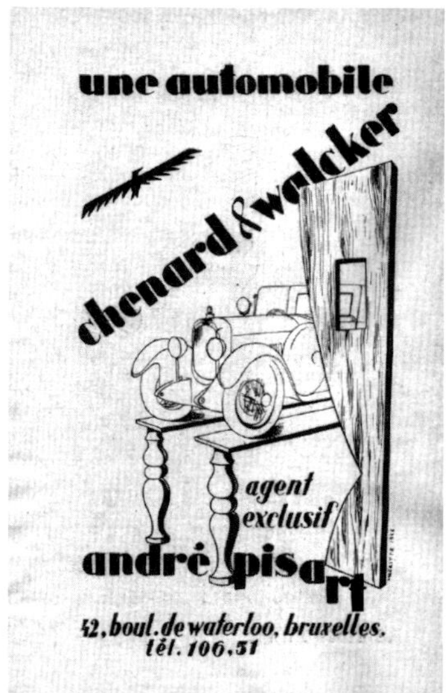

42. René Magritte: advertisement for automobiles, published in *Le Centaure*, 1926. Photo courtesy of Gallery Patrick Derom, Brussels.

The Belgians embraced popular music, rejecting the "aura" of high art, which Walter Benjamin identified in his famous essay of 1936, "The Work of Art in the Age of Mechanical Reproduction."[152] Likewise, René Magritte frequently disparaged the pretensions of the "artiste-peintre" of the academy. In the 1920s and 1930s, Magritte illustrated many examples of sheet music, including the

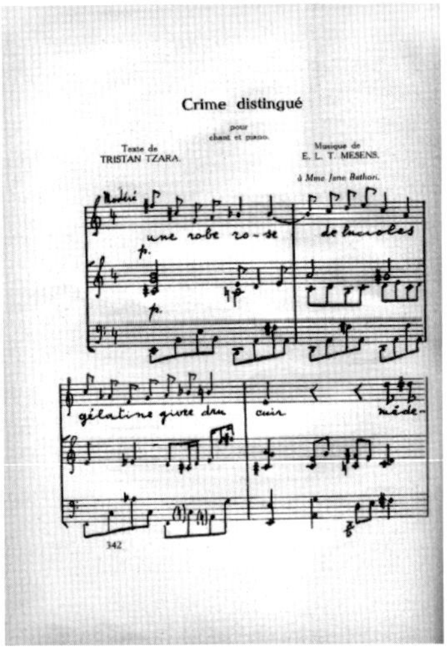

43. "Crime distingué," 1924, words by Tristan Tzara and music by E.L.T. Mesens, published in *Variétés*. Photo courtesy of Gallery Patrick Derom, Brussels.

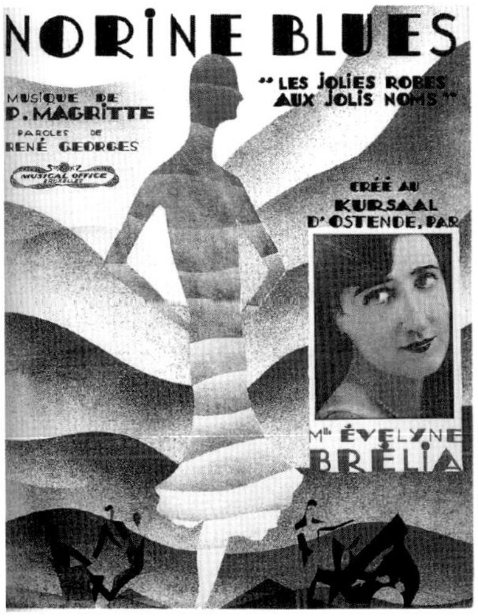

44. René Magritte: *Norine Blues*, sheet music cover, music by Paul Magritte, 1925. Photo courtesy of Gallery Patrick Derom, Brussels.

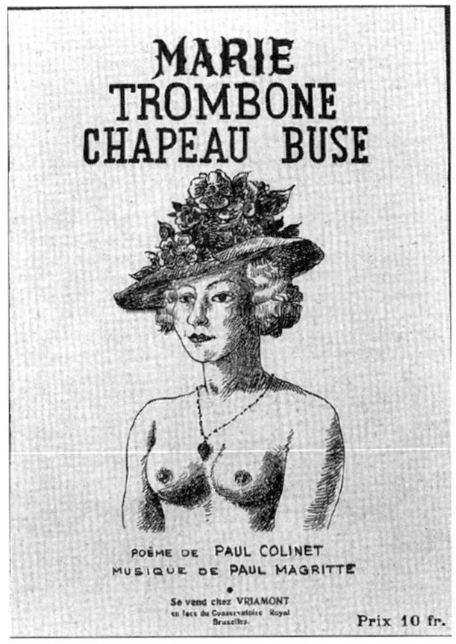

45. René Magritte: "Marie Trombone," sheet music cover, music by Paul Magritte, 1936. Photo courtesy of Gallery Patrick Derom, Brussels.

song "Norine Blues," which was a collaboration with his brother, Paul, who wrote the music, while he and Georgette Magritte wrote the words (credited as "René Georges"). The piece was dedicated to Norine Van Hecke (fig. 44).

Magritte's brother, Paul, was a professional musician, and René illustrated several other of his compositions, including "Marie Trombone Chapeau Buse" in 1936 (fig. 45). The influence of music on Magritte's art is broader than that, however. Magritte used musical staffs and notation as elements in many of his collages. The flaming tuba which appears in several works is another example. Music, like the cinema, provided alternate means for escaping the constrictions of bourgeois society and creating new artistic effects.

Paul Delvaux – The Gaze of Desire

Second only to Magritte, the most highly regarded Belgian Surrealist is Paul Delvaux (1897-1994). Delvaux created somnambular depictions of nude figures, who glide through dreamlike settings, often juxtaposed with clothed people engaged in everyday activities. He disregarded the normal boundaries governing desire and behavior. He also frequently painted skeletons, which move about freely in the world, continuing their daily activities. His work clearly shares affinities with that of both Ensor and Magritte.

Delvaux was the son of a lawyer and an extremely protective mother. He studied at the Academy of Fine Arts in Brussels from 1920-1924. At the insistence of his parents, who wanted him to have a practical career, he first studied architecture, but soon switched to painting. He took classes from Jean Delville at night while completing his military service, and later studied with Constant Montald. As a student, he painted with his class at the same Rouge-Cloitre outside Brussels where the fifteenth-century artist Hugo van der Goes had been treated for melancholia. His earliest works were relatively dark Impressionistic landscapes followed by more Expressionistic figure studies.

Belgian Expressionist painters, such as Gustave van de Woestyne, Constant Permeke, and James Ensor, influenced Delvaux in the 1920s. He began painting large scale, stylized nude figures, such as *Le Couple* (*The Couple*) of 1929. By 1932, he focused increasingly on these large scale nudes, and he painted a *Sleeping Venus* which prefigured much of his later work. At about this time he discovered the art of the Surrealists, and he began painting his figures in a more realistic style, but in a dream-like atmosphere. Around 1934, he destroyed many of his early works, making a definitive break with his past. Delvaux joined the Belgian Surrealist group in 1936, although he continued to remain rather independent. His first retrospective exhibition was in December 1944 at the Palais des Beaux-Arts in Brussels, made possible by the liberation of Brussels from the Nazis on September 4. Although events of the war overshadowed this exhibition, Delvaux's fame increased, and for a time even surpassed that of Magritte. He was awarded a chair in Fine Arts at the Belgian Royal Academy, where he taught from 1950-1962. Delvaux's technique is academic, but his imagery is personal, obsessive, erotic, and replete with Freudian symbolism. There is now a museum dedicated to his works near his former summer home at St. Idesbald (near Dunkirk).

Delvaux was a timid person, dominated by his parents for many years. His mother, Laure Jamotte, frequently warned him of the dangers of women and sexuality. In 1930, he agreed to stop seeing the woman he loved, Anne-Marie de Maertelaere, a woman from Antwerp nicknamed Tam, and acquiesced to his parents' demand that he not wed her even after their deaths.[153] His mother died at the end of 1932 and his father in 1937. Delvaux made an unhappy marriage in 1937 with another woman, Suzanne Purnal. This destructive union lasted until an unexpected reunion with Tam ten years later, which eventually led to their marriage.

Both Delvaux and Magritte introduced elements from popular culture, as well as high art, into their works. One of the strongest influences on Delvaux was the curious traveling exhibition called the Musée Spitzner, which he discovered about 1929-30. This was a carnival-like sideshow with medical and wax-figure exhibits created in France in the late nineteenth century. Delvaux observed that "The Musée Spitzner was a formidable revelation for me. It was really a very important turning point and I can perhaps tell you that it preceded the discovery of Giorgio de Chirico, but it was in the same sense."[154]

The Musée Spitzner was founded in France in 1856 and began touring Belgian carnivals and fairs regularly in 1885. Under a veneer of science, it presented wax figures of nude women, anatomical freaks, and diseased sexuality. The exploitation of the display was justified by the scientific knowledge that it popularized. The "Sleeping Venus" was a wax figure with a mechanical interior that made her breasts rise and fall as if she were alive and breathing. The Musée Spitzner was in part a museum of horrors; its medical exhibits evoked a nightmarish sense of the terrors of nature gone awry. They represented the Other, as well as a mirror for the public's secret fears and neurotic self-image. The Musée Spitzner's stark contrast of medical exhibits with the gaiety of the fair atmosphere haunted Delvaux for years, and he admitted that: "The discovery of the Musée Spitzner made me completely change my conception of painting."[155]

The juxtaposition of erotic images, freaks of nature, and scientific dissections in the Musée Spitzner corresponded to Delvaux's inner anxieties about sex and death. Modern psychology has shaped the world view that is reflected in the content of these images. When Hieronymus Bosch painted nudes and deformed beings in his hallucinatory paintings, they were symbols of sin and demonic nature. The Musée Spitzner exhibited such figures under the guise of scientific objectivity. They were also, however, objects of desire. In the midst of the carnival setting, this provided a thrilling spectacle of forbidden knowledge.

As he himself often admitted, many of Delvaux's mature works echo the imagery and sense of voyeurism of the Musée Spitzner. Eroticism was a major preoccupation for Delvaux:

> Without eroticism, painting would be impossible for me [...]. The eroticism of my works resides in the evocation of youth and of desire [...]. A painting...must be seen and that is how it fulfills its function. It is a pleasure to contemplate a painting and, it is undoubtedly important that one names this pleasure for one's self—I think of women when I paint, young and attractive, beautiful to see...[156]

Delvaux admitted that his father had been known for his propensity to admire young women, which occasionally provoked trouble with his mother, and he himself liked to gaze at women: "I loved to look at them. But I was too timid to risk anything further."[157]

Of course, the contrast of nude women and clothed men, which is undeniably used for erotic purposes, also reflects the commonplace world of the art studio, wherein clothed men (the artists were primarily men) gaze at and paint nude women. Delvaux was asked directly if his unhappy relations with his first wife Suzanne were reflected in his paintings, but answered guardedly: "I do not know. There must be a difference between a work which blossoms from joy and that which is created in sadness. Whatever is brought to life in us, that which surges in our imagination or even the music which chants in us, is not necessarily tied to the momentary state of the spirit."[158]

Delvaux discovered a laconic mode of expression, wherein nude women and clothed men are juxtaposed in a dream-like manner. Wandering about like sleepwalkers, obsessively preoccupied, they ignore each other in the manner of the men and women in Manet's *Luncheon on the Grass* of 1863. In Delvaux's *Phases of the Moon I* of 1939 (Museum of Modern Art, New York), the scientists ignore the gift-wrapped nude woman in front of them, while in the background a male piper leads a troop of naked women. Although the male figures within the painting ignore the nearly nude female,

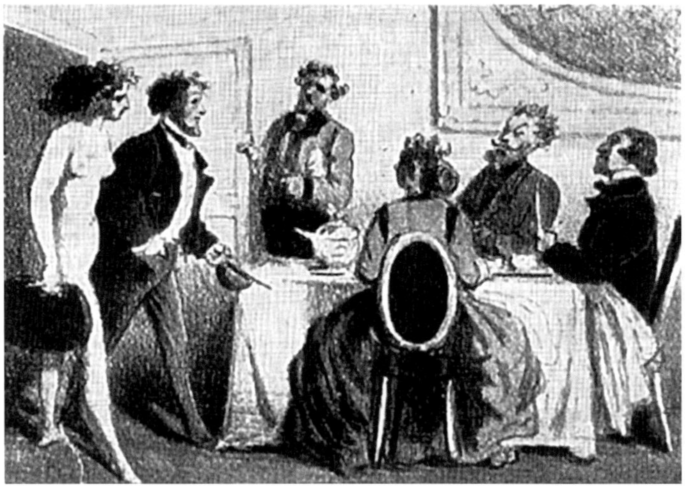

46. Hervey de Saint-Denis: drawn representation of a dream, originally from *Les Rêves et les moyens de diriger* (1867), republished in *Variétés*, Brussels, 1929.

the artist himself and viewers of the painting are able to gaze on her endlessly. Delvaux once explained that the men in his pictures are often clothed because they represent himself: "The men are often shown clothed in my pictures. Why not? The response is simple: I am presenting myself, the painter, recognizable or not."[159]

The oneiric quality of Delvaux's imagery is certainly deliberate. Voyeurism and unexpected nudity was a mainstay of early twentieth-century psychology and even had roots in the nineteenth century. A famous book on lucid dreaming by Hervey de Saint-Denis, *Les Rêves et les moyens de diriger* (1867), included a drawn representation of a dream (fig. 46). This image was republished in the Belgian modernist journal *Variétés* (Brussels, 1929).

Beyond initial appearances, nude women play a complex, symbolic, even allegorical role for Delvaux:

> The painting of the nude, the nude itself, can never be for me [...] anything but an opportunity, rather a means to an end. I am convinced that the *figures* in a painting must be clothed in the appearances of poetry and mystery, and thus be intercessors. It is this, it seems to me, which gives the work its altitude and confers upon it its powers; so that the nude in itself doesn't exist.[160]

The nudes in Delvaux's paintings are a mediating force, intermediaries between the viewer and the mystery of life.

Contemporary viewers may find Delvaux's compulsive voyeurism disquieting. An anomaly in an era dominated by abstract, non-representational art, his paintings remained fixated on representing a dream-like fantasy world of nude women, a nearly pornographic paradise. The Surrealist emphasis on sexuality and psychoanalytic imagery gave him permission to follow his private obsessions. It should also be noted that the theme of the privileged gaze and its connection to power and freedom is an old one in Flemish art. The nude woman is not always powerless: Peter Paul Rubens, who himself is well known for his portrayal of female nudity, illustrated the Old Testament Apocryphal story of Susanna and the Elders as an archetype of sexual harassment avenged, when Susanna refuses to give in to her attackers and has them executed.

In May of 1940, Belgium was quickly overrun by the German invasion, and Delvaux withdrew into an internal world, refusing to exhibit. He was forced to rely on his imagination during the war; as he later observed: "That which

I seek above all, is to bring out the poetry of certain elements of my life. The war was paradoxically for me charged in a particularly intense fashion."[161] During the war, Delvaux began painting and drawing skeletons with increasing frequency, often at the natural history museum of the Park Leopold. He was reacting to current events, which made death seem to be all around.[162] Delvaux once admitted that: "I have always been fascinated with the medieval Dances of Death. It is a theme so intense, so rich in lessons."[163] Skeletons continued to be an important theme in his work even after the war.

In *The Conversation* (1944, **no. 52**), Delvaux posed a half-nude model and skeleton in exactly the same position, so that their gestures create a visual rhyme. There is a third repetition of the pose on the wall behind, made by the cast shadow of the skeleton. The "echo" of the nude woman diminishes with the distance, becoming less and less substantial. This work is also a meditation on the fleeting passage of time, mortality, and memory.

The casual relationship between the woman and the skeleton places them in the realm of an artist's studio, where artist and model could improvise in a playful manner. The art studio contrasts dramatically with the other contexts where one might see a skeleton, the medical laboratory or hospital is a much more controlled environment. As Martin Kemp and Marina Wallace remind us, medical anatomical studies were ritualistic, carefully monitored, and semi-public, performed in anatomical "theaters."[164] Artists have more latitude to create poses that grow from, but also help mediate, our fears of mortality.

The juxtaposition of nude female and skeleton can also be found in *vanitas* imagery in earlier northern painting. Here it signifies the fragility and transience of life, memorably seen in Hans Baldung-Grien's allegorical painting of the *Woman and Death* from the early sixteenth century (fig. 47). The picture presents an elegant young woman with a fashionable hat and jewels, holding a blindfolded baby while a skeleton stands behind her. The artist seems to be implying that death comes even to the young and beautiful. The presence of the blindfolded baby, however, suggests that the woman may in fact be Venus, for Cupid was frequently shown blindfolded in the art of this period to symbolize the fact that love is blind.[165] Neoplatonists interpreted this as an allegorical statement about divine love, which is blind and accepts everyone, in contrast to earthly love, which discriminates on the basis of appearance. Therefore, this allegory of love and death may have Christian over-

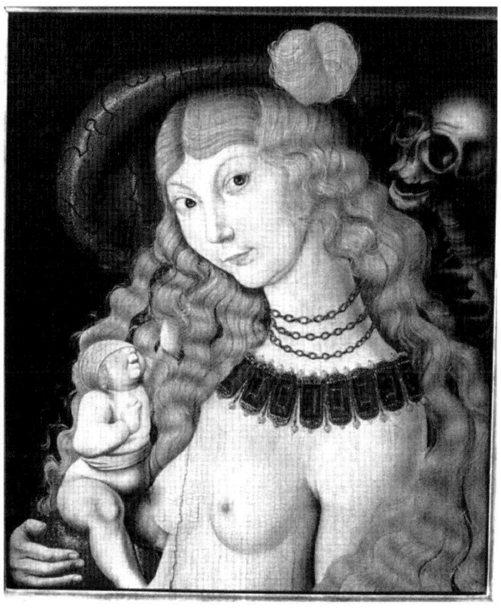

47. Hans Baldung-Grien, *Death and the Maiden*, early 16th century. Royal Museums of Fine Arts of Belgium, Brussels.

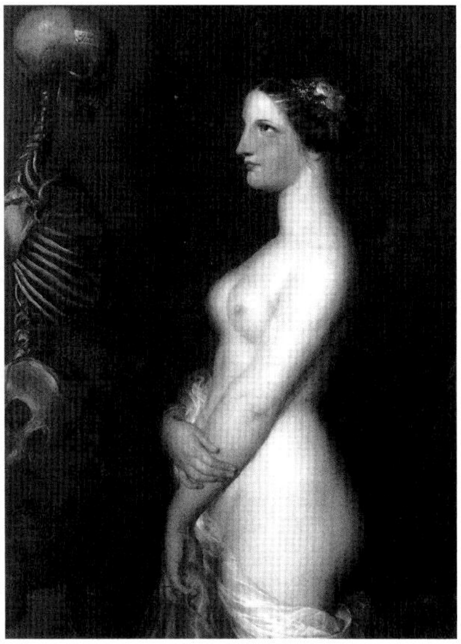

48. Antoine Wiertz, *La Belle Rosine*, 1847. Wiertz Museum, Brussels.

tones, despite the eroticism of the subject. Considering the gender biases of the era, the beautiful woman may also be intended to symbolize the snares of earthly pleasure, which distract the (male) soul and lead to death. In that case, the blindfolded child might signify the willful blindness of men. The woman's direct gaze at the viewer suggests that she may be a *femme fatale,* and that the viewer might be her next conquest.

The juxtaposition of sensuality and death also surfaced in the macabre images of the Romantic Antoine Wiertz in the mid-nineteenth century (fig. 48). *La Belle Rosine* clearly derives from the same tradition of *vanitas* imagery as Baldung-Grien's painting. The picture is also known as "The Two Beauties." Presumably set in an artist's studio, the Rubensian young model confronts a skeleton, which has a label pasted to her skull identifying her as "La Belle Rosine." Wiertz's painting depicts an intense, almost perverse, bond between the woman and her skeletal double. The unexpected encounter of two realities is similar to the shock of surrealist juxtapositions and prefigures Breton's concept of "convulsive beauty."

The fusion of love and death approached an almost hysterical pitch in Symbolist art of the late nineteenth century. The Norwegian artist Edvard Munch made several images that combined death and sexuality, including *Death and the Maiden* (fig. 49). They are truly an ill-matched couple. At the turn of the century, a new interest in public health led to a widespread awareness of the threat of syphilis and other venereal diseases. At the same time, new studies of human sexuality by Sigmund Freud, Richard Krafft-Ebing, and Havelock Ellis highlighted the complexity of sexual desire. Freud even claimed that all people have an unconscious desire for death that is inextricable from the sex drive. This image of a naked woman embracing a skeleton suggests both the promise and peril of human regeneration. Munch has lightly drawn spermatozoa and fetuses in the border of the print, suggesting that, on the one hand, through lovemaking, men and women can transcend themselves and become "a link in the chain that binds a thousand generations."[166] On the other hand, the dark, angular form of the skeleton is a vivid reminder of the dangers of human sexuality. Desire is entwined with anxiety, jealousy, and the pain of loss, intercourse can transmit disease, and conception can pass degenerative traits on to the next generation.

Although not drawn to themes of decadence and morbid obsession with death in the way that Munch was—there remains a kind of innocence about Delvaux's fascination with sexuality—Delvaux is nonetheless a worthy match to Munch when it came to obsession and anxiety. Many of Delvaux's paintings seem to illustrate Freudian theories of the unconscious, particularly in terms of the scientific exploration of inner depths. One of Freud's metaphors for the psychoanalytic recovery of the contents of the unconscious was the comparison to an archaeologist exploring a buried city such as Pompeii. In his famous essay on *Gradiva* Freud wrote: "There is no better analogy for repression, which at the same time makes inaccessible and conserves something psychic, than the burial which was the fate of Pompeii, and from which the city was able to arise again through work with the spade."[167]

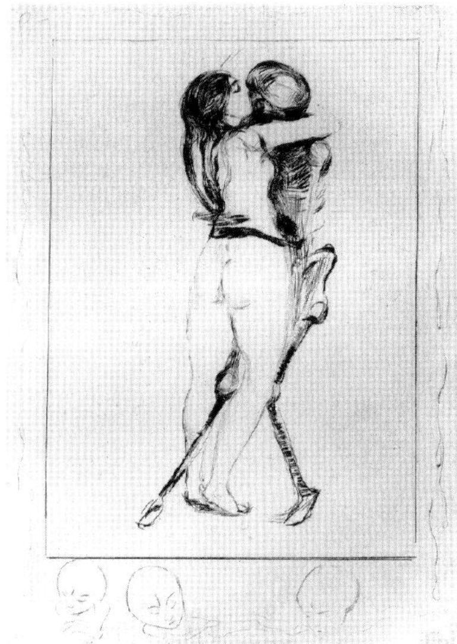

49. Edvard Munch: *Death and the Maiden*, drypoint, 1894. Private collection.

The Surrealists admired Freud's essay on *Gradiva* for its analysis of the power of obsession and the ability of the unconscious to recreate reality by superimposing subjective images on external scenes. This was perfectly congruent with their own poetic and artistic projects, and they opened a gallery called Gradiva in Paris in the 1930s.[168] Delvaux expressed his fascination with the skeletal remains of Pompeii: "It has all been there for two thousand years. Antiquity is present, still living; one can see it, sense it... Pompeii is the only place where there is nothing inauspicious. It is not an ensemble of ruins, but the skeleton of a civilisation. And for me, the skeleton is a very intense element of life."[169]

A woman who modeled frequently for Delvaux from 1966 into the mid-1980s, Danielle Caneel, noted that Delvaux was quiet around women and easily shocked by modern sexual mores. She felt that Delvaux represented an extreme case of the social constraints which shaped gender relations for an earlier generation, and that he believed that true communication between men and women was impossible.[170] This is perhaps somewhat contradicted by his long and happy relationship with his second wife, Tam, whom he finally married despite the promise extorted by his parents, but it is undeniable that many of his works depict a gulf between men and women.

Delvaux's art was essentially escapist and personal. Unlike René Magritte, he never sought to change the world through revolutionary images: "When I paint, I seek to escape from modernity. I leave the exterior world, and enter into my painting. I stroll about and I live there. No one can demand that of a spectator, because each one is free to think what he wishes. I exhibit what I make: if it may be beautiful, ugly, good, bad, I really do not know."[171] The personal overshadows the political in Delvaux's art; he reflects the high development of bourgeois culture in the twentieth century, with his broad knowledge of history and culture and emphasis on personal psychology. He translated his personal obsessions into monumental images, drawing the viewer into his own private odyssey in search of self-knowledge. *The Riddle* of 1946 (**no. 51**) projects his fascination with sexuality and dreams in a fantasy of a classical but timeless golden age.

Paul Delvaux never sought to depict Belgian national identity explicitly, but his visionary imagination and individualism nonetheless exemplifies one aspect of it. The increasing subjectivity of Modern art accompanied a widely recognized retreat into personal, rather than public, concerns in society. The late nineteenth century was torn between the poles of socially oriented art, in the workers of Constantin Meunier and the landscapes of Emile Claus, as well as the idealist withdrawal from materialism and conflict in the Symbolist movement. One of the primary impacts of the First World War was to make that ivory tower withdrawal less viable. Artists such as Frits van den Berghe and René Magritte sought to balance social concerns and psychological realities. Modern Belgian art is a unique microcosm of the critical tensions of the modern world, and much of the power of the art of this era stems from this. It is truly "a new key."

I would like to express my personal thanks to Patrick Derom and Gilles Marquenie in Belgium for their generous assistance with this exhibition, and astute contributions to this essay. Thanks are also due to Frederik Leen in Brussels. In Boston, my colleague Katherine Nahum kindly read early drafts and offered valuable suggestions. My best editor, as always, is my wife Reva Dolobowsky. Of course, without the collection of Henry and Françoise Simon, none of this would have happened.

Notes

1 Francis Haskell, *History and Its Images, Art and the Interpretation of the Past* (New Haven and London: Yale University Press, 1993) chapter 15, "Huizinga and the 'Flemish Renaissance,'" 431-495.

2 Henri Pirenne, "La Nation Belge," *Compte rendu de la distribution des prix qui a eu lieu le 1er octobre 1899* (Brussels: E. Guyot, 1899) 4-26. Reprinted in *La Belgique artistique et littéraire,* ed. Paul Aron (Brussels: Editions Complexe, 1997) 98-119.

3 Edmond Picard, "L'âme belge," *La Revue*, supplement to *Revue encyclopédique* (Paris: Larousse, 1897) 595-599; reprinted in *La Belgique artistique et littéraire* 90.

4 Chantal Kesteloot, "Growth of the Walloon Movement," *Nationalism in Belgium. Shifting Identities, 1780-1995,* eds. Kas Deprez and Louis Vos (New York: St. Martin's Press, 1998) 142. Kesteloot is quoting M. Bologne.

5 Max Rooses, *Art in Flanders* (New York, 1914) 2.

6 Christian Berg, "The Symbolic Deficit. French Literature in Belgium and 19th Century National Sentiment," *Nationalism in Belgium,* eds. Deprez and Vos 63.

7 José Fontaine, "Four Definitions of Culture in Francophone Belgium," *Nationalism in Belgium,* eds. Deprez and Vos 153.

8 José Fontaine, "Four Definitions of Culture in Francophone Belgium" *Nationalism in Belgium,* eds. Deprez and Vos 154.

9 Louis Vos, "The Flemish National Question," *Nationalism in Belgium,* eds. Deprez and Vos 83.

8 José Fontaine, "Four Definitions of Culture in Francophone Belgium" *Nationalism in Belgium,* eds. Deprez and Vos 154.

9 Louis Vos, "The Flemish National Question," *Nationalism in Belgium,* eds. Deprez and Vos 83.

10 *Le Romantisme en Belgique, Entre réalités, rêves et souvenirs*, catalogue of exhibition, (Brussels: Royal Museums of Fine Arts, 2005).

11 Rooses, *Art in Flanders* 288. Beyaert was born in Courtrai (Kortrijk) and studied first at the academy in Tournai and then at the Royal Academy in Brussels.

12 Deborah Silverman, *Art Nouveau in Fin-de-siècle France. Politics, Psychology and Style* (Los Angeles: University of California Press, 1989).

13 Lut Pil, "Painting at the Service of the New Nation State," *Nationalism in Belgium,* eds. Deprez and Vos 45.

14 David Nicholas, *Medieval Flanders* (London and New York, 1992) 8.

15 Robert Herbert, "Method and Meaning in Monet," *Art In America* (Sept. 1979) 90-108. Paul Hayes Tucker, *Monet in the '90s* (New Haven: Yale University Press, 1992).

16 Paul Greenhalgh, ed., *Art Nouveau. 1890-1914* (Washington, DC: National Gallery of Art, 2000), ch. 3, "The Cult of Nature" 54-71.

17 Piet Boyens has extensively studied this movement; see his exhibition catalogue, *Masterpieces of Modern Belgian Art, The Simon Collection* (Brussels: Musée d'Ixelles, 2003) 11-13. Also, by the same author: *Flemish Art: Symbolism to Expressionism at Sint-Martens-Latem* (Tielt [Belgium]: Lannoo; Sint-Martens-Latem [Belgium]: Art Book Co., 1992) and *In de voetsporen van de Latemse Kunstenaars* (Gent-Amsterdam: Ludion, 2003).

18 Boyens, *Flemish Art, Symbolism to Expressionism* 26.

19 Max Nordau's book *Degeneration* (1893) blamed urban life for a host of psychological and medical problems. This criticism was continued by the sociologist Georg Simmel in his 1903 book *Die Grössstadte und das Geistesleben* (*The Metropolis and Mental Life*). See Gill Perry, "Primitivism and the Modern," *Primitivism, Cubism, Abstraction. The Early Twentieth Century* (New Haven and London, 1993) 35.

20 Boyens, *Masterpieces of Modern Belgian Art* 11.

21 Boyens, *Flemish Art, Symbolism to Expressionism* 19.

22 Boyens, *Flemish Art, Symbolism to Expressionism* 207.

23 Boyens, *Flemish Art, Symbolism to Expressionism* 12. Michel Draguet, *Le Symbolisme en Belgique* (Antwerp: Fonds Mercator, 2004) 305-315, has important insights into this first group.

24 Lieve Gevers, "The Catholic Church and the Flemish Movement," *Nationalism in Belgium,* eds. Deprez and Vos 117.

25 Boyens, *Flemish Art, Symbolism to Expressionism* 62, 263.

26 See Linda Jessup, ed., *Antimodernism and Artistic Experience, Policing the Boundaries of Modernity*, (Toronto, Buffalo and London: University of Toronto Press, 2001).

27 Elizabeth Gilmore Holt, ed., *From the Classicists to the Impressionists: A Documentary History of Art and Architecture in the Nineteenth Century* (New Haven and London: Yale University Press, 1986) 387-388.

28 Johan de Smet, *Emile Claus 1849-1924* (Antwerp: Pandora, Snoek-Decaju & Zoon, 1997) 7, 9.

29 Emile Verhaeren in *La Jeune Belgique*, qtd. by Serge Goyens de Heusch, "Impressionism, Neo-Impressionism and Luminism in Belgium," *Impressionism to Symbolism: the Belgian Avant-garde 1880-1900*, eds. Mary Anne Stevens and Robert Hoozee (London: Royal Academy of Arts, in association with Ludion Press, Ghent, 1994) 33.

30 Boyens *Flemish Art, Symbolism to Expressionism* 20.

31 Boyens, *Flemish Art, Symbolism to Expressionism* 19.

32 Serge Goyens de Heusch, "Impressionism, Neo-Impressionism and Luminism in Belgium" 37.

33 Michael Palmer, *Ensor to Alechinsky: The Simon Collection of Belgian Art* (Privately printed by Heinrich Simon, 1998) 12.

34 Dominique Marechal, "Fernand Khnopff: From Bruges to Fosset," *Fernand Khnopff*, ed. Frederik Leen, catalogue of exhibition, (Brussels: Royal Museums of Fine Arts of Belgium, 2004) 35-44.

35 *Stimmungsmalerei*, or mood painting, in the nineteenth century has roots in Romantic theories of empathy, and was furthered by Charles Baudelaire's poem "Correspondences" in *Les Fleurs du Mal* (1857).

36 Ludwig Hevesi referred to Khnopff as the *obermystiker* of Brussels, in *Acht Jahre Sezession* (Vienna, 1906) 30.

37 Luc and Paul Haesaerts, qtd. by Francine-Claire Legrand, *Symbolism in Belgium*, (Brussels: Laconti, 1972) 207.

38 Boyens, *Flemish Art, Symbolism to Expressionism* 226.

39 Boyens, *Flemish Art, Symbolism to Expressionism* 58.

40 The Belgian Symbolist poet Grégoire LeRoy refered to the "ancient houses of his soul" in a poem, "Noëls éteints," in *La Rouet des Brume,* (Brussels, 1901) 201. A striking visual image of a man's torso dissected to parallel the rooms of a house is found in Tobias Cohn's medical treatise, *Maaseh Tobiyyah*, published in Venice in 1707. The architecture of the human body is clear: the hair is likened to the roof, the eyes to the windows, and the mouth to a door.

41 Qtd. by Boyens, *Flemish Art, Symbolism to Expressionism* 224.

42 James Gleick, *Chaos, Making a New Science* (New York: Viking Penguin, 1987).

43 Frederik Leen, "Cercles en Coteries, Groupes et associations d'artistes d'avant-garde en Belgique 1917-1929," *L'Avant-garde en Belgique 1917-1929*, eds. Frederik Leen, Anne Adriaens-Pannier and Gisèle Ollinger-Zinque, catalogue of exhibition, (Brussels: Musée d'Art moderne, 1992) 15.

44 Willy van den Bussche, "The Three from Ostend: Ensor, Spilliaert and Permeke," *From Ensor to Delvaux*, catalogue of exhibition (Ostend: Museum voor moderne kunst, 1996) 23.

45 Qtd. by Francine-Claire Legrand in *Léon Spilliaert, Symbol and Expression in 20th Century Belgian Art*, catalogue of exhibition (Washington, D.C., 1980) 43.

46 Jollivet-Castelot, qtd. by Frank Edebau in *Léon Spilliaert, Symbol and Expression in 20th Century Belgian Art* 13.

47 De Smet subscribed to *Das Kunstblatt* 1917-1920; Boyens, *Flemish Art, Symbolism to Expressionism* 103.

48 Wilhelm Worringer, *Abstraction and Empathy* (1908), qtd. in Donald Gordon, *Expressionism, Art and Idea* (New Haven and London: Yale University Press, 1987) 51.

49 Gordon, *Expressionism, Art and Idea*, highlights these characteristics of Expressionism: "That is why it is misleading to attribute to Expressionists, without qualification, a Romantic 'quest for unity' or 'feeling for the whole,'" 169.

50 Boyens, *Flemish Art, Symbolism to Expressionism* 136.

51 James Lindgren, *Preserving Historic New England. Preservation, Progressivism and the Remaking of Memory* (New York and Oxford: Oxford University Press, 1995).

52 Michelle Facos, *Nationalism and the Nordic Imagination, Swedish Art of the 1890s* (Berkeley and Los Angeles: University of California Press, 1998).

53 The oldest such museum existing today is that of Skansen in Stockholm, Sweden. It was founded in 1891, and was modeled on an earlier Norwegian example created by King Oscar II in Oslo, which was later incorporated into the Norsk Folkemuseum in the 1890s.

54 Lieve Gevers, "The Catholic Church and the Flemish Movement," *Nationalism in Belgium* 116.

55 Sophie de Schaepdrijver, "Occupation, propaganda and the idea of Belgium," *European Culture in the Great War,* eds. Aviel Roshwald and Richard Stiles (Cambridge: Cambridge University Press, 1999) 289.

56 See Eugenia W. Herbert, *The Artist and Social Reform in Belgium and France, 1885-1898* (New Haven, 1961) 9-11 and *passim.*

57 Jules Destrée, qtd. in Sura Levine, "Politics and the Graphic Arts of the Belgian Avant-Garde," *Les XX and the Belgian Avant-Garde: Prints, Drawings and Books, c. 1890,* ed. Stephen Goddard (Lawrence, KS: Spencer Museum of Art, 1992) 55-74.

58 Jakob Smits, letter of May 18, 1921, qtd. in Boyens, *Masterpieces of Modern Belgian Art* 48.

59 Herbert, *The Artist and Social Reform in Belgium and France* 31.

60 In his Memoirs, Horta recalled the commission: "They chose me to build the Maison du Peuple, because they wanted something expressive of my aesthetic style. The choice was not at all political. My friends and I simply had the same ideas, and there was no question of interest — we were 'reds' without having thought about Marx or his theories.... I could see immedi-

ately that the work would be interesting: to build a palace, which wouldn't be a palace but a 'house' where air and light, too long excluded from workers' hovels, would be the luxuries. The house would lodge the administrative offices, cooperative offices, political and professional meeting rooms, and a cafe where the price of drinks would be in keeping with the directors' desire to combat alcoholism, still a great problem among the people. There would be conference rooms for instruction and to crown it all, an immense auditorium for political meetings and the party's congress, as well as for the musical programs and theatrical events the members would produce." Victor Horta, *Memoirs*, qtd. in *Art Nouveau Belgium France,* ed. Yvonne Brunhammer, catalogue of exhibition (Houston, 1976) 349.

61 Other examples can be found in the catalogue *Art Nouveau Belgique* (Brussels, 1981) 96-97. See also *Architecture pour le Peuple. Maisons du Peuple. Belgique, Allemagne, Autriche, France, Grande-Bretagne, Italie, Pays-Bas, Suisse* (Brussels: Archives d'Architecture Moderne, 1984).

62 Sura Levine, "Monumental Transformations: The Changing Status of Constantin Meunier's Monument to Labor" (unpublished Ph.D. dissertation, University of Chicago, 1996).

63 Vincent Van Gogh, Letter 610, [November 1889?], *The Complete Letters of Van Gogh*, vol. 3 (Greenwich, CT: New York Graphic Society, 1959) 222.

64 Amy Ogata, *Art Nouveau and the Social Vision of Modern Living. Belgian Artists in a European Context* (Cambridge, UK: Cambridge University Press, 2001) 29.

65 See Adam Hochschild, *King Leopold's Ghost* (Boston: Houghton Mifflin Co., 1999) for an account of this tragic colonial venture.

66 Donald Gordon, "German Expressionism," *"Primitivism" in 20th Century Art, the Affinity of the Tribal and the Modern,* ed. William Rubin, vol. II, catalogue of exhibition (New York: Museum of Modern Art, 1984) 373, 379.

67 Willy van den Bussche, "Permeke Biography," *From Ensor to Delvaux* 220.

68 Not just African art, but also the art of fifteenth century Flemish painters, and that of Giotto and even Botticelli, was labeled "primitive" in the early twentieth century.

69 Kenneth Craig, "*Pars Ergo Marthae Transit:* Pieter Aertsen's 'Inverted' Paintings of *Christ in the House of Martha and Mary,*" *Oud Holland,* 97 (1983) 25-39. See also Craig's article "Pieter Aertsen and *The Meat Stall,*" *Oud Holland* 96 (1982) 1-15.

70 Most notably, Svetlana Alpers, *The Art of Describing: Dutch Art in the Seventeenth Century* (Chicago: University of Chicago Press, 1983).

71 Eddy de Jonghe, qtd. in Simon Schama, *The Embarassment of Riches, An Interpretation of Dutch Culture in the Golden Age* (New York, 1987) 162.

72 Amy Ogata, *Art Nouveau and the Social Vision of Modern Living* 48.

73 Some of Rops's dress designs are illustrated in Claudine Lemaire, "Abandon, grace, souplesse," *Art Nouveau belgique*, catalogue of *Europalia* exhibition (Brussels: Palais des Beaux-Arts, 1980) 183.

74 See Debra N. Mancoff, *Flora Symbolica, Flowers in Pre-Raphaelite Art* (Munich: Prestel, 2003) 68-75, for examples of the Aesthetic mania for sunflowers.

75 Albert Alhadeff, "George Minne: Fin-de-siècle Drawings and Sculpture" (unpublished dissertation, New York University, 1971) 183ff.

76 Boyens, *Flemish Art, Symbolism to Expressionism* 84.

77 Willy van den Bussche, "The Three from Ostend: Ensor, Spilliaert and Permeke," *From Ensor to Delvaux* 28.

78 Palmer, *Ensor to Alechinsky: The Simon Collection of Belgian Art* 85.

79 A major exhibition in London recently explored the connections of synaesthesia and the art of Kandinsky: *Kandinsky: The Path to Abstraction, 1908-1922* (London: Tate Modern, 2006). I summarized nineteenth-century precedents in an earlier essay, "Nocturnes: Munch and Melancholia, and the Mysteries of Life and Death," *Edvard Munch: Psyche, Symbol, Expression*, catalogue of exhibition (Chestnut Hill, MA: McMullen Museum of Art, 2001) 53-57.

80 Charles Baudelaire, "Richard Wagner et Tannhäuser," *Curiosités esthétiques. L'art romantique*, 1861; qtd. in Günther Metkin, "Music for the Eye, Richard Wagner and Symbolist Painting," *Lost Paradise. Symbolist Europe*, catalogue of exhibition (Montreal: Montreal Museum of Fine Arts, 1995) 118.

81 *Paul Gauguin. The Writings of a Savage*, ed. Daniel Guérin (New York: Viking, 1978) 146-147.

82 Scriabin's *Prometheus* was partly inspired by the Belgian Symbolist artist Jean Delville; it was written while Scriabin was staying with Delville during the period when the artist was creating a mural of Prometheus for the Université Libre in Brussels. See Olivier Delville, *Jean Delville, Peintre 1867-1953* (Brussels: Laconti, 1984) 26.

83 Leen, "Cercles en Coteries" 15.

84 Boyens, *Flemish Art, Symbolism to Expressionism* 94.

85 Boyens, *Flemish Art, Symbolism to Expressionism* 53.

86 Amy Ogata, *Art Nouveau and the Social Vision of Modern Living* 15.

87 I am indebted to Gilles Marquenie for this reference.

88 Boyens, *Flemish Art, Symbolism to Expressionism* 98.

89 Sophie de Schaepdrijver, "Occupation, propaganda and the idea of Belgium" 270.

90 Klaus Thewelheit, *Male Fantasies, Volume 1: Women, Floods, Bodies, History* (Minneapolis: University of Minnesota Press, 1987).

91 A recent example is Larry Zuckerman. *The Rape of Belgium. The Untold Story of World War I* (New York and London: New York University Press, 2004). See also *European Culture in the Great War,* eds. Roshwald and Stiles.

92 See Stanley Weintraub, *Silent Night: The Story of the World War I Christmas Truce* (New York: Free Press, 2001). A recent film directed by Christian Carion, *Joyeux Noel,* also released as *Happy Christmas* (2005), depicts this story.

93 Boyens, *Flemish Art, Symbolism to Expressionism* 109.

94 The Belgian artists in Wales was the subject of a recent exhibition: *Art in Exile, Flanders, Wales and the First World War,* eds. Oliver Fairclough, Robert Hoozee, and Caterina Verdickt (National Museum and Galleries of Wales, Cardiff, 2002).

95 J.W. Gamble, letter of 1915, qtd. in Modris Eksteins, *The Rites of Spring: The Great War and the Birth of the Modern Age* (New York and London: Doubleday, 1989) 214.

96 Quotation taken from wall label at the exhibit *Innocent Landscape* at the In Flanders Fields Museum, in the Cloth Hall, Ypres, July 2006.

97 E.H. Kossmann, *The Low Countries, 1780-1940* (Oxford, 1978) 654.

98 Martial Lekeux, *Le Patelin de Notre Dame* (Bruges, [1927] reprint 1993). Father Lekeux wrote many other books, including *Mes Cloitres dans la Tempête*, and *Maggy*. Lekeux died in 1957.

99 Sophie de Schaepdrijver, "Occupation, Propaganda and the Idea of Belgium" 273.

100 Leen, "Cercles en Coteries" 15.

101 Leen, "Cercles en Coteries" 20.

102 Leen, "Cercles en Coteries" 21.

103 Sophie de Schaepdrijver, "Occupation, Propaganda and the Idea of Belgium" 267-294.

104 Stephen Schloesser, *Jazz Age Catholicism* (Toronto and London: University of Toronto Press, 2005) 10.

105 Jay Winter, *Sites of Memory, Sites of Mourning, The Great War in European Cultural History* (Cambridge: Cambridge University Press, 1995).

106 A point emphasized by Stephen C. Foster, "World War I: The Grand Illusion, the Great War, and the Formal Revolution," *The Ideological Crisis of Expressionism: The Literary and Artistic German War Colony in Belgium 1914-1918*, eds. R. Rumold and O.K. Werckmeister (Columbia, S.C., 1990) 281-295.

107 Modris Eksteins, *The Rites of Spring*; Kenneth Silver, *Esprit de Corps: The Art of the Parisian Avant-Garde and the First World War, 1914-1925* (Princeton, NJ: Princeton University Press, 1989). Jay Winter, *Sites of Memory, Sites of Mourning, The Great War in European Cultural History* (Cambridge: Cambridge University Press, 1995); Schloesser, *Jazz Age Catholicism.*

108 Eksteins, *The Rites of Spring* 165-166.

109 Leen, "Cercles en Coteries" 56.

110 There were many more; see Leen, "Cercles en Coteries" for an extended study of these journals.

111 Leen, "Cercles en Coteries" 45-46.

112 Letter to Albert Croquez, qtd. in Diane Lesko, *James Ensor: The Creative Years* (Princeton, N.J., Princeton University Press, 1985) 43.

113 James Ensor, qtd. in *Artists on Art, From the XIV to the XX Century*, eds. Robert Goldwater and Marco Treves (New York: Random House, 1972) 387.

114 Patricia Berman, *James Ensor: Christ's Entry into Brussels in 1889,* Getty Museum Studies on Art (Los Angeles: J. Paul Getty Trust Publications, 2002).

115 Ensor spent only two days in jail; Erich Heckel was one of these who intervened for him. Rainer Rumold, "Introduction," *The Ideological Crisis of Expressionism* 11.

116 Michael Holquist, "Prologue," Mikhail Bakhtin, *Rabelais and His World.* Trans. Helene Iswolsky (Bloomington: Indiana University Press, 1984) xviii.

117 Even the newest survey of twentieth century art by Hal Foster, Rosalind Krauss, Yve-Alain Bois, and Benjamin H.D. Buchloh, *Art Since 1900* (London: Thames and Hudson, 2004), reinforces this canon. See reviews in *The Art Bulletin* (LXXXVIII, 2, June 2006) 373-89.

118 Michel Draguet, *Le Symbolisme en Belgique* (Antwerp: Fonds Mercator, 2004) 305-319.

119 Boyens and Marquenie, *Frits van den Berghe,* catalogue of exhibition (Ostend: Museum voor moderne kunst, 1999) 19.

120 Willy van den Bussche, "Introduction," *Frits van den Berghe,* Boyens and Marquenie 9.

121 Piet Boyens, *Flemish Art: Symbolism to Expressionism at Sint-Martens-Latem* (Tielt [Belgium]: Lannoo; Sint-Martens-Latem [Belgium]: Art Book Co., 1992) 398.

122 Boyens and Marquenie, *Frits van den Berghe,* 20-21. Also, Boyens, *Flemish Art: Symbolism to Expressionism* 5, 167.

123 Boyens, *Flemish Art, Symbolism to Expressionism* 106.

124 Willy van den Bussche, "Introduction," *Frits van den Berghe,* Boyens and Marquenie 9.

125 Perry, "Primitivism and the Modern" 63.

126 Willy van den Bussche, "Introduction," *Frits van den Berghe,* Boyens and Marquenie 13.

127 Marianne W. Martin, *Futurist Art and Theory* (Chicago: University of Chicago Press, 1968).

128 Umberto Boccioni, "The Technical Manifesto of Futurist Sculpture," *Futurist Manifestos*, ed. Umbro Apollonio (New York: The Viking Press, 1970) 63. "Let's split open our figures and place the environment inside them."

129 Jean Seznec, *The Survival of the Pagan Gods* (Princeton, NJ: Bollingen Press, 1953) 49ff. Other visual examples of man as a microcosm include Johannes de Ketham, *Fasiculo de medicina* (Venice: Gregori, 1493).

130 René Magritte, *Magritte / Torczyner: Letters Between Friends*, trans. Richard Miller (New York: Abrams, 1994) 120-21, Letter of 18 September 1965: "If one wants to talk about Max Ernst's influence, better talk about the influence of Frits van den Berghe, who was very much removed from the Surrealist spirit: he only used the outer aspect of Ernst's painting and yet he is regarded by some as a "precursor" of Surrealism in Belgium."

131 Boyens, *Flemish Art, Symbolism to Expressionism* 458. Qtd. from an interview in *Le Centaure* (Brussels), I, no. 7 (1927) 135-139.

132 Joke Van Pamel, "Confronting Dualities of the Flesh: '*De Vrouw*' 1924-25, a Gouache Series by Frits van den Berghe," unpublished M.A. Thesis (University of Cincinnati, 2006) 28.

133 Hollis Clayson, *Painted Love: Prostitution in French Art of the Impressionist Era* (Los Angeles: Getty Trust Publications, 2003).

134 Leo Steinberg, "The Philosophical Brothel," *Art News*, vol. 71, Sept./Oct. (1972) 20-29; 38-47.

135 Donald Gordon, "German Expressionism" 370-374.

136 The literature on Surrealist art and sexuality is extensive; especially noteworthy are: Xavière Gautier, *Surréalisme et sexualité* (Paris: Gallimard, 1971); and *Investigating Sex. Surrealist Discussions, 1928-1932,* ed. José Pierre (London and New York: Verso, 1992).

137 See the essay by Claude Cernuschi, "Freudian Themes In The Symbolist Work Of George Minne" in this volume for a penetrating exposition of Freudian theories of narcissism.

138 Willy van den Bussche, "Introduction," *Frits van den Berghe,* Boyens and Marquenie 12.

139 Leen, "Cercles en Coteries" 28.

140 André Breton, *Manifestoes of Surrealism* (Ann Arbor: University of Michigan Press, 1972) 26.

141 Breton, *Manifestoes of Surrealism* 15.

142 David Sylvester, *Magritte, The Silence of The World* (New York: Abrams, 1992) 58.

143 Sylvester, *Magritte, The Silence of The World* 163.

144 Letter to Marcel Mariën, 21 August 1940; qtd. in Sylvester, *Magritte, The Silence of The World* 251.

145 Torczyner, *Magritte: Words and Images* 22.

146 "Headless. And also footless. Often armless too; and almost always unarmed, except with poetry and passion. There they are, the surrealist women so shot and painted, so stressed and dismembered, punctured and severed…" Mary Ann Caws, "Body: Seeing the Surrealist Woman," *The Surrealist Look: An Erotics of Encounter* (Cambridge, MA: MIT Press, 1997) 53.

147 René Magritte, *écrits complets*, ed. André Blavier (Paris: Flammarion, 1979) 259. Translation mine; original text follows: "Les titres des tableaux ne sont pas des explications et les tableaux ne sont pas des illustrations des titres. La relation entre le titre

et le tableau est poétique, c'est-à-dire que cette relation ne retient des objets que certaines de leurs caractéristiques habituellement ignorés par la conscience, mais parfois pressenties à l'occasion d'événements extraordinaires que la raison n'est point encore parvenue à élucider."

148 An excellent survey of Magritte's commercial work may be found in George Roque's *Ceci n'est pas un Magritte* (Paris: Flammarion, 1983).

149 Sylvester, *Magritte, The Silence of The World* 84-85.

150 Louis Scutenaire, 1947, qtd. in Jan Ceulers, *René Magritte, 135 rue Esseghem, Jette-Brussels* (Antwerp: Pandora, 1999) 19.

151 Ceulers, *René Magritte, 135 rue Esseghem.*

152 Briony Fer, "The Language of Construction," *Realism, Rationalism, Surrealism. Art Between the Wars* (New Haven and London: Yale University Press, 1993) 166.

153 Maurice Debra, *Promenades & Entrétiens avec Delvaux,* (Paris and Louvaine-la-Neuve : Duculot 1991) 63.

154 Delvaux qtd. in Barbara Emerson, *Delvaux* (Antwerp: Fonds Mercator, 1985) 57. Translation mine; original text: "Ce Musée Spitzner a été pour moi un révélation formidable. Cela a été vraiment un tournant très important et je peux peut-être vous dire qu'il a précédé la découverte de Giorgio de Chirico, mais c'était dans le même sens."

155 Emerson, *Delvaux,* 57-58. Translation mine; original text: "La découverte du Musée Spitzner m'a fait virer complètement dans ma conception de la peinture."

156 Qtd. by Jacques Sojcher, *Paul Delvaux* (Paris: Ars Mundi, 1991) 13. Translation mine; original text: "Sans l'érotisme la peinture serait, pour moi, impossible [...] L'érotisme de mon oeuvre réside dans l'évocation de la jeunesse et du désir [...] Un tableau... doit être regardé et c'est ainsi qu'il remplit son office. Il y a plaisir à contempler un tableau et, sans doute, est-il important que celui-ci appelle lui-même ce plaisir — je pense aux femmes que je peins, jeunes et attrayantes, belles à regarder..."

157 Debra, *Promenades & Entretiens avec Delvaux* 130; translation mine. Original text: "J'aimais les regarder. Mais j'étais trop timide pour m'aventurer plus loin."

158 Debra, *Promenades & Entretiens avec Delvaux* 134. Translation mine; original text: "La tournure malheureuse de son mariage avec Suzanne eut-elle une influence sur son oeuvre? 'Je l'ignore. Il doit exister une différence entre un travail qui s'épanouit dans la joie et celui qui se crée dans la tristesse. Quoique ce qui se met à vivre en nous, ce qui surgit dans notre imagination ou même la musique qui vient chanter en nous, n'est pas nécessairement lié â l'état d'esprit du moment.'"

159 Emerson, *Delvaux* 236; translation mine. Original text: "Les hommes se montrent souvent vêtus dans mes tableaux. Pourquoi pas? La réponse est simple: je me présente moi-même, le peintre, reconnaissable ou non."

160 Qtd. by Sojcher, *Paul Delvaux* 13. Translation mine; original text: "La peinture de nu, le nu lui-même, ne peut jamais être pour moi [...] qu'une occasion, un moyen plutôt qu'une fin. Je suis convaincu que les figures, dans le tableau, doivent revêtir

les apparences de la poésie et du mystère, et en être ainsi les intercesseurs. C'est cela, me semble-t-il, qui donne à l'oeuvre son altitude et lui confère ses pouvoirs; de sorte que le nu n'existe pas, en soi."

161 Delvaux, qtd. in Emerson, *Delvaux* 101; translation mine; original text:"Ce que je cherche surtout, c'est à faire ressortir la poésie de certains éléments de ma vie. La guerre paradoxalement en est pour moi chargée de façon particulièrement intense."

162 Emerson, *Delvaux* 111, quotes Suzanne Houbart-Wilkin's observation that the war turned people's spirits toward the idea of death.

163 Emerson, *Delvaux* 161; translation mine; original text: "J'ai toujours été fasciné par les Danses macabres du Moyen Age. C'est un thème si intense, si riche en enseignements." [Interview with Jo Gérard].

164 Martin Kemp and Marina Wallace, *Spectacular Bodies* (Berkeley, Los Angeles and London: University of California Press, 2000) 23 and *passim*.

165 Erwin Panofsky, "Blind Cupid," chapter in *Studies in Iconology; Humanistic Themes in the Art of the Renaissance* (New York: Harper and Row, 1972) 95-128.

166 Edvard Munch, "St. Cloud" (1889), qtd. in *Edvard Munch: The Frieze of Life*, ed. Mara-Helen Wood (London: National Gallery Publications, 1992) 12.

167 Wilhelm Jensen, *Gradiva,* and Sigmund Freud, *Delusion and Dream in Wilhelm Jensen's Gradiva* (Los Angeles: Sun and Moon Press, 1993) 166-67.

168 This gallery, run by André Breton, featured an entrance designed by Marcel Duchamp. Over the door the name GRADIVA was spelled out over the names of various Surrealist women: Gisèle, Rosine, Alice, Dora, Ines, Violette, and Alice. See Whitney Chadwick, *Women Artists and the Surrealist Movement* (Boston: Little Brown and Company, 1985) 50-51.

169 Emerson, *Delvaux* 93; translation mine; original text: "'Depuis deux mille ans tout est là. L 'Antiquité est présente, encore vivante; on peut la voir, la sentir... Pompéi est le seul endroit où elle n'a rien de néfaste. Ce n'est pas un ensemble de ruines, mais le squelette d'une civilisation. Et pour moi, le squelette est un élément de vie très intense.'"

170 Emerson, *Delvaux* 199.

171 Delvaux, qtd. by Emerson, *Delvaux* 241. Translation mine; original text: "Lorsque je peins, je cherche à m 'échapper de la modernité. Je quitte l'extérieur, et j'entre dans mon tableau. Je m'y promène et j'y vis. Personne ne peut exiger cela d'un spectateur, car chacun est libre de penser ce qu'il veut. Je montre ce que je fais: que cela soit beau, laid, bon, mauvais, je n'en sais strictement rien."

Ensor's Parrot

Katherine Nahum

> *My grandparents kept a shop in Ostend's Kapucijnenstraat where they sold seashells, lace, rare stuffed fishes, old books, engravings, weaponry, Chinese porcelain—a confused mess of anomalous objects constantly being overturned by several cats, some screeching parrots and a monkey. I spent long hours there in the company of the monkey and the parrots and the cats. The store reeked of mold, and the acrid pee of the monkey filled up the seashells and the cats lounged among the most precious laces. However, this peculiar shop was frequented by the most distinguished visitors. I could name the Emperor Wilhelm, then the Prince of Prussia, Leopold I, King of Belgium, the Duke of Brabant, the Count of Flanders.... My grandmother amused them all with her wit. She would often rig me up in bizarre costumes, as she also carefully dressed her monkey—she had taught him hundreds of tricks. This wicked animal, the terror of the neighbors, accompanied her on her walks. She adored masquerades. I can see her still, standing at the foot of my little bed during the night of carnival parade, dressed as a coquettish peasant, but her mask was ghastly. I was around five, she was more than sixty. My childhood was stocked with marvels, and visiting my grandmother and her shop, iridescent with reflections of shells and sumptuous laces, with strange stuffed beasts and the terrible weapons of savages affected me deeply. Often the monkey would perch on a gigantic stuffed fish to great satiric effect [...]. Strangers decked out in gold, great Russian lords, Polish Jews would begin arriving [...]. Then the crazy race to the sea where could be found yet more seashells of thousands of colors. Indeed, these exceptional surroundings developed my artistic faculties, and my grandmother was my great inspiration.* [1]

THE POLITICAL, RELIGIOUS, AND PSYCHOLOGICAL ASPECTS OF THE ART OF JAMES ENSOR (1860-1949) evolve, if they do not explode from the early poetic experiences described above. Attempts will be made in this essay to expose the complex layerings of Ensor's art that have issued from an unusual childhood. It is already evident that the seashells, fish, basket, and pottery depicted in his *Still Life with Fish and Shellfish* (1895, **no. 23**), one of four Ensor paintings in the Simon Collection, evoke these peculiar domestic circumstances, and evoke as well the entire seaside, carnival culture of Ostend where Ensor was born, lived, and worked.

Ostend, a resort town on the North Sea, attracted the monied classes from England and the Continent. It was also famous for the extravagance of its Carnival. Before Lent in February, Ensor's family catered to the Ostend revelers, selling them carnival masks and other outré objects that Ensor lists in his letter. Behind the still life stand, not just the grandmother he describes, but also a formidable female world of the Haeghemans, Ensor's mother's family: grandmother, mother, aunt, and sister. His mother, Maria Catharina, ran a profitable business and kept the family together.

Traces of the the artist's father, James Frederic Ensor, are harder to detect. An English subject born in Belgium, Ensor's father trained as a doctor, had experience as a civil engineer, read and wrote in several languages, and maintained all his life a deep and abiding interest in the arts. He was an accomplished musician. The father came from an independently wealthy family, from the same economic and social class as the tourists who swarmed Ostend each summer. It is not surprising that the artist's grandparents disinherited their son when he married Maria-Catharina,[2] the daughter of illiterate lace-makers and shopkeepers. Ensor's father found the hardscrabble yet glittering Ostend repugnant, and attempted to find work in America as an engineer in 1861—the worst moment, since it was the eve of the American Civil War. He returned to Ostend and collapsed, spending his days reading and walking, and his nights drinking himself to death.

Nevertheless it was Ensor's father, alone, who recognized and supported his son's talent. Unbeknownst to his wife and her family,[3] who did not value the seascapes and drawings that the boy had begun to make, the father arranged lessons with two local artists. The women considered the artist's images valuable only later, and then as inventory to be sold in the souvenir shops along with masks, puppets, and shells. Ensor went on to attend for little more than two years, the Brussels Académie Royale des Beaux-Arts. He found the curriculum frustrating and dry, but got to know several artists, including Fernand Khnopff, with whom he later founded Les Vingt or Les XX (The Twenty), the Brussels avant-garde association, in 1883.

While studying at the academy, he also met the intellectuals Ernest and Mariette Rousseau and their son, Ernest. The Rousseaus' informal soirées attracted radical thinkers, poets, and artists involved in discussions of recent scientific progress, and the political, social, and religious divisions among francophone populations, and between Walloons and Flemings. The increasing Catholic control within the government was always a charged topic. Here also Ensor may have become aware of anarchism. The artist found it all stimulating, and he fell half in love with Mariette Rousseau.

Nevertheless, he returned home to Ostend, as if drawn back by Circe herself, to the very same apartments above the family souvenir and carnival shops where he had always lived.

Traveling little and essentially living out his life in Ostend, Ensor acquired his prodigious knowledge of art history not from exchanges with other artists, but primarily from engaging with the images he found in books, an activity through which he must have formed the most rewarding relationships, since those with his parents were frustrating. Family life was characterized by emotional coldness and distrust.[4] Nevertheless, Ensor's visual acuity and pleasure in art must have flourished during his childhood home schooling. His father's library included philosophy, religion, science, literature, the best of continental and English art books, and art journals like the *Gazette des Beaux-Arts.*[5]

The 1895 *Still Life with Fish and Shellfish* (**no. 23**)—in fact, his entire oeuvre—may represent and owe its existence to Ensor's father, his library, and his secret initiative to find instruction for his son. He set the artist on his path. That decision may have been the father's only assertive, fulfilling action.

Ensor's still life derives from venerated traditions of northern *vanitas* imagery wherein symbolic objects point to the moral, Christian conduct of one's life before the inevitable. *Vanitas* might include literal representations of skeletons and bones to symbolize death, as in a *memento mori. Still Life with Fish and Shellfish* can be related to two other of Ensor's marine still lifes, *Skate and Herring* (1880, Koninklijk Museum voor Schone Kunsten, Antwerp) and *The Skate* (1892, Musée d'Art Moderne, Bruxelles).

All three are indebted to Chardin's widely admired *The Ray Fish* (1728, Musée de Louvre), which the eighteenth-century artist Nicholas de Largillière implicitly compared, as Ensor might have known, to the colorists of the Flemish school.[6] Ensor's own handling of color derives from the Flemish colorists and Jean-Baptiste-Siméon Chardin. Light seems to emanate from within the richness of colors that modulate from the browns at the lower right to the pearly pinks at the upper left; this relation of light and color gives the painting its immediate visual impact. Ensor felt that light dominated his vision; it was the "queen of our senses."[7] Two flounders, one brown, the other overlaid upon the first and brilliant white because its underbelly is exposed, have displaced the sting rays, both in Chardin's painting and in Ensor's. Ensor's earlier painting (1880) depicts the skate overturned on straw with its poisonous and still dangerous tail inserted into the dark interior of a basket, a suggestive motif. Here, in the Simon Collecton still life, however, both Chardin's and Ensor's dangerous sting rays have been replaced by mere flounders that hang over the table edge. Ensor shows us opposite sides of two fish, like two aspects of the same flounder, which he turns over, flip-flop, before our eyes, as if he were working out some ambivalent assessment. Two mackerel lie nearby; a rouget or mullet is upright and aligned with the front edge of the simple wooden table. It looks like one of those stuffed fish his grandmother had collected, as Ensor mentions in his letter.

Small shells are placed in isolation around the fish to allow us to identify them: mussel and oyster shells form spots of color against the dull brown wood. A glorious conch shell with its beribboned pinks and salmons dominates the shells before it. It is aligned with various vessels: at left, a stout pot with handle and spout that looks like a miniature ship's prow carved as a woman's form; at right, a basket, the weave threaded with strange blue characters that may spell out "Ostend." The additive placement of these objects bespeak the curiosities for sale in the Haegheman's shops. The conch from some exotic shore and the pots symbolically suggest the female sex, and they exist behind the pale, prominent flounder, "an image of utter sexual exhaustion,"[8] a symbol of the suffering Christ, and an image that is linked to the artist because it is closest to his stance before the canvas. The painting telescopes multiple themes, an artistic habit that will continue to inform Ensor's work.

Heaps of lowly straw flow from the basket, but Ensor has refashioned the straw into something like gold tinsel that seems to radiate an abstract light for the entire painting. Having studied Rembrandt carefully, Ensor was aware of the distorting and dissolving properties of light that could suggest another, spiritual or ghostly world. At right are overlapped ceramic jars, examples of the grandmother's Chinese porcelain, objects brought forward from the female realm of Ensor's childhood. They suggest how specific physical needs were attended to: in isolation and perfunctorily. He described how his hardworking mother, the only support of the family, spoiled him with sweets and left unsaid that emotional nurturing and relationships were hardly the coin of the land. They were unavailable from either parent:[9] one was industriously running a business, the other reading and ruminating in his study, or out with the Ostenders drinking. The local burghers and fishermen would take the father around the seaside bars to get him drunk and would gleefully deposit him, unconscious, at the door to the Haegheman's souvenir shop. The artist reacted to these repeated excursions with bitter irony, recalling that his father "was really a superior man, finally preferring to be drunk rather than to be like the rest of us."[10] By quoting Paul Claudel's wry comment on Verlaine, Ensor was attempting to defend and distance himself from this unpleasantness and undo his humiliation by placing his father in the company of these admired poets and intellectuals.

The still life background is filled by energized diagonal strokes of salmon pinks shot through with white and some blue, a sea of color—it seems the North Sea itself has washed up these fish and shells. From within the brilliance of the color field emerges the faint outlines of a figure, a man swathed in blue drapery. He looks fatherly, or like a sacred figure who appears to lean left toward others, their heads inclined toward him. Above, shapes fly heavenward. The eye is led from the foreground gold filaments to the figure in blue in the background. In other ways, color ties these two domains, the realm of the strange pots and shells of his mother's souvenir shops, and the amorphous, surging, soothing realm of the sea, perhaps god's realm, or some fantasied realm of emotional sustenance that was not available to him in a household alternately contentious or deathly silent.[11] Ensor was "above all, deeply moved by the sea nearby, immense and

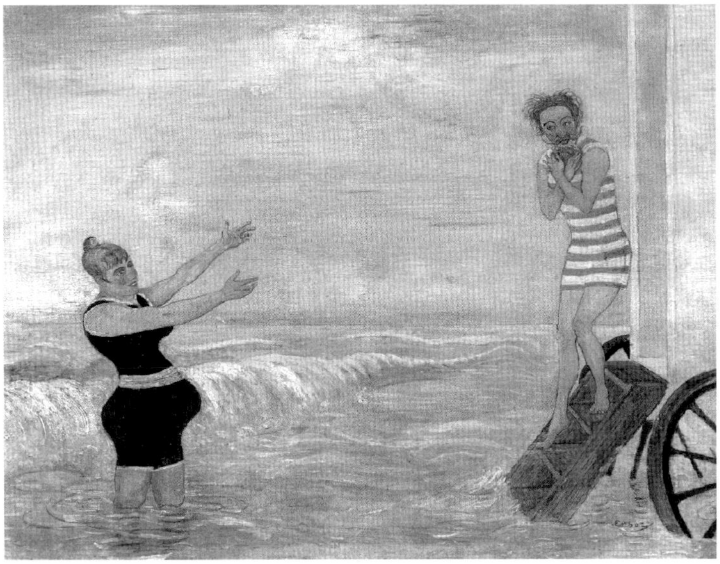

1. James Ensor: *The Call of the Siren*, 1893. Oil on panel, 38 x 46 cm. Private Collection.

always there."[12] As is true of most of Ensor's images, several themes intersect within this still life. Its layers refer to the sexual caution implied in the *vanitas*, to Christianity, and to the artist's own divided world comprised of his hardworking mother, and then his father, whom Ensor could barely grasp for all his besotted vagaries, but who seemed linked to the creative life source of the sea—always there. The artist may inject another personal meaning as well if the sexual symbolism modulates his mother's prudery regarding nudity and his own resistance to painting it.

Both issues are addressed in a rare image of nudity, the suggestively symbolist and luminous *Children Washing* (1886, private collection), a satirical deep dig at two female members of his family because the faces of the pre-adolescent nude girls shown sensuously washing are those of his mother and his sister, Mitche.[13] In fact, this may be a literal and black humored response to his mother's advice that, "if you need proper feminine models—take your sister, your aunt, or me."[14] It is an early image, but not the first,[15] in which the natural face is replaced with a false one, a kind of mask—at any rate, a misrepresentation—since the women were considerably older than the girls depicted.

Ensor's relationship with his companion of sixty-one years, Augusta Boogaerts, may be suggested in the still life by the glowing pink conch, traditional symbol of a woman's labia, from which the moribund flounder is turned away. Writers question if their relationship was sexual at all.[16] Ensor's sexual uncertainty and ambivalence is suggested in a number of his paintings and caricatures.

The Call of the Siren (fig. 1), a powerful example of self-mockery, shows Ensor wearing a ridiculous striped bathing costume and arms chastely crossed on his chest, unwilling to test the waters where the opulent Augusta stands with open arms. How could Ensor be anything but wary of the opposite sex, given an early life dominated by strong women? Whatever the couple's relationship, it surely was intimate and long lasting. Augusta eventually had a part to play in the artist's work, becoming his business manager, and, by the 1930s, actually setting up the compositions for Ensor's still lifes.[17] Surrendering the composing of still lifes to Augusta bespeaks not only passivity, but a degradation of artistic quality.

Still life is associated with the sacred: symbolic elements within sacred paintings of the fifteenth century became isolated as independent subjects. Another convention held that foreground and background (say, in the form of paintings shown within a painting) commented upon one another, expanded a narrative. Such a relation of foreground to background corresponds to daily lived experience, as when we understand the "now" in terms of a background or a context, a family or a culture in which it has occurred. Conversation has a background. It is created and monitored by both partners, and needs, against the history of their relationship, constant disambiguation. Meanings emerge from the tilting of the conversation toward implicitly known goals. Mikhail Bakhtin, whose *Rabelais and His World* demystifies the world of folk humor and with whose ideas of Carnival other writers see parallels to Ensor's art,[18] avowed elsewhere that "beneath the generalized meanings of words lies a history of 'past communicational exchanges [that] cling to our words.'" Likewise, evolving psychoanalysis has suggested that "every word has a hidden glow of feeling that has been built from the specific relational encounters in which it has been embedded."[19] For any nineteenth-century visual artist, however, images are the primary means of communication, not words. "Feelings" attached to words correspond to feelings attached to artists' imagery. Ensor's shapes, colors, lines and their dispersal in illusionistic space, their register by brushstroke—whether hidden, overt, or pressed into bold expression—all comprise the artist's communication and convey his emotional state. A history of feelings form the background and are made specific in what is immediately before us, the objects of his still life. Both of these domains have "a hidden glow of feeling" that is the result of many forces: the wish to be cared for and to be relieved of both anxiety and fear, Christian belief, the history of art, and the still life genre within it. The painting is the result of all that has occurred within the "now" set against a deep background.

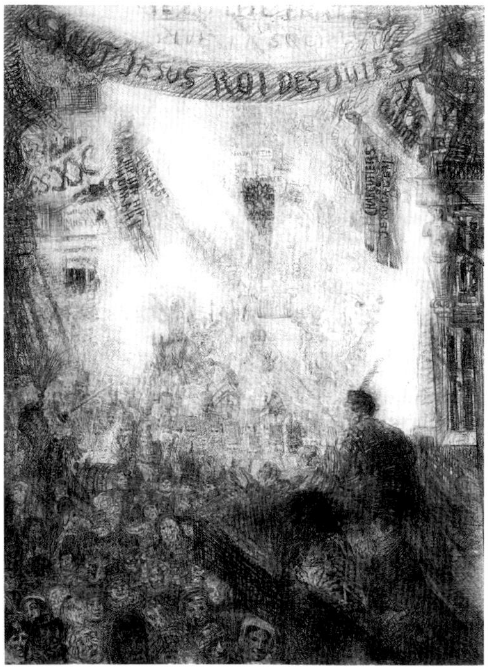

2. James Ensor: *The Lively and Radiant: The Entry of Christ into Jerusalem*, 1885. Black and brown crayon, with paste on paper; paper mounted on canvas, 206 x 150.3 cm. Museum of Fine Arts, Ghent. © 2006 Artists Rights Society (ARS), New York/SABAM, Brussels

Ensor's feelings of personal religious devotion are unknown,[20] although he spent hours walking and communing with the sea. The sea and its coast were his earliest subjects, ones to which he kept returning as if for consolation. In *Christ Calming the Storm* (1892, Museum voor Schone Kunsten, Ostend), a direct response to J.M.W. Turner's *Steamboat Off a Harbor's Mouth* (1842, Tate Gallery, London), Ensor solves the romantic quandary of man in a heartless, godless world by reintroducing Christ to calm the waters. Since the figure of Christ is indistinguishable from the light, however, what is seen and what is imagined is unclear. There is a parallel, too, in the sky above: elongated, masked horrors of his childhood, like the grotesques Ensor was painting at this time, can be glimpsed in the colored streamers of dissipating clouds. A lurch from safety to terror, from benevolence to cruelty is distinctly Ensorian.

The religious theme underpinning the 1895 still life also recalls a series of large-scale drawings, entitled *Visions: the Halos of Christ or the Sensibilities of Light* (1885), which ultimately led to Ensor's great and most famous painting, *The Entry of Christ into Brussels in 1889* (1888, J. Paul Getty Museum, Los Angeles). These drawings and the large painting initiate, as Robert Rosenblum has pointed out, a concern with the noxious aspects of the city, urban anxiety, overpopulation, and the city's ugly, menacing throngs of "the living dead."[21] Ensor's caricatured figures filling the streets were executed in the teeth of governmental control by the Catholic party and francophone monied classes after the elections of 1884.[22] Both drawings and painting are highly subjective and insert within these religious subjects contemporary issues, portraits of friends, political figures, and self-portraits.

The drawings of *Visions* demonstrate Ensor's wish to avow Christ's vulnerable humanity and his import as a socially creative, concerned individual whose mission was to further the common social good.[23] *Visions* was meant to elicit public awareness and action concerning current social issues. With Ensor's past experiences at the Rousseaus' gatherings in Brussels, his wish to participate in and effect such changes alone could explain his identification with the suffering Christ, overwhelmed by an uncomprehending and hostile crowd—infidels. A similar self-identification was shared by his contemporaries, Odilon Redon, Vincent van Gogh, and Paul Gauguin.

Ensor's identification with Christ seems more personal. *The Lively and Radiant: The Entry of Christ into Jerusalem* (fig. 2) proclaims changes for the social realm—the portrait of the anarchist and social philosopher Emile Littré is collaged into the foreground—as well as for the artistic realm: a banner with the name Les XX waves in the distance. Nevertheless, the image is a symbolist and personal expression, and the originary sources of Ensor's art are embedded in it. The figure of "Jesus, King of the Jews," as another banner reads, signals the role of the outcast that both Jesus and Ensor occupied.[24] The artist's paintings were increasingly rejected by Les XX, the group that he had helped to form, and were misunderstood by the critics and the public. Ensor had become marginalized. In the drawing, Jesus' figure is nearly lost within the surging whole. An area of dominant, obliterating light, the "queen of our senses," further weakens Jesus' form and presumable effectiveness as political and artistic leader. He has become passive, he retreats from our view and our engagement with him. As the focus of Ensor's identification, he is like the artist's father and like what Ensor, too, has become.

Ensor avoided Brussels, and any city of artists, and returned to Ostend to take up his English father's stance, becoming a somber semi-recluse in a place that had "a faded side, mean, a stinginess, also an odor [...]. One lived poorly in the kitchen cellar which always smelled a little of gas and boiled fish, where one gossiped, where one served hot and sweet smelling cups of coffee, with bad humor, with sullenness, with suppressed spite [...]."[25]

Withdrawal to a degraded circumstance within Ostend was necessary to the creation of his art: both carnival masquerades and loyalty to his father had to be kept alive. Ensor never ventured very far from Holland, Brussels or London, the city of his father's family. In 1892, five years after the senior Ensor's death, the artist went to London for four days to meet and to talk to his paternal grandmother who received him politely but cooly.[26] Ensor's artistic choices were determined also by his identification with his father. English sources informed his art. Constable and J.M.W. Turner were important antecedents for Ensor's seascapes and landscapes. British eighteenth-century satirists Hogarth, Rowlandson, Cruikshank, and Gillray were all sources for his caricatures, paintings, and general skewerings of the government and the uncomprehending art community. Ensor himself said that his etchings and paintings had an "English character" and that he "felt more English than most English artists" then practicing.[27]

There is a 1908 reprise (private collection) of the original version of the Simon Collection still life that precisely repeats the engulfing background with its figures emerging through the mist, as well as the fish, shells, basket, and pottery in the foreground, but these individual elements have a harder linearity than the same objects depicted in1895.

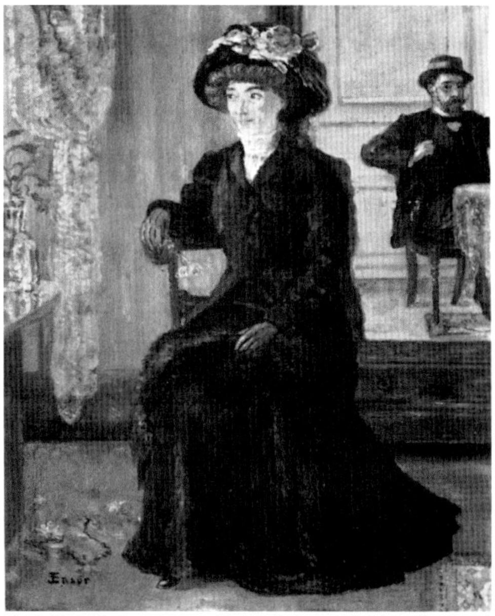

3. James Ensor: *Our Two Portraits*, 1908. Oil on panel, 41x 33.5 cm. M. Mabille Collection, Rhode-St-Genèse. © 2006 Artists Rights Society (ARS), New York/SABAM, Brussels

The copy of the still life was painted just after *Our Two Portraits* (fig. 3),[28] aptly titled because it shows Augusta Boogaerts seated and looking out a window, while behind her appears Ensor's image reflected in a mirror. The painting is not titled "Double Portrait," because the portraits are separate and unequal: Augusta is the admired, even beloved, focus, but the mirror catches Ensor looking at her warily. This handling speaks to Ensor's earliest circumstance of an isolated childhood, and now to the nature of his relationship to Augusta. Its temporal proximity to the 1908 copy of the original still life with its sexual connotations suggests, despite the difference in subject, an affinity in meaning between the two paintings. While painting *Our Two Portraits*, Ensor was reminded of the symbolic meanings of the still life's conch and flounder, perhaps, but reminded of something that he wanted to recapture. These sequential paintings are the visual equivalent of mental associations.

Ensor also painted *Still life with Vegetables and Lamp* (1908, **no. 24**) during this time. There are no ethereal figures in the later still life, although the background, like an abstract theatrical scrim, has a boldly angular, haunting shadow suggesting a figure raising its arms in threat. The shape cannot be accounted for by any objects within the composition. The harsh background is emotionally consistent with the painting's color organization of cold reds and blues. Lacking the warmth and radiance of the earlier still life, the painting seems to signal a transition from moody tonal painting to cooly modern, colored abstraction. The threat implied in the angular figure haunting the foreground objects is chilling. They seem chosen anachronistically according to iconographic traditions: the snuffed candle and a darkened lamp suggest death, and the lemon, bitterness; the peach and the pomegranate signify, respectively, Truth and the Resurrection. What remains seems mere humble produce that would form part of a hearty Flemish meal were these objects not so coldly isolated, and did not the red cabbage assert itself, raising its leafy arms in response to the lamp and to the threatening figure behind. All are set upon two tablecloths, one blue, one white,[29] and the cloths are spread over two tables.

At right and left are forms that suggest instability. The glass at right is too close to its shadow and seems to lack support. In this area all forms, including the menacing shadow, have been subjected to a kind of transparent geometric abstraction. From the left another blue table intrudes; it holds a green teapot, something from the Haegheman shops that Ensor may have kept over his long life. It becomes apparent that the blue tablecloth beneath the peach, the pomegranate, a goblet, the cabbage, and the oil lamp has something to do with the blue menacing shadow; these two blues isolate and organize the primary objects of the still life. The oil lamp, although unlit, reminds us that Ensor felt light dominated the senses and brought forth color, as it has brought forth the colors of the vegetables shown here, especially the cabbage.

The active red cabbage is placed just at the painting's center, and it, like much else, is anthropomorphized. The cabbage was considered a healthful source of food, known to counter the effects of alcohol.[30] It may represent Ensor's wished-for solution to the derangements of his father's drunken behavior. Placed with glasses, goblet, and a decanter for wine, the cabbage—along with the oil lamp—suggests the subtle theme informing the painting: Ensor's expression of his enraged disappointment in his father through the use of cold color, sharp forms, and disruptive elements in the painting. The lamp—so personal to Ensor's artistic enterprise because it signals his work's central tenet, light—is repeated in at least three other still lifes of 1905-07. All have as complementary subjects various Commedia del Arte figures, especially Pierrot, and skeletons.[31] In sum, the 1908 still life shares with other Ensorian works a sense of the macabre, the grotesque, the surreal—and autobiography.

Similar dramatic renderings of cabbages focus on their red leaves in divergent ways. *Red Cabbages and Onions* (1913, Walter M. Bockhorn Collection, Switzerland) is a stunning color composition of reds and yellows. The cabbage leaves are compacted into a dense and mysterious form of reds, pinks, and touches of blue; a rosy pink halo radiates into the pale, bluish background.

Ensor's Parrot

"Monumental cabbages with their admirable veins and triumphant shapes haunted me [...],"said Ensor in 1925, around the time he painted *Red Cabbage and Masks* (1925-30, private collection).[32] Here, the cabbage leaves have opened to make an ill-kempt form. Placed on the same table as the first, the cabbage is surrounded by fruit and flowers and beyond the table, masks hover in the air and reach up from below. One mask leans toward the cabbage and pokes its long nose into the red leaves. Behind, in a detail from *Christ's Entry into Brussels*, a woman puckers up to kiss the man next to her: he startles. Everything is different. Ensor's dissonant colors and intrusive forms satirize his earlier coherent work with its subtle color organization, atmosphere, and mood.

This contrast of handling is not a matter of a neutral "variation on a theme," a search for new "visual solutions," or a "reworking of a theme more deeply,"[33] examples of current thinking that have swung back from earlier scholarship. Earlier writers limited Ensor's most creative period to the last twenty years of the nineteenth century, after which they deemed his work weak and repetitive. A consultation of the catalogue raisonné tends to confirm this evaluation, but there are exceptions and bursts of late creativity. However, the comparison of these two paintings reveals Ensor's trivializing of his own accomplishments and creative talents. The mockery previously used to lambaste social ills and the naïve artistic community is now turned on his own work.

"My grandmother was my great inspiration," said Ensor, because she was linked to all those shells, lace, fish, costumes, exotic weapons, a parrot, and luxuriating cats. She dressed up the monkey she had taught tricks, rigged out the child Ensor in bizarre costumes as well, as if he were the same order of being. The significant relationships he had as a child were formed with bizarre animals and inanimate objects. But his experience with his grandmother also opened his eyes, "the queen of our senses," to curiosities elsewhere, to the Netherlandish masters of the grotesque, like Bosch and Brueghel, and to his immediate predecessors Antoine Wiertz and Félicien Rops. He copied the acerbic images of Daumier and Goya. Ensor's grandmother was the woman of the mask, she created a theatre of masks as he came to create his own. At Ensor's bedside she acted the coquettish peasant who wore the mask that terrified him at the time of Carnival. She was the doyenne of Carnival, the purveyor of masks to revelers who turned the world upside down, before the dull chill of Lent set in.

Ensor replaced faces with masks for the first time in *Scandalized Masks* (fig. 4). Writers have frequently questioned whether the painting depicts anonymous drunks, shows a carnival scene, or exposes a confrontation between Ensor's father and grandmother.[34] The painting, like other works, merges all three themes.

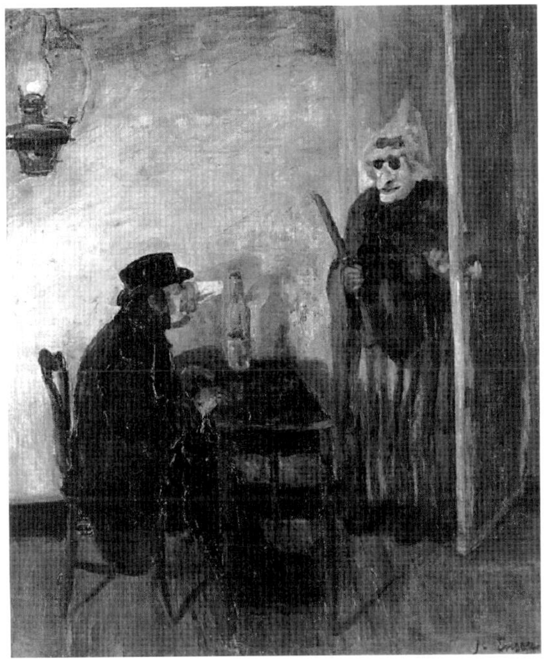

4. James Ensor: *Scandalized Masks*, 1883. Oil on canvas, 135 x 112 cm. Royal Museums of Fine Arts of Belgium, Brussels. © 2006 Artists Rights Society (ARS), New York/ SABAM, Brussels

Scandalized Masks shows a shabbily dressed man sitting at a table in a working class bar. He wears a hat, and there is a bottle on the table that casts a shadow on the wall behind, scratched with yellow, orange, green, and at the top, graffiti to the right of an kerosene lamp hanging from the ceiling. The man clearly *wears*[35] a mask with a mouth agape, its very large nose connoting stupidity and sloth. He looks up, as if frightened, at the woman who has just entered the room. He is cowed, humiliated to be found in this circumstance. She is dressed in dark clothing, holds a carnival horn, and sports a curious mask that includes dark sunglasses; her eyes cannot be seen, and she appears blind. There is a bow on her conical hat that echoes the shape of her darkened glasses; this creates a visual ambiguity whereby opaque bow and opaque eyes are compared. Her smile is sinister. Is this grandmother redux, the very figure with a hideous mask who appeared to the artist at the age of five? This mask displays a pointed chin and nose, but one not as long as the man toward whom she directs her unseeing gaze.

The woman has intruded upon the space of the man and yet does not seem to acknowledge him. His hands, placed at the edge of the table, indicate he is about to push back his chair and flee. Fear speaks through the man's body language and is frozen in the features of his mask. The mask's expression has been described as embodying the irrational fear of nightmares and of childhood,[36] and it may bring to light similar frightening experiences of the grandmother that the father and son unknowingly shared. Ensor's memoir above describes his grandmother's masked appearance at his bedside as "*affreux*," ghastly.

The images of masks that his grandmother inspired, which are seen repeatedly in Ensor's work, conflated both the female repertoire of curiosities found in the souvenir shops with the peculiar appearance of being inebriated, as carnival revelers were, and more personally, as his father often was. The mask, overdetermined for the artist as one of his grandmother's curiosities, is also an important remnant of Ensor's seeing his father drunk. The faces of drunks assume the rigidity of a mask—a mask of restraint, a mask of mirth, a mask of concern for another, a mask of self-pity. The expression of the mask does not change, and the drunk tries hard not to change a set expression that may pass as sobriety, or the appearance of propriety. People let us know how they feel through facial expressions and body language that are fluid and immediately readable as part of an implicit communication. When these become frozen into rigid behavior and into an expression that looks like a mask, the exchange is impaired. We read the expression and understand that we are meant to assume what we know to be false.

Following *Scandalized Masks*, Ensor used masks as rigid emblems of human folly, duplicity, and emptiness, to set the expressions of character types and to describe laughter, crying, wonder, stupidity, and fear. The overwhelming *Christ's Entry into Brussels in 1889* (1888) is the prime example. Ensor's vision was encoded in the huge painting's artistic, religious and political themes, its broader social questions,[37] and certainly encoded within the painter's mature expressive style of intensely colored and heavily troweled pigment. Reds, greens, and yellows scream. The painting uses excoriating irony, mockery, and scatological imagery to denounce the "unholy alliance" of political, military, and church authorities, and to lampoon the Bourgeoisie enriched and empowered by their policies—all of whose representatives appear as hideously distorted masks in the first tiers of the oncoming crowds.[38] The painting "reveal[s] Ensor's rage as well as his humor," as Jeffery Howe puts it succinctly,[39] but as far as Les XX and the public were concerned, the meaning of Ensor's art had become ever more coarse and obscure.[40] Today we evaluate his imagery as richly innovative, anticipating Edvard Munch, German Expressionism, Edouard Vuilliard, l'Art Brut, the CoBrA group, and Surrealism.[41] The crowd of masked grotesques is so corrupted that its throngs ignore the return of Christ, shown with the features of Ensor. His brightly lit figure, as in the *Visions* drawing, is small and insignificant. The crowd is disgorged from the street into our space before the canvas. Much has been written about Ensor's depictions of excreted bodily fluids, and, hidden in this large image of drunken hilarity, are revelers on a green balcony in the background who vomit and defecate on a banner bearing the sign, XX (Les Vingt).[42] Intended for an exhibition of Les XX in 1889 but never actually shown there, the entire painting dumps on many groups, along with the avant-garde group, and now we are included. We spectators feel vomited upon, for the scene is framed by a predominance of reds forming a large mouth, and within it, spots of color for the masked figures—red, blue, yellow ochre, green—that merge visually according to pointillist theory to form something like projectile vomitus. (This gives new meaning to the term "expressive.")

Georges Seurat's *Sunday Afternoon on the Island of La Grande Jatte* (1884-86, Art Institute of Chicago) had been shown the previous year at the 1887 exhibition of Les XX to great acclaim and to Ensor's great consternation. He resented the effect Seurat's work was having on Belgian artists like Léon de Smet, Emile Claus, and Théo van Rysselberghe, some of whose works are included in the Simon Collection—and resented particularly that his friend, Willy Finch, responded so positively to Seurat. Ensor bristled at the painting's basis in the cold science of optics, its classical ordering, its "overly restrictive procedure."[43] Ensor's painting, measuring 8 ¼ by 14 feet, is a monumental response to *La Grande Jatte's* mere 6 ¾ by 10 feet. Both paintings include many figures within an exaggerated perspective, but Ensor's perspective is violent and his space more distorted. Ensor's painting argues with the cool emotional tone, the color, and the light of *La Grande Jatte*. Ensor felt Seurat's painting exemplified the rules of art, and "all rules, all canons of art vomit death."[44] Ensor's subject is Carnival, the drunken blast before Lent. His use of the body and its functions again refers to the effects of alcohol; it also refers to those earthy common folk for whom Carnival was truly meant. It was their métier, their expression.[45] *The Entry of Christ into Brussels* displaces to the periphery the folk that Rabelais described, and puts on center stage the pretentious grand Bourgeoisie, the military behind them, the over-scaled Bishop leading all, as the celebrants in Brussels.[46]

Christ's Entry into Brussels was a direct attack on the Belgian political and religious elite, a sly dump on Les XX, which had rejected Ensor's work, and a rivalrous jab at Seurat, the so-called "Communard," whose sympathies for the people were represented by those idealized, calm, clean workers bathing in the Seine opposite the island of La Grande Jatte (*The Bathers*, 1883-84, National Gallery, London). Real peasant folk were "cunning, coarse, dirty," given to "endless coupling," picking their noses and farting, and their effective response to fear or to any socially repressive shenanigans was laughter.[47] "Rabelais interested me too, with his Brueghel side. They made me think of old Flemish paintings: oily, greasy, embossed, stamped, grimy,"[48] Ensor recalled with some diffidence, as if rivalrous with Rabelais, too. Here, "Rabelaisian" describes both Ensor's way, and his imagery, not Seurat's. Ensor felt he saw through Seurat, whom he considered not revolutionary but retrograde.

Whereas *The Entry of Christ into Brussels in 1889* (1888) projects toward us a glut of revelers, *From Laughter to Tears* (**no. 46**) sets out a restrained frieze of masks. Ensor has reigned in rivalrous feelings for his worthy artistic opponent, Seurat, and has thoughtfully articulated his own response to life and death. Painted in 1908, the same year as *Still Life with Vegetables and Lamp*, the imaged masks retain Ensor's forceful expression of horror and humor.

There are three masks ranged left to right following the sequence in the title: laughter; a skull as perhaps the transitive preposition "to"; then a masked figure crying. The skull serves as a fulcrum balancing Laughter and Tears. The painting is succinct, to be read as a simple equation: human awareness of death, whatever death may mean, changes laughter to tears. Ensor's work translates this awareness.

All three masks float above vaguely defined bodies in obscure drapery, but the central, quite energized skull wears a white coat and blue shirt and tie. The skull figure, so formally dressed, is Ensor. Laughter and Tears, the flanking masks, hide nothing, but the skull is accurately used as a mask because it hides something behind, a pair of living, ill-

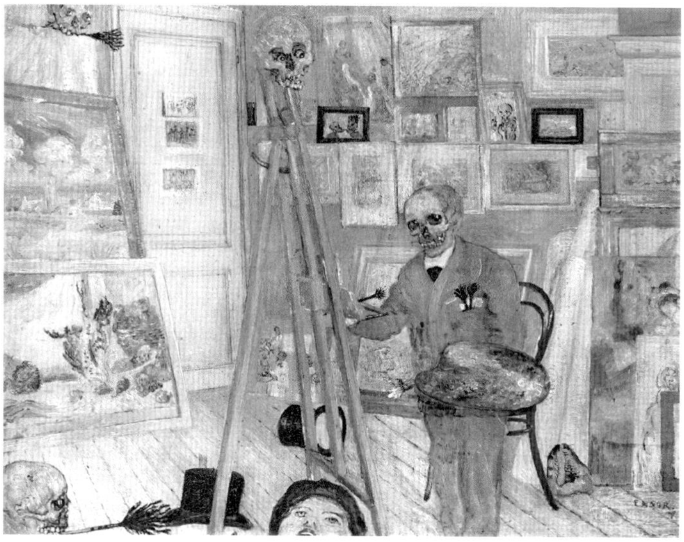

5. James Ensor: *Skeleton Painter,* 1896/97. Oil on panel, 38.5 x 45.5 cm. Koninklijk Museum voor Schone Kunsten, Antwerp. © 2006 Artists Rights Society (ARS), New York/SABAM, Brussels

matched, crossed and terrified eyes.[49] A fleshy gullet can also be seen behind the skull's missing teeth.

How paradoxical that a skull, the very definition of yawning emptiness and the symbol of death, should mask life, mask fear in life. And surely that fear is Ensor's own fear of death—Ensor's worried eyes peer out from behind the boney cavities. The two paintings from the Simon Collection discussed above implicitly, subtly speak of death but within revered still life traditions. The skull here is a terrifying emblem of death that hides many other fears unique to Ensor: those tensions in the divide between the matrilineal realm and the paternal that were addressed in *Scandalized Masks*, and the divide between aesthetic wonder and fear inscribed in Ensor's memory of his grandmother's scintillating shells and her frightful carnival mask. It must hide Ensor's fear of death in life that he witnessed not just in his father's alcoholic surrender, but also in the retreat to nullifying propriety by his mother, grandmother and sister, and in the throngs of living dead glutting the streets during carnival. All this is far from Rabelais's masks, supreme images of medieval folk culture that were associated with playfulness, joy, change, and reincarnation.[50]

Ensor often portrayed himself as a skeleton. *Skeleton Painter* (fig. 5) was based on a photograph showing Ensor looking outward as he sat at an easel that was topped by a skull. In the painting Ensor stands as he works, and the skull, with a horrified expression in his eyes, looks down at the artist: the living head has also become a skull, one with eyes that look at us meaningfully. All the same objects—many identifiable paintings hung and leaning on the walls, other skulls, a mask, top hats—surround him as they do in the dim photograph.[51]

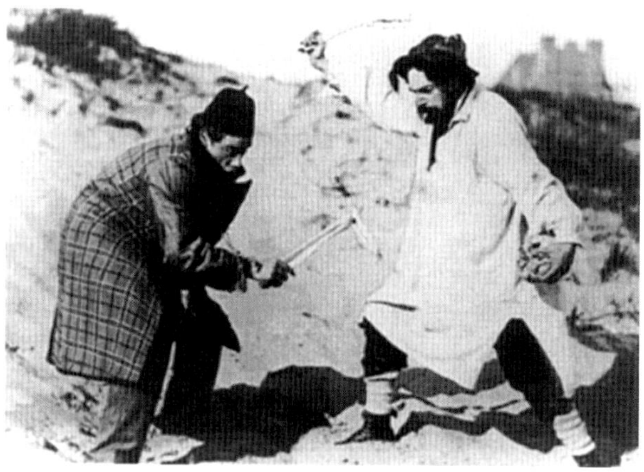

6. James Ensor and Ernest Rousseau Jr. in the dunes at Ostend, 1892. Photograph. Patrick Florizoone, James Ensor Archief, Ghent.

Skeletons bring us back to history and biography. Skeletons from as early as the seventeenth-century Spanish siege of Ostend were constantly turning up on its beaches. There are several photographs of Ensor and his friend Ernest Rousseau Jr. horsing around on the dunes using skeleton bones (fig, 6).

Reminders of death's power were everywhere, part of Ensor's landscape. The fear in Ensor's skull eyes and the comic parody of the dance of death on the beach were opposing poles of response. The only way to deal with death, whether his parents' deaths in life or those spectacles and institutions that represented death in life—oppressive, corrupt, and elitist governments, uncomprehending art societies—was to laugh, poke fun at all of them. That was the solution par excellence of the folk of Carnival. But laughter was hard to achieve, hard to maintain, and turned quickly to terror.

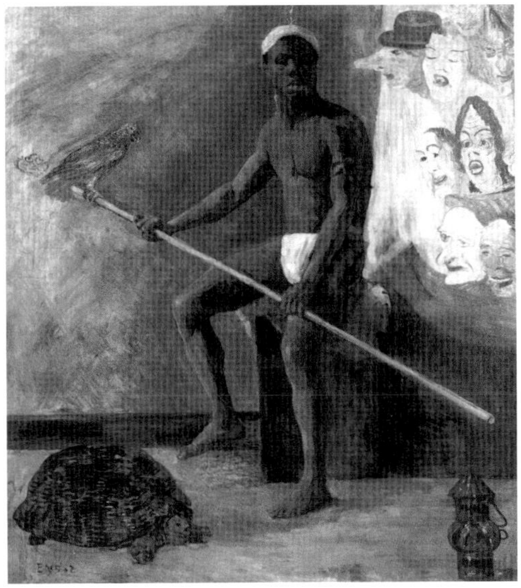

7. James Ensor: *Masks Watching a Negro Minstrel*, 1878-79. Oil on canvas, 115 x 96 cm. Private Collection. © 2006 Artists Rights Society (ARS), New York/SABAM, Brussels

A brilliant blue parrot perches on the cranium of the skull and looks downward at something Tears holds in his hand, flowers or a toy that conforms to the same scale of the parrot. Thus each figure appears with an attribute as if each were a saint: Laughter holds a rose. Laughter and Tears are representations of set emotions like the set expressions of drunks, like the masks from the souvenir shops that became Ensor's repertory[52]—but they neither hide nor disguise anything, there is nothing behind them.[53]

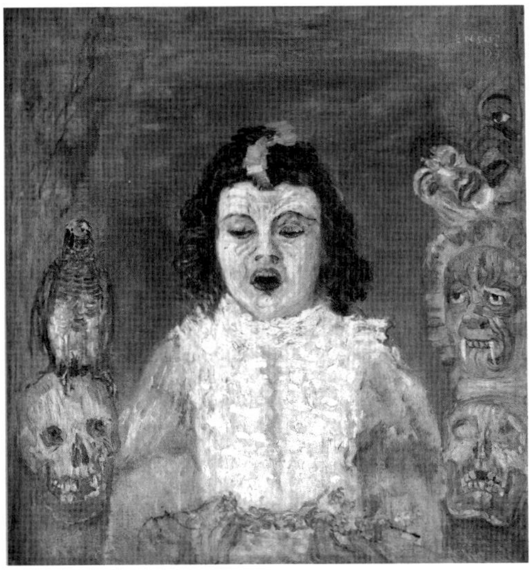

8. James Ensor: *The Girl with Masks*, 1921. Oil on canvas, 57 x 53 cm. Städtische Galerie im Städelschen Kunstinstitut, Frankfurt am Main. © 2006 Artists Rights Society (ARS), New York/SABAM, Brussels

The parrot first appears sitting on a pole in *Masks Watching a Negro Minstrel* (fig. 7), Ensor's project for a live model assignment at the Brussels Academy, and it was not, like the masks, tortoise, and kerosene lamp, one of the additions made to the painting in 1890.[54] The parrot's original inclusion in 1879 suggests its personal meaning for the artist. Afterward, Ensor used the parrot infrequently but in association with his own self-image.[55]

A parrot surmounting a skull appears in the left foreground of *The Girl with Masks* (fig. 8), while masks line its right edge. The eyes of the skull gaze upward at the pasty white face—almost a mask itself—of a young girl, perhaps Ensor's niece,[56] who seems to be singing and looking down at the flowers she holds. The parrot looks away.

The parrot turns out to be a loaded symbol,[57] well suited to characterize shifting and layered aspects of Ensor's art and his life. A parrot may suggest embarassment, even humiliation, as when the parrot repeats a phrase that exposes a secret. Within Ostend it was impossible to keep secret his father's alcoholism—as much as the artist might have yearned for it—and it was the source of much humiliation.

Once a mere streak of blue forming the hair for the laughter figure, it has rematerialized on the skull as a bird, a blue parrot that gazes, intrigued, by the toy in Tears's hand. Parrots parrot words and phrases but they cannot engage in a real give-and-take, in conversation, in an ongoing, sustaining relationship.[58] This was the nature of Ensor's relationships with the stuffed fish, shells, and exotic porcelains, as well as the screeching parrots with which he kept company as a child. A move toward another, an invitation to engage, went unacknowledged and became generalized to the stilted relationships with his female relatives, with Augusta Boogaerts, and with his father, in individual ways. Ensor felt only the art reproductions in his father's study and his own drawings and paintings repaid his engagement. These images seemed to speak to him.

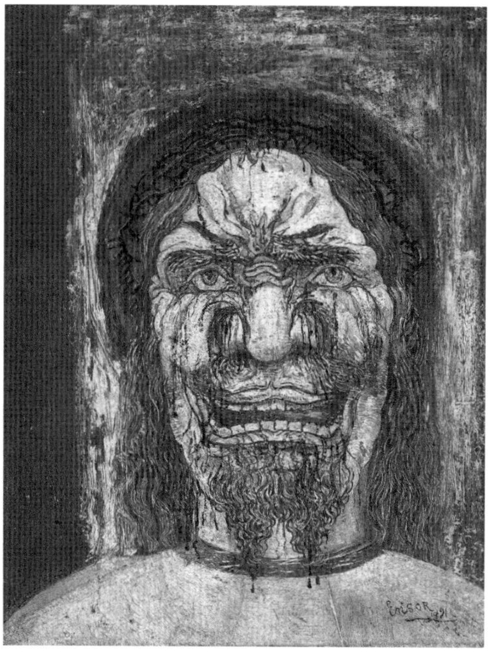

9. James Ensor: *The Man of Sorrows*, 1891. Oil on panel, 21.5 x 16 cm. Koninklijk Museum voor Schone Kunsten, Antwerp. © 2006 Artists Rights Society (ARS), New York/SABAM, Brussels

Because parrots repeat our words and phrases they appear to mock us. "I have happily confined myself to the land of mockery where everything is brilliant but violent masquerade," the artist said.[59] Mockery became the canon of Ensor's oeuvre.

The parrot is associated with docility because it can be trained. Ensor had artistic training, but he was hardly considered docile—quite the opposite: he was the hypercritical rebellious innovator who set new terms for art of the twentieth century. We may interpret docility to mean and embody Ensor's curious retreat into passive solitude in Ostend. Parrots can fly, but are often held captive. Ensor recognized his own self-imposed captivity in Ostend and used the parrot as self-symbol.

Ensor must have known the parrot to be an exotic bird, which had come across the sea and to his grandmother's shops where Ensor spent long hours in its company. Pirates had parrots; Ensor has a parrot on the top of his head. The parrot eyes something in Tears's hand; will he snatch it? Ensor sneered that he was more English than those English artists who pirated early renaissance masters,[60] but he also "pirated" a gamut of continental and English art.

The parrot was taken as proof of the Virgin birth of Christ because it can say *Ave*. Ensor as Christ is avowed by his parrot, as the artist has shown himself in many paintings and etchings (fig. 9). Some of these self-representations go beyond the suffering Christ to Christ as an angry and degraded being (the etching *Christ Tormented by Demons*, 1895).

The parrot is associated with foolishness and foolish laughter, terms which conjure not only the comic aspects of Ensor's humor, but also the fool as medieval jokester who tells the truth. Yet foolishness suggests Ensor's fearful superstitiousness. He dreaded the number thirteen. The drawing and etching of *Devils Teasing Me* (1895) that recall the above-mentioned etching of *Christ Tormented*, and *Me and My Circle* (1939, private collection)—where, it might be noticed, a blue parrot appears at the upper right—both confirm that Ensor truly felt beset by devils, demons, and frightening masks.[61] The title and subject of the latter painting refer also to the inadequate companions of Ensor's childhood, of whom he still thinks at the age of seventy-nine.

Did Ensor know that W.B. Yeats, the Anglo-Irish writer, used a black parrot to embody the horrors of the forces of disruption?[62] "Foolishly" believing in omens, Ensor often repeated the ominous story from his childhood of the black seabird that flew into his room as he lay in bed, knocking out the lighted candle to plunge the room into darkness. "I was crazed with fear. I can still see that horrible apparition and feel the impact of the black bird. It leaves me terribly shaken."[63] The black seabird bringing darkness is the foil to light which otherwise dominated Ensor's senses and his painting, revealing the purity and strength of his colors. The black seabird is death. To the deaths feared and listed above can be added death of his own creative forces, a darkening of which Ensor "can still see and feel the impact."

All these meanings of death—disruption, physical dissolution, death in life, and death of creativity—inhere in Ensor's painting. His art, emerging from Carnival, conjures his own concerns with foolishness, humor, the permutations of death and the deadening lack of recognition by his family and understanding of his art by the community of artists. Through Christian imagery made grotesquely carnival, Ensor wished to overturn any disrespect to the public, even sadistic attacks upon it by elitist and repressive governments. The wider social realms were the macrocosm of the personal realm.

In contrast to *From Laughter to Tears, The Fantastic Ballet* (1919, **no. 47**), the fourth and last painting by Ensor in the Simon Collection, is as light-hearted as its title suggests, despite the inclusion of some raunchy but puerile carnival figures. "Light hearted" does not describe the color etching of the same title made almost thirty years earlier.[64] The etching technique, which uses biting acid, tends to result in caustic imagery, and the earlier print projects a feeling of bitter anger concerning something dramatic happening in 1889. Ensor dug into the surface of the plate in such a way as to suggest not only unruly feelings, but also the chaos of figures moving on stage, and to create an overall grainy surface that obscures the identity of some of them.

The later painting is clearer, and it has an altogether different emotional tone. Fourteen figures drawn from the Commedia del Arte, from Carnival, and from Ensor's personal life appear on a stage strangely bound by a theatrical backdrop of blue sky and clouds and a spandrel of an archway that continues upward beyond the painting's frame. Pierrot, in white with his hat pierced by an arrow, occupies center stage, and he is shown as if spread eagled, but he is actually standing. His right foot is raised pointing in one direction while he looks in the opposite direction at other characters. As is true of the skull in *From Laughter to Tears*, he forms a kind of pivot between figures on either side.

The painting's lyrical tone can be explained by time and circumstance: Ensor was creating *La Gamme d'Amour*, a ballet for which the artist provided the scenario, music, costumes, and set design.[65] This musical enterprise had begun in January of 1905 with an initial, slow waltz; later pieces were added, given musical notation and orchestrated by others. By 1911, the project was completed and soon performed. The entire ballet was published in Brussels in 1929. Because he was working on his musical score, Ensor's *Fantastic Ballet* is infused with a gentle melodic tone, a sense of pleasurable fantasy and memory.

Ensor's musical interests are evoked by his painting, interests that must have begun with his awareness of his father's musical accomplishments. From childhood he had picked out tunes and improvised on the piano, and an 1881 photograph shows Ensor playing a penny whistle or pipe while seated atop a chimney (fig. 11). Probably because he had an ear for music he never learned to read or write it. He also fearfully avoided the instrument's white keys, only playing the black keys—closer to hand—with stiff and flattened fingers. His friends Albin and Emma Lambotte must have known of his growing passion for music and of his efforts to create the ballet, for they presented him with a gift of a harmonium in March of 1906, a year after he had begun work on the score. Often Ensor was photographed happily playing his harmonium placed immediately in front of the huge *Entry*

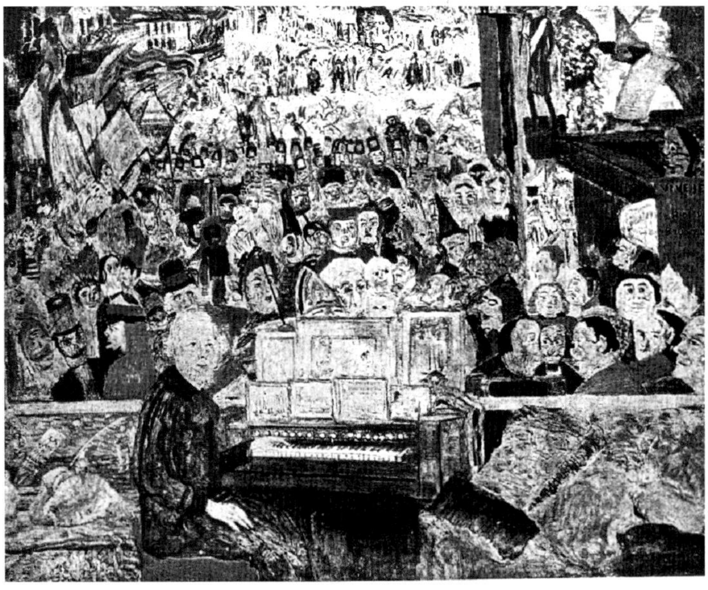

10. James Ensor: *Ensor at the Harmonium*, 1933. Oil on canvas, 80 x 100 cm. Menard Art Museum, Komaki City, Aichi, Japan. © 2006 Artists Rights Society (ARS), New York/SABAM, Brussels

of Christ into Brussels in 1889 that hung within his apartment for many years. The contiguity of painting and instrument suggests that during these early decades of the twentieth century Ensor naively considered his musical productions aesthetically equivalent to the masterwork of his career.[66] The artist seems to have shifted his creative interests to music in the first years of the new century.

Based on these many photographs, his painting, *Ensor at the Harmonium* (fig. 10), juxtaposes Ensor's visage with Pierrot's mask in the painting's foreground. They look remarkably alike. Many images of Pierrot appear in Ensor's oeuvre, as in *The Fantastic Ballet*, and in most instances can be understood as self-representations.

The Pierrot of *The Fantastic Ballet* looks directly to the right at a gendarme with epaulets, breeches and—absurdly inappropriate—sabots. The gendarme looks over his shoulder suspiciously at a figure with a huge head. He wears white and his head is white; he leans over and snot drips from his nose. This then, is one of the Rabelaisian common folk of Carnival, for behind him a figure blows the carnival horn. Directly behind him and sliced by the frame, appears a face with a worried expression and a long nose. Appearing just below the spandrel of the arch, the figure wears a hat that looks clerical.

In front of these three palely painted figures are a man in red and a woman in a blue mask who bow to each other. Is this the love interest who often consumes Pierrot? Downstage right, a man wearing green lies on his back and raises his legs to us in such a way that his bottom connecting the two legs forms a large "U." He is the same figure, but reversed, that appears on stage to the right in *Christ's Entry into Brussels*. There he leans over so that his backside, drawn with a smiley face, is presented to us.

On the left side of *The Fantastic Ballet*, some figures appear dressed in street clothes. A man and a woman wearing hats seem to have walked on stage and into Ensor's personal life, while a blond ingenue holds a collapsed fan and looks out at us with a knowing, if jaded, glance. The couple appear with goofy, satirized expressions in the earlier etching and are linked to a masked character, Zanni from the Commedia del Arte, whose giddy expression and long nose is sliced by the left edge of the etching. He seems to correspond to the worried face at the right edge of the etching and painting. The two hatted figures are less caricatured in the painting, while the Zanni mask is barely discernible.[67]

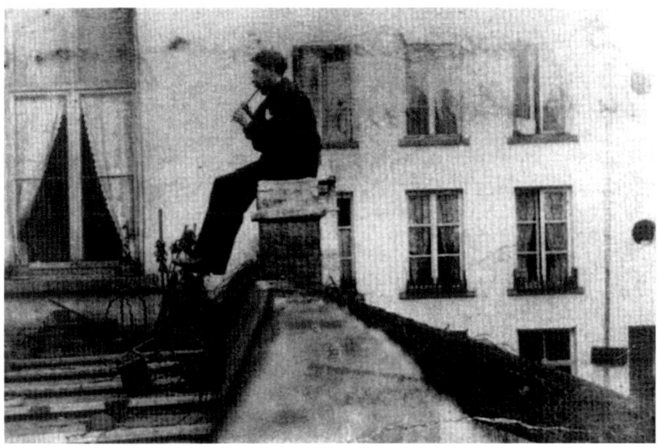

11. Ensor playing the flute while seated on a chimney pot in Ostend, photograph, c. 1885. Patrick Florizoone, James Ensor Archief, Ghent.

Behind the ingenue stands a male figure draped in white: another Pierrot, whose features are more identifiable as Ensor's own. The figure has no ruffled collar, and Ensor's familiar features are handled differently from those shown in the 1889 etching. There Pierrot looks out at us quizzically and seems to have his arm around the smiling ingenue: Ensor/Pierrot's love interest at that earlier time? Here Ensor's gaze looks inward, as though he is remembering with pleasure not so much the earlier etching as his artistic career and what these intimate and carnival characters have meant to him.

Behind the second Pierrot/Ensor figure stands an older woman in pink, perhaps a maternal figure. A disgruntled woman in the painting, she is an absurd masked figure in the etching: Ensor's grandmother? Downstage left, a clown in pink stretches out diagonally on his stomach. He vomits at us, recalling the two examples of vomiting, large and small, in *Christ's Entry*. Finally, diagonally opposite to the vomiting figure, within the spandrel of the arch, another bizarre male figure, really a diamond-shaped head resting on pink shoulders, is presented full face, austerely to us: he is like a Byzantine Christ. He has authority because he forms part of the architectural frame to the scene. His totemically rigid appearance as against the boisterous exertions below may refer to the centrality of Catholicism to social control and the potential overturning of it—for Ensor, imagistically through paintings concerning Carnival. The iconic, upright figure and prone vomiting figure are dramatically, diametrically opposed, one representing rectitude, order, propriety and the other, inebriation, dissolution, the earthy common folk. In fact, the supine figure in green presenting his bottom to us is another earthy carnival type; together they both form a paradoxically stable base for the more palely rendered, elusive figures above. Now in 1919 Ensor is alluding to the events and political structures and strictures that pertained to the 1880s and remembering his various responses to them as depicted in *Visions: The Entry of Christ into Jerusalem* and the great painting *The Entry of Christ into Brussels in 1889*, among many others. And he is remembering and picturing these scenes happily, because he no longer fears losing his creative powers; music has become his new means of creative expression, and the means to "soothe the savage breast."[68] Music has displaced Light, the queen of our senses.

Ensor summons lively, brightly colored figures from crucial images of his artistic past and casts them within a sonorous ballet of his retrospective imagination; it is a ballet of memory and fantasy that is immensely pleasurable. Parallel to works by Paul Gauguin and Edvard Munch,[69] the painting is a summing up of the artist's creative life.

Who was to know that Ensor would live until 1949? As far as Ensor was concerned, his painting career was completed, having somehow staunched the wounds of the past. He would continue remembering and repeating earlier visual compositions, but would turn to light music based on operettas and the tunes of the café concert to express his talent. What did it matter that he over-valued his musical gifts?[70] By the end of his long life, Ensor had exhibited far and wide, mounted several retrospectives, and was considered a great artist in many countries, by heads of state, and most important, by many artists. Recognition, honors, and awards accumulated: King Albert I made Ensor a hereditary baron in 1929. James Ensor had become the equal to those European princes he had seen there among the seashells, porcelains, weaponry, and parrots that his imagery later memorialized.

I thank Jeffery Howe for bringing to my attention many meanings associated with parrots, and for sensitively guiding this essay to its completion. I thank Jeremy Nahum for his insightful comments regarding the assumptions underlying this essay. Adeane Bregman is gratefully acknowledged for her assistance in gathering bibliographic references, and Naomi Blumberg is to be thanked for her keen editing. This essay is dedicated to the memory of Susan Appleton Harding (1947-2004).

Notes

1 Letter to Louis Delattre, 4 August 1898, qtd. in Gisèle Ollinger-Zinque, "Moi et mon milieu," *Ensor* (Brussels: Royal Museums of Fine Arts of Belgium, 1999) 14-15, author's translation.

2 David S. Werman, "James Ensor, and the Attachment to Place," *The International Review of Psychoanalysis*, 16.3 (1989) 287. Werman is the only author who mentions that Ensor's father was disinherited. He does not cite his source.

3 Werman 288.

4 Ulrike Becks-Malorny, *James Ensor (1860-1949): Masks, Death and the Sea* (Taschen, 1999) 10.

5 Becks-Malorny 21-22.

6 Pierre Rosenberg, *Chardin 1699-1779* (Cleveland: Cleveland Museum of Art and Indiana University Press, 1979) 116.

7 Qtd. by Patricia G. Berman in *James Ensor, Christ's Entry into Brussels in 1889* (Los Angeles: J. Paul Getty Trust, 2002) 79. Of course it is vision, and not light, that is one of the human senses.

8 As contemporary artist Robert Berlind, reacted to it, June 9, 2006.

9 David S. Werman, "Edgar Allen Poe, James Ensor, and the Psychology of Revenge," *Annual of Psychoanalysis* 21 (1993) 310.

10 Qtd. by Diane Lesko, *James Ensor: The Creative Years* (Princeton: Princeton University Press, 1985) 18, note 19.

11 The silence within darkened interiors is captured in paintings of the early 80s. The women knit and sew and look down at their hands. *Portrait of the Artist's Father* (1881) shows the father formally dressed and seated, his eyes lowered to a book.

12 Qtd. by Rudolf Schmitz, "'You Words without Rhyme and Reason, I Love You, I Love You': The Deregulated Language of James Ensor," *James Ensor*, eds. Ingrid Pfeiffer and Max Hollein (Hatje Cantz, 2005) 155.

13 Lesko 26-27.

14 Qtd. by Lesko 26-27.

15 The first painting to include masks is *Scandalized Masks* (1883) discussed below.

16 Lesko 66. Apparently Ensor took Augusta Boogaerts to hotels in Brussels.

17 See Lesko's sensible description of their relationship, 66-68 and 146-148.

18 Timothy Hyman, "A Carnival Sense of the World," *James Ensor 1860-1949: Theatre of Masks,* ed. Carol Brown (London: Barbican Art Gallery, 1997) 17.

19 Mikhail Bakhtin and Peter Hobson qtd. by the Boston Change Process Study Group, "Response to Commentaries," *Journal of the American Psychoanalytic Association*, 53.3 (2005) 761-770. See also Mikhail Bakhtin, *The Dialogic Imagination*, ed. Michael Holquist (Austin: University of Texas, 1981) 276-282 and *passim*.

20 "Ensor was certainly no mystic—perhaps he was even an atheist [...]." Gisèle Ollinger-Zinque, *Ensor by Himself* (Brussels: Laconti, 1976) 29.

21 They are a bold contrast to earlier, impressionist depictions of the city as beautiful and harmonious, and they go on to influence later artists, the first being Edvard Munch. See Robert Rosenblum, "James Ensor: An International Perspective," *Ensor* (Brussels: Royal Museums of Fine Arts of Belgium, 1999) 25.

22 See Susan M. Canning, "Visionary Politics: The Social Subtext of James Ensor's Religious Imagery," *James Ensor, 1860-1949: Theatre of Masks*, ed. Carol Brown (London: Barbican Art Gallery, 1997) for a thorough discussion of the relation between social, religious, and personal issues in *Ensor's Visions*.

23 D. F. Strauss and Ernest Renan had both written books titled "The Life of Jesus," and both were devoted to describing Jesus as a socially active person, not God. These authors heavily influenced the cultural world of late nineteenth-century France and Belgium. Ensor must have been aware of their ideas.

24 Gustave Courbet also saw himself as the outcast, wandering Jew. See *The Meeting, or Bonjour Monsieur Courbet* (1854, Musée Fabre, Montpellier).

25 Jean Stevo, qtd. by Lesko 19.

26 Werman, "James Ensor, and the Attachment to Place," 291-292. Again, Werman does not cite his source for this information.

27 James Ensor, Letter to the art critic Pol de Mont, Ostend, 4 Oct. 1900, qtd. in *James Ensor, Theatre of Masks* 98.

28 See Xavier Tricot, *James Ensor, Catalogue Raisonné of the Paintings* (London: Philip Wilson, 1992) nos. 397, 399.

29 The two tablecloths probably indicate Ensor's awareness of Cézanne who used bunched, active tablecloths to bring isolated obects intimate relation. Mary Kovacs articulated these ideas in her 2003 unpublished Boston College paper, "Cézanne: Conversations on the Table."

30 Ad de Vries, *Dictionary of Symbols and Imagery* (Amsterdam: Elsvier, 1984) 74.

31 See Tricot, *Catalogue Raisonné*, nos. 396, 410, 411, 412.

32 Schmitz 154.

33 Ingrid Pfeiffer, "James Ensor Seen as a Whole—an Attempt at a Resumé," *James Ensor,* eds. Pfeiffer and Hollein 18. The catalogue's comparison of early and late paintings of *Christ Calming the Storm*, cited as examples of merely different approaches to the same subject, show the 1906 painting to be decidedly weak, a gestural mnemonic of the coloristic and expressive power of the painting of 1891.

34 Lesko 23; Becks-Malorny 38.

35 Gert Schiff, "Ensor the Exorcist," *Art the Ape of Nature: Studies in Honor of H.W. Janson* (New York: Harry N. Abrams, 1981) 722. Schiff makes distinctions among figures who wear masks, those who are "transformed into masks, and masks as autonomous, spectral beings." His mask taxonomy includes "objects, spirits, and caricatures of real people." Such rational classifications seem unlikely for an artist whose originary experience of masks is described in his memory fragment at the beginning of this essay.

36 Jean Stevo, qtd. by Lesko 19.

37 Patricia G. Berman has written the definitive, book-length essay on the painting.

38 Berman 52.

39 See Jeffery Howe's introductory essay in this volume.

40 The public was not responding to this painting, however, because it was not exhibited until 1929.

41 Rosenblum 24-31. However, we know that Goya, not Ensor, was the first modernist to explore "terrifying domains," although it is clear the Belgian paid careful attention to the Spaniard's work.

42 See Susan Canning, "The Ordure of Anarchy: Scatological Signs of Self and Society in the Art of James Ensor," *Art Journal* 52.3 (1993) "Scatological Art," 47-53.

43 Berman 48.

44 Qtd. by Berman 48. Berman feels "it would be an overstatement to claim that [the painting] was created as a direct answer to Seurat's masterpiece."

45 Mikhail Bahktin, "Introduction," *Rabelais and his World*, trans. Helene Iswolsky (Bloomington, IL: Indiana University Press, 1984) 18-20.

46 However, a Grand Pierrot, Ensor's *Doppelganger*, stands just behind the Bishop.

47 Michael Holquist, "Prologue," *Rabelais and His World* xix-xxiii.

48 Qtd. by Xavier Tricot in "A Portrait of the Artist as a Skeleton," *James Ensor*, eds. Pfeiffer and Hollein, 85.

49 Lesko 7. The author points out that Ensor's charcoal study of a plaster cast of a classical head, executed while he was at the Académie shows a similar handling, eyes intensely focused and penetrating, far beyond what could have pertained in the plaster, already at a second remove from the classical statue. In both cases Ensor imbues "dead" objects with life, character and feeling.

50 Bahktin 39-40.

51 However, the conch shell, also seen in *Still Life with Fish and Shellfish* (1895), seems an addition to *Skeleton Painter*.

52 The same skull-as-mask is found in *Death and the Masks* (1897), and uses the same handling of the eye cavities. The "Tears" mask is one of those surrounding the skull.

53 Ingrid Pfeiffer counters this idea, saying "in comparison to the masks, [a skull or skeleton] is always precisely what it is, and therefore more honest, less concealed." She may not be taking into account these particular renderings of the skull. Pfeiffer, "James Ensor Seen as a Whole" 38.

54 Tricot, *James Ensor* 166.

55 Tricot, *Catalogue Raisonné*, nos. 421, 497, 517, 560.

56 Tricot, *James Ensor* 184.

57 Ad de Vries 358.

58 R. S. Nahum, verbal communication 21 July 2006.

59 Qtd. by Lesko 4.

60 "[...] The taste of some of the English artists today is extraordinarily perverted. Under the influence of the work of Botticelli the majority of today's artists turn their noses up utterly at the great masters and satirists like Turner, Constable, Crome, Gainsborough, Hogarth, Rowlandson, etc. [...]," Ensor qtd. in *Theatre of Masks* 98.

61 Ensor's many images of himself with surrounding devils depend on Goya's *Caprichos*, particularly plate 43, *The Sleep of Reason Produces Monsters* (1797).

62 Ad de Vries 358.

63 From a letter to André De Ridder (August 1928) qtd. by Gisèle Ollinger-Zinque, "Me and My Circle" 14. Much has been made of this memory by psychoanalysts. Its resemblance to Leonardo's memory of the kite/vulture as interpreted by Freud suggests that Ensor read Freud's *Leonardo da Vinci and a Memory of his Childhood* (1910), identified with Leonardo, and created or reshaped his own childhood memory—keeping out of awareness that he was doing so. Nevertheless, we recognize that the black seabird and darkness are expressions of Ensor's innermost concerns.

64 *The Apparition: Vision Preceding Futurism* (1886, The Art Museum, Princeton University), a mixed media on paper anticipating later, related works, includes colorful ghoulish figures. There are other etchings and a painted repetition of the composition in 1925-30. See Tricot, *Catalogue Raisonné*, no. 524.

65 See Robert Wangermée, "La Gamme d'Amour and Ensor's Music" *Ensor* (Brussels: Royal Museums of Fine Arts of Belgium, 1999) for a lively and comprehensive description of Ensor's musical career. My ideas are based on his essay.

66 Wangermée 57.

67 My discussions with Carolyn Bonacci regarding the Zanni mask were most helpful for identifying this figure.

68 William Congreve (1670-1729), *The Mourning Bride* I.1.

69 *Where Do We Come From? What Are We? Where Are We Going?* (1897, Museum of Fine Arts, Boston); and *Dance of Life*, (1899-1900, National Gallery, Oslo).

70 He was encouraged to do so by admiring, but misguided friends, as Wangermée describes, 62.

"Laughter Liberates Us from Fear"[1] —*The Place of Carnival in Our Lives*

Susan A. Michalczyk

CARNIVAL—AS SPOKEN WORD, AS VISUAL IMAGE—calls forth visions of the fantastic, the grotesque, the world of masquerade, excessive revelry and above all, escape. As symbolic representation of human defiance toward the uncertainties of daily existence and the perils of sin and death, the presence of Carnival reminds participant and voyeur of the perpetual struggle between the sacred and the profane. Debauchery, role-reversals, and exaggerated laughter become part of the cyclical parody of our mortality.

"Carne vale," a farewell to the pleasures of the flesh, beckons one and all to a conversion and repentance that can only occur after tasting the fruits of temptation. Renunciation of material and lustful desires comes after the seduction. Excessive indulgence in sinful and forbidden behaviors fosters greater desire for penance. As revelers don masks and sink into acts of fantastic deception and depravity, the Carnival assumes a paradoxical role. Use of the mask provides transcendence from mere mortal existence, as mortality disappears behind eternal caricature and fantasy. Mockery and deception dominate the world of masquerade as individual identity dissolves and the universal awareness of the human condition intensifies. The masks worn during the celebration of Carnival allow momentary escape. The recreations of such primordial experiences by Ensor visually eternalize the role of the carnivalesque, both past and present, clearly expressed by Mircea Eliade in his discussion of symbolism, art, and myth: "[...] the time implied by the mask is ecstatic time, removed from the here and now. Whatever its type, every mask proclaims the presence of some being who does not belong to the everyday world."[2] The rapture of the carnivalesque sense of light, color, and fluid motion cannot be sustained, distorting the terror of death, turning light to darkness and laughter to tears.

James Ensor's paintings, *From Laughter to Tears* (1908, **no. 46**) and *The Fantastic Ballet* (1919, **no. 47**), reveal these carnivalesque and fantastic themes, as swirls of vibrant color and soft pastels dissolve into patterns of light amid grotesque masquerade. In Ensor's works, the meaning of Carnival deepens in order to transcend the calendar dates as merely pre-Lenten celebration and expands to encompass, in the words of Mikhail Bakhtin, "a process, a view of the world in which all important value resides in openness and incompletion, as well as mockery of all serious, 'closed' attitudes about the world."[3] Openness, incompletion, and mockery describe Ensor's artistic style with its basis in caricature. The figures, masked and stylized by Ensor, seem quasi-alive, only mannequins positioned in exaggerated and shocking behaviors.

In *The Fantastic Ballet,* honest emotion and sincere feeling are replaced by contrived laughter and scandalous flirtation. Ensor effectively creates the Carnival mood by incorporating features that accentuate the bold and defiant spirit of celebration, through dance, movement, and laughter. Death, in *From Laughter to Tears,* is portrayed as a skeletal head perched upon an amorphous body and takes center stage, positioned as a grim reminder to the impassioned revelry and masquerade. Caricatured grins, leaking nasal cavities, enlarged orifices, and fluids flowing freely mask the terror while encouraging participant and voyeur to defy mortal limitations.

At the most basic level, the primary focus of Carnival stems from the Church's interpretation of mortification of the flesh as the only road to salvation. Within the established boundaries of proper etiquette and religious sentiment, the season of Carnival appeases all social classes by sanctioning brief periods of excessive uncivilized and sinful behavior. The lowliest of sinners and the most devout among Church and local officials both profit from the brief interlude away from societal constraints and religious dogma. Once translated into artwork, the theme of Carnival extends beyond the limitations of fixed moments in time to encompass the eternal expression of revelry and mortification.

The etymological origins of Carnival derive from the Latin phrase "carne levare," meaning to take away or lift up meat,[4] eventually shortened during the Middle Ages to "carne vale."[5] Clearly the emphasis throughout the centuries moves from pure escapism from the drudgery of daily life, as experienced in early Roman rituals, to the more religious ascetic dimension manifested through the Renaissance. Though not decisively linked to Carnival, the Roman celebration of Saturnalia and the customs surrounding the raucous mid-winter to early spring display suggest strong parallels to the religious tradition of Mardi Gras (Shrove Tuesday) and Ash Wednesday. At the turn of the last century, "the last day of the Carnival was the customary season in Central Europe for promoting the growth of the crops by means of leaps and dances."[6] As with many pagan celebrations, the association with the purely natural deepens to include a more sacred quality as religions assume a central role within evolving social hierarchy.

Ensor's stylized depiction of orgiastic indulgence, captured in *The Fantastic Ballet*, transforms the ancient fertility rituals of the farmers into contemporary parody as weaknesses of the flesh. In spite of centuries of development and civilization, the "belief in the sympathetic influence which human conduct, and especially the intercourse of the sexes, exerts on the fruits of the earth,"[7] continues to affect the rhythm of human existence. *The Fantastic Ballet* exudes the rhythmic connection that provides respite from the disconcerting reality of *From Laughter to Tears*. The reinterpretation of such symbolism in Ensor's grotesque study of the masquerade is a far cry from the primitive assessment of the feasting and fasting customs so lyrically interpreted by Sir James Frazer in his classic work, *The Golden Bough*, and offered as antithesis to the modern artist's chaotic depictions of revelry and retribution:

> Every man, every woman, every child, has hard work of some kind or another. With the custom of Lent, everyone stays at home. It is the time for prayer, for fasting, for improving the soul. Many men during these months will live even as the monks live. There are no plays during Lent, and there are no marriages. It is the time for preparing the land for the crop; it is the time for preparing the soul for eternity.[8]

The harmonic expression of the natural connection between plants and animals, between the sower and the seed, translate into more outrageous allegory in Ensor's works. Entering Ensor's world of Carnival and the fantastic demands a turning away from the clarity of balance and embracing the absurdity of laughing and dancing with death. With this revised attitude toward caricature and fantasy, the focus shifts to the grotesque body so that "the organs that matter most are the nose and the mouth, which protrude into the world or ingest from the world,"[9] thus forming "the grotesque image."[10] *The Fantastic Ballet* reveals exaggerated, hooked noses and elongated, pointed shoes and caps. Stylized horns and instruments extend carefully from open and rounded mouths and lips, with the most grotesque mouth featured on the swollen face of a man wrapped within a large pinkish cone shape, strangely reminiscent of a much smaller version lying prone on the table in Ensor's *Still Life with Vegetables and Lamp* (1908, **no. 24**). Fluids oozing from nasal cavities and from protruding tongues blur the boundaries between witnessing what is deemed acceptable human behavior and what is considered bizarre or obscene. Focus upon such excessive motion and detailed fluidity paradoxically heightens the sense of discomfort and fascination thrust upon the audience.

Though apparently deadened and devoid of authentic emotion and expressiveness, the characters behind the masks in *From Laughter to Tears* and those swallowed up within the dance of *The Fantastic Ballet* radiate incredible vitality and physical movement, as if entrapped by the swirling colors of the painted scenes. Their paradoxical status, of a close bond between laughter and death, offers an artistic interpretation of the tightly woven historical connection between Carnival and Lent. Ensor rejects the standard interpretation of Life understood through the experience of Comedy and Tragedy by inserting Death as the defining element between the comic and tragic masks in *From Laughter to Tears*. "In carnival, laughter and death are intertwined; death and pain are everywhere to be found and are grimly real, only death never has the final word."[11]

The Humanist view with strict and detailed guidelines for etiquette and appropriate social interactions as presented in Castiglione's *Book of the Courtier* (*Il Libro del Cortegiano*) further intensifies the satirical dimension of Carnival. Fools and clowns replace lords and ladies in the sumptuous world of the masquerade. As Christian tradition replaces pagan, the revelry and excessive feasting that precedes the Lenten renunciation of worldly pleasures grows more elaborate and unruly, at times lasting more than a week. As a result, from the fifteenth to the seventeenth century, Church officials, panicked by lewd behavior and drunkenness, attempt to institute greater control in order to prevent any association with the ancient pagan rituals, with little success. "In these uninhibited festivities the tendency is to 'confuse forms' by means of the inversion of the social pattern, the juxtaposition of opposites and the unleashing of the passions—even in their destructive capacity."[12] Ensor's artistry projects the *confused forms* and *unleashed passions* of the revelers, while preserving the uneasiness from close proximity to death.

Unable to achieve mastery over the excesses of temptation and the weaknesses of the flesh, Pope Benedict XIV, in the mid-eighteenth century, established stronger regulations and defined rituals more clearly in an effort to increase awareness among the revelers of their sinfulness and need for atonement. Designated as an opportunity for penance and absolution during the final three days of the festivities, the "Forty Hours of Carnival" marks a new ecclesiastical policy of evening services within each church welcoming all to enter, confess, and repent.[13]

Within the Christian tradition, the observance of Lent, beginning on Ash Wednesday and continuing for six weeks, offers a partial explanation for the heightened role for the season of Carnival throughout history. Along with adapting to the sacred dimension, Carnival, since its origins, continues to address the profane expression of human existence as well. With the pressures created by communal living amid ever-evolving civilization, the human psyche falls prey to repression and neuroses. Inevitably efforts to tolerate inequality among the social classes and between the sexes lead to outrageous displays of misconduct sanctioned only during Carnival. The inevitable tension that arises between orgiastic indulgence of the flesh and ascetic renunciation of such pleasures emerges quite dramatically in literary and artistic endeavors from the Renaissance onward.

The paradox of accepting the duality of man's carnal and spiritual potential manifests itself in Pieter Bruegel's ornate and symbolic work, *Battle of Carnival and Lent* (1559, Royal Museums of Fine Arts of Belgium, Brussels). The choice of the word *battle* echoes the theological and sociological attitudes toward the seasons of sin and repentance that Bruegel incorporates into a visually seductive display of mortality and immortality. The human body in all its fullness and folly frolics and atones in carefully detailed depictions of the vast array of Renaissance figures: young and old, male and female, merchant and man of God, servant and noble. The harsh limitations of life, experienced by some members of society, momentarily dissolve into the frenzied display of the fantastic and grotesque. Bruegel paints the maimed and the mighty, the gaunt and the deformed, as well-fed and neatly robed religious move among flamboyant, masked revelers. With keen attention to the full range of daily life, *Battle of Carnival and Lent* records the duality and tension of existence, of earthly and spiritual desires bound within the unending cycle of pleasure and pain. With accuracy and artistry, Bruegel recreates a metaphor of life. Decadence and deprivation, role-reversals of gender and of class, vivid reenactments of illusory escapades immortalized in a carnivalesque romp of costumed and masked figures are juxtaposed against somber clusters of religious and penitents. Fools, clowns, and even mock kings and queens madly fling anything at hand: water, dirt, beans, beads, and flowers. As in written recordings of these festivities, symbolic characters, such as Pierrot, Harlequin and Punchinello, highlight the fantastic atmosphere.

In a more contemporary and stylized interpretation, Ensor's paintings of masks and the world of the fantastic revolve around similar elements of the grotesque and fantastic. The plight of human existence inspires extremes of fascination and revulsion, evidenced within the popular culture and within Ensor's works. The grotesque body appears in defiance of stringent and authoritarian attitudes toward acceptable behavior and societal constraints. Ensor chooses visual images of distorted facial expressions, hollow eyes that appear removed from the highly charged dynamism created amid the juxtaposing of enlarged noses and wide open mouths that offer glimpses of oozing fluids, fractured teeth, or swollen and protruding tongues in both *From Laughter to Tears* and *The Fantastic Ballet*. The painter and the eyes of his subjects remain removed from the world, as if somehow tainted by an ever-present knowledge of death. The masks, inextricably supported by decay and death, as illustrated in *From Laughter to Tears*, reappear in other works by Ensor, which offer more explicit connections between temptation and the need for repentance, such as his etchings *The Seven Deadly Sins Dominated by Death* (1904, Museum voor Schone Kunsten, Ghent, inv. 1998-B 176) and *The Devils Dzitts and Hihahox leading Christ into Hell* (also known as *Christ Descending into Hell*; 1895, Museum voor Schone Kunsten, Ghent, inv. 1998-B 134).[14] Focus upon bodily functions, orgiastic fantasies, and ascetic purgation reflects the emerging tension surrounding Carnival as a source of heightened awareness of all the corporeal pleasures, forbidden, yet desired, while at the same time a constant reminder of the threatening reality of mortality, suffering, and death. Certainly parallels exist in the hurling of dirt and flour among the crowds, with the well-known words spoken during Ash Wednesday services: "Ashes to ashes and dust to dust," a somber warning, a death knell to call the lost souls back from the masquerade.

With his etchings, Ensor moves from purely symbolic and suggestive allusions to mortality and death, understood in portrayals as the carnivalesque, to direct expression of death, parodied in the midst of skeletal decay and grotesque characters. Ensor's insistence upon the grotesque elements reinforces the contemporary understanding of Carnival, with all the underlying theological, philosophical and psychological meanings, as the glorification of all things carnal and taboo. The starkness of the black ink on a sepia background creates a somber tone amid the shadows and lifelessness of the masks. In *The Deadly Sins Dominated by Death*, the pivotal figure is the skeleton mask of death, depicted as a winged creature in flight. Ensor offers a visual interpretation of the symbolism of birds in flight to human souls by cleverly attaching blackened soaring wings to the sinister mask of Death. It seems as if Ensor's caricature of Death, spreading its wings in flight, is capturing and claiming the very souls of the grotesque Seven Deadly Sins, who bear striking resemblances to so many of Ensor's other masked creatures. Carnival, as symbolic of human experience, cannot be separated from sin and death, as the human soul loses the distinctly separate nature of the blue parrot in *From Laughter to Tears* and merges with the horrific and familiar skull. Metaphorically, then, the mask of death devours the soul that once rested upon it.[15]

Through the creation of a sea of masks, as in *The Fantastic Ballet*, or simply with the unholy trinity of *From Laughter to Tears*, Ensor tests the limits of propriety and comfort. Both masked figures, expressing laughter and tears, seem forced and affected as if their responses are controlled or somehow directed by the central skeletal-masked figure. In the midst of such lifelessness and desperation rests the blue parrot, alert atop Death's skull, perhaps a reminder of transcendence or the human soul, perhaps merely a parody of the insignificance of existence. The intensity of expression in the eyes of Death and in his visionary parrot offer sharp contrast to the hollow and closed eyes of the figures representing Comedy and Tragedy, suggesting perhaps Death's greater power and vision in matters of life and death.

The contorted masks positioned on either side of the foreboding and defiant image of Death display similar characteristics seen in the masquerade of *The Fantastic Ballet*. Brush strokes of vibrant color dance across the canvas of both paintings, as if suggesting in caricature, human emotion and connectedness, deliberately hidden behind the masks. At first glance, the palette of colors, primarily pastels, used by Ensor is reminiscent of childhood escapades and dreams of fantasy. Only upon closer examination do the perversely painful details emerge, of protruding nasal cavities and cavernous sockets that once held cartilage for noses, mouths, or eyes. With incredible directness and simplicity of scene, Ensor projects through the comic and tragic masked figures of *From Laughter to Tears* a comic nonchalance and cynical acceptance toward the yellowing skull of Death that dominates the portrait. The metaphorical war waged in the splendidly evocative display of figures and symbols within Bruegel's *Battle of Carnival and Lent* reappears in Ensor's art with less emotional clutter. *From Laughter to Tears* acknowledges the same battle and the same results: triumph of death over the physicality of human life, but ultimate triumph of the spirit of Carnival. Ensor's use of softer colors and caricatured forms transports both participant and viewer into the realm of the imagination and the senses, guided by fantasy not fear.

As the only sanctioned release from the prison of a highly structured and repressed society, Carnival, as interpreted in Ensor's works, offers momentary escape from the drudgery of life by emphasizing a complete disregard for the punishment of death. Forever frozen in a grotesque masquerade or in debauched dance, Ensor's masked figures blend together to create a surreal expression of unity and balance, in much the same way as his brushstrokes permeate the canvas with color and light. Ultimately, it is the overwhelming presence of light, through a balance of open brushstrokes of soft colors fading into white that lifts the heaviness and horror inextricably linked to the significance of Carnival throughout history. Ensor parodies the periods of feasting and fasting, understood as the human condition, as if he himself is merely an observer, a chronicler of life's absurdities and frailties.

In earlier centuries, when the eternal struggle between Carnival and Lent—succumbing to temptation of the flesh or renouncing all carnal desires—seemed more naïve and integrated within the natural rhythms of life, the *death* of Carnival was the final act before the initiation of the Lenten observance. An actual funeral was held, as symbol acquired form, to present a visual and sensory image to the masses. Body and soul were solemnly connected, as revelers turned into penitents and the risks of damnation outweighed the transitory pleasures of life. Dying to the self in this life, by turning away from all natural bodily functions, occurred quite naturally and spontaneously with the awareness of and indulgence in sinful behavior. Eventually the literal enactment of the *death* of Carnival transitioned to purely symbolic catharsis, ever-more stylized and distant.

As civilization has evolved and lost the immediacy of connection with nature, the disconnection between body and soul has widened. Contemporary society cannot experience fully the ancient rituals and customs, fossilized over time. The arts, then, serve as a means of reconnecting the original experience or form with the symbol. Ensor's dynamic use of color and motion amid scandalous and stylized actions recalls the central meaning of Carnival, the disconcerting mystery of Dostoevsky's *The Brothers Karamazov*, that indeed, "all is permitted." The paradoxical element emerges in the transformation of Carnival from a celebration that permits all forbidden pleasures to one that languishes near death due to excessive permissiveness.

Ensor delights and disturbs the viewer with his imagery of masks and masquerade, and addresses the seductive power of his masks in a letter from 1932: "And my suffering masks, scandalized, insolent, cruel, wicked [...]. And the mask shouts at me: freshness of tone, intense expression, sumptuous décor, large, unexpected gestures, disordered movements, exquisite turbulence. Oh! the animal masks of the Ostend carnivals!"[16] Ensor relies upon the boldness of his masks to convey the exaggerated emotions—laughter and passion, sorrow and tears—that so often lie hidden behind the masked balls and the grotesque mannerisms. "Carnival, therefore, does not and cannot hope to change the world; it can only change our inner relationship to that world."[17]

Notes

1 Caryl Emerson, *The First Hundred Years of Mikhail Bakhtin* (Princeton: Princeton University Press, 1997) 96.

2 Mircea Eliade, *Symbolism, the Sacred, and the Arts*, ed. Diane Aposolos-Cappadona (New York: Crossroad Publishing Company, 1985) 71.

3 Gary Saul Morson and Caryl Emerson, *Mikhail Bakhtin: Creation of a Prosaics* (Stanford: Stanford University Press, 1990) 443.

4 Tanya Gulevich, *Encyclopedia of Easter, Carnival and Lent* (Detroit: Omnigraphics, 2002) 52.

5 Gulevich, *Encyclopedia of Easter, Carnival and Lent* 52.

6 Theodor H. Gaster, *The New Golden Bough: A New Abridgement of the Classic Work by Sir James George Frazer* (New York: Mentor, 1964) 654.

7 Gaster, *The New Golden Bough* 655.

8 Gaster, *The New Golden Bough* 656.

9 Morson and Emerson, *Mikhail Bakhtin* 450.

10 Morson and Emerson, *Mikhail Bakhtin* 450.

11 Emerson, *The First Hundred Years of Mikhail Bakhtin* 96.

12 Juan Eduardo Cirlot, *Dictionary of Symbols*, trans. Jack Sage (New York: Dorset Press, 1991) 233.

13 Cirlot, *Dictionary of Symbols* 56.

14 Rudi Fuchs and Jan Hoet, eds., *Flemish and Dutch Painting: From Van Gogh, Ensor, Magritte and Mondrian to Contemporary Artists* (New York: Rizzoli, 1997) 178, 180.

15 See references to blue parrot in Katherine Nahum article "Ensor's Parrot" in this volume.

16 Fuchs and Hoet, eds., *Flemish and Dutch Painting* 312.

17 Emerson, *The First Hundred Years of Mikhail Bakhtin* 103.

Occupied Belgium: The Art of War

John J. Michalczyk

World War I (1914-1918), "The Great War," and "The War to End All Wars," left an indelible scar on the collective soul of the Europeans, with over eight million killed and twenty-one million wounded, and with devastation of the land spreading both east and west. The intense development of technology (aircraft, bombs, artillery, machine guns) was most responsible for these deaths. Belgium, one of the smallest embattled countries, especially felt the horrors of this war. The Armistice of 11 November 1918 and the controversial Treaty of Versailles in 1919 unfortunately only temporarily and superficially solved the conflict for the Europeans whose land was ravaged and its people traumatized. The conditions of the treaty only helped lay the groundwork for yet another conflict. Germany was embittered with its large war reparations, division of land, and the stigma as a war-mongering country, and soon Europe, for a second time in the twentieth century, fell victim to the demons of war.

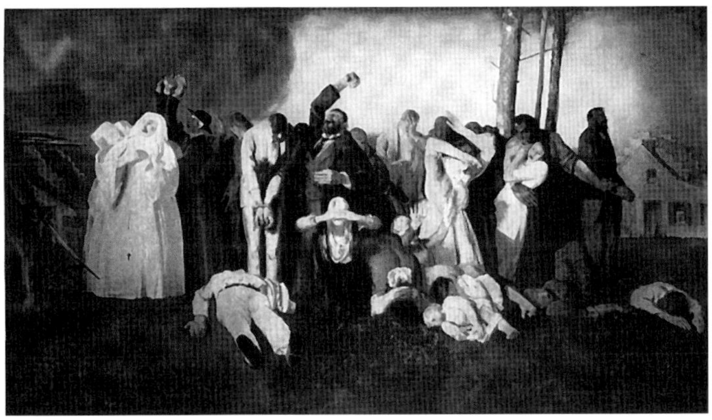

1. George Bellows: *Massacre at Dinant,* 1918. From *Art and the Great War* (New York: E.P. Dutton, 1919).

War wounds would be re-opened on 1 September 1939, and Belgium soon would be caught up again in war, occupation, and resistance. This apocalyptic and destructive war on its territory, soon overshadowed "The Great War," and eventually the tragic memory of the first major European war of the century would gradually sink into oblivion as citizens and governments made feeble attempts at peace and healing. The art of Belgian painters as well as of other European artists nonetheless has vicariously kept the image of World War I alive, while obliging us to look at the ramifications of four years of occupation and intense suffering on the part of the civilian populations.

Occupied Belgium: The Art of War

In order to grasp the power of the artist to reveal the drama of war and occupation, we must provide an historical portrait of a small country, such as Belgium, dominated by a powerful, mechanized country, such as Germany. As Larry Zuckerman recounts in his very detailed study of the country under occupation, it was truly the "Rape of Belgium" that the world had witnessed, and often passively watched and ignored as the bystander.[1]

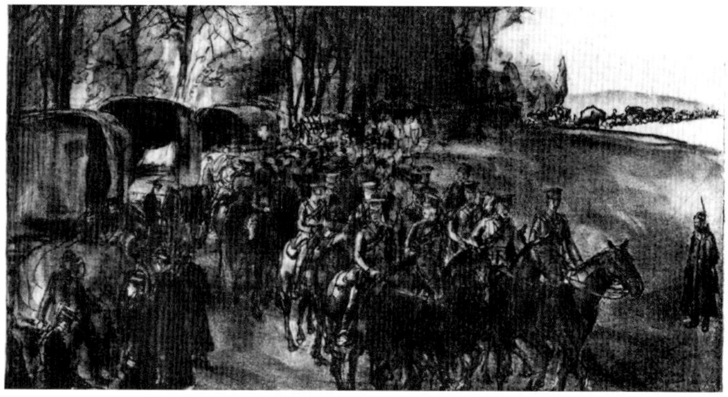

2. G. Spencer Pryse: *Retreat of the Seventh Division and Third Cavalry on Ypres*. From *Art and the Great War* (New York: E.P. Dutton, 1919).

In August 1914, Germany viewed neutral Belgium as a mere stepping stone to France. A geographically miniscule nation compared to France, Great Britain or Germany, Belgium nonetheless, with its 7.5 million population and wealth of resources, was still the sixth-ranked industrial power in the world. It would soon be reduced to shambles. When Germany marched into Belgium in August, it would mark the beginning of the end in many ways. More than 5,000 Belgian civilians were shot, towns and cities such as Dinant,[2] Antwerp, and Louvain (Leuven) were looted and burned, and 100,000 workers were deported to Germany as forced labor. "In and around Leuven 2,441 houses were burned; 2,722 were looted; 251 civilians were killed, the majority summarily executed or just murdered without any pretext of judgment; and 831 civilians were deported to an internment camp in Germany. Almost 40 percent of the destruction occurred in the city itself."[3] The Gothic architectural institutions like the University of Louvain suffered severe damage on 26 August 1914, including a large part of its historical library dating back hundreds of years. In view of these statistics, British historian Arnold Toynbee articulates his understanding of the sweeping power of the mechanized German army—"the destruction of Louvain (Leuven) was the greatest organized outrage which the Germans committed in the course of their invasion of Belgium and France."[4] Of the medieval city of Ypres (Ieper), only ruins remained following the military skirmishes there.[5]

Soon bank accounts were frozen, equipment removed and taken to Germany for the war industry, and food supplies requisitioned. Economic disaster prevailed. Through it all, with blatant propaganda, Germany justified the invasion, occupation, and deportation. For four years, a hungry and traumatized citizenry saw no hope, with lukewarm support from other countries. The United States would not become involved until the third year of the conflict. Even when a German submarine sank the British liner "Lusitania" on southern Ireland's shores in 1915, killing 1,200 people, among them 128 Americans, the United States did not enter the conflict. It should be said, however, that Herbert Hoover, as Chairman of the Commission for Relief in Belgium, did organize relief assistance for the Belgians. Belgium still felt truly brutalized and isolated.

Throughout the war the resistance movement of the Belgians, the underdog, kept chipping away at the occupying forces. Germany took drastic measures against those who did not buckle under the repressive force. The German response to the resistance of the Belgian government and people was brutal. There were atrocities. Hostages were taken and, at times, used as human shields. Individuals suspected of being guerrillas, of performing acts of sabotage, or of giving active support to Belgian soldiers were summarily executed. Houses, towns, and parts of cities were put to the torch. Among those executed were priests and women.[6]

The final cost of the war was significant, especially the toll on humans: military and civilian casualties together totaled 50,000 dead; out of 267,000 Belgian men mobilized, 13,716 were listed dead, 44,686 wounded, and 34,659 missing. The physical destruction of Belgium, proportionately, was the greatest in terms of all of the Allies: 100,000 houses were destroyed, 300,000 acres of fertile land were laid barren, livestock was drastically depleted by the Germans, and the entire infrastructure of railways and industrial production was decimated.

An artistic response to the war emerged from all over Europe, as artists and writers reacted to the tragedy during and after the war. Most well-known of the World War I literature is that of German lance-corporal Erich Maria Remarqué's pacifist novel *All Quiet on the Western Front* (1929), burned in Nazi Germany in May 1933. In England, Wilfred Owen ("Dulce et decorum est") and Siegfried Sassoon ("They") revealed their anti-war feelings in powerful verses, at times brutally graphic. One of the more popular poems, Lt. Col. John McCrae's "Flanders Fields," evoked the specter of Death that now haunts the resting place of those who fought and died valiantly.

In Flanders Fields the poppies blow
Between the crosses row on row,
That mark our place; and in the sky
The larks, still bravely singing, fly
Scarce heard amid the guns below.
We are the Dead. Short days ago
We lived, felt dawn, saw sunset glow,
Loved and were loved, and now we lie
In Flanders fields.[7]

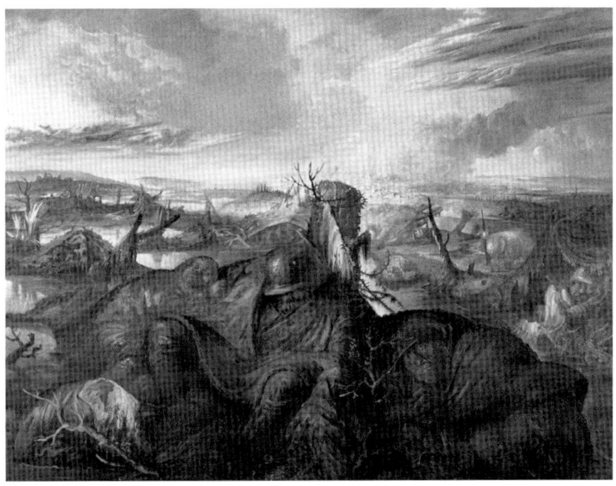

3. Otto Dix: *Flandern (Flanders)* (after *Le Feu* by Henri Barbusse), 1934-36, Oil and tempera on canvas, 200 x 250 cm, Nationalgalerie, Staatliche Museen zu Berlin, Germany. Bildarchiv Preussischer Kulturbesitz / Art Resource, NY. © 2006 Artists Rights Society (ARS), New York/VG bild-Kunst, Bonn

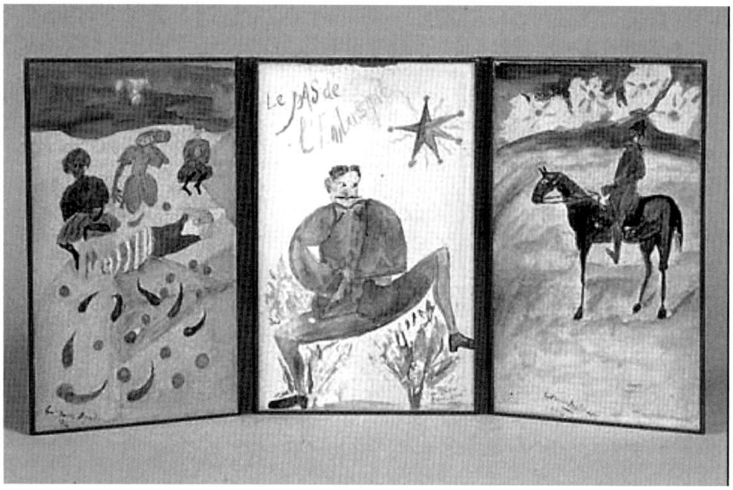

4. Guillaume Apollinaire: *Le brigadier marqué, Le pas de l'embusqué* et *Sans titre (The Marked Brigadier, The Shirker's Step* and *Untitled)*, triptych, Centre Mondial de la Paix, Verdun.

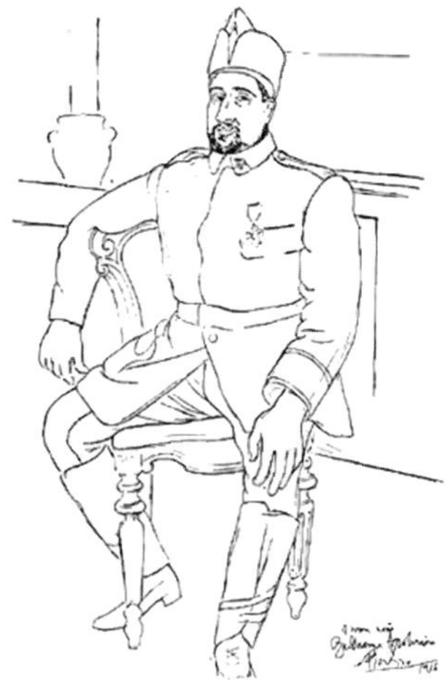

5. Pablo Picasso: *Apollinaire blessé (Apollinaire Wounded)*, 1916. Pencil on paper, 48.8 x 30.5 cm. © 2006 Estate of Pablo Picasso/Artists Rights Society, New York.

German veteran Otto Dix, who had completed a powerful anti-war triptych, in the midst of the Third Reich's militarist build-up toward war, created a visual parallel to McCrae's work, in *Flandern* (fig. 3). One can detect here the style of the old German masters.[8]

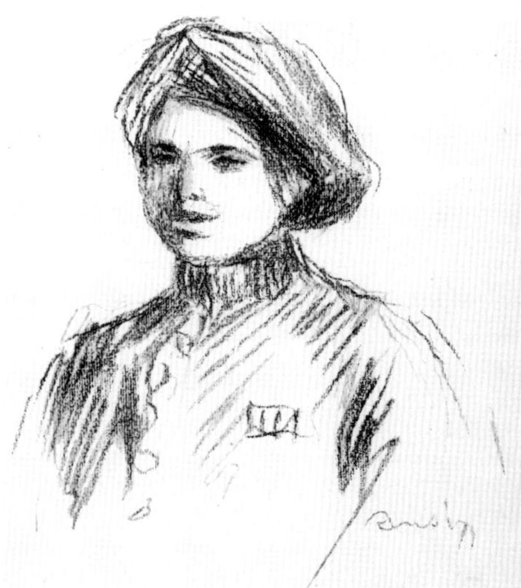

6. Pierre-Auguste Renoir: *Portrait of his son wounded in war*. From *Art and the Great War* (New York: E.P. Dutton, 1919).

Other European conscripts included many artists who left their mark through their paintings and drawings. Their styles run the full gamut—Impressionism, Fauvism, Cubism, Futurism, and Abstract Expressionism. Many of the painters had fought and suffered the effects of war on their minds and bodies. Among the more noted can be found Guillaume Apollinaire who painted *Le brigadier marqué*, (fig. 4), and Pablo Picasso who painted *Apollinaire blessé*, (fig. 5) in a similar pose as the brigadier, seated with legs spread apart. Once Apollinaire enlisted in the French army and joined the artillery unit, Picasso felt that his circle of artist friends had been totally disrupted by the war.[9]

This absence was felt all over Europe. Pierre Bonnard painted *Un village en ruines près de Ham* (*A Village in Ruins near Ham*) and Marc Chagall, *Soldat blessé*, (*Wounded Soldier*). Otto Dix[10] and Ernst

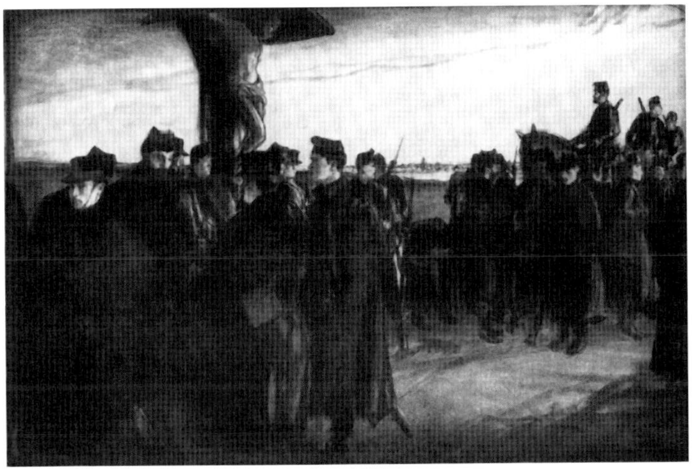

/. G. Spencer Pryse: *The Wayside Crucifix—Belgium*, 1914. From *Art and the Great War* (New York: E.P. Dutton, 1919).

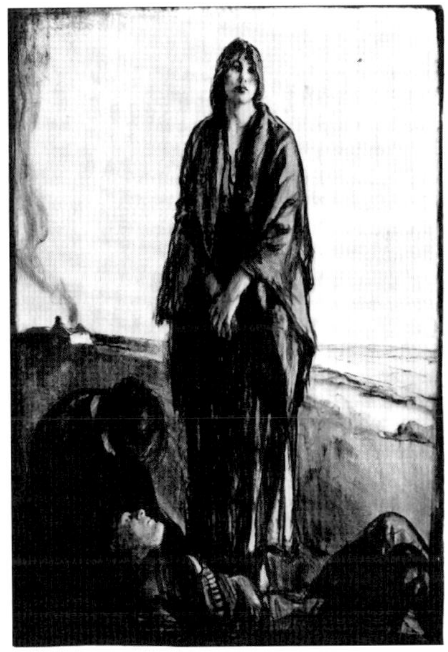

8. G. Spencer Pryse: Belgium, 1914. Lithograph. From Art and the Great War (New York: E.P. Dutton, 1919).

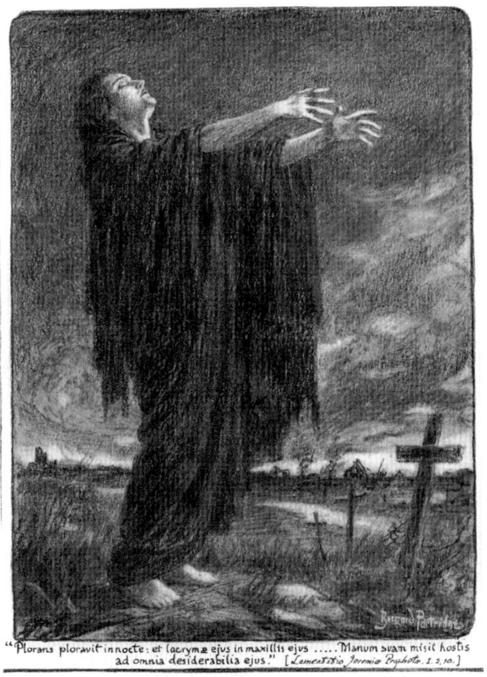

9. Bernard Partridge: *La Belgique: 1914.* From *King Albert's Book* (New York: Hearst's International Library, 1915).

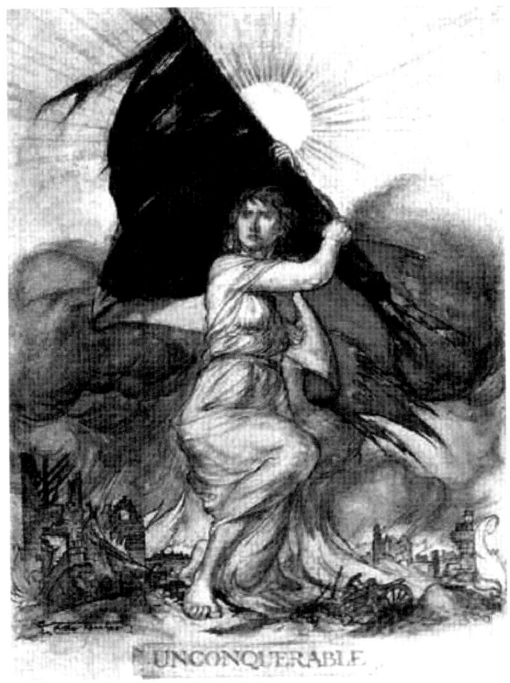

10. Arthur Rackham: *Unconquerable.* From *King Albert's Book* (New York: Hearst's International Library, 1915).

Ludwig Kirchner both painted a similar personal image of the war in *Selbsbildnis als Soldat* (*Self-portrait as a Soldier*). There was also George Grosz with his *Soldats morts sur le champ de bataille* (*Dead Soldiers on the Battlefield*), Oskar Kokoschka *Isonzo-Front*, Fernand Léger "*Sur la route de Fleury, deux morts*" (*On the Road to Fleury – Two Men Killed*), who, among others artists, captured the Great War with stirring images. Renoir's portrait of his wounded son is a poignant artistic recollection of the pain of war (fig. 6).

Two drawings by British artist Gerald Spencer Pryse, *The Wayside Crucifix—Belgium, 1914* and *Belgium, 1914* (figs. 7-8) offer an outsider's view of military engagement and the tragic impact of war upon the civilian population, respectively. Pryse's *Belgium, 1914* graphically indicts the occupying Germans by showing two women mourning over a soldier's death, with other corpses strewn along the countryside. A burning house in the background characterizes the German's destructive march through Belgium in August 1914. *La Belgique: 1914,* by Bernard Partridge, captures the lamentation of a woman in mourning, with outstretched hands, in a field of crosses (fig. 9). The Latin caption to the drawing about cries in the night reads: "Plorans ploravit in nocte: et lacrymae in maxiillis ejus…Manum suam misit hostis ad omnia desiderabilia ejus."

In their paintings, drawings, and lithographs, often completed between the wars, the European artists vividly illustrated the tragic effects of fear, gassing, mutilation, and death in provocative ways to reinforce the theme, "War is Hell!" Despite the trauma of war and occupation, however, the Belgians still shared a ray of hope and felt that they were "unconquerable," as British artist and illustrator Arthur Rackham portrays Belgium rising out of the ashes (fig. 10).

It is the same unbreakable spirit that another non-Belgian, Edith Wharton, portrays in her short poem, "Belgium":

La Belgique ne regrette rien
Not with her ruined silver spires,
Not with her cities shamed and rent,
Perish the imperishable fires
That shape the homestead from the tent.

Wherever men are staunch and free,
There shall she keep her fearless state,
And, homeless, to great nations be
The home of all that makes them great.[11]

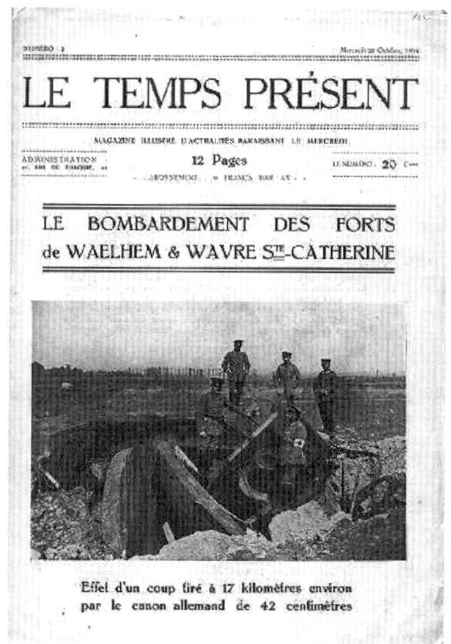

LE TEMPS PRÉSENT

MAGAZINE ILLUSTRÉ D'ACTUALITÉS PARAISSANT LE MERCREDI

12 Pages

LE BOMBARDEMENT DES FORTS de WAELHEM & WAVRE Ste-CATHERINE

Effet d'un coup tiré à 17 kilomètres environ par le canon allemand de 42 centimètres

11. The effects of a German cannon, *Le Temps Présent*, October 1914.

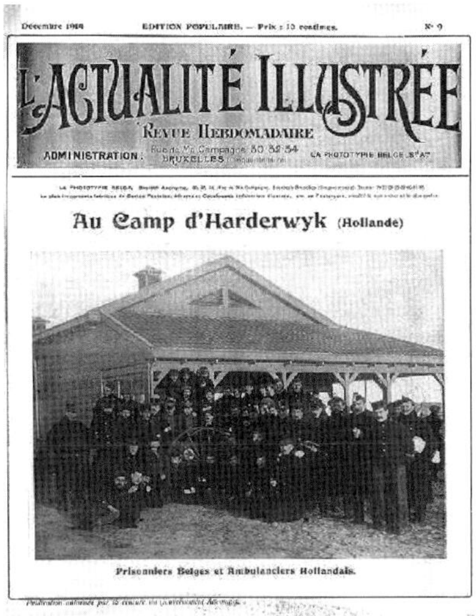

12. Belgian prisoners of war interned at Harderwyck, Netherlands, *L'Actualité Illustrée*, (Brussels), December 1914.

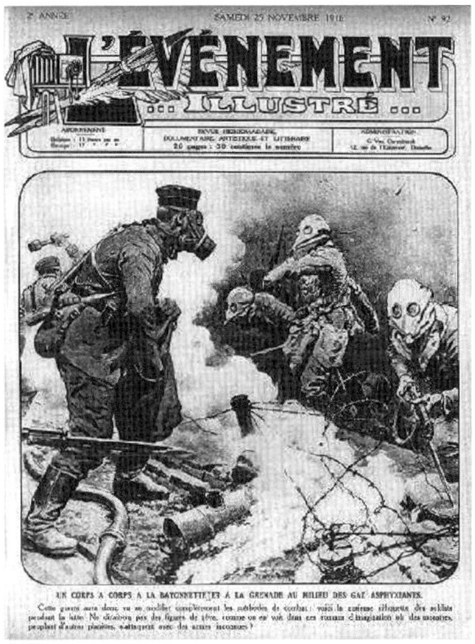

13. Gas Attack, *L'Evénément*, (Brussels), November 1916.

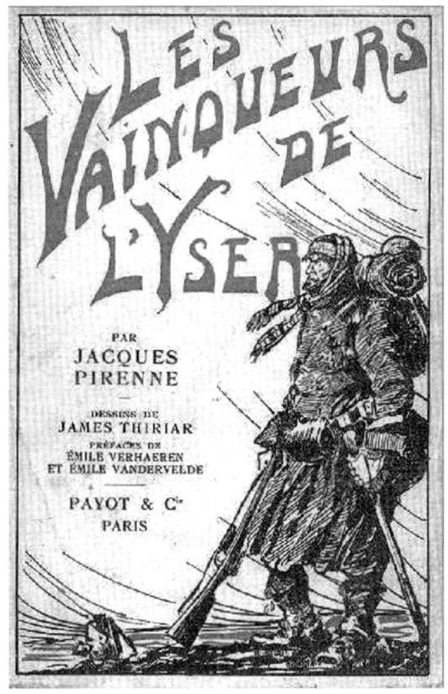

14. Cover of *Les Vainqueurs de l'Yser* (*The Victors of the Yser*, 1917).

French painter Claude Monet also saluted the heroic Belgians and their king caught up in this strife: "Très honoré de l'occasion qui m'est offerte, de pouvoir crier toute mon admiration à l'héroique Belgique, et d'adresser très respectueusement la même admiration au noble et vaillant roi de la nation Belge. Vive la Belgique! Vive les Alliés! Vive la France!"[12]

Belgian artists used their drawings and paintings not only to inform the world about the war, but to express their own personal sentiments about a society torn asunder by conflict. Artists designed covers and other illustrations for magazines and periodicals such as *Le Temps Présent* (*Present Days*), *Actualité Illustrée* (*Illustrated News*), *L'Evénément* (*The Event*) (figs. 11-3), and *Notre Pays* (*Our Country*). This was a challenge, since they had to publish their work with the occupying force censoring their art and content. At the same time, the artists were able to dramatize the war more graphically in the newspapers which sought the sensationalism that helps sell newspapers.

Some Belgian artists who are recognized in particular for their contributions of war art are André Leynen (1888-1984), Alfred Bastien (1873-1955), Henri de Groux (1867-1930), and James Thiriar (1889-1965). Thiriar, for example, was a Belgian soldier artist who made the commercial and artistic connection of art and media. He was wounded in action and published his work in the *Illustrated London News,* for example, "L'Arrivée au Contonnement" ("Belgian Troops Arrive at a Cantonment"). He also illustrated Jacques Pirenne's novel *Les Vainquers d'Yser*, with the image of a fatigued but bold-looking soldier in winter (fig. 14).

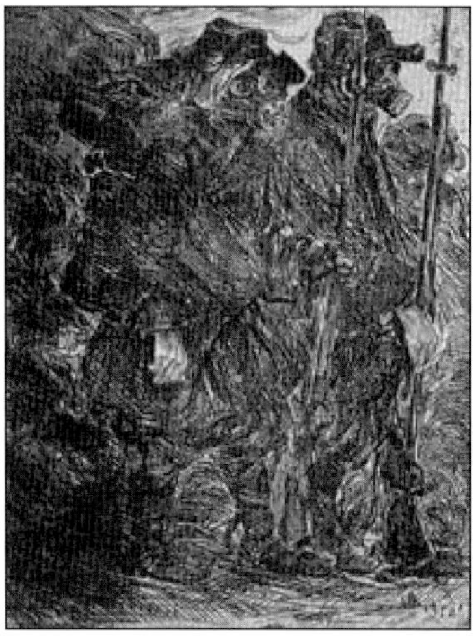

15. Henri de Groux: *Masques à gaz (Gas Masks).* Etching, Royal Army and Military History Museum, Brussels. © SESAM, Paris, 1998.

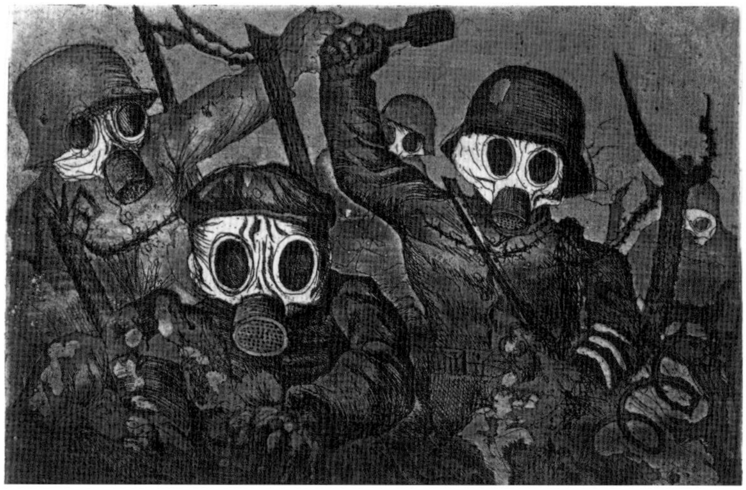

16. Otto Dix: *Sturmtruppe geht unter Gas vor (Assault under Gas),* 1924. Watercolor, 35.3 x 47.5 cm. Kupferstichkabinett, Staatliche Museen zu Berlin, Berlin, Germany. Bildarchiv Preussischer Kulturbesitz / Art Resource, NY. © 2006 Artist Rights Society (ARS), New York/VG Bild-Kunst, Bonn

The three panoramic, multi-colored drawings of the Yser battlefield by Alfred Bastien give the reader of the illustrated journal a feel for the war. The etching *Masques à gaz (Gas Masks)* of Henri de Groux (fig. 15) reveals soldiers with rifles and bayonets poised for action, having donned gas masks. Their pig-like features with snouts dehumanize the men. After 22 April 1915, the first time Germans used poison gas on the enemy near Langemarck, this was a common sight, when the dreaded cry, "Gas!," was shouted in the trenches.[13] One can compare De Groux's image with those of Otto Dix, who paints the haunting, nightmarish images of the soldiers with their masks as well (fig. 16), and the Irish artist Sir William Orpen, who served as an artist in the British Army with the rank of Major during the Great War (fig. 17).

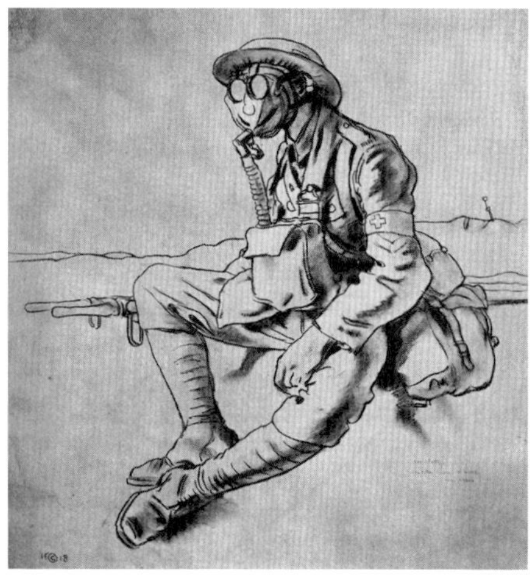

17. William Orpen: *The Gas Mask.* Drawing. From *Art and the Great War* (New York: E.P. Dutton, 1919).

Among the Belgian painters represented in the McMullen Museum of Art exhibition who captured various dimensions of the war, we find Edgard Tytgat (1879-1957), Jakob Smits (1856-1928), and Frits van den Berghe (1883-1939).

Rarely does one find the war-time paintings of Tytgat included in catalogues or exhibitions outside Belgium. Artistically, he evolved from Impressionism, to Fauvism, to Expressionism, but all at his own pace and with his own unique sensitivity. Geographically, he moved a very short distance from Brussels to the suburb of Watermael in 1907. There he continued his connection with the group La Libre Esthétique, especially linked with the painter Rik Wouters, who was most prominent as a painter at the time, and whose *Woman with Gray Gloves* (1911, **no. 32**) dates from this period. Tytgat was part of this quasi-revolutionary art group, initiated in 1893 and guided by the strong will and energy of Octave Maus. This group promoted the independence of the artist and the renunciation of pastiche and formulae and continued its exhibitions for two decades. At times with great audacity, it broke away from the reserve and circumscription of the traditional artists in both subject and material. Jane Block situates Tytgat and his fellow avant-garde colleagues at the beginning of the war:

> However, the twenty-first exhibition of La Libre Esthétique in 1914 turned out to be the last. Maus's great experiment of establishing a laboratory for all that was new in Belgium came to an end—as did so much else in Europe—with the outbreak of World War I in August 1914. Indeed, the German occupation led to the self-imposed exile to Holland and England of some of Belgium's brightest stars of the future, among them the pillars of Belgian Expressionism—Frits van den Berghe, Rik Wouters, Gustave and Léon de Smet, Edgard Tytgat, Valerius de Saedeleer, and Gustave van de Woestyne.[14]

When Octave Maus gave his final exhortation in Lausanne, where he was a part of the Belgian delegation to the Swiss Embassy, his words of wisdom, of encouragement, and of passion for his world of art rang out clearly: "Love Art, Strive to Serve It, and to Promulgate It."[15] This appeal would certainly be in harmony with Tytgat's continued efforts at painting during and after the war.

At the outbreak of the war in August 1914, Tytgat sketched out the basis for his later work, *The First Invaders of Watermael* (**no. 43**). He completed the painting in 1918 (**no. 42**), having spent the duration of the war in England where he made a living by designing woodcuts for book illustrations and graphic works.[16] The folkloric and naïve tone of the painting belies the occupation as described above. It is very much in the anecdotal style of his other works *Souvenir d'un Dimanche (Memory of a Sunday)* and *Le Clown melodieux (The Melodious Clown),* and his *Une fille d'Eve (Daughter of Eve),* which evokes Paul Gauguin's primitive, expressionist style in Tahiti. It stands in stark contrast to the graphic and, at times, satirical work of the German artists Otto Dix and George Grosz. In general, Tytgat's work reflects a jovial, light-hearted spirit, whether it be in *Invitation au paradis* (*Invitation to Paradise,* 1922), which has an Eden-like appearance, or in his mythological narratives as in *La Conquête de Troie* (*The Conquest of Troy,* 1950), based on the Homeric subject. The playful embarrassment of a man accidentally coming across a semi-naked woman sunning herself in *The Interrupted Walk* (1936, **no. 40**) is very humorously awkward. For his seemingly casual and light-hearted approach to his work, he is referred to by Paul Haeserts as a part of an artistic group "dont le maître incontesté demeure le sourriant et narquis peintre conteur," as well as "le malicieux et poétique Tytgat."[17] Other critics, such as Marnix

Gijsen, saw him as someone who observed and took delight in the "trivialities of day-to-day life," so well depicted in the little details of *The First Invaders of Watermael* (**no. 42**).[18]

Marc Eemans, in *La Peinture Moderne en Belgique,* appreciates some of the more popular aspects of Tytgat's work that are also reflected in *The First Invaders of Watermael*:

> Avec Edgard Tijtgat (Bruxelles, 1879-1957), qui fut l'ami de Rik Wouters, dont il retraça la vie en des gravures sur bois pleines d'esprit, nous abordons un tout autre aspect de l'expressionisme, un aspect anecdotique et folklorisant qui nous rapproche de l'imagerie populaire, mais qui a une saveur des plus délicieuse. C'est à juste titre que l'on a pu parler de "Tijtgat l' Enchanteur."[19]

In appearance, the scene in the painting seems innocent enough—a calm day with a few horsemen riding through town. In essence, however, Tytgat offers just a hint of the pain of occupation. The action in the painting takes place on several levels. The two spike-helmeted German cavalry make their presence known as they ride into town, their standards erect in their hands, a reflection of the movement of the German forces in August 1914. As was common for the marauding German army looting and pillaging its way toward France, one German soldier plucks the fruit from a tree, filling a large basket with his "just rewards," while another uses the outdoor toilet. On one side of the street are small shops, where one shopkeeper places a shutter on the façade of the grocery store. Do the merchants feel the ominous presence of the Germans? Across the street a woman, seen from behind, is bending down in the front of her house, working away. Behind the house, the gardens and fields are unattended. The trolley moves along its tracks, although trolley and train transportation soon will become more and more limited as the occupation continues. Above the scene, a couple watches the German soldiers as they go about their business. "What will be next?" they may inquire.

A second Flemish artist represented in the McMullen Museum of Art exhibition, Frits van den Berghe, reflects a much darker side of the war and occupation than does Tytgat. Yet he, like Tytgat, spent the war years in self-imposed exile. When the Germans invaded Belgium, Van den Berghe was in America where, in desperate straits, he copied old paintings for various art dealers.[20] Instead of settling back in Belgium, "He came back, found his country occupied, and went off to Holland where new trends like German Expressionism seemed to be in vogue. He dropped Impressionism and became an Expressionist."[21] Yet, it is difficult to situate Van den Berghe in any one movement. Paul-Gustave van Hecke comments on his ambiguous style: "The place occupied by the work of Frits van den Berghe in the development of modern art is not to be situated alternately in expressionism and surrealism, but extends over both fields, in defiance of all theories."[22] Of all of the Flemish painters from Laethem-Saint-Martin (Sint-Martens-Latem), he is considered the most prone to "intellectualism" in his work.

Van den Berghe's expressionist sensitivities are very obvious as he contemplates the more grim physical and psychological residue of the war. His *Obsession III* (1919, **no. 44**) and later work, *The Last Gunner* (1929, **no. 45**), visually document his interest in the Great War. In *Obsession III*, Van den Berghe portrays the stress of war on a man in the forefront of the painting, while his faceless wife sits at a table beneath a colorful work of abstract art. The troubled person is Van den Berghe's close friend, artist Gust de Smet, whose son was killed accidentally on his way to a recruiting station.

In *The Last Gunner* (1929), a decade after the dust of the Great War had settled, Van den Berghe creates a caustic view of the war, although not as graphic and brutal as in works by Germans Otto Dix and Max Beckman. His rusted helmeted soldier has a broken torso. In his shadow is another one-eyed warrior looking on, producing an almost string-like effect. This is a fragmented image of the soldier who was once technologically advanced. He is reduced to a mere collapsed reflection of the soldiers who were later convinced that they were lambs led to the slaughter.

Born in Holland, Jakob Smits became a naturalized Belgian in 1902. Following the death of his wife in 1899, his palette, once full of life, color and light, took on more sobering tones. From a plastic part point of view, light is of central importance in his work, a light which he depicts by accumulating thick layers of paint. In this regard his art heralds Expressionism. Yet Smits was never to do violence to reality in order to increase expressive power. He did simplify and compose it in such a way as to internalize it.[23]

This is certainly evident in his *Pond in a Park at Brussels* (1921-1925) and *Sunrise in the Kemp-Brabant*. In *Armistice* (1919, **no. 41**), he paints an image of the center of a Belgian town at the close of the war. A handful of the residents, sketchily painted in blues, greens and reds, mill about the area. The Belgian flags are hung aloft on homes and a church tower, with a patriotic salute to the end of hostilities and the brutal occupation of the Germans. Bold strokes outline the structures of the white houses. Yet there is a darkness that is apparent here in the layers of paint, giving a simple and yet somber tone to an otherwise jubilant moment. Johan Fleerakers addresses Smit's sense of beauty in starkness: "I am sure that Jakob Smit's work again will uphold, for 21st century generations, a form of beauty that was not generated by wealth, but rather by scantiness, relinquishment, deliberate renunciation, in short by a certain form of asceticism."[24] The simplicity of *Armistice* stands out as a tribute to an artist who searched for and found this quality throughout his life, until he died at the age of seventy-two, four years after the disturbing war came to a close.

The portrayal of World War I from the beginning of occupation to the close of the war with the signing of the Armistice in 1919 is not extensive in the McMullen exhibition, but it does give a flavor of the various styles of and impressions of the war upon the artists, some of whom lived in exile in order to survive and continue their artistic endeavors. From the light-spirited work of Tytgat at the presence of the Germans in the suburb of Brussels to the caustic tones of Frits van den Berghe in *Obsession III* and *The Last Gunner*, to the last rays of warfare in a Belgian town in *Armistice*, the Great War is interpreted in Expressionistic tones for the most part. Through their views of the tragedy of war, these artists in the avant-garde in Belgium will have made an impact upon the art world of Europe during the Great War and the period between the wars.

Notes

1 Larry Zuckerman, *The Rape of Belgium: The Untold Story of World War I* (New York: New York University Press, 2004).

2 See George Bellows's foreboding painting of the death of civilians in *Massacre at Dinant* (1918) in Richard Cork, *A Bitter Truth: Avant-Garde Art and the Great War* (New Haven: Yale University Press, 1994) 190.

3 Bernard A. Cook, *Belgium: A History* (New York: Peter Lang Pub., 2004) 95.

4 Arnold J. Toynbee, *The German Terror in Belgium: An Historical Record* (New York: G.H. Doran, Co., 1917) 88. See also Viscount Bryce's preface to Toynbee's *The Belgian Deportations* (London: Unwin, Ltd., n.d.), which calls the deportation of the Belgians "virtual slavery," 5. Toynbee ends his plea for understanding by lamenting: "They have gone. But where? No one knows. What to do? No one knows. Will they ever come back? No one knows. No one knows. No one knows. What we do know is that from now on we shall live with the heartrending memory, and the anguish" 95.

5 Ian F.W. Beckett has grasped the political, military and, at times, psychological impact of the first of three major battles in *Ypres: The First Battle, 1914* (Harlow, England: Pearson Education Limited, 2004). Beckett (99-100) also notes a famous German at this battle, one who received his "baptism of fire," temporarily blinded by British gas bombs—Adolf Hitler. He regained his sight after the 13 October 1918 battle and recovered in a military hospital near Berlin when the war ended a month later.

6 Cook, *Belgium: A History* 101.

7 John McCrae, *The Oxford Book of War Poetry*, ed. Jon Stallworthy (Oxford: Oxford University Press, 1984) 165. The war poems of other World War I poets, such as Wilfred Owen and Siegfried Sassoon, are also collected in this volume.

8 In this painting, Dix stylistically imitates the work of French communist and veteran Henri Barbusse in *Le Feu (Fire).*

9 Cork, *A Bitter Truth* 59.

10 See Cork, *A Bitter Truth* 272-280 for graphic images of warfare from 1920-24, such as *The Trench, Wounded Man Fleeing, Seen at the Steep slope at Cléry-sur-Somme, Shell*, and *House Destroyed by Bombs (Tournai).*

11 Qtd. in *King Albert's Book* (New York: Hearst's International Library Co., n.d.) 165.

12 *King Albert's Book* 56.

13 See John Singer Sargent's painting *Gassed* (1917, Imperial War Museum, London), a linear parallel to Bruegel's painting *The Parable of the Blind Leading the Blind* (1568, Galleria Nazionale, Naples).

14 Jane Block, "Les XX and La Libre Esthétique: Belgium's Laboratories for New Ideas," *Impressionism to Symbolism: The Belgian Avant-Garde 1880-1900*, eds. Mary Anne Stevens with Robert Hoozee (London: Royal Academy of Arts, 1994) 55.

15 Block, "Les XX and La Libre Esthétique" 55.

16 For more biographical details, see Marnix Gijsen, "Edgar Tijtgat," *Flemish Art from Ensor to Permeke*, Albert Smeets (Tielt: Uitgeverij Lannoo, 1971) 202-212.

17 Paul Haesaerts, "Le Temps de la Subversion et de la Diversité," *Huit Siècles de Peintures: Trésors des Musées de Belgique* (Brussels: Arcade, 1969) 116 and 114, respectively.

18 Gijsen, "Edgar Tijtgat" 11. Gijsen further describes him personally as someone caught up in the lower middle class world, one where there is hardly any passion, distortion or speculation.

19 *La Peinture moderne en Belgique* 96.

20 For a fuller view of Van den Berghe's life and work, see H. Lampo, "Frits van den Berghe," *Flemish Art from Ensor to Permeke* 188-201.

21 *Flemish and Dutch Painting: From Van Gogh, Ensor, Magritte and Mondrian to Contemporary Artists*, eds. Rudi Fuchs and Jan Hoet (New York: Rizzoli International Publications, Inc., 1997) 335.

22 P.-G. van Hecke, qtd. in *Flemish Art from Ensor to Permeke* 188.

23 Fuchs and Hoet, *Flemish and Dutch Painting* 334.

24 Johan Fleerackers, qtd. by Pieter Geert Buckinx, "Jakob Smits," *Flemish Art from Ensor to Permeke* 117.

Freudian Themes in the Symbolist Work of George Minne

Claude Cernuschi

I Minne and Freud

IN 1910, THE CAREER OF THE SYMBOLIST SCULPTOR GEORGE MINNE (1866-1941) was in a state of acute crisis. After two decades of indulging the vagaries of his imagination—depicting attenuated adolescents in contemplative or physically tormented poses, or mothers desperately clutching their children—Minne came to suspect his art of having lost all meaningful contact with "reality." Covetous, some art historians believe, of the success and popularity enjoyed by his "rival" Constantin Meunier[1] (a Realist sculptor renowned for his uncompromising depictions of the working class suffering under the yoke of the industrial revolution), Minne reverted to empirical experience with a vengeance. Whether he was disillusioned with the Symbolist movement as a whole is not clear. But well into his forties, he spurned the simplified renditions of the human body he had favored until now, immersed himself in the study of anatomy, attended courses on dissection at the University of Ghent, and even took in a model on a permanent basis to scrutinize the details of his vigorous worker's physique without recourse to idealization or stylization (fig. 1).

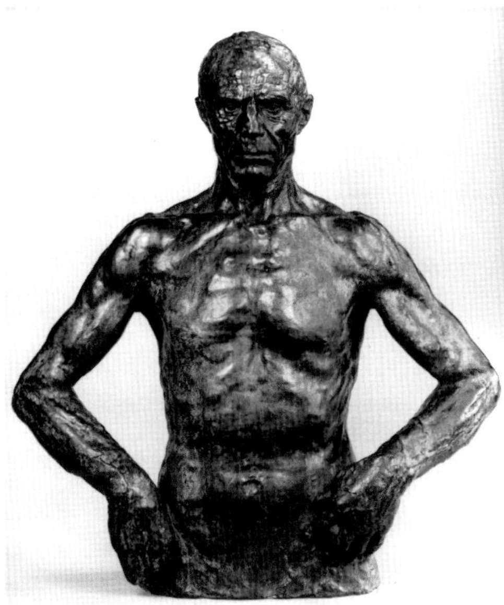

1. George Minne: *Laborer*, 1910. Bronze, 102 cm. Royal Museums of Fine Arts of Belgium, Brussels. © 2006 Artists Rights Society (ARS), New York/SABAM, Brussels

Lasting barely four years—but at a time of civil unrest[2]—Minne's "crisis" reflects how powerfully two rival ideologies had permeated the political and intellectual life of early twentieth-century Europe. For one, art's responsibility was to draw attention to current socio-economic conditions, expose the unjust distribution of resources under capitalism, and demystify the false consciousness the ruling class perpetuates in order to maintain its grip on power. No middle ground was permitted. Any work of art unable to relate its own minor acts of aesthetic rebellion to the larger issues of revolutionary class struggle was susceptible to dismissal as bourgeois, escapist, or irrelevant. For the other, art was an undeniable, albeit inadvertent, expression of the artist's unconscious, that layer of the psyche where instinctual drives and undesirable thoughts are repressed on account of their incompatibility with what civilization decrees as normative, moral behavior. On this account, human mentation is continually and inevitably scissored by inner conflict, and everyday conduct—be it intellectual or aesthetic achievement, or even the larger trends of social, political, or historical dynamics—is but a superficial manifestation of this deeper, more fundamental schism. These two ideologies, of course, are most commonly associated with the names of Karl Marx and Sigmund Freud. And Minne's crisis, even if short-lived, and even if the artist might never have conceptualized it in such terms, demonstrates how poignantly these two competing worldviews affected his own.

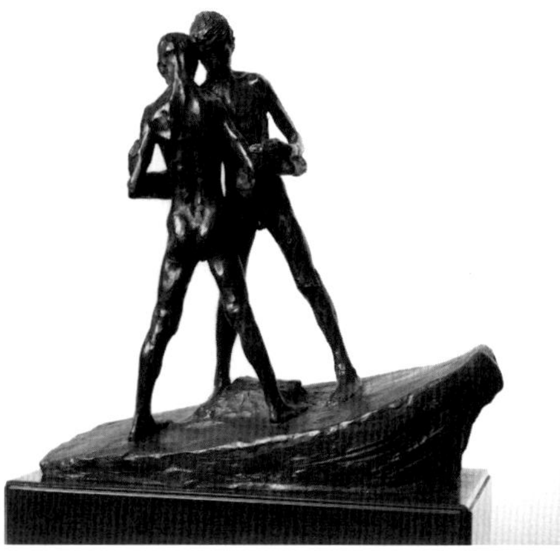

2. George Minne: *Monument to Jean Volders*, 1898. Bronze, 68 cm. Museum voor Schone Kunsten, Antwerp. © 2006 Artists Rights Society (ARS), New York/SABAM, Brussels

Of the two, however, Minne falls squarely in the Freudian camp. Which is not to say that Minne scorned or was at all insensitive to the concerns of the working class. In fact, he enjoyed more intimate contacts with peasants and laborers than many an armchair Marxist,[3] and, perhaps for this reason, was commissioned to sculpt a monument in the memory of Jean Volders (fig. 2), the founder of the *Parti Ouvrier Belge* (the Belgian Worker's Party). In spite of the sincerity with which he undertook this project, Minne came upon a solution so highly idiosyncratic—two men facing each other, wobbling precariously in an uncertain embrace on the bow of a ship—that it could not help but run afoul of the party's expectations; Minne's funds were withheld and the commission, not surprisingly, was withdrawn. In many respects, the incongruity between Minne's vision and that of the Worker's Party could be attributed to the competing worldviews mentioned above, and, as a result, to the widely divergent opinions they held about the role and function of art. Along these lines, Minne's situation could be construed as symptomatic of the phenomenon the social theorist Richard Sennett described as the "fall of public man": the idea that modern individuals no longer tend to measure their sense of self-worth in terms of their role in the public sphere, but in terms of their own private and psychological wellbeing.[4] Sennett's thesis also dovetails nicely with the argument articulated by the historian Carl Schorske in his seminal book *Fin-de-Siècle Vienna: Politics and Culture*. For all the political upheaval of the late nineteenth century, Schorske argues that: "Traditional liberal culture has centered upon rational man, whose scientific domination of nature and whose moral control of himself were expected to create the good society. In [the twentieth century], rational man has given place to that richer but more dangerous and mercurial creature, psychological man. This new man is not merely a rational animal, but a creature of feeling and instinct. We tend to make him the measure of all things in our culture. Our intra-subjectivist artists paint him. Our existentialist philosophers try to make him meaningful. Our social scientists, politicians, and advertising men manipulate him. Even our advanced social critics use him, rather than the criterion of rational right, to judge the worth of a social order. Political and economic oppression itself we assess in terms of psychological frustration."[5]

Schorske's account describes Minne's situation most poignantly.[6] Numerous students of the period have described his generation as politically disconnected and disillusioned. Not only did the sculptor portray human beings as psychological rather than rational animals; he also interpreted the broader questions of society and politics (as in the Volders project) through a more intimate, psychological lens. Minne's *Monument de la Paix* (*Monument of Peace*) of 1930 (fig. 3), to cite another example, uses an interpersonal situation, a mother and child locked in an affectionate embrace, to visualize a much broader idea or concept. On that score alone, Minne's concerns intersect Freudian preoccupations far more powerfully than Marxian ones. Freud, after all, also construed social forces in terms of interpersonal dynamics, and even wrote extensively on many of the themes to which the artist repeatedly, if not obsessively, returned: narcissism, inner conflict, adolescent sexuality, religion, parent/child interactions, the interchangeability of the physical and psychological, the motif of the double, the difference between individual and group psychology, just to name those addressed in the following pages. These connections notwithstanding, Freud is barely mentioned in the Minne literature.[7] Although references abound, and justifiably so, to the symbolist writers he befriended, and whose texts he occasionally illustrated—George Rodenbach, Charles van Lerberghe, Grégoire Le Roy, Karel van de Woestijne, and, most notably, Maurice Maeterlinck—any potential correlations between Minne's work and Freudian thought have remained largely unexplored.

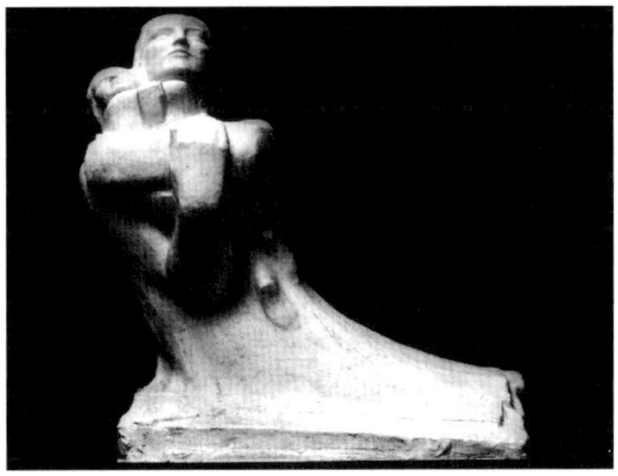

3. George Minne: *Monument de la Paix (Monument of Peace)*, 1930. Granite, 70 cm. Location unknown. © 2006 Artists Rights Society (ARS), New York/SABAM, Brussels

This is all the more surprising since, in many ways, Minne would prove a prime candidate for psycho-biographical investigation. He allegedly spoke little and only very softly.[8] Some of his acquaintances recalled him as shy, taciturn, reclusive, introverted, acetic, naïve, innocent, child-like, misanthropic, agoraphobic, and so fearful of human contact as to suffer from what, in current-day jargon, we call "social anxiety disorder." Determined to follow a career in the arts over stern paternal objections, moreover, Minne enacted the stereotypical Oedipal scenario: when their conflicting positions over his vocation became irreconcilable, Minne broke relations with his father. He could not even count on support from his family when, as a young parent himself, Minne faced acute financial difficulties. As he turned to Maeterlinck for assistance, the latter, despondent over his own inability to help, wrote to Le Roy: "I know not what to do…[Minne's] father is horrible!"[9] The parental relationship was so fraught with resentment that, following his mother's death, Minne spurned any inheritance, preferring to leave the few remaining pieces of furniture left to him on the sidewalk for anyone to filch.[10] Many art historians speculate that the simplicity and reductiveness of his work also echoes the reticence of his personality and austerity of his lifestyle—an indication, in other words, of how closely Minne's art reflects the man.[11] "Like his figures," Lynne Pudles writes, "he seems to have been psychologically isolated and turned in on himself."[12]

On the technical side, Minne regularly practiced a drawing method akin to automatism: i.e., the use of improvisation and accident in order to create marks allegedly independent of conscious control. Minne, Leo van Puyvelde recalled, "told me one day that his drawings are born, so to say, of themselves. It happened that drawings were begun without a clear idea of the final form they would take on paper; by making circles and marks, he saw an inner image manifest itself: sometimes the image of a nude, sometimes that of a mother and child, would emerge. The truly definitive form, dreamt of by the artist, all too often presented itself too late." In light of these experiments, it is perhaps not surprising that Puyvelde expressed the view that "the genesis of a work of art takes place in the unconscious."[13] It is, of course, unclear as to whether this passage, published in 1930, reflects Minne's own working process, or Puyvelde's knowledge of the latest artistic trends: namely, the contemporaneous rise of Surrealism and its purported abandonment of conventional modes of execution to access the unconscious mind. But Minne could easily have anticipated Surrealist ideas. Maeterlinck, the writer with whom he admitted having the greatest affinity, declared, speaking specifically of Minne, that "the work of genius is nothing but the work of the unconscious."[14] If the sculptor's ethos and technique were—as insinuated by Puyvelde and Maeterlinck—indeed comparable to those of the Surrealists, then this affinity would bring a significant correspondence between his worldview and theirs, and, by extension, between his and Freud's, to light.

But as tempting as a psychoanalytic approach may be, this essay will neither psychoanalyze Minne nor employ Freudian theory to understand his work along psychoanalytic lines. In the present context, psychoanalysis will not be used as a mode *of* interpretation—as a kind of master-narrative that subsumes other objects of interpretation within its "imperialistic" purview[15]—but as *an object* of interpretation. The premise is not that Freudian theory offers a suprahistorical perspective from which all objects of culture (regardless of chronological period or geographical origin) can be investigated.[16] The premise, rather, is that psychoanalysis is *itself* historical, that its intellectual premises are, of necessity, time- and culture-bound, and that, as such, it stands on no less exalted (or ideologically-neutral) ground than the art it ostensibly attempts to interpret. Considering the severe (and often devastating) criticisms psychoanalysis has received at the hands of the scientific community,[17] it would—accordingly—be exceedingly naive to use Freudian theory as a mode of interpretation in any context. All the same, many of the themes recurrent in Freudian psychoanalysis, as intimated above, betray remarkable points of intersection with those explored in Minne's Symbolist work, and thus establish a link between Symbolism and Surrealism. As such, these points of intersection may provide an exegetical nexus from which some of the specific motifs and broader implications of Minne's own idiom may emerge in sharper relief.

II Body and Mind

It is a leitmotif of Minne's work, for example, that human figures are depicted without reference to an explicit narrative.[18] "His art," as Grégoire Le Roy put it, "is, above all, an art of suggestion."[19] Minne's sculptures, Le Roy wrote elsewhere, "do not explain their subject; they allow it to be felt; their mysticism takes hold of us; they obsess us by the imprecision of mystery and conquer us by a gripping but unresolved eloquence."[20] In the two pieces included in this exhibition (**nos. 27** and **28**), *The Kneeling Pair, or Adam and Eve* (1889) and the *Small Relic Bearer* (1897), body language plays a major, if not indispensable, role.[21] The more so since Leo van Puyvelde has it on good authority (namely, the sculptor himself) that the title *Adam and Eve* was added to the former, not just after the fact, but in blatant violation of the artist's intent. Although "someone wanted to see Adam and Eve after the Fall in this group," Puyvelde insists, "...I have it from the artist that [the work] was inspired by the sight of a man and woman praying in church. This motif became a generalized image of those who are resigned to accept pain as a trial. These human beings have been stripped of their clothing, which would either date or individualize them. They find themselves in a state of primal nudity."[22]

Based, as it is, on personal interactions with the sculptor himself, Puyvelde's admonition carries considerable weight.[23] Even so, the proverbial "someone" responsible for connecting Minne's group with the Expulsion should not be judged too harshly. The number, age, gender, pose, and facial expressions of his figures are remarkably consistent with previous depictions of that Biblical scene; and to conceive of Adam and Eve as existing in "a state of primal nudity," or as being forced to endure "pain with resignation," is hardly incongruous.[24] Thus, even if Minne did not intend the group to represent Adam and Eve specifically—which, of course would be in keeping with the Symbolist penchant for elusiveness and ambiguity[25]—the closeness with which his own figures approximate the body language of the original pair in Western art makes that very association near-inescapable (to anyone familiar with the Judeo-Christian tradition, at

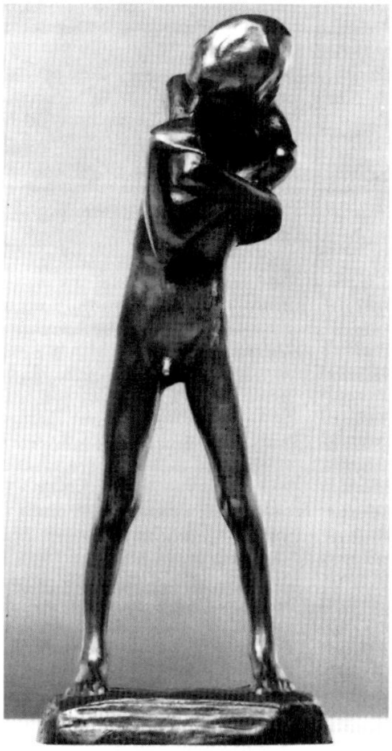

4. George Minne: *The Small Wounded One II*, 1898. Bronze, 25 cm. Private Collection. © 2006 Artists Rights Society (ARS), New York/SABAM, Brussels

any rate). Puyvelde's rebuke, in fact, was not enough to dislodge that connection, and the frequency with which a Biblical reference is attached to Minne's group in the art historical literature attests to how closely the emotional valence the artist hoped to communicate approximates that communicated by conventional depictions of Adam and Eve.

In other instances, however, Minne's audience did not have it so easy. Spectators present at his first exhibitions found it exceedingly difficult to interpret his work or connect it with recognizable iconographical prototypes.[26] In 1891, a reviewer complained of Minne's "erotico-ambiguous" scenes that "transcended all limits of meaninglessness."[27] Karel Lybert singled out *The Prayer* and *The Small Wounded One* (fig. 4) as being "two works of remarkable strangeness. The spectator shakes his head trying to understand, all the while asking himself to which world these beings possibly belong."[28] Commenting on the *Fontaine des agenouillés* (fig. 9, *Fountain of the Kneeling Youths*), moreover, Charles Buls declared: "I don't understand anything of this piece. I only see five kneeling individuals ready to spit into a basin."[29] Since some scholars find themselves at a loss whether to categorize Minne's work as allegory, sign, or symbol,[30] interpretive problems even bedevil criticism to this day. For his part, Minne saw his work as raising no interpretive obstacles. He foreswore any interest in psychology or intellectualism in order to "better turn to myself and work in absolute sincerity."[31] His defenders, like Le Roy, even deemed his work to be readily intelligible on account of the "intensity of its direct sentiment."[32] But despite Le Roy's comment, and for all of Minne's goodwill, it should be said that "sincerity" or "directness" cannot simply be literally "transcribed" in bronze, wood, or marble. No matter what the artist seeks to express or communicate, if no common ground exists between the artist's intellectual assumptions and those of the audience, communication breaks down.

Insofar as Minne was concerned, he must have resolved this dilemma for himself by endorsing the view, if only tacitly, that the language of the human body itself—independently of any other clue—might provide the spectator with enough of an interpretive scaffold to construct the meaning of his work.[33] (Not surprisingly, his teacher, Charles Van der Stappen, called him "the sculptor of the gesture"[34]). In that respect, of course, Minne betrays a great affinity with Auguste Rodin, a sculptor he greatly admired and from whom he directly sought advice. But even if he exploited physicality to its extreme—depicting human beings in poses of exaggerated extension and contraction—Rodin often attached a title to his figures (e.g., *Adam*, *The Prodigal Son*, *Iris: the Messenger of the Gods*, etc.). In the process, he firmly located his sculptures (especially those depicting a nude body without recognizable attributes) within a clearly intelligible narrative context.

To be sure, Minne occasionally provided similar information. But not always. Much of his production—such as *The Kneeling Pair, or Adam and Eve* and the *Small Relic Bearer* in this exhibition, as well as a host of other depictions of nude adolescents—leaves the audience guessing as to the precise narrative (if any) into which these figures were meant to fit. As Puyvelde put it: "These figures evoke no particular idea, no definitive sentiment."[35] Even more poetically, André Fontainas suggested that, for Minne, "plasticity is but the appropriate intermediary to reveal something more profound, more intangible, the vitality of instinct or the obscure impulses of the spirit."[36] It is in this particular respect—in his ostensible belief that the physical body could effectively translate emotional states independently of symbolic, allegorical, or narrative codes—that Minne has much in common with Freud. A great admirer of Darwin, Freud, after all, endorsed the biologist's view, articulated in *The Expression of the Emotions in Man and Animals* (1872), that the body could provide a key to the mind. In *Studies on Hysteria* (1895), he explained hysterical symptoms as "the effects and residues of excitations which have acted upon the nervous system as traumas." These symptoms emerge, he continues, when "a sum of excitation impinging on the nervous system is transformed into chronic symptoms in so far as it has not been employed for external action in proportion to its amount....in hysteria...a considerable part of this 'sum of excitation' of the trauma is transformed *into purely somatic symptoms*. It is this characteristic of hysteria which has so long stood in the way of its being recognized as a psychical disorder [italics mine]."[37] Thus, following a principle Freud calls conversion, *physical* symptoms such as paralysis, pain, cramps, and irritability can actually be attributed to hysterical—i.e., psychical—causes.[38] If traumatic reminiscences have no opportunity to be abreacted (i.e., to be discharged) and have been repressed into the unconscious, then the "sum of excitation, being cut off from psychical association, finds its way all the more easily along the wrong path to a somatic innervation."[39] Even if some symptoms have a demonstrably organic origin, hysterical symptoms may attach themselves to them so as to merge organic and hysterical causes beyond easy detection.

Since Freud construed these principles as revealing basic aspects of human mentation, they did not pertain to hysterical patients alone. On the contrary, Freud was convinced that the physical manifestation of psychological states brought "the behavior of hysterical people nearer to that of healthy ones."[40] Hence, the permeability of the physical and psychological dovetailed with the permeability of the normal and abnormal, and the distinction between normality and pathology was no longer absolute. "Hysteria of the severest type," Freud writes, "can exist in conjunction with gifts of the richest and most original kind."[41] On this account, since Minne fashioned figures whose body language could (or so he believed) effectively communicate emotional states without any explicit reference to symbology or narrative, it is, arguably, because he, like Freud, endorsed the possibility that psychological states could be expressed in terms of physical analogs; and, further, that such findings applied, not only to pathological patients, but to normative human behavior.

This principle, of course, was not unique to Freud. In fact, it is very likely that Freud himself appropriated it from the philosophy of Arthur Schopenhauer, who, after decades of neglect, was becoming progressively more influential in fin-de-siècle culture, and was known to some of the writers and poets in Minne's intellectual circle. Endorsing Kant's division between reality (the thing-in-itself) and our own *sensations* of reality (the phenomenon), and concluding that human forms of knowledge (space, time, causality) apply *only* to our sensations rather than to reality proper—or only to phenomena rather than to things-in-themselves—Schopenhauer separated the world between "will" and "representation." For him, the will was the real world, the Kantian thing-in-itself; everything else, the entirety of our experience—even the physical sensation of living inside a human body—was nothing more than representation. We may experience the world through the senses, and we may delude ourselves into thinking that this experience exists independently of our minds, yet that experience, he insisted, is always internal; it is always constructed by us.

But although Schopenhauer conceded that the thing-in-itself—the will—is inaccessible to us on an intellectual plane, he did not, paradoxically, abandon our ability to know the thing-in-itself. He got around this potential contradiction by arguing that even if our forms of knowledge are, of necessity, limited, and even if our categories and intellectual constructs describe our experience (the phenomenon) rather than the thing-in-itself, this does not prevent *us* from also being an example of the will. We ourselves, for all intents and purposes, *are also* the thing-in-itself. Thus, even if the body is nothing but representation, it still comprises the first and most immediate source of human understanding, an understanding whose primary experience was physical. Knowledge, writes Schopenhauer, "is nevertheless given entirely through the medium of a body, and the affections of this body are, as we have shown, the starting point for the understanding in its perception of this world."[42] "The act of will and the action of the body," he continues, "are not two different states objectively known, connected by the bond of causality; they do not stand in the relation of cause and effect, but are one and the same [...]. The action of the body is nothing but the act of will objectified [...] will that has become representation."[43] Accordingly, although the contrast between will and representation corresponds to the distinction between reality and sensation, the body is precisely where will and representation meet. "The identity of the body and the will further shows itself," he writes, "[...] in the fact that every vehement and excessive movement of the will, in other words, every emotion, agitates the body and its inner workings directly and immediately, and disturbs the course of its vital functions."[44]

There is no evidence to suggest that Schopenhauer directly influenced Minne's worldview. By all accounts, Minne was no great reader. But he could have been exposed to variants of Schopenhauer's ideas through the writers and intellectuals he befriended. Schopenhauer, for example, believed that the form of knowledge that exists "outside and independently of all relations...the Ideas that are the immediate and adequate objectivity of the thing-in-itself...is *art*, the work of genius."[45] Emile Verhaeren, a great defender of Minne's in print, and whose poems the sculptor illustrated, wrote approvingly of the artist using remarkably similar terminology. Minne's figures, he wrote, "are practically beyond what is possible to be...They are disengaged from their milieu; they come and go beyond the other side where only the Idea...can live."[46] Against this background, it would not be difficult to interpret a sculpture such as Minne's *Le grand blessé* (*Large Wounded One*) of 1894 (fig. 5) as informed by analogous ideas. In keeping with Minne's penchant for ambiguity, the nature of the wound itself, the implement employed to inflict it, and the larger context in (or reason for) which its victim received it, remain completely unclear. Nonetheless, the body, with head thrown back and limbs extending into the surrounding space, appears so overcome with pain that no literary or Biblical narrative is necessary to communicate that point. No less consistent with the intellectual tenets of Freud and Schopenhauer, is the assumption under which the majority of Minne scholars are operating: that the wound referenced in the title *Large Wounded One* is as much psychical as physical.[47] Although Lynne Pudles states that it "is unclear whether the boy's wound is physical or psychic," she nonetheless concedes that the sculpture's bodily contortions "suggest a pain that far exceeds the physical."[48] Along the same lines, Albert Alhadeff described Minne's *Man with a Watersack* (1897) this way: "His convulsed condition suggests a transcendent vision—a dialogue with the invisible, hallmark of symbolism; hence its hunger, a hunger born of the soul rather than the body."[49] If this reading is persuasive, it would reinforce one of the basic premises of this essay: that, like Freud, Minne construed the physical and psychological as interchangeable.

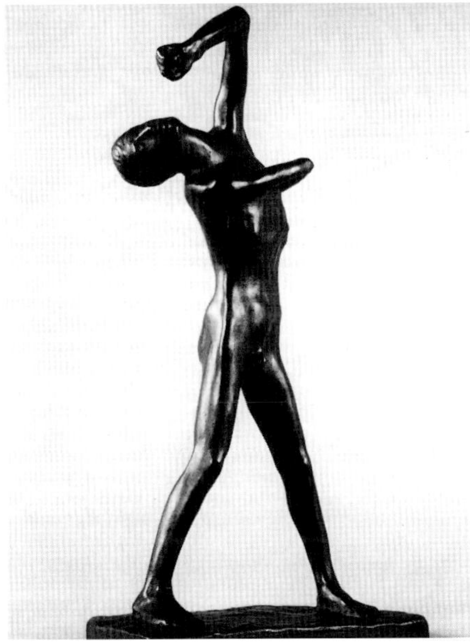

5. George Minne: *Large Wounded One*, 1894. Bronze, 39.5 cm. Private Collection. © 2006 Artists Rights Society (ARS), New York/SABAM, Brussels

III Sexuality and Adolescence

But Freud and Minne do not simply share a similar belief in the interchangeability of the physical and psychological. They also seem to share a similar belief in *what* the physical—specifically—reveals about the psychological. The figure in *L'adolescent I* of 1891 (fig. 6) is again portrayed as if writhing in pain, and the pain, as in the wounded figures mentioned above, seems as much emotional as physical—perhaps even more so, given that the figure does

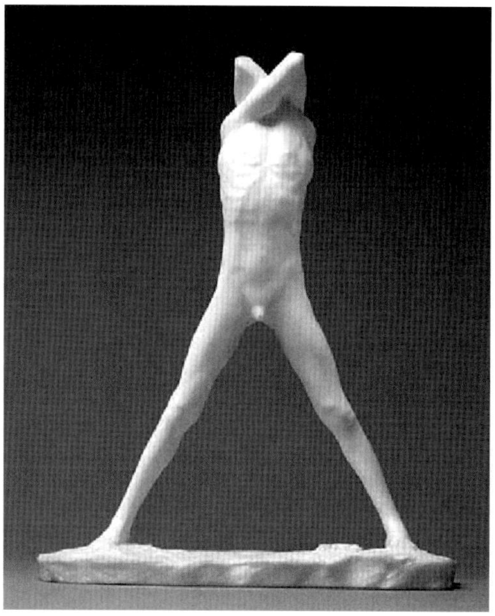

6. George Minne: *L'adolescent I*, 1891. Marble. Getty Museum, Los Angeles. © 2006 Artists Rights Society (ARS), New York/SABAM, Brussels

not, as in the *Large Wounded One*, clutch a part of the body where the "wound" may be localized. What differentiates this adolescent even more emphatically from his wounded counterparts, however, is not simply the greater emphasis on the emotional rather than physical trauma to which he responds, but the extent to which the figure seems to be wrestling, not with some external threat, but with an internal one: namely, with himself. The body language of the adolescent, for instance, appears bitterly divided against itself. If the spreading of the legs and exposure of the genitals bespeak unabashed sexual exhibitionism, the crossing of the arms over the face, conversely, bespeaks shame and disgust. In this sculpture, Minne seems to be conveying an idea not altogether different from one central to Freud's psychoanalysis: namely, that the Ego is not master of its own house.[50]

Indeed, as psychoanalysis is a "science of the symbolizing activity of the mind,"[51] awarding primacy and interpretive relevance to *mental* as opposed to *factual* reality,[52] it is essentially concerned "with the nature and causal interrelations of such entities as wishes and beliefs."[53] More specifically, the mental states of interest to psychoanalysis (i.e., those that define its interpretive and diagnostic purview) are an individual's sexual wishes or desires. These wishes and beliefs are not only multiple, but often mutually incompatible; they may be considered culturally unacceptable, or even revolting to the very individual who harbors them (such as the primordial Oedipal wish). It follows, therefore, that Freud identified the destabilizing experience of multiple and contradictory impulses, as well as the desire to satisfy personally repugnant or socially objectionable wishes, as the very root-causes of neuroses. As the analyst Kurt Eissler so aptly put it: "For Freud, man is a system in conflict."[54]

Against this backdrop, the contradictory, even antagonistic, aspects of Minne's *Adolescent*—intro- versus extroversion, exhibitionism versus prudery—could be construed as also reflecting a view of the mind as irreparably divided. Of course, such a view need not be connected exclusively with Freud. Being a good Platonist, Schopenhauer also endorsed the correlation used in the *Phaedrus* between the divided nature of the human soul and a charioteer attempting to control his steeds. "One of them is noble and good," Plato writes, "and of good stock, while the other has the opposite character, and his stock is opposite. Hence the task of our charioteer is difficult and troublesome."[55] Schopenhauer, in fact, employed a near-identical metaphor in *The World as Will and Representation*: "what bridle and bit are to an unmanageable horse, the intellect is to the will in man; it must be led by this bridle by means of instruction, exhortation, training, and so on; for in itself the will is as wild and impetuous an impulse as is the force appearing in the plunging waterfall."[56] And Freud, correspondingly, referenced the very same analogy: he saw the ego's "relation to the id [...] like a man on horseback, who has to hold in check the superior strength of the horse."[57] But what makes Freud's view of human nature that much more pessimistic than Plato's, and more in line with Schopenhauer's, is its insistence on humanity's ignorance of the very problems that plague it most acutely.

Subject to contrary impulses, human beings will, according to Freud, marshal their mental energy to resolve any ensuing tensions or conflicts. Although individuals seek to satisfy their wishes and desires, they are invariably forced by expediency to defer gratification, compromise, or even renounce certain wishes and desires altogether. "Generally speaking," Freud writes, "our civilization is built up on the suppression of instincts. Each individual has surrendered some part of his possessions—some part of the sense of omnipotence or of the aggressive or vindictive inclinations of his personality."[58] But foregoing the satisfaction of instinctual drives comes at a price. According to Marshall Edelson, it is unlikely that attempts to resolve mental conflicts or dilemmas will prove "totally successful" or "effected without some cost in frustration, pain, or misery."[59] In the majority of cases, if wishes remain unsatisfied, or if wishes elicit feelings of guilt or shame, the individual's *repressing* and turning wishes away from consciousness is the most immediate resolution to mental conflict. The discovery of the process of repression is among the key principles in psychoanalytic theory; in Freud's words, it "is the cornerstone on which the whole structure of psycho-analysis rests...*the most essential part of it* [italics mine]."[60] Likewise, it is no less important to point out that psychoanalytic theory further postulates that once a wish becomes the target of repression, not only is the content of the wish no longer conscious, but the *very fact* of its repression is also made inaccessible to consciousness. "It is one of the conditions of the illness," Freud insists, "that the person who is obeying a compulsion carries it without understanding its meaning."[61]

Along similar lines, one may hypothesize that the ambiguity resulting from Minne's reluctance to associate his adolescents with a particular Biblical or literary narrative serves, not just to convey that physical stress can convey psychological stress, or that the human mind is bedeviled by inner conflict. Maintaining the spectator's ignorance[62] of the true nature or cause of their anxieties and frustrations may also be Minne's way of communicating that the adolescents are no less ignorant of these causes themselves. Speaking of the *Small Wounded One* (fig. 4), for example, Albert Alhadeff observes that the figure, "subject to unknown sources of affliction...appears threatened by forces beyond its understanding."[63] All of which, of course, exacerbates the mental suffering these figures have ostensibly no other choice but to endure. It is always easier, after all, to find a solution to a problem once its particular source or nature becomes apparent. Like Freud, Minne seems to be insinuating that it is humanity's own ignorance of (and refusal to face) the exact character of its own predicaments—not the predicaments per se—that make them all the more severe.

But although ideas pertaining to the conflicted nature of the mind, and to humanity's own general lack of self-knowledge, can be traced back to a long tradition of philosophical writings, there is another, specifically Freudian, spin that can also be discerned in Minne's adolescents: namely, the importance awarded to their sexuality. Lynne Pudles has argued that the work of Minne (and of many of the Belgian symbolists he befriended) was especially marked by a concern with sin, guilt, and damnation, an obsession she traces to their common Jesuit education.[64] Particularly powerful in this context is Maeterlinck's recollection of how obsessed the Fathers to whom the children's education was entrusted were with chastity: "The slightest carnal thought," Maeterlinck recalled, "hurled you into eternal flames. All the sermons were concerned only with hell." Even while taking baths, students were allowed to wash only below the knees. "The rest," Maeterlinck continues, "which seemed not to exist, was relegated to a dark mystery. Summer baths were taken...under a heavy garment of cardboard-like wool...[a symbol] of a stubborn and hermetic chastity."[65] If he were indeed reacting to having grown up in such an ambiance, Minne might very well have attempted to give form to what had been forbidden him during his student days. In parallel, it is often said that Freud's views on sexuality were also born of, and inextricable from, the excessively repressive Victorian morality of fin-de-siècle Viennese culture. Even so, what binds Minne and Freud is not simply an interest in sexuality; it is, rather, an interest in *adolescent* sexuality. In his "Three Essays," for example, Freud positioned psychoanalysis as the first psychological theory to have argued for the sexual appetites of pre-pubescents. It is generally assumed, he declares, that sexuality "only awakens in the period of life described as puberty. This, however, is not a simple error but one that has had grave consequences, for it is mainly to this idea that we owe our present ignorance of the fundamental conditions of sexual life."[66] Whether Freud's assertions of priority in this matter ("So far as I know, not a single author has clearly recognized the regular existence of a sexual instinct in childhood"[67]) are entirely justifiable is, of course, open to debate. But, irrespective of Freud's honesty, the propensity of children to be sexual provides another point of connection between the worldviews of Minne and Freud. It also explains why Minne's exhibitions in Vienna proved so influential. In his book *The Fin-de-Siècle Culture of Adolescence*, John Neubauer persuasively argued that: "the culture of the Viennese *Jungen* was *adolescent*, both in a literal sense, for its adolescent artists and its thematization of adolescence."[68]

IV Primitivism and Recapitulation

But Belgium was not immune to this same tendency. Just as magazines such as *Jugend* (*Youth*) appeared in central Europe, so did Belgium produce its own counterparts to celebrate the potential of a new generation: e.g., *La Jeune Belgique* (*Young Belgium*), *La Société Nouvelle* (*The New Society*), *L'Art Moderne*. This fascination with youth was, of course, symptomatic of a more general fascination with things primordial and atavistic. Minne's work was often described as "primitive," "Gothic," or "child-like."[69] The designation "Gothic" was unlikely to have displeased the artist—he was a great admirer of medieval sculptors such as Claus Sluter and Jean de Béthune. Yet references to regressive or archaizing tendencies were not always laudatory. Georges Verdavainne, for example, lambasted Minne for having "pleased himself by competing with savages from central Africa." Minne, he continues in a tone of extreme censure, "has transported the practices of the Africans among us."[70] Adept and clever, Minne's defenders managed to put a positive spin on Verdavainne's diatribes. Emile Verhaeren, for instance, praised the sculptor for "going back to the source (of art), to naiveté and childhood" and redressing the "presently phlegmatic" state of contemporary art.[71] And as early as 1890, an anonymous reviewer proclaimed that Minne "appears like a primitive. Thus all the suffering, the faith, of the first centuries of existence reappear in his plasters....There is the exasperation of emotion commonly found among newer beings, still barbaric."[72] These words encapsulate the defensive lines upon which the supporters of Minne's work made their stand. Albert Alhadeff summarized the trend this way: "The primitive, understood as everything awkward and crude, permits us to perceive the world anew; it allows us to see with the untainted vision of a child or, as was said of Minne [by Maeterlinck], of a *minus habens*."[73]

Against this backdrop, Minne's art could be interpreted as "elemental"[74] (Demolder), "eternal" like "the static and primitive sculpture of Egypt"[75] (Le Roy), or "naturally"[76] like the art of the Flemish Renaissance (Maeterlinck). For Maeterlinck in particular, Minne did not even need to imitate the artists of the past: "they relive spontaneously in him."[77] In his view, the young and naïve sculptor somehow remained at the same creative stage as artists of previous epochs, and, by dint of his innocence, was far more likely to capture what is elementally human than the overly sophisticated artists of his own time. In retrospect, this rhetorical spin seems to have been the weapon of choice among Minne's champions. But there was more at work here than the brandishing of a rhetorical device. Maurice Vanderleyden, for example, wrote that, "like [Maeterlinck], he [Minne] has ancestral souvenirs."[78] Making the same point himself, Maeterlinck interjected that, although Minne "was ignorant of everything, nonetheless, in his very early drawings and sketches, all of his art could already be found in full force, all he became, and all he will become hereafter."[79] For his part, Charles van Lerberghe made the claim that Minne's sculptures could be used to "illustrate Darwin."[80]

Although such remarks may appear perplexing to a present-day audience, they actually betray how strongly Minne's supporters believed the science of the time could be marshaled to defend his art. The same can be said of Freud, who, intriguingly enough, referenced the very same theories. Freud, as insinuated earlier, was a great admirer of Darwin,[81] and, on this basis, endorsed the (now discredited but then heralded) view that ontogeny recapitulates phylogeny, or, to put it another way, that each individual human being reenacts the evolution of the species at an accelerated rate. "The prehistory into which the dream-work leads us back," writes Freud, "is...the individual's prehistory, his childhood, and on the other, in so far as each individual somehow recapitulates in an abbreviated form the entire development of the human race, into phylogenetic prehistory too...symbolic connections, which the individual has never acquired by learning, may justly claim to be regarded as a phylogenetic heritage."[82] "Primal phantasies," he adds, "are a phylogenetic endowment. In them the individual reaches beyond his own experience into primaeval experience [...]."[83] In this particular context, it becomes clear that Maeterlinck, Vanderleyden, and van Lerberghe's were referencing evolutionary science to promote the idea that Minne's purported child-like innocence should be prized, not disdained, and that the artist was actually closer to that basic human "essence" being gradually obfuscated by modern civilization. Given the respect accorded Darwin's theory of evolution in fin-de-siècle culture, this weapon proved, or so Minne's admirers must have reasoned, a powerful one to wield against those intent on impugning the artist's naïveté. Indeed, a reviewer in the *Mercure de France* wrote: "Minne, I believe, transcribes in sculpture the afflictions of man, and what is animalistic about them, as they were felt, certainly, by those races living in centuries when the artificial had not yet taken hold."[84] Maeterlinck even referred to the artist's talents as a "prenatal gift."[85] Just as the child was seen as the father of the man, so was Minne's "primitivism" and thematization of adolescence (to borrow John Neubauer's phrase) a testimony to his proximity to things primordial.

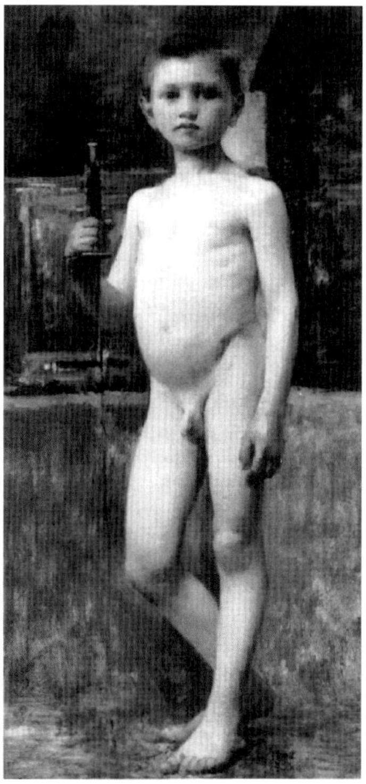

7. Franz von Stuck: *Nude Boy*, c.1900. Oil on canvas, 85.1 x 40 cm. Private Collection.

But the "thematization of adolescence" of which Neubauer speaks was not the celebration of an idealized innocence emblematic, say, of the Romantic era.[86] As Bram Dijkstra has already observed, representations of children in fin-de-siècle European culture soon displayed as much erotic charge as representations of adults (as in the work of the German artist Franz von Stuck [fig. 7]),[87] and, no doubt, began to foster the views of psychologists—Freud among them—that children were no less sexual than adults. In *The Female Offender*, for example, Cesare Lombroso and William Ferrero declared: "What terrific criminals would children be if they had strong passions, muscular strength, and sufficient intelligence."[88] Writing in 1895, Paul Adam concurred: "virtually all vices fester in the mind of the child [...] evil in adults is a sign of their not having grown up. In the taverns, in the places of debauchery, in the prisons, it is the mental tone of the child which animates and motivates."[89] In the late nineteenth century, the image of the child (visualized by Minne and conceptualized by Freud and others) reverted to pre-Enlightenment ideals, and thus frequently mutated from one of fragility and innocence to one of criminality and perversion—not a state of grace before the fall, but one of bestiality and instinct before civilization.[90]

V Masochism, Free-Will, and Narcissism

Speaking of things bestial, another nexus around which Freud and Minne's views seem to gravitate is the concept of masochism. Perhaps the most compelling, if controversial, interpretation yet offered of a Minne sculpture has been Lynne Pudles's reading of *Adolescent I* (fig. 6) as both engaging in an act of self-strangulation, and fighting against that strangulation at the same time.[91] Of course, such conflicting signals could be reflective (as explained above) of how severely the idea of "rational man" had been shaken in late nineteenth- and early twentieth-century culture. Even so, the concept of masochism takes the concept of the divided personality to another power. Along similar lines, Pudles also construes the gesture of Minne's *Large Wounded One* (fig. 5) as representing a figure directing a blow toward its own head.[92] And just as *Adolescent I* seems to be fighting the very same strangulation he initiated, so does the *Large Wounded One* strive to evade the very same blow he launched. Taking this line of argumentation one step further, one could even construe *Le petit blessé* of 1896 (fig. 4) as either licking his own wound, or, more poignantly, as even inflicting it on himself (i.e., as a form of self-mortification of the flesh, an atonement for sins, or as a kind of precursor to the various forms of auto-mutilation enacted by later performance artists such as Vito Acconci, Chris Burden, or purported by others such as Rudolf Schwarzkogler). Whether any of these—admittedly forced—interpretations are legitimate remains an open question. But in view of Freud and Minne's proclivity to see humanity as haunted by inner conflict, any insinuation that human beings can harbor masochistic tendencies simply takes that same concept to another level. "Clinical observations led us," Freud writes in *The Pleasure Principle*, "…to the view that masochism, the component instinct which is complimentary to sadism, must be regarded as sadism that has been turned round upon the subject's own ego."[93]

In other words, the obstacles that culture and civilization place before the gratification of our aggressive instincts force us, either to repress those very instincts, or to redirect them in ways that obfuscate their original object or intent. Since we may feel honest revulsion at our own desire to injure others, that revulsion can compel us to redirect those desires of injury toward ourselves (protecting us from the embarrassment and shame of admitting that we even harbor such desires in the first place). The censorship of the Ego will guarantee that neurotic symptoms not betray their real meanings, but constitute compromise formations between the Id's compulsion to satisfy a particular drive and the Ego's equal determination to deflect it from consciousness. On this account, if masochism represents, as Freud intimates, a kind of aggressive sadism redirected toward one's own self, then this surface behavior actually belies another, deeper (and often contrary) motivation—a motivation unknown even (nay, especially) to the very individual engaging in such behavior. If Minne's adolescents are indeed perpetrating analogous acts of self-injury, and yet resisting those acts at the same time, then this seeming contradiction could be construed as somehow equivalent to that most Freudian of notions: namely, that we behave, often without knowing why, in ways inimical to our own self-interests.

But the view of human nature endorsed by Freud, and visualized by Minne, does not just radically undercut the Rationalist ideal of self-knowledge. It also undercuts that of free-will and evokes the specter of predestination. Critics have frequently mentioned how effectively Minne's figures evoke a sense of extreme submission and powerlessness. That so many are positioned on their knees exacerbates, not only a mood of helplessness, but, even more generally, their fatalistic acceptance of a burden and destiny over which they have little, if any, control.[94] "So many," Puyvelde writes, "…are imprisoned within rigid forms. They are dominated, subjugated. Are they still endowed with a will? Are they even capable of straightening their muscles, of redressing themselves?"[95] Intriguingly, the extreme physical constraint and atmosphere of emotional surrender symptomatic of Minne's sculptures echoes the strict determinism that Freud saw ruling over human psychological (and even biological) experience. In his *Introductory Lectures on Psychoanalysis*, for example, Freud warned his audience that, although many human beings "nourish a deeply rooted faith in undetermined psychical events and in free will," such a naïve notion is ultimately "quite unscientific and must yield to the demand of a determinism whose rule extends over mental life."[96] It may sound ironic that Minne and Freud would betray so many points of intersection while one was working in so intuitive a way and the other insisted on his employing a mode of investigation no less objective and rigorous than those practiced in the hard sciences. Yet many of his detractors argue that Freud actually deluded himself when it came to the scientificity of his discipline. Even if psychoanalytic explanations are purportedly based on causal relationships, analysts often overlook the extent to which their interpretations of those relationships are contaminated by their own ideological biases and social prejudices. Freud, for example, believed his interpretations of human behavior to be guided exclusively by empirical evidence. But what should be made of the following passage: "the feminist demand for equal rights for the sexes does not take us far, for the morphological distinction [between men and women] is bound to find expression in differences of psychical development. 'Anatomy is destiny.'"[97] Freud, in other words, held that his belief in the inferiority of women was not a time-bound and culturally specific attitude, but a genuine "scientific" claim confirmed by biological fact. This is not say, of course, that Minne's ideas and Freud's were identical (at least, as far as women's rights, or any other political issue, was concerned), but to underscore how close Minne's fatalism[98] could parallel Freud's rigorous determinism—in spite of the latter's misguided belief that his domain was science rather than art.

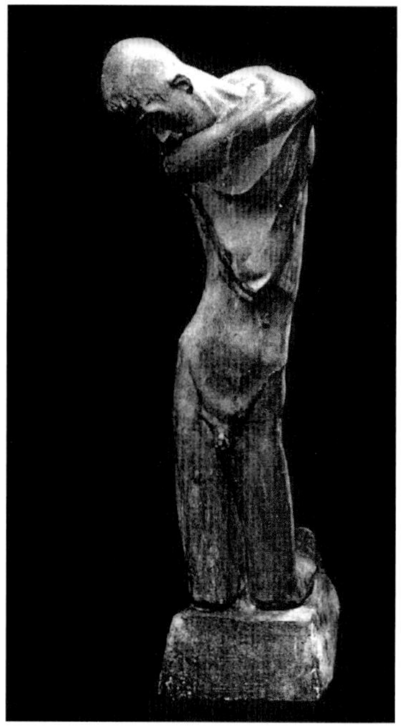

8. George Minne: *Le grand agenouillé (Kneeling Youth)*, 1898. Kunsthistorisches Museum, Vienna. © 2006 Artists Rights Society (ARS), New York/SABAM, Brussels

In addition to questions of inner conflict, adolescent sexuality, and masochism, another key issue of obvious interest to both Minne and Freud was narcissism. The *Small Relic Bearer* in this exhibition, for example, is a variant on what is arguably Minne's most famous sculpture: *Le grand agenouillé* (*Kneeling Youth*) of 1898 (fig. 8). With downcast eyes and arms tightly wrapped around his torso, the figure—often described as paradigmatic of emotional withdrawal and self-absorption[99]—had, not surprisingly, already been connected with the mythic character of Narcissus by the poet and friend of Minne, Karel van de Woestijne.[100] Minne may not have made the association himself, but he powerfully, even if inadvertently, cemented that connection by replicating the figure into five examples and arranging them around a reflecting pool: *La fontaine des agenouillés* (*The Fountain of the Kneeling Youths*) of 1898 (fig. 9). Since Narcissus fell in love with his own image, and died unable to tear himself away from his reflection in a pool of water, it stands to reason that Minne's sculpture was often mentioned in tandem with that particular mythological figure. (And if that sculpture had indeed become Minne's most famous piece—i.e., the one with whom he was most commonly associated—that very celebrity might explain his "crisis" of 1910: perhaps he came to see the entirety of his art as having turned away from the world no less than his *Kneeling Youths*.)

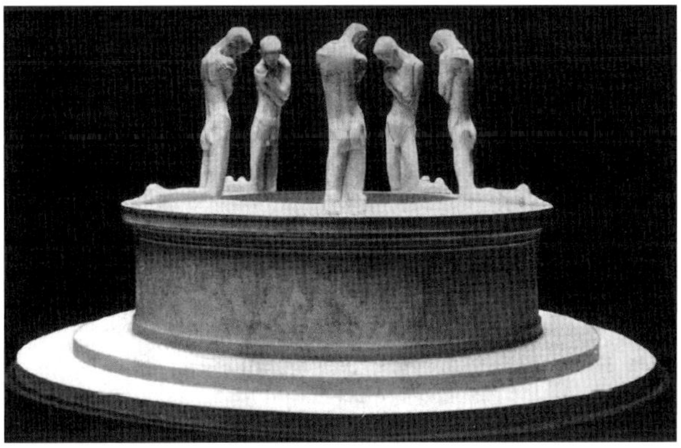

9. George Minne: *Fountain of Kneeling Youths*, 1898. Marble. Folkwang Mseum, Essen. © 2006 Artists Rights Society (ARS), New York/SABAM, Brussels

As is well known, Freud wrote extensively on the concept of narcissism, and can be credited for disseminating that term in common, everyday parlance. What is especially intriguing for our purposes, however, especially given the strong evocation of both self-centeredness and despondency in Minne's figures, is the intimate connection Freud established between narcissism and melancholy. "[T]he melancholic," Freud writes, "has, it is true, withdrawn his libido from the [sexual] object, but that, by a process we must call 'narcissistic identification,' the object has been set up in the ego itself, has been, as it were, projected on to the ego."[101] In other words, just as masochism is a form of sadism redirected from an external toward an internal target, so is narcissism nothing but love likewise redirected. And if Freud provides an intellectual framework wherein self-absorption and self-love can be connected with melancholia—as they are in Minne's sculpture—he also provides another to connect both with another of the kneeling figure's most remarkable traits: its effeminacy. Indeed, Freud drew an intimate link between femininity and self-love. But he was scarcely the only psychologist to do so; Havelock Ellis also relied on the myth of Narcissus to define and provide the appropriate nomenclature for a specific psychological fixation that (despite its masculine name) he associated most readily with women. There is a tendency, he writes, "sometimes found, more especially perhaps in women, for the sexual emotions to be absorbed, and often entirely lost in admiration. This narcissus-like tendency, of which the normal germ in women is symbolized by the mirror, is [...] rarely found in men."[102] The very same point was stressed by Freud, who actually had co-opted the term "narcissism" from Ellis before making it a mainstay of his own diagnostic investigations: "we attribute a larger amount of narcissism to femininity, which also affects women's choice of [love] object, so that to be loved is a stronger need for them than to love."[103]

The melancholic and androgynous, almost "feminine," look of Minne's adolescents thus mirrors the way contemporary psychologists ascribed melancholy and narcissism primarily to women rather than men, a blatantly derogatory connection symptomatic of fin-de-siècle culture. The contemporary prejudice that women were passive (since their responsibilities were confined to the domestic sphere, they were allegedly more susceptible to self-admiration than men who, active and engaged in the public arena, had no time for such indulgence) may be as much to blame as the countless numbers of women gazing into mirrors portrayed in the academic and Symbolist art of the time.[104] Taking that dubious association and prejudice to another level, Freud even coupled narcissism with homosexuality: "Homosexual object-choice originally lies closer to narcissism," he writes, "than does the heterosexual kind. When it is a question, therefore, of repelling an undesirably strong homosexual impulse, the path back to narcissism is made particularly easy.... A strong libidinal fixation to the narcissistic type of object-choice is to be included in the predisposition to manifest homosexuality."[105] Otto Weininger made a somewhat analogous link in his notorious book, *Sex and Character*, lashing out against the Viennese Secessionist proclivity to idealize "tall lanky women with flat chests and narrow hips."[106] There is little doubt that Weininger had work such as Minne's in mind, and was, by extension, decrying the powerful influence Minne exerted on Viennese artists such as Gustav Klimt (an influence later exerted on Egon Schiele and Oskar Kokoschka [fig. 10]). In Weininger's view, the effeminate body-type was "un-manly" and objectionable on moral grounds. "The enormous recent increase in a kind of dandified homo-sexuality," he states, "may be due to the increasing effeminacy of the age."[107] Not surprisingly, Mario Amaya reasoned that, in late nineteenth-century culture, the "androgyne acted as counterfoil to the sadistic female [or femme fatale]. Impotent and epicene, these ephebes offered themselves up like sacrificial lambs to the cause of decadence."[108]

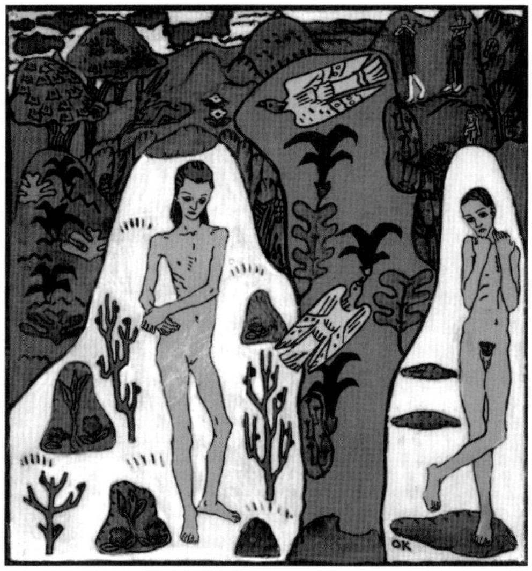

10. Oskar Kokoschka: *The Girl Li and I* from *The Dreaming Youths*, 1908. Color lithograph, 24 x 22 cm. Private Collection

On this account, Minne's adolescents drew negative criticism by running afoul of the stereotypical concept of the ideal male: virile, active, self-confident. Effeminate, passive, and conflicted, they could be construed, rather, as direct reflections of the crises mentioned at the outset of this essay: the "fall of public man," the "downfall of 'rational' man and birth of 'psychological' man," the "breakdown of traditional liberal culture," the "disintegration of Enlightenment ideals," etc. But these "crises" were not only echoed in new cultural phenomena (Symbolism, decadence, occultism, spiritualism, psychoanalysis, and so on); they also provoked a violent political backlash of their own (anti-feminism, anti-Semitism, homophobia, racism, and so on), a backlash of which Weininger provides no better example. His tendency to project the cause of cultural "degeneracy" (a common form of invective at the time) on marginalized groups—women, children, Jews, homosexuals, non-Western races, etc.—typifies the nefarious edge of this cultural counterattack, as do the ideas of August Strindberg. In an essay of 1895, Strindberg argued that the latest scientific and anthropological research left no doubt that between "the child, woman, and inferior races there exists a not negligible analogy."[109] Even Freud, despite professing to practice a cool and dispassionate scientific approach, was not above voicing such prejudices himself (as the above citations indicate). Where Minne stood, however, is a murkier issue, especially as we have so little evidence upon which to base any assessment. At the very least, the combination of self-love, melancholy, and effeminacy so integral to, and unmistakable in, his *Kneeling Youths* provided Weininger with a certain degree of ammunition. But whether these associations were ones Minne celebrated or censured remains an open question; if anything, his "crisis" of 1910 demonstrates how complex these questions were, even for him.

VI Repetition

Easier to trace, perhaps, is the parallel between the fivefold repetition of the kneeling figure in Minne's Narcissus fountain (fig. 9) and Freud's ideas on group psychology and repetition compulsion. To be sure, from Greek caryatids to Rodin's *Three Shades* (the threefold replication of the same figure—an autonomous piece called *Adam*), there is no shortage of precedents in the history of art for this form of exact duplication.[110] All the same, if Rodin's three Shades converge toward one another, or toward an undetermined but central focal point, Minne's figures appear oddly disconnected and unaware of each other. Even so subtle an adjustment as breaking the symmetry of their individual poses by having their head lean slightly to the side prevents any interaction between the protagonists. As one youth leans in the direction of another, that one leans away, as does the next, and so on around the circle. By this delicate amendment, Minne reinforces their alienation, both from one another and from the outside world.[111] Even so, the identical repetition of each figure's stance betrays another key aspect of the group: the degree to which they partake, albeit individually, of a similar, if not to say identical, emotion. As Lynne Pudles remarked: the overall "mood is intensified by the replication of the figures."[112] In this way, it should be said that Minne's personae look strikingly different from those of Ferdinand Hodler, an artist to whom Minne is, not without justification, frequently compared.[113] Indeed, even as Hodler's "eurythmic" compositions rely upon a certain degree of repetition, the figures are always differentiated, however subtly, in age, disposition, or facial expression, thus avoiding the identical repetition favored by Minne in the *Fountain*. Walking a tightrope between singularity and collectivity, Minne seems, miraculously, to have kept his balance; his figures may have no physical or emotional contact with one another, but, paradoxically, they are no less psychologically unified than any group sharing a common cause. "Echoing pain by parallel union," Aldaheff writes, "is one of Minne's principal themes."[114]

Relating this aspect of the fountain to Freud's ideas may, at first glance, seem incongruous. During psychoanalysis, after all, therapeutic progress is contingent on the free-associations made possible by the interactive dialogue between analyst and *individual* patient. Since there is no practical way of putting an entire group on the couch, analysis of the Freudian sort seems to have shied away from group therapy. But this did not deter Freud's meta-psychological musings in the least. No matter how restrictive on the pragmatic level, the characteristic methods of psychoanalytic therapy could, or so he reasoned, provide enough information upon which broader conclusions could be extrapolated. What are groups, in the end, if not a cluster of individuals? Accordingly, there was no logical reason why psychoanalytic laws governing one should not, *mutatis mutandis*, govern the other. "When individuals come together in a group," Freud writes, "all their individual inhibitions fall away and all the cruel, brutal, and destructive instincts, which lie dormant in individuals as relics of a primitive epoch, are stirred up to find free gratification."[115] "The contrast between individual psychology and social or group psychology," he continues, "[...] loses a great deal of its sharpness when it is examined more closely."[116] Ultimately, he concludes, "individual and social psychology are, for all practical purposes, identical."[117]

It is, of course, perplexing that the very person who held that repression works in a highly individualized manner, and who warned against excessive generalization, would also posit the argument that individual and group psychology work in intimate lockstep. Regardless, Freud established a tenet according to which groups, for all their diversity and plurality, behave in a manner either analogous, or even identical, to individuals. If one were to construe the emotive resonance of the Narcissus fountain along Freudian lines, the argument might run something like this: the loss of self is experienced *individually* by all members of the group, but also *collectively* by the group itself. The group in its entirety thereby manifests all of the emotive characteristics particular to the very individual upon whose repetition the collective unit is built: melancholy, introspection, narcissism, alienation, and so on. Even the very configuration of figures around the fountain itself—namely, the serial, replication of the same pose, and, by extension, of the same emotion—echoes a syndrome Freud frequently employed to describe the proclivity to repeat the same neurotic behavior: "repetition compulsion." When pathogenic material is not remembered, or disconnected from the original situation in which it arose, patients, Freud writes, are "obliged to *repeat* the repressed material as a contemporary experience."[118] On this account, repetition compulsion is indicative, again, of our mental life being unhinged by drives and impulses of which we have no cognizance. By extrapolating this mode of behavior from the individual to the group, Freud seems to be saying, and perhaps Minne as well, that repression is as much of a collective—or societal—issue as an individual one; that it is not simply singular, but entire classes of, human beings who are ignorant of the mental predicament in which they find themselves. Not an easy claim to verify, to be sure, but a rhetorically powerful one nonetheless.

Another issue of interest to Freud that may be brought to bear on any interpretive reading of the Narcissus fountain—and, even more appropriately, of the Volders monument (fig. 2)—is the literary theme of the double or *döppelganger*.[119] This theme is present, Freud writes, when we are confronted with "characters who are considered identical because they look alike. This relation is accentuated by mental processes leaping from one of these characters to another—by what we call telepathy—so that the one possesses knowledge, feelings and experience in common with the other. Or it is marked by the fact that the subject identifies himself with someone else, so that he is in doubt as to which his self is, or substitutes the extraneous self for his own. In other words, there is a doubling, dividing, and interchanging of the self. And finally there is the constant recurrence of the same thing—the repetition of the same features or character-traits or vicissitudes."[120] In the *Volders monument*—also known as *Solidarity*—it seems as though both figures are not only striking the same pose and enduring the same trial; it is as if their very survival depends on a delicate choreography whereby any move by one must be immediately intuited and counter-acted by the other. One has the sense that the slightest misstep, the most trivial of missed signals, will be enough to throw both figures completely off balance. And just as Freud speaks of "mental processes leaping" from one person to another, Minne's piece conveys that both figures can communicate without speech, just as two dancers who know each other intimately can practically move as one.

But the theme of the double also betrays a powerful ambiguity. Even if individuals in a group, according to Freud, "behave as though they were uniform, tolerate the peculiarities of its other members, equate themselves with them, and have no feelings of aversion towards them,"[121] such behavior (or an encounter with one's double) would be profoundly disconcerting to anyone who prizes his or her individuality. On the one hand, there is security in numbers, in knowing that one's lot is intertwined with that of a community; on the other, there is the necessity to conform, to relinquish personal concerns for those of the collective, to even lose one's self completely. It is this very ambiguity, too, that Minne, although without providing any resolution, made subliminally present when repeating his figure, identically and without variation, in the Narcissus fountain and, to a lesser degree, in the Volders monument.

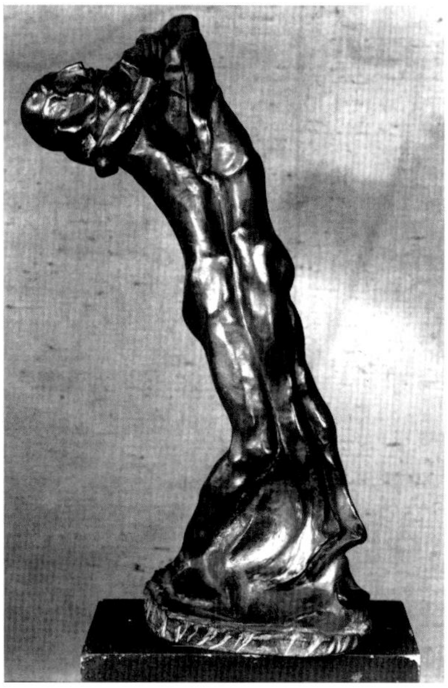

11. George Minne: *Prodigal Son*, 1896. Plaster, 58.7 cm. Museum voor Schone Kunsten, Ghent. © 2006 Artists Rights Society (ARS), New York/SABAM, Brussels

VII Parents and Children

The last parallel this essay covers is no less laden with emotional ambiguity: namely, parent/child interactions. Since Minne's relationship with his father was irreparably strained on account of the artist's choice of career, it stands to reason that Minne, like Rodin before him, would have been tempted to illustrate the parable of the prodigal son (fig. 11). Unlike Rodin's prototype, however, Minne's image is nearly unintelligible. The son and father are so physically close as to undermine the audience's ability to distinguish one figure clearly from the other.[122] This proximity endangers, not simply the legibility of the individual characters, but also the crucial set of dualities upon which the very point of the story hinges: youth versus old age, rashness versus serenity, innocence versus experience, the inclination to dispense versus the need to receive forgiveness. If this lack of legibility was intentional—and there is no reason to think that it was not—what could Minne have meant by it? That these absolute dualities need to be re-thought? That the complex relations between father and son cannot be boiled down to overly simplistic labels such as "moral" or "dissolute"? It is, of course, difficult, or even impossible, to answer these questions with any degree of certainty. But given Minne's own personal background, and in view of the idea of the divided self he seems to have shared with Freud, it would hardly be surprising if the artist sought to problematize (or at least find alternative meanings in) the Biblical parable.

In view of Minne's estrangement from his own father, moreover, it is surprising that the majority of his depictions of parent and child interaction focus not on father-and-son, but, almost exclusively, on mother-and-son. Yet this discrepancy does not necessarily mean that the artist's biography bears no connection to his art. If his relationship with his father was wrought with too much emotional baggage, Minne might have avoided its representation precisely for this reason, or made it unrecognizable by projecting it onto another image altogether: that of mother and child. As already indicated above, psychoanalytic theory postulates that the Ego works to repel any unconscious impulses from emerging into conscious awareness, so much so that those very same impulses emerge only in oblique and unintelligible ways (e.g., in dreams or neurotic symptoms). If Minne did indeed re-channel his own repressed feelings about his father in so roundabout a manner, the theme of the Madonna and Child, given its prominence in the Christian tradition, would have provided the artist with a clever disguise (fig. 12). It should be stated, for the sake of clarity, that, had Minne

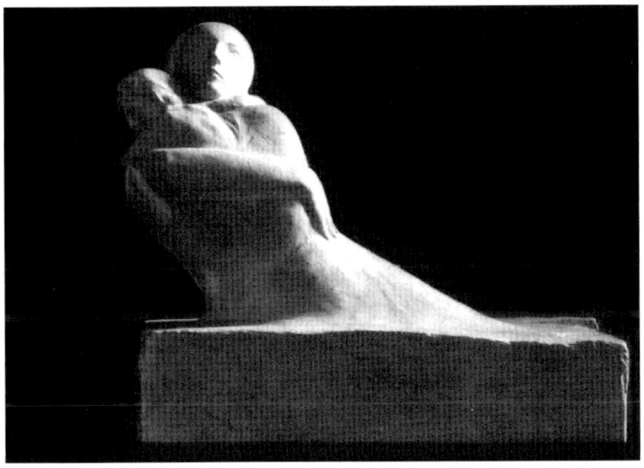

12. George Minne: *Maternal Ecstasy*, 1923. Marble, 48 cm. Location unknown. © 2006 Artists Rights Society (ARS), New York/SABAM, Brussels

implemented such symbolization, according to strictly Freudian dictates, he would have done so subliminally and inadvertently. In which case, the artist himself would have been completely unaware that the appearance in his work of either the Pietà motif or any generically vague representations of mother/child interaction was actually a stand-in for his relationship with his own father.

But the mother and child image need not be explained in so convoluted a way. Far from being repressed, Minne's feelings of resentment toward his father seemed to have been fully conscious; and the appearance of the mother and child theme in the sculptor's work may even have denoted, or transcribed, a first-hand experience. It is often mentioned in the literature that among the most powerful incidents Minne recalled from his childhood was witnessing the plight of French refugees during the Franco-Prussian War of 1870-71. His most vivid memory of that event, in fact, was of a mother and child in extreme emotional distress.[123] Years later, even as he resided in England to avoid the carnage of World War I, Minne could not have been more personally affected by the conflict. Having, like Freud, children at the front—three in his case—proved a source of perpetual anxiety for him and his wife.[124] Even so, the recurrence of this motif throughout Minne's career belies any attempt to limit it to a specific biographical episode, be it the Franco-Prussian or the Great War. More intriguingly for the purposes of this essay, Minne's images of mothers and sons, despite betraying a wide range of emotions, can easily be divided among two groups: mothers either mourning their dead child (fig. 13) or enjoying the rapturous delight of motherhood (fig. 12).

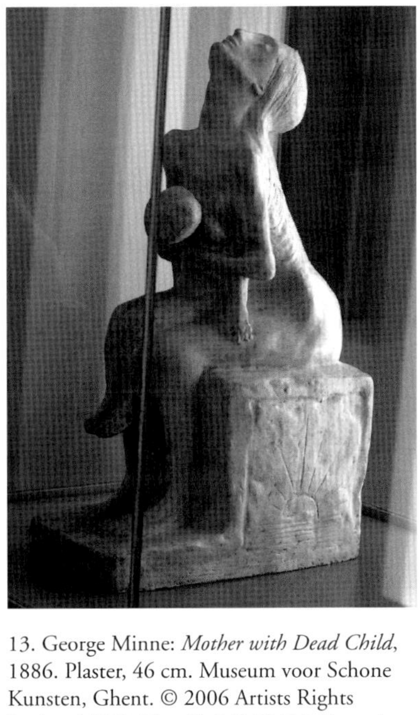

13. George Minne: *Mother with Dead Child*, 1886. Plaster, 46 cm. Museum voor Schone Kunsten, Ghent. © 2006 Artists Rights Society (ARS), New York/SABAM, Brussels

In a way, this dichotomy echoes that all-important Freudian dyad of Eros and Thanatos: the life- versus the death-instinct. The theme of death is indeed significant in Minne's art, and not restricted to the depiction of dead children; even the self-absorbed figures in the Narcissus fountain have also been compared to funerary sculpture.[125] (Along these lines, and given the frequent references to death in Symbolist art and literature, these figures could

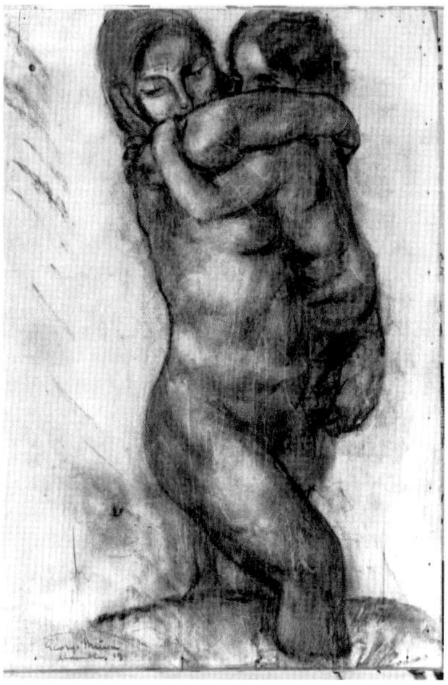

14. George Minne: *Mother with child*, drawing, 1928.

also be contemplating the possibility of their non-existence, perhaps as a corollary to their loss of self already embodied in the repetition of their identical poses.) But Minne's mother-and-child images strike perhaps an even more effective parallel with the way psychoanalysis tends to view the nature of all human relationships as having been powerfully impacted by mother-child interactions, and, conversely, to view those interactions from an adult, rather than child-like, perspective. In some of Minne's groups, for example—e.g., *L'extase maternelle* (*Maternal Ecstasy*) of 1923 (fig. 12) or *Monument de la Paix* (*Monument for Peace*) of 1930 (fig. 3)—the bond between mother and child assumes a markedly sexual dimension (fig. 14). In Minne's late work, as Pierre Baudson has already remarked: "du couple mère-enfant se dégage parfois une extrême sensualité, un certain érotisme latent issu du contact étroit de leur corps, seule expression de la jouissance dans une oeuvre volontairement ascétique."[126] For Freud, of course, sexual desire toward one's mother comprised one of the two inescapable, mirror components of the Oedipal Complex; the other, hostility toward one's father, was already mentioned above. Using Sophocles' *Oedipus Rex* as his model, Freud extrapolated the idea of a universal and ubiquitous aspect of child psychology from Oedipus' inadvertent marrying his mother Jocasta and killing his father Laïus.[127]

The idea was taken up again in the *Interpretation of Dreams* and, ever since, has functioned as an inescapable interpretive pillar of psychoanalytic exegesis.[128] Sophocles' tragedy, Freud writes, "is one in whom these primaeval wishes of our childhood have been fulfilled, and we shrink back…with the whole force of the repression by which those wishes have since that time been held down within us. While the poet, as he unravels the past, brings to light the guilt of Oedipus, he is at the same time compelling us to recognize our own inner minds, in which those same impulses, though suppressed, are still to be found."[129] Within a Freudian framework, then, Minne's images of ecstatic mothers clutching their infants would easily be construed as visualizing the very themes occluded by civilized norms of behavior, but nonetheless enacted in artistic forms such as Sophocles' play. By some inexplicable power, art cuts through the repression that holds our mental life tightly in its grip, and manages to dispel the illusions imposed by social conditioning and show humanity its true face.

Yet Freud believed that the psychological role of art, or even of adult recreational games, was more important than simple catharsis. It is not simply that works of art "compel us to recognize our own inner minds"; they can also help us master our anxieties by permitting us to rehearse anxious situations in a less threatening context. Freud found evidence to corroborate this theory in his observation of children's games—specifically, from what has come to be known as the "fort-da game" in the psychoanalytic literature. In *Beyond the Pleasure Principle*, Freud described a child who, although generally well behaved, adopted the annoying habit of casting his toys aside. The sound he emitted while discarding his playthings resembled the German word "fort" (gone), while the one emitted as he retrieved them resembled the word "da" (here). As these two sounds inevitably accompanied the repetition of this seemingly innocent ritual, Freud came to interpret the game as playing an important compensatory role for a child who, in reality, was revisiting the dis- and re-appearance of the parent to whom he was most attached: his mother. Intriguingly, Freud provided different alternatives explanations for this form of play. When the boy had to endure the absence of his mother, "he was in a *passive* situation—he was overpowered by the experience; but, by repeating it, unpleasurable though it was, as a game, he took an *active* part. These efforts might be put down to an instinct for mastery that was acting independently of whether the memory was in itself pleasurable or not."[130] Since the objects thrown aside could function as stand-ins for the mother, the discarding of the toy could, Freud surmised, also indicate the child's indirect means of taking revenge upon her for leaving him. Regardless, Freud concludes by drawing an analogy between such children's games and works of art created by adults. "[A] reminder may be added," Freud continues, "that the artistic play and artistic imitation carried out by adults, which, unlike children's, are aimed at an audience, do not spare the spectators (for instance, in tragedy) the most painful experiences and can yet be felt by them as highly enjoyable. This is convincing proof that, even under the dominance of the pleasure principle, there are ways and means enough of making what is in itself unpleasurable into a subject to be recollected and worked over in the mind."[131]

Against a Freudian background, Minne's divergent images of the pain and rapture of motherhood could thus be construed as a more intense, adult form of the "fort-da" game. On the one hand, the child's need to stage (and thereby rehearse) the mother's disappearance is recreated in the artist's representation of the motif of the Pietà: the most extreme kind of separation between mother and child. This solution would be analogous to Freud's claim that, as in representations of tragedy, "the most painful experiences can yet be felt as highly enjoyable," as well as reinforce his alternative hypothesis that, no matter how distressing an experience may be, the ability to control it lessens the level of distress. On the other, the graphic visualization of the primordial Oedipal wish in, say, *Maternal Ecstasy* could connote the joy of the mother's return, and allow, as most art is wont to do, the blatant representation of feelings otherwise subject to repression.

Minne, however, also took these images to another power. It is not only the relationship between mother and son that gives these pieces their edge; it is also the interconnection between their bodies. "Minne succeeds," Puyvelde writes, "in unifying both beings. They are connected and almost conjoined by the folds of their clothing."[132] On this score, it may be proposed that Minne transgresses the domain of Freudian thought proper in order to intersect that of

"Object-Relations" theory, a theory usually associated with the work of Melanie Klein, W.R.D. Fairbairn, and D.W. Winnicott. For the Object-Relations school, it was not the child's unconscious fantasy of intercourse with, but the actual nurture and affection provided by, the mother that was psychologically determinative. In that case, it was the impact exerted by the literal physical environment, and the actual affective relationships between human beings, that trumped the imaginary, inner life of the child. If "a satisfactory object-relationship during the period of infantile dependence" is established, Fairbairn argued, the child would grow to become well adjusted and emotionally healthy; if, on the other hand, the child did not feel "really loved as a person, and that his own love" was "not accepted," a "traumatic situation"[133] would ensue. In parallel, Minne, who suffered from parental distance and censure, may be visualizing an ideal situation in his art, one where mother and child enjoy a near-symbiotic relationship. By means of her empathy, the mother would thus anticipate her child's needs and create an idyllic environment where the beneficial is provided and the harmful avoided. That Minne would have looked to such a model of parental behavior longingly is perhaps too obvious a conclusion to draw. More interesting, arguably, is the way in which such a model might have functioned for him as paradigmatic of *all* interpersonal relations. If the title *Monument to Peace* is to be taken seriously, then Minne, like some of the psychoanalysts of the Object-relations school, might be intimating that actual relations between human beings have inordinate effects on our emotional and psychological lives; and, more broadly, that universal peace might be achieved if the nurturing touch of a mother were somehow adopted as paradigmatic for all human relations.

VIII Religion

On this account, the ways in which themes of inner conflict, adolescent sexuality, narcissism, repetition, and parent/child interactions appear in Minne's work, as well as its underlying assumptions about the interchangeability of the physical and psychological, and the similarity between individual and group psychology, sustains the argument that significant connections can be drawn between his oeuvre and ideas articulated in Freudian psychoanalysis. Which is not to say, of course, that the worldviews of Freud and Minne coincided perfectly. There is one particular matter, for example, upon which they could not have been more different. Confident only in the power of science, Freud, an avowed atheist, was so suspicious of religion as to have dismissed it as an "illusion." "Religion," he wrote, "is an attempt to master the sensory world in which we are situated by means of the wishful world which we have developed within us as a result of biological and psychological necessities. But religion cannot achieve this. Its doctrines bear the imprint of the times in which they arose, the ignorant times of the childhood of humanity. Its consolations deserve no trust."[134] Minne, on the other hand—if his work, replete as it is with explicit and implicit religious references, is any indication—must have held religion in the highest regard. In fact, he once declared that, while he could not literally pray himself, his works were tantamount to prayer.[135] His introspective personality and solemn demeanor, moreover, even earned him the nickname "God the Father" when he resided in the artist's colony in Laethem-Saint-Martin near Ghent.[136]

Yet Minne's religiosity was not of a traditional kind. Puyvelde wrote that "Minne's religious art remains an art largely and absolutely human,"[137] and Paul Haeserts that it "squares with our modern preoccupations and is therefore more secular than religious."[138] For all their differences on this issue, therefore, a point of intersection may nonetheless be discerned between Minne and Freud, a point that brings us back to the questions of fatalism and determinism already raised above. Even Freud conceded that the majority of human beings seek psychological support from some form of belief system (however delusional that support or system may be); but, in Minne's universe, no such support is apparent. His figures enjoy neither emotional certainty nor confidence in the solidity of the earth underneath them. They stand precariously on the ground, some slip and are even in danger of losing their equilibrium.[139] This lack of certitude, be it a reflection of Minne's religious philosophy or not, betrays a worldview according to which humanity is conceived as having lost its bearings. Likewise, Freud also saw humanity as existing in a state of utter desperation. As indicated above, he felt the Ego was not a master in its own house. Freud, in fact, felt that his discoveries had disturbed the sleep of the world; and had dealt humanity so severe a blow to its self-esteem as to be on a par with Copernicus' displacement of the earth from the center of the solar system, and Darwin's of man from his special status conferred by God.[140] In view of the above, Minne and Freud's diametrically opposed views on religion did not prevent their beliefs from bringing them to the same conclusion: i.e., that humanity is helpless, thrown, with little support, in a world hostile or, worse, entirely indifferent to its needs or concerns.

IX Conclusion

Arguing for so many thematic connections between Minne's work and Freudian ideas has, no doubt, engendered the expectation among readers of this essay that, at some point, evidence will be adduced and documentation presented to support the contention that Minne was conversant with, and informed by, the basic tenets of psychoanalysis. If readers did indeed work under such an expectation, an apology is in order because no such evidence will be adduced and no such documentation presented. Implicit in the argument of this essay is the underlying assumption, not that Freud influenced Minne, but, rather, that Minne, or, more accurately, Minne and countless artists like him, influenced Freud.

To make this point, we need to return, albeit briefly, to the concepts of Narcissism and the Oedipal complex already elucidated above. Reading Freud, one may get the impression that his reliance on these specific diagnostic tools was deduced from and refined during his long years of treating actual, living analysands. But it is just as likely that Freud's love of Classical mythology culturally predisposed him to project this form of behavior on, as much as to detect it in, his patients. Bram Dijkstra already made this critical point with respect to Havelock Ellis, the psychologist, it will be recalled, who coined the term "narcissism," and who primarily associated that syndrome (as did Freud) with women. Although Ellis believed that he had "identified a pathological condition characteristic of woman," he had, according to Dijkstra, simply codified "a condition whose 'symptoms' and characteristics had been developed and categorized progressively over a period of several decades by artists and writers who were themselves responding to the 'betrayal' by woman of ideals of behavior imposed on her during an earlier historical period."[141] In other words, the relationship between visual art and scientific texts is particularly significant—not because artists were necessarily influenced by the anti-feminine prejudices postulated by contemporary scientists—but because the images created by artists over the centuries *themselves informed the ideas of the scientists.* "Both the emblem of the mirror," Dijkstra posits, "and the glance of Narcissus had been impressed upon Ellis' mind, as the structure of his remarks makes abundantly clear, not by the direct study of human behavior but by the art and literature produced by his contemporaries."[142]

The same could be said of Freud. It was not so much the symptoms of his patients, but his admiration for Sophocles' *Oedipus Rex* (as well as Shakespeare's *Hamlet*) that led him to concoct the idea of the Oedipal complex. And much the same could be said of narcissism, the death-instinct, the double, and so on, themes that abound in the literary traditions of which Freud was so fond. If the preceding appraisal seems severe, or gives the impression that Freud's theories lose probative value and explanatory force as a result, it would nonetheless be in tune with much of the literature published in recent decades on psychoanalysis. As insinuated at the outset of this essay, any use of Freudian concepts to elucidate Minne's art in the present study should not be taken as an uncritical endorsement of Freud's (or even Minne's) assumptions. Indeed, many of these assumptions should strike a contemporary observer as highly dubious. The very idea that the body provides a transparent avenue to understanding the mind, for example, is patently problematic. To be sure, Schopenhauer's identification of physicality with the thing-in-itself reinforced the view that physicality provided an epistemological template for a philosophy of truth, as well as an aesthetic basis for establishing a transparent, unequivocal, and unmediated form of artistic communication. And by articulating a visual language based on the physical nature of the human body, so Minne must have reasoned, an artist was more likely to reveal "truth" than by using a pictorial idiom grounded in arbitrary signs or symbolic codes. But the poses of many of Minne's figures appear to comprise variations on a theme: the *Small Relic Bearer* in this exhibition (1897), as noted above, is connected to that of the *Kneeling Youth*, to the Narcissus fountain, and to an earlier, kneeling figure of John the Baptist. Not surprisingly, Albert Alhadeff points out that, in Minne's art, "Gestures may be arbitrarily transferred from figure to figure."[143] And as the titles of the works change, so do the "meanings" of those gestures. Unlike the *Kneeling Youths* of the Narcissus fountain, whose burdens remain unseen and invisible, the *Small Relic Bearer* gives visual and material form to the burden oppressing him by the literal presence of the relic.[144] Even if the exact nature of that burden remains unclear, the implication is that the

Small Relic Bearer is oppressed by external concerns, while the *Kneeling Youths* of the Narcissus fountain by internal ones. The physical pose of the body may be the same, but the slightest change in title or attribute can actually convey widely different meanings. In his *Philosophical Investigations*, Ludwig Wittgenstein made an analogous point. If we think of an individual with a smiling face, we may readily assume that such a facial expression is clear, unambiguous, and in no need of interpretation. But what would we make of that face, the philosopher questions, if we saw it smiling at a small child, and, then again, smiling at the demise of an enemy? [145]

One should be careful—analogously—not to endorse all assumptions made during the nineteenth century about the interchangeability of the physical and psychological. When directly applied to clinical or psychological therapy, these same assumptions were notoriously unreliable, and, in fact, led to a variety of medical *mis*diagnoses. George Frederick Drinka, for instance, argues that, on account of their belief in the interchangeability of the physical and psychological, nineteenth-century thinkers gave to neurosis "a general, all-embracing meaning." Such lack of precision, he continues, "lingered throughout the nineteenth century; the term 'neurosis' applied not only to those illnesses we modern would call neuroses but also to diseases such as epilepsy and chorea, which now are tied conclusively to brain pathology. Even disorders such as goiter, resulting from an iodine deficiency, and tetanus, an infectious illness, were called neuroses throughout the nineteenth century."[146] Drinka's point is hardly insignificant. In a footnote to *The Psychopathology of Everyday Life*, Freud related a sobering example of a case history not altogether different from the scenario just described: "M__L was a fourteen-year-old girl, [...a case] which taught me a lesson I am not likely ever to forget and whose outcome cost me moments of great distress. The child fell ill of an unmistakable hysteria, which did in fact clear up quickly and radically under my care. After this improvement the child was taken away from me by her parents. She still complained of abdominal pains which had played the chief part in the clinical picture of her hysteria. Two months later she died of sarcoma of the abdominal glands. The hysteria, to which she was at the same time predisposed, used the tumor as a provoking cause, and I, with my attention held by the noisy but harmless manifestations of the hysteria, had perhaps overlooked the first signs of the insidious and incurable disease."[147] Not surprisingly, according to present-day neurophysiologist J. Allan Hobson, Freud's psychoanalytic ideas on repression were derived "from an erroneous picture of the nervous system [...]. Freud assumed [...] that the nervous system was devoid of either synaptic contact or inhibition; that *it was incapable of losing, discarding, or canceling information*; that it was, in fact, a passive receptacle of both energy and information; able to create neither and to get rid of either one only via some motor action. We now know that none of these ideas is correct."[148]

No less problematic is Freud's connection between individual and group psychology. The sociologist Emile Durkheim lambasted this very form of explanation as profoundly misleading: "Every time that a social phenomenon is directly explained by a psychological phenomenon, we may be sure that the explanation is false [...]. The group thinks, feels, and acts quite differently from the way in which members would were they isolated.... If we begin with the individual in seeking to explain phenomena, we shall be able to understand nothing of what takes place in the group."[149] If Durkheim's point is at all persuasive, and many believe that it is, then the Freudian parallel between group psychology and individual psychology founders disastrously. But this analogy no doubt led Freud to believe that his own ideas—to return to the polarity mentioned at the outset of this essay—would subsume those of Marx. How could there be peace and justice among peoples, nations, or social classes, Freud must have reasoned, unless peace and justice reigned within the individual first? And the inner state of the individual falls, quite conveniently, within the exclusive purview of psychoanalysis. Instead of seeing the individual as the state in miniature, as Plato did in the *Republic*, Freud saw the state as the individual writ large.[150] In his view, it is harmony in the latter that predicates harmony in the former.

Minne may have thought along similar lines. Just as the Volders monument (fig. 2) visualizes the individual's need to rely upon others—a call for mutual understanding and interdependence—the image, in light of Minne's interest in repetition and doubling, could also signify the two sides—torn asunder and disconnected—of the same individual's personality. In that case, the individual's survival would depend, not on its solidarity with the larger social fabric, but on the inner harmony struck between the multiple aspects of its own personality. It is that harmony, not a mandate dictated from outside, which, in turn, could serve as a basis or blueprint for political harmony and social justice. But the very possibility of this insinuation would probably have sufficed to secure the Belgian Worker's Party's disapproval. To hint that social and political accord is contingent on emotional and psychological accord (or that the Freudian worldview subsumes the Marxian one) was enough to torpedo Minne's commission.

It is perhaps no wonder that Minne's work, though his recognition was long in waiting in his native Belgium—Le Roy even proclaimed that "his native land did not deserve that he be born on its soil"[151]—was so popular in Vienna.[152] By all accounts, social life in Habsburg Austria was stifled by an ossified Imperial bureaucratic system that left most of its subjects feeling politically disconnected and disempowered (the satirist Karl Kraus coined the word "bureaucretinism" to convey the system's widespread reputation for incompetence). In such a situation, many Habsburg subjects felt unable to alter either the socio-political conditions at hand or the very system whose organization held those same conditions in place. According to William McGrath, Austrian Liberalism differed from its counterparts in England, France, and Germany by "its relative weakness vis à vis the traditional power centers of monarchy, aristocracy, and church."[153] It has been argued, therefore, that the arts were especially eulogized in Viennese culture because they provided a welcome refuge from the political inefficiency and stagnation of the time. In a state where public activity was almost preordained to grind to a halt, and where daily life was stifled by an entrenched bureaucracy out to hinder the remotest possibility of change, artistic activity, according to Carl Schorske, "became a substitute for the life of action." "As civic action proved increasingly futile," he continues, "art became almost a religion, the source of meaning and the food of the soul."[154]

What Schorske sees happening to turn-of-the-century Viennese cultural figures, interestingly enough, was a mirror image of what he saw happening to the radical intellectuals of his own generation. After 1945, he writes, "liberals and radicals, almost unconsciously, adapted their world-views to a revolution of falling political expectations."[155] Nothing, he continues, "was more striking than the turn from Marx to Freud. For here the search for and understanding of the ills that plague mankind tended to be translated from the public and sociological domain to the private and psychological one."[156] If Schorske's account does indeed describe the conditions particular to the Viennese fin-de-siècle, it may also explain why Minne, long ignored in his own country[157] was so popular in Vienna. Vienna, after all, was the city of Freud.

I would like to thank all of those individuals who have assisted me in the preparation of this essay: Jeffery Howe and Nancy Netzer, for inviting me to submit this piece for the catalogue, and for numerous suggestions for improvement; Adeane Bregman, Bapst Librarian, Boston College, as always, for her invaluable assistance; Jessica Langella, my research assistant, for her remarkable diligence in tracking down such a vast number of bibliographical references; Naomi Blumberg and John McCoy, of the McMullen Museum, for editorial comments and dealing with photographic reproductions; Ursula Cernuschi and Suzy Forster, for their help and moral support. Lastly, I would like to dedicate this essay, in friendship, to Marietta Cambareri.

Notes

1 See André de Ridder, *George Minne* (Antwerp: Sikkel, Monographies de l'art Belge, 1947) 9, and Albert Alhadeff, "Meunier and Minne: Subterranean Visions and the Blue Summits of the Soul," *Bulletin of the Detroit Institute of Arts* 65 (1989) 22-35.

2 Leo van Puyvelde, *George Minne* (Brussels: Editions des "Cahiers de Belgique," 1930) 29.

3 Puyvelde, *George Minne* 22-23, 38.

4 See Richard Sennett, *The Fall of Public Man: On the Social Psychology of Capitalism* (New York: Vintage, 1976).

5 Carl Schorske, *Fin-de-Siècle Vienna: Politics and Culture* (New York: Alfred A. Knopf, 1985) 4-5.

6 In fact, in his introduction to the exhibition *Constantin Meunier/George Minne: Dessins et sculptures* (Bruxelles: Musées Royaux des Beaux-Arts de Belgique, 1969), non-paginated, Pierre Baudson saw both Meunier and Minne as relecting these two very poles: "Contemporains, ils sont ainsi comme les deux poles de cette fin de siècle. L'un devenu l'expression de la revolution industrielle, de la prise de conscience sociale, du machinisme triumphant, de la condition ouvrière et humaine en general, l'autre perdu dans l'anxiété latente et narcissique d'une époque qui se cherche toujours, où l'homme se réfugie au fond de lui-même."

7 One of the few exceptions, and then only in a footnote, is Paul Haesaerts, *George Minne ou le repliement sur soi-même* (Amsterdam & Antwerp: Het Kompas & De Spieghel, 1938) f.n. 2, 6.

8 Paul Haesaerts, *Laethem-Saint-Martin: Le village élu de l'art Flamand* (Brussels: Editions "Arcade," 1965) 86.

9 Maeterlinck Foundation Archives, Ghent, B. LXVII – 19.

10 Paul Eeckhout, "La Mère, dans la vie et l'oeuvre de George Minne," *Bulletin des Musées Royaux des Beaux-Arts de Belgique* 38-40 (1989) 507.

11 Leo van Puyvelde, *George Minne* 37.

12 Lynne Pudles, "The Symbolist Work of George Minne," *Art Journal* 45 (Summer 1985) 120.

13 Puyvelde, *George Minne* 43.

14 Maurice Maeterlinck, "George Minne," *La Nervie*, September/October 1923, 205.

15 See Françoise Meltzer's "Introduction: Partitive Plays, Pipe Dreams," *The Trial(s) of Psychoanalysis,* ed. F. Meltzer (Chicago: University of Chicago Press, 1988) 1-7.

16 As Laurie Schneider Adams puts it: "if the psychoanalytic method is valid, it must apply to all periods of human history." *Art and Psychoanalysis* (New York: Harper/Collins, 1993) 12.

17 See, for example, Adolf Grünbaum's *The Foundations of Psychoanalysis: A Philosophical Critique* (Berkeley: University of California Press, 1986); Hans Eysenck's *The Decline and Fall of the Freudian Empire* (New York: Penguin, 1991); Frank Sulloway's *Freud: Biologist of the Mind* (New York: Basic Books, 1983); R. Webster's *Why Freud Was Wrong* (New York: Basic Books, 1995); Malcolm McMillen's *Freud Evaluated: The Completed Arc* (Cambridge, Mass.: MIT Press, 1997); Richard Wilcocks's *Maezel's Chess Player: Sigmund Freud and the Rhetoric of Deceit* (Lanham, Maryland: Rowman & Littlefield, 1994); and Allan Esterson's *Seductive Mirage: An Exploration of the Work of Sigmund Freud* (Chicago and Lasalle, IL: Open Court, 1993).

18 Andrea Vagianos, "The Sculpture of George Minne," *Canadian Journal of Netherlandic Studies* 9-10 (Spring 1988) 54: "The individuality of Minne's representations is even more pronounced in his sculptures; they are self-referential since they are not related to a literary text, and therefore are much purer statements." See also Udo Kultermann, "Der Bildhauer Georg Minne," *Das Kunstwerk* 9 (1955-56) 54, and André de Ridder, *George Minne* 10.

19 Grégoire Le Roy, "George Minne," *L'Art Moderne*, September 28, 1890, 308.

20 Le Roy, "George Minne," *Bulletin et catalogue des expositions* (Brussels: Galerie Georges Giroux, 1920) 2.

21 See Paul Desmeth's short but poignant essay, "Notes sur quelques oeuvres de George Minne," *Paysages Bruxellois* (Brussels: Vromant & Co, 1937) 43-46.

22 Puyvelde, *George Minne* 52.

23 The same point was made by Le Roy: "...l' impression qu'il fait naitre est toujours générale. Ce n'est pas l'histoire de tel ou tel sentiment, ni de tel épisode d'une vie quelconque même, non, c'est la légende de la douleur à travers les temps..." Grégoire Le Roy, "George Minne," *L'Art Moderne*, September 28, 1890, 308.

24 See also, Albert Alhadeff, *George Minne: Fin de Siècle Drawings and Sculpture*, Ph.D. Thesis, Institute of Fine Arts, New York University, 1971 (Ann Arbor: University Microfilms, 1972) 38-39.

25 See Maurice Vanderleyden, "Le salon des XX," *La Mosaique*, February 19, 1891, qtd. in Alhadeff, "George Minne: Maeterlinck's fin de siècle Illustrator," *Annales de la Fondation Maurice Maeterlinck* 12(1966): 8; see also Anne Marie Musschot, "L'art de l'évocation: le movement symboliste en Belgique," *Septentrion* 25, No. 1 (1996) 55.

26 See Puyvelde, *George Minne* 16.

27 Champal, "Chez Les XX," *La Réforme*, February 11, 1891 qtd. in Albert Alhadeff, "Minne and Gauguin in Brussels: An Unexplored Encounter," *La Sculptura nel XIX secolo* (Bologna: Atti del XXIV Congresso Internazionale di Storia dell'Arte, 1979) 185.

28 Karel Lybert, *De Vlaamsche Kunstbode* XIX (1889) 569.

29 See Georges Chabot, "Les mésaventures de diverses oeuvres de Minne," *La Métropole*, January 23, 1953, qtd. in Alhadeff, *George Minne: Fin de Siècle Drawings and Sculpture* 186.

30 Arnold Lutz, "Der Wasserträger von George Minne in Karl-Marx-Stadt," *Bildende Kunst* 31 No. 6 (1983) 281.

31 George Minne, letter of 8 June 1919, qtd. in *George Minne en de kunst rond 1900* (Ghent: Museum voor Schone Kunsten, 1982) 208.

32 Le Roy, *La Nation*, 5 January 1891, qtd. in Puyvelde, *George Minne* 18.

33 Monique Tahon-Vanroose, "George Minne," *Wilhelm Lehmbruck/George Minne/Joseph Beuys* (Ghent: Museum voor Schone Kunsten, 1991) 243: "Ses personages ne sont ni des figures héroïques ni des demi-dieux, mais des êtres frêles résistant avec une force opiniâtre. C'est pourquoi il les représente nus, dépouillés de toute reference extérieure. Leur nudité dévoile leur âme."

34 Charles Van der Stappen cited in anonymous, "Le sculpteur George Minne est mort," *Action Française*, March 9-10, 1941, qtd. in Puddles 121.

35 Puyvelde, *George Minne* 55.

36 André Fontainas, "La vision mystique du sculpteur George Minne," *L'Art et les Artistes*, 17, 1923, 318.

37 Sigmund Freud and Joseph Breuer, *Studies on Hysteria*, in *The Standard Edition of the Complete Psychological Works of Sigmund Freud*, trans. J. Strachey (London: Hogarth Press, 1953-74), Vol. 2, 86. [Hereafter, referred to as S.E.]

38 See also "Three Essays on the History of Sexuality" S.E. 1905, 7: 164: " The removal of the symptoms of hysterical patients by psychoanalysis proceeds on the supposition that those symptoms are substitutes—transcriptions as it were—for a number

of emotionally cathected mental processes, wishes and desires, which, by the operation of a special psychical procedure (*repression*), have been prevented from obtaining discharge in psychical activity that is admissible to consciousness. These mental proceses, therefore, being held back in a state of unconsciousness, strive to obtain expression that shall be appropriate to their emotional importance—to obtain *discharge*; and in the case of hysteria they find such an expression (by means of the process of 'conversion') in somatic phenomena, that is, in hysterical symptoms."

39 Freud, *Studies on Hysteria* 116.

40 Freud, *Studies on Hysteria* 174.

41 Freud, *Studies on Hysteria* 103.

42 Arthur Schopenhauer, *The World as Will and Representation* (New York: Dover: 1969), Vol. I, 99.

43 *The World as Will and Representation*, Vol. I, 100.

44 *The World as Will and Representation*, Vol. I, 101.

45 *The World as Will and Representation*, Vol. I, 184.

46 Emile Verhaeren, "Constantin Meunier," *L'Art Moderne*, December 5, 1891, qtd. in Emile Verhaeren, *Pages Belges* (Brussels, 1926) 137.

47 A similar debate occurred in the 18th century; see, for example, Gotthold Ephraim Lessing's *Laocoön*.

48 Pudles, "The Symbolist Work of George Minne" 123.

49 Alhadeff, "Meunier and Minne: Subterranean Visions and the Blue Summits of the Soul" 29.

50 Freud, *Introductory Lectures on Psychoanalysis*, [1917], trans. J. Strachey (New York: Norton, 1966), 285.

51 Marshall Edelson, *Psychoanalysis: A Theory in Crisis* (Chicago: University of Chicago Press, 1988) xxxiv.

52 See for example, Freud's remark: "It remains a fact that the patient has created these phantasies for himself and this fact is of scarely less importance than if he had really experienced what the phantasies contain. The phantasies possess *psychical* as contrasted with *material* reality, and we gradually learn to understand that *in the world of the neuroses it is psychical reality which is the decisive kind.*" S.E. 16 (1917): 369.

53 Edelson xxii.

54 Kurt Eissler, *Leonardo da Vinci: Psychoanalytic Notes on the Enigma* (New York: International Universities Press, 1961) 58.

55 Plato, *Phaedrus*, E. Hamilton, and H. Cairns, eds., *The Collected Dialogues of Plato* (Princeton: Princeton University Press, 1961) 493.

56 *The World as Will and Representation*, Vol. II, 213.

57 Freud, *The Ego and the Id* [1923], trans. J. Riviere, (New York: Norton: 1960) 15.

58 Sigmund Freud, "'Civilized' Sexual Morality," S.E. 9 (1906-09): 186.

59 Edelson, *Psychoanalysis: A Theory In Crisis* 105.

60 S. E. 14 (1914): 77.

61 Freud, "Obsessions and Religion," S.E. 9 (1906-09): 122.

62 Pudles, in "The Symbolist Work of George Minne," makes a somewhat similar point with respect to the *Fountain of the Kneeling Youths*, which will be discussed below. On 126, she writes: "In contrast to Rodin's Burghers of Calais, where one may penetrate and interact with the figures, whose expressions and postures open up to the outside, Minne's five figures are closed and directed inward, turning their backs to the spectator and shutting him out."

63 Alhadeff, *George Minne: Fin de Siècle Drawings and Sculpture* 35-36.

64 Pudles, "The Symbolist Work of George Minne" 120.

65 Maeterlinck, *Bulles bleues* (Monaco: 1948) 83-88.

66 Freud, "Three Essays on the Theory of Sexuality," *Pelican Freud Library Vol. 7: Sexuality* (London: Penguin, 1977) 173.

67 Freud, "Three Essays" 173.

68 John Neubauer, *The Fin-de-Siècle Culture of Adolescence* (New Haven and London: Yale University Press, 1992) 106.

69 See Eugène Demolder, "Chronique artistique: Les XX," *La Société Nouvelle*, 6, 1980, 117.

70 G. Verdavainne, "L'Exposition des XX," *La Fédération Artistique*, January 26, 1890, 163.

71 Emile Verhaeren, "Aux XX," *La Nation*, February 20, 1891, qtd. in Alhadeff, "Minne and Gauguin in Brussels: An Unexplored Encounter" 187.

72 Anonymous, "Une exposition annuelle des XX," *Le Journal de Charleroi*, January 30, 1890, qtd. in Alhadeff, "Minne and Gauguin in Brussels: An Unexplored Encounter" 188.

73 Albert Alhadeff, "Minne and Gauguin in Brussels: An Unexplored Encounter," *La Sculptura nel XIX secolo* (Bologna: Atti del XXIV Congresso Internazionale di Storia dell'Arte, 1979) 180.

74 Demolder,"Chronique artistique: Les XX." *La Société Nouvelle*, 6, 1890, 117.

75 Le Roy, "George Minne," *L'Art Moderne*, qtd. in *George Minne en de kunst rond 1900* (Ghent: Museum voor Schone Kunsten, 1982) 49.

76 Maeterlinck, *La Nervie*, 1923, qtd. in *George Minne en de kunst rond 1900* 52.

77 Maeterlinck, *La Nervie*, 1923, qtd. in *George Minne en de kunst rond 1900* 52.

78 Maurice Vanderleyden, "Le Salon des XX," *La Mosaique*, Feb. 19, 1891, qtd. in Alhadeff, *George Minne: Fin de Siècle Drawings and Sculpture* 30.

79 Maeterlinck, "George Minne: L'imagier de la douleur," *La Nervie*, September/October 1923, 205.

80 Letter addressed to Albert Mockel, *Fonds Van Lerberghe*, Bibliothèque royale, Brussels, qtd. in Alhadeff, *George Minne: Fin de Siècle Drawings and Sculpture* 37.

81 See Frank Sulloway, *Freud: Biologist of the Mind* (New York: Basic Books, 1983).

82 Freud, *Introductory Lectures on Psychoanalysis*, trans. James Stratchey (New York: Norton, 1977)199.

83 Freud, *Introductory Lectures on Psychoanalysis* 371.

84 Daland, "Le Salon des XX, Bruxelles," *Mercure de France*, 1(March 1890) 91.

85 Maeterlinck, "George Minne," *La Nervie*, September/October 1923, 205.

86 See also Edward Timms, "The 'Child-Woman': Kraus, Freud, Wittels, and Irma Karczewska," *Vienna 1900: From Altenberg to Wittgenstein*, eds. E. Timms and R. Roberston (Edinburgh: Edinburgh University Press, 1990) 87ff.

87 Bram Dijkstra, *Idols of Perversity: Fantasies of Feminine Evil in Fin-de-Siècle Culture* (New York: Oxford University Press, 1986) 178-200. For additional comments on the images of children, see also Alfred Weidinger's *Oskar Kokoschka: Dreaming Boy and Enfant Terrible: Oskar Kokoschka at the Vienna School of Applied Arts,* exhibit catalogue (Stenersen Museum, Oslo and Amos Anderson Art Museum, Helsinki, 1997) 42ff.

88 Cesare Lombroso and William Ferrero, *The Female Offender* (Littleton, Colorado: Fred Rothman, 1980) 151.

89 Paul Adam, "Des enfants," *La Revue Blanche* IX (1895) 350-53.

90 On the negative image of youth in turn-of-the-century Vienna, see also Stefan Zweig's *The World of Yesterday* (Lincoln and London: University of Nebraska Press, 1964) 33: "The world about and above us, which directed all its thoughts only to the fetish of security, did not like youth; or rather it constantly mistrusted it. Proud of its systematic 'progress' and of its order, bourgeois society proclaimed moderation and leisure in all forms of life as the only virtues of man; all hasty efforts to advance ourselves were to be avoided [...] young people, who always instinctively desire rapid and radical changes, were therefore considered a doubtful element which was to be held down or kept inactive for as long as possible [...]. This distrust that every young man was 'not quite reliable' was felt at that time in all circles."

91 Lynne Pudles, "Solitude, Silence, and the Inner Life: A Study of Belgian Symbolist Artists," diss. University of California, Berkeley, 1987. 195.

92 Pudles, "The Symbolist Work of George Minne" 123.

93 *Beyond the Pleasure Principle*, [1920] trans. J. Stratchey (New York: Norton: 1961) 66.

94 In *George Minne* 37, Puyvelde made a slightly different point: "D'autres personages se jettent à genoux et ce qu'ils croient être la fatalité du destin leur enlève le courage de lever la tête. Ils s'abandonnent à une force qu'ils ne peuvent comprendre."

95 Puyvelde, *George Minne* 38.

96 Freud, *Introductory lectures on Psychoanalysis* 106.

97 "The Dissolution of the Oedipal Complex," *Pelican Freud Library Vol. 7: Sexuality*, 320. The same idea is reiterated in the *New Introductory Lectures on Psychoanalysis* [1933] trans. J. Strachey, New York: Norton, 1964, where Freud writes, 110: "After all, the anatomical distinction [between the sexes] must express itself in psychical consequences [...]. [Women] feel seriously wronged, often declare that they want to 'have something like it too', and fall victim to 'envy for the penis', which will have ineradicable traces on their development and the formation of their character [...]." "The wish to get the longed for penis eventually in spite of everything may contribute to the motives that drive a mature woman to analysis, and what she may reasonably expect from analysis—a capacity, for instance, to carry on an intellectual profession—may often be recognized as a sublimated modification of this repressed wish [111]."

98 Puyvelde, *George Minne* 37.

99 In his landmark study, *Symbolism* (Boulder, CO: Westview Press, 1979), Robert Goldwater, 212, 215, remarked: "Minne's figures are characteristically oblivious of anything but their own emotion; clasping to themselves their regretful emaciated bodies, they contemplate a world within."

100 See Pudles, "The Symbolist Work of George Minne" 126; Udo Kultermann, "The Fountain of Youth: The Folkwang Fountain by George Minne," *Konsthistorik Tidskrift* 46(1977)144; F.-C. Legrand, *Symbolism in Belgium* (Brussels: 1972) 157; and Robert Schmutzler, *Art Nouveau* (London: Thames and Hudson, 1978) 12.

101 *Introductory Lectures on Psychoanalysis* [1917] 427.

102 Havelock Ellis, "Auto-Eroticism, A Psychological Study," 1898, qtd. in Dijkstra 145.

103 Freud, *New Introductory Lectures on Psychoanalysis* 117.

104 See Jeffery Howe, "Mirror Symbolism in the Works of Fernand Khnopff," *Arts Magazine* 53 (September 1978) 112-118.

105 Freud, *Introductory Lectures on Psychoanalysis* 426-27.

106 Otto Weininger, *Sex and Character* (London: William Heinemann, 1906) 73.

107 Weininger, *Sex and Character* 73.

108 Mario Amayo, "Flesh and Filigree," *ArtNews* 68 (1969) 27.

109 August Strindberg, "De l'inferiorité de la femme," *La Revue Blanche* (January 1895) 14.

110 Goldwater, *Symbolism* 216.

111 See also Andreas Hünecke, George Minne—Der große Kniende: Die Entfaltung eines bildnerischen Themas," *Bildende Kunst* 28 (1980) 609, and Pudles, "The Symbolist Work of George Minne" 124.

112 Pudles, "The Symbolist Work of George Minne" 124.

113 See, for example, Andrea Vagianos, "The Sculpture of George Minne" 60; Udo Kultermann, "Der Bildhauer Georg Minne" 55; and Robert Hoozee and Monique Tahon-Vanroose, "George Minne en de kunst rond 1900," *George Minne en de kunst rond 1900* 175.

114 Alhadeff, *George Minne: Fin de Siècle Drawings and Sculpture* 156.

115 Freud, *Group Psychology and Analysis of the Ego*, trans. James Stratchey (New York: Norton, 1959) 11.

116 Freud, *Group Psychology and Analysis of the Ego* 1.

117 Peter Gay, *Freud For Historians* (Oxford; Oxford University Press, 1985) 159.

118 Freud, *Beyond the Pleasure Principle*, trans. James Stratchey (New York: Norton, 1989) 19.

119 Pudles, "The Symbolist Work of George Minne" 125.

120 Freud, "The Uncanny," *The Pelican Freud Library, Vol 14: Art and Literature* (London: Penguin, 1988) 356.

121 Freud, *Group Psychology and the Analysis of the Ego* 34.

122 Pudles, "The Symbolist Work of George Minne" 124.

123 Paul Haesaerts, *Laethem-Saint-Martin: Le village élu de l'art Flamand* 88.

124 Eeckhout, "La Mère, dans la vie et l'oeuvre de George Minne" 507.

125 See Udo Kultermann, "Der Bildhauer Georg Minne," *Das Kunstwerk* 9 (1955-56) 54.

126 Pierre Baudson, "Introduction," *Constantin Meunier/George Minne: Dessins et sculptures*, n. pag.

127 In a letter of October 15, 1897, Freud wrote to his friend Wilhelm Fliess: "A single idea of general value dawned on me. I have found, in my own case too, being in love with my mother and jealous of my father, and I now consider it a universal event of early childhood [...]. If this is so, we can understand the gripping power of Oedipus Rex [...] the Greek legend seizes upon a compulsion which everyone recognizes because he senses its existence within himself. Everyone in the audience was once a budding Oedipus in fantasy and recoils in horror from the dream fulfillment here transplanted into reality." Jeffrey Moussaieff Masson, *The Complete Letters of Sigmund Freud to Wilhelm Fliess, 1887-1904* (Cambridge: Harvard University Press, 1985) 272.

128 If a child loves one parent and hates the other, Freud writes, this state "is confirmed by a legend that has come down to us from classical antiquity: a legend whose profound and universal power can only be understood if the hypothesis I have put forward in regard to the psychology of children has an equally universal validity. What I have in mind is the legend of King Oedipus [...]. His destiny moves us only because it might have been ours [...]. It is the fate of all of us, perhaps, to direct our first sexual impulse towards our mother and our first hatred and our first murderous wish against our father." *The Interpretation of Dreams* [1900], trans. James Strachey, (New York: Avon Books, 1965) 296, 298.

129 Freud, *The Interpretation of Dreams* [1900] 296.

130 Freud, *Beyond the Pleasure Principle* 15.

131 Freud, *Beyond the Pleasure Principle* 17.

132 Puyvelde, *George Minne* 63.

133 W. R. D. Fairbairn, *Psychoanalytic Studies of the Personality* (London: Tavistock and Routledge and Kegan Paul, 1952) 55-56.

134 Freud, *New Introductory Lectures on Psychoanalysis* 148.

135 Puyvelde, *George Minne* 40.

136 Eric Rowan and Carolyn Stewart, "Belgian Artists Exiled in Wales: A Unique Opportunity Missed?" *An Elusive Tradition: Art and Society in Wales* (Cardiff: University of Wales Press, 2002) 109.

137 Puyvelde, *George Minne* 61.

138 Haesaerts, *George Minne et le repliement sur soi-même* 7.

139 Haesaerts, *Laethem-Saint-Martin: Le village élu de l'art Flamand* 113-14.

140 Freud, *Introductory Lectures on Psychoanalysis* 284-85.

141 Dijkstra 146.

142 Dijkstra 146.

143 Alhadeff, *George Minne: Fin de Siècle Drawings and Sculpture* 148.

144 See Andreas Hünecke, "George Minne—Der große Kniende: Die Entfaltung eines bildnerischen Themas," *Bildende Kunst* 28 (1980) 609.

145 Ludwig Wittgenstein, *Philosophical Investigations*, trans. G. E. M. Anscombe (New York: Macmillan, 1958) 145.

146 G. F. Drinka, *The Birth of Neurosis: Myth, Malady, and the Victorians* (New York: Simon and Schuster, 1984) 40.

147 Freud, *The Psychopathology of Everyday Life* [1901], trans. A. Tyson (New York: Norton, 1960) 146.

148 J. Allan Hobson, *The Dreaming Brain* (New York: Basic Books, 1988) 53, 62.

149 Emile Durkheim, *The Rules of Sociological Method* (Glencoe, IL: Free Press, 1962).

150 Gay, *Freud For Historians* 147-48.

151 Le Roy, 1920, qtd. in *George Minne en de kunst rond 1900* 53.

152 See also Marian Bisanz-Prakken, "Khnopff, Toorop, Minne und die Wiener 'Moderne,'" *Sehnsucht nach Glück/Wiens Aufbruch in die Moderne: Klimt, Kokoschka, Schiele*, ed. Sabine Schulze (Vienna: Verlag gerd Hatje, 1995) 172-78.

153 William McGrath, *Dionysian Art and Populist Politics in Austria* (New Haven: Yale University Press, 1974) 7.

154 Carl Schorske, *Fin-de-Siècle Vienna: Politics and Culture* (New York: Alfred A. Knopf, 1985) 9.

155 Schorske, *Fin-de-Siècle Vienna* xxiii.

156 Schorske, *Fin-de-Siècle Vienna* xxiv.

157 In 1920, for example, Grégoire Le Roy exclaimed: "Il faut vraiment être initié aux incompréhensions officielles pour s'expliquer qu'un artiste d'une si haute valeur, dont nombres de musées étrangers exposent les oeuvres, dont un notament lui a consacré une sale entière. ait pu être méconnu aussi longtemps et aussi gravement par son pays." Grégoire Le Roy, "George Minne," *Bulletin et catalogue des expositions* (Brussels: Galerie Georges Giroux, 1920) 1; see also Olaf Peters, "George Minne," *New Worlds: German and Austrian Art, 1809-1940,* ed. Renée Price (New York: Neue Galerie, 2001) 32-37.

Works in the Exhibition

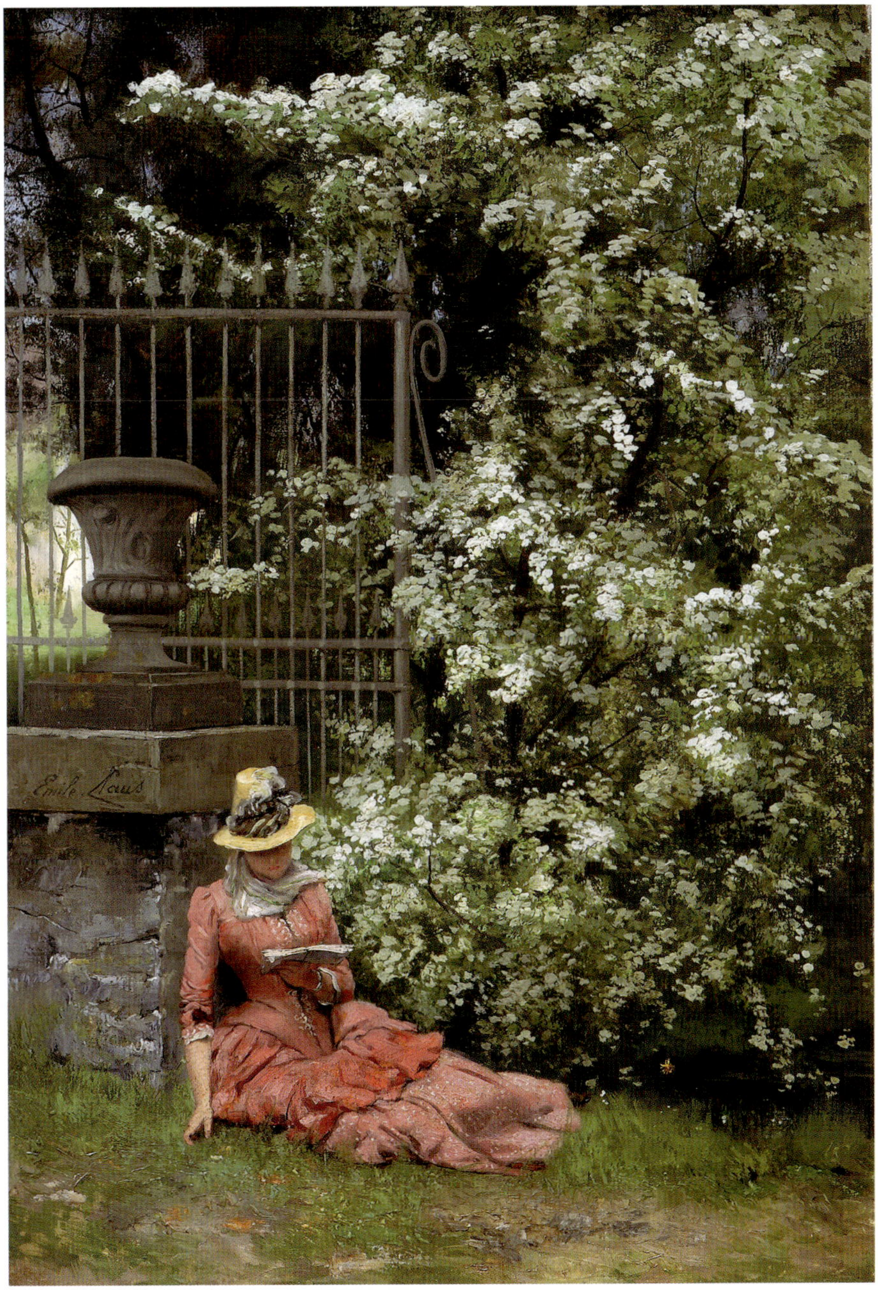

1. Emile Claus (1849-1924)
Woman Reading, c.1890
Oil on canvas, mounted on panel, 70.8 x 47.4 cm

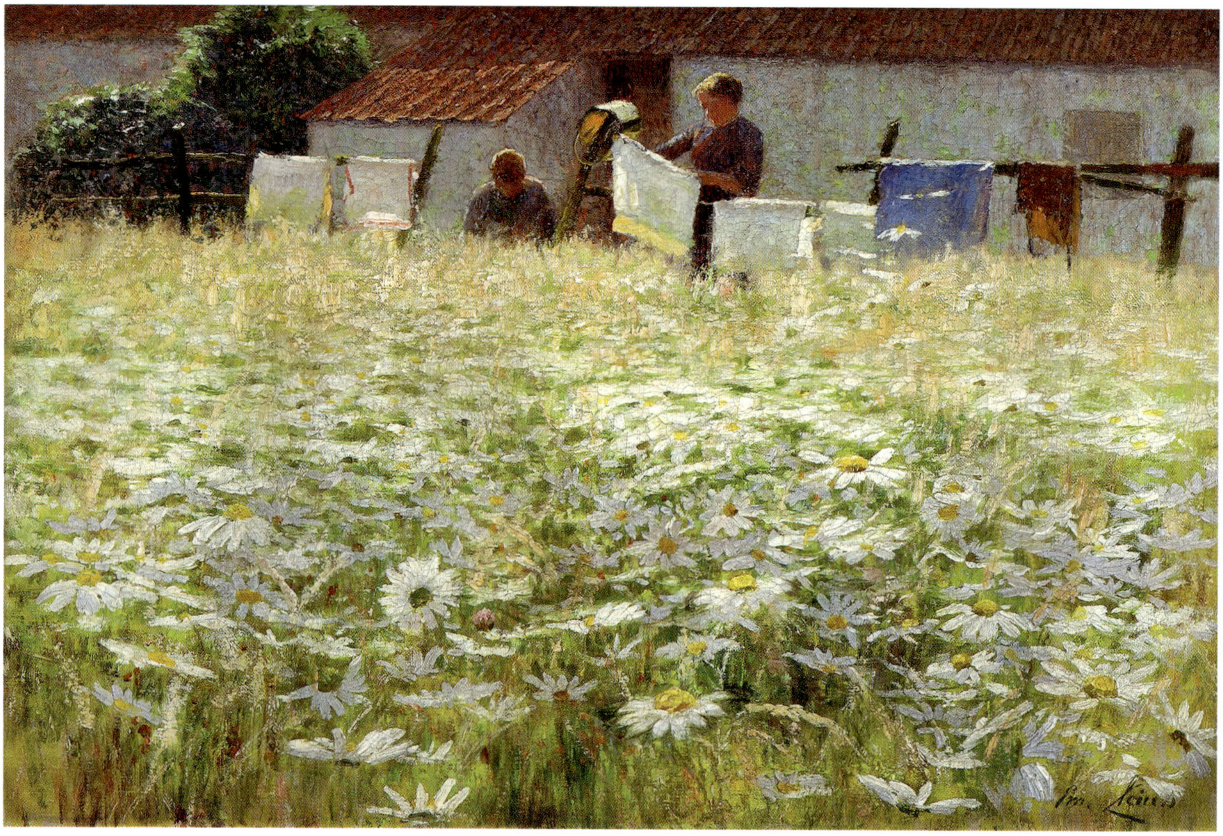

2. Emile Claus (1849-1924)
Daisies, 1897
Oil on canvas, 50.5 x 73.5 cm

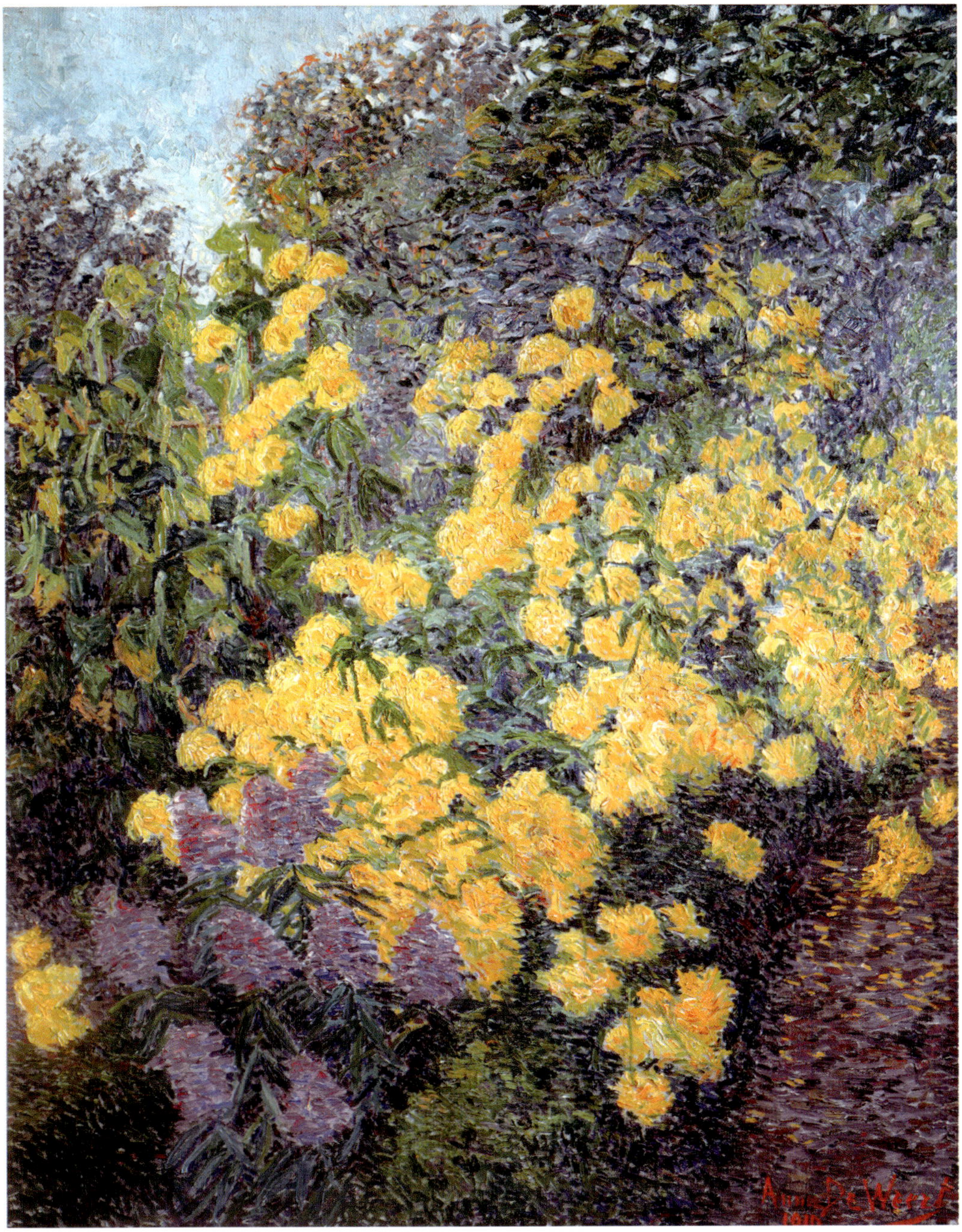

3. Anna de Weert (1867-1950)
Garden in Bloom, 1910
Oil on canvas, 114 x 89 cm

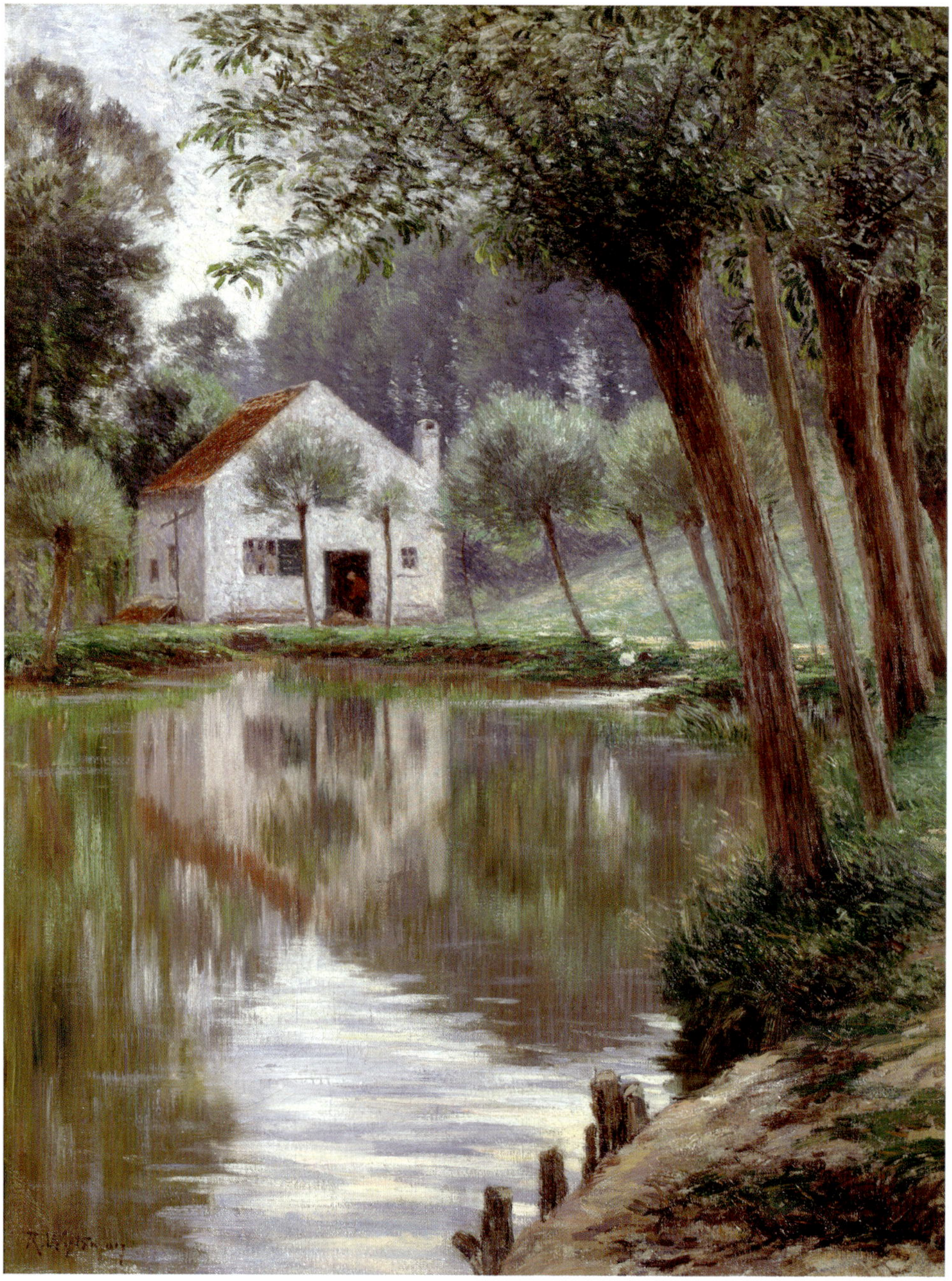

4. Rodolphe Wytsman (1860-1927)
Pond at Linkebeek, 1894
Oil on canvas, 81 x 60.5 cm

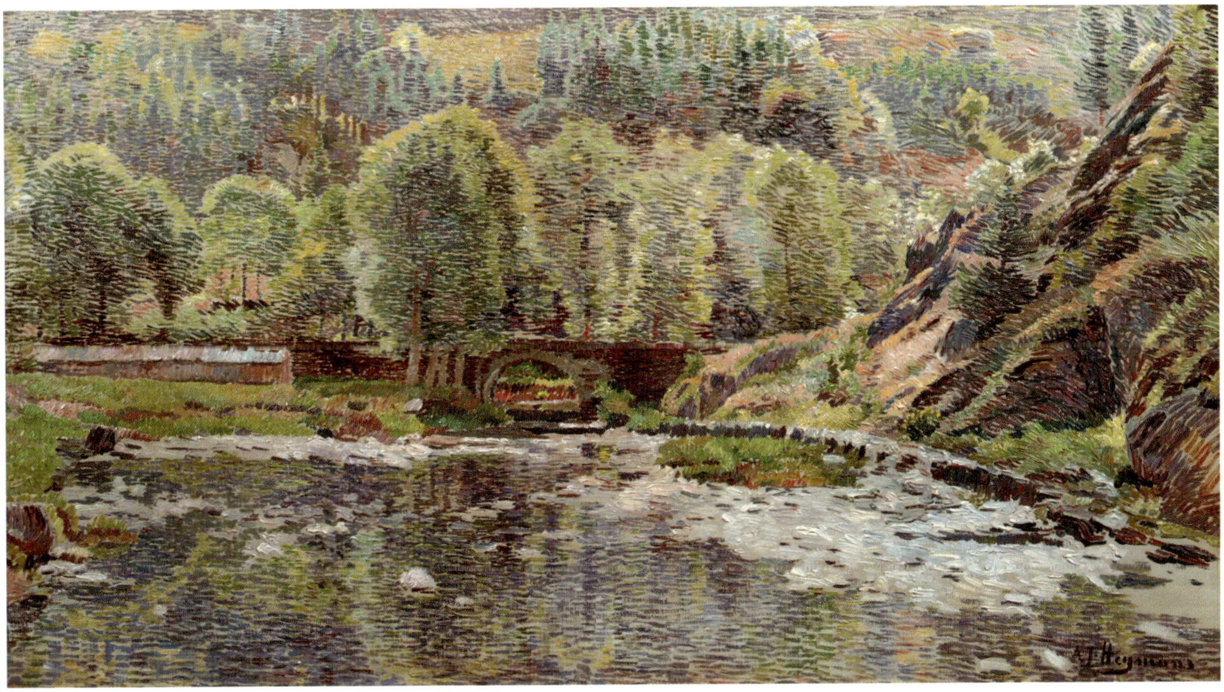

5. Adrien-Joseph Heymans (1839-1921)
The Bridge in the Valley, n.d.
Oil on canvas, 52 x 92 cm

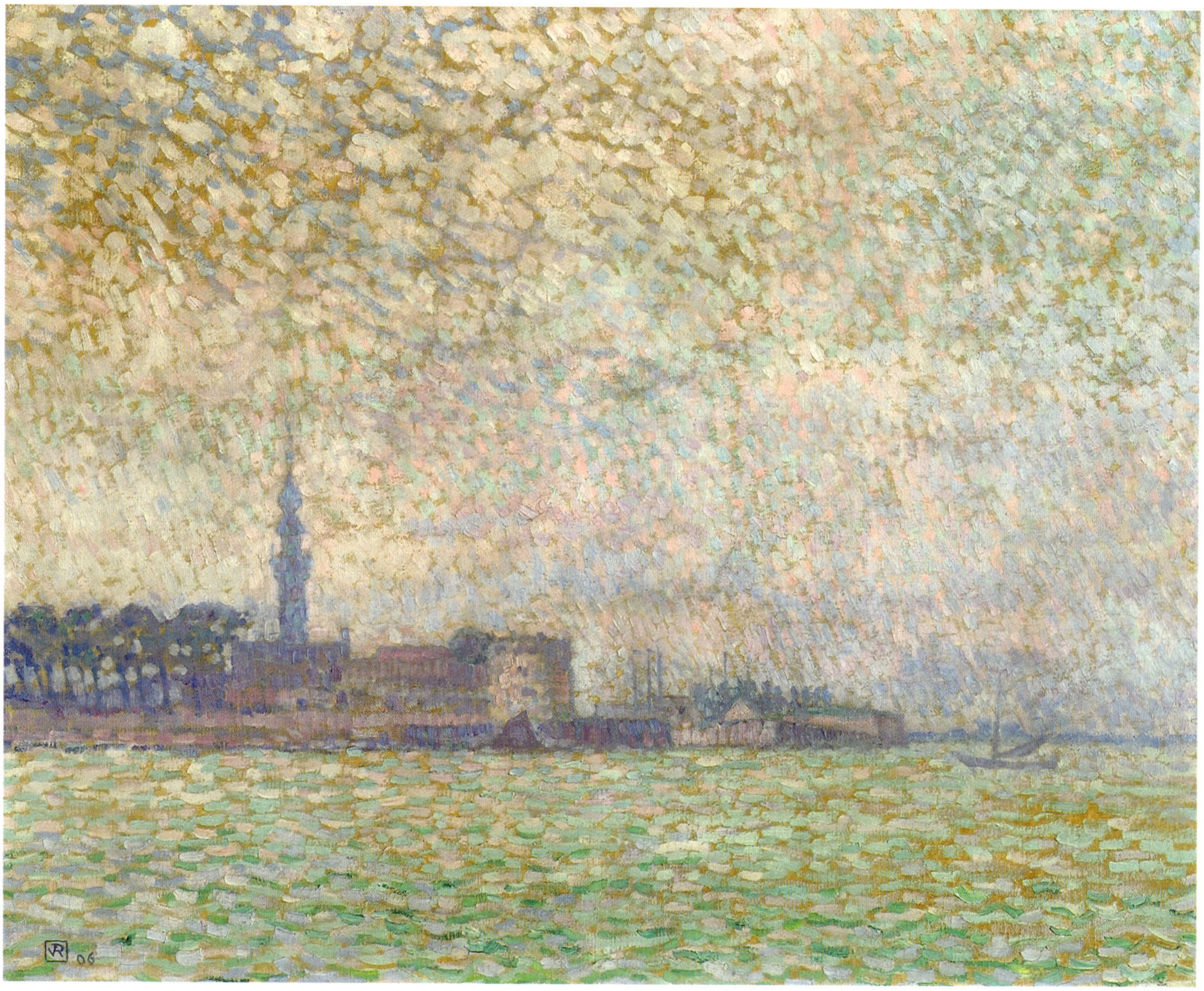

6. Théo van Rysselberghe (1861-1926)
Veere in the Morning Mist, 1906
Oil on canvas, 60.5 x 73 cm

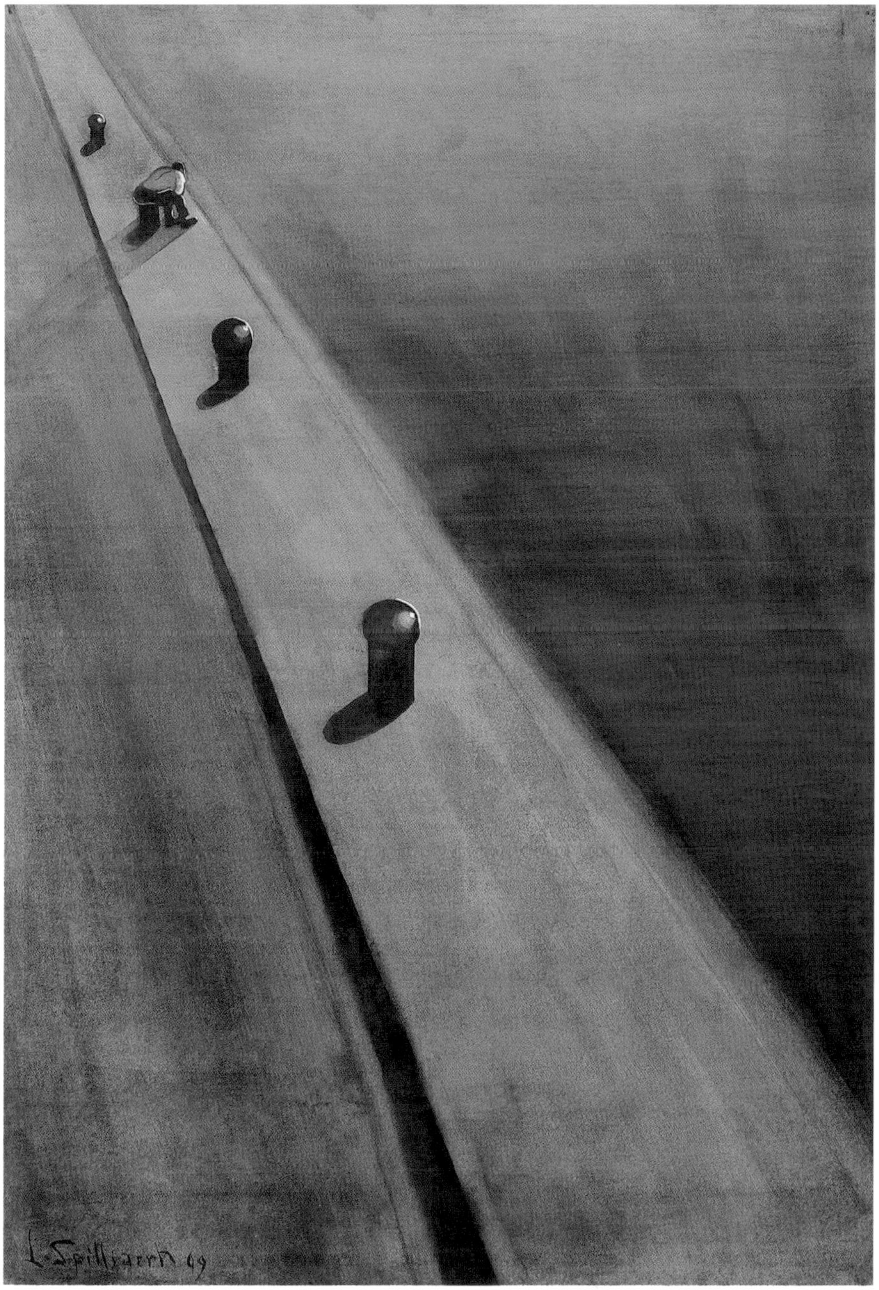

7. Léon Spilliaert (1881-1946)
Wharf with Fisherman Seated on a Mooring Post, 1909
India ink wash and brush, pastel, crayon and gouache on paper,
68.6 x 46.1 cm

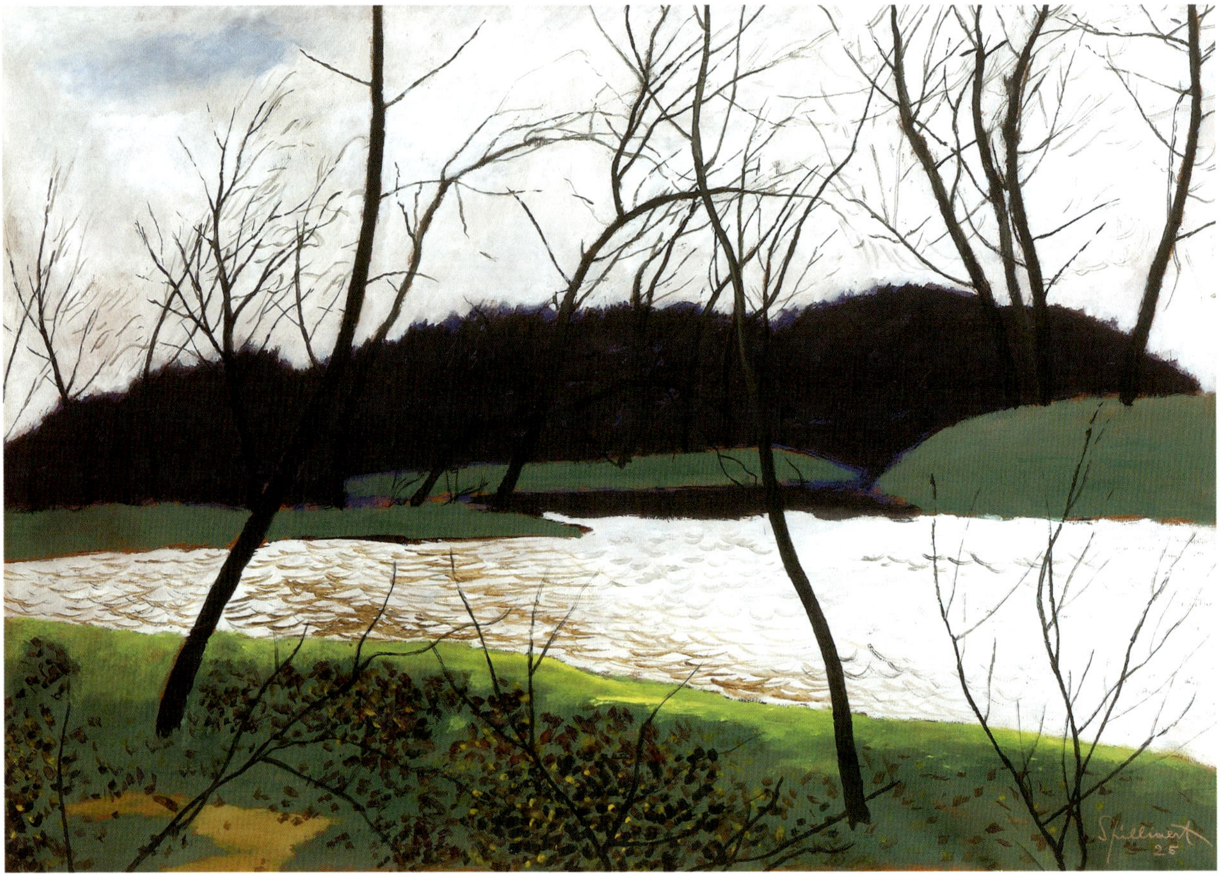

8. Léon Spilliaert (1881-1946)
Park in Autumn, 1925
Gouache on paper, 56 x 77 cm

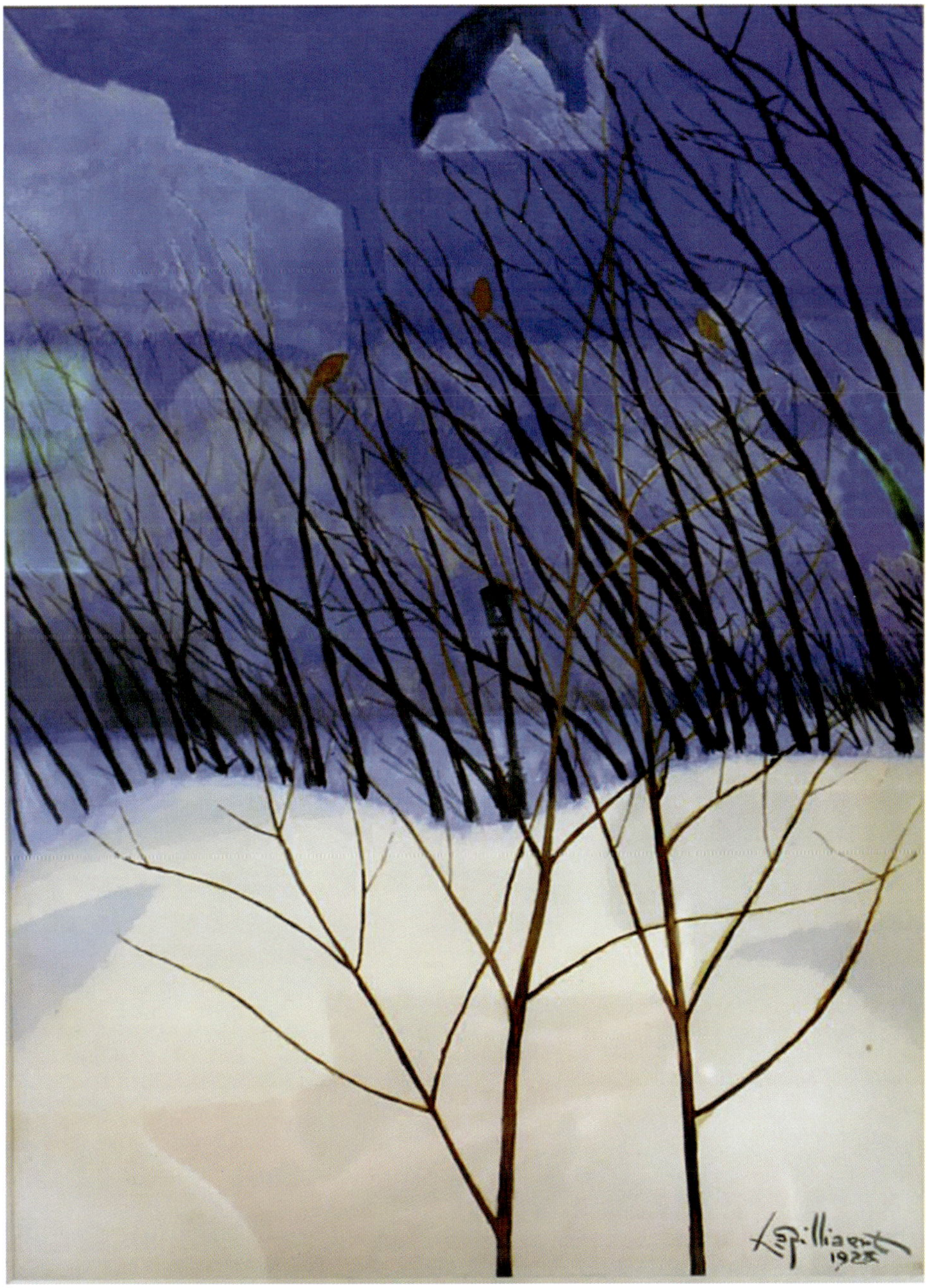

9. Léon Spilliaert (1881-1946)
Dream Landscape in the Snow, 1928
Watercolor and gouache on paper, 74 x 53 cm

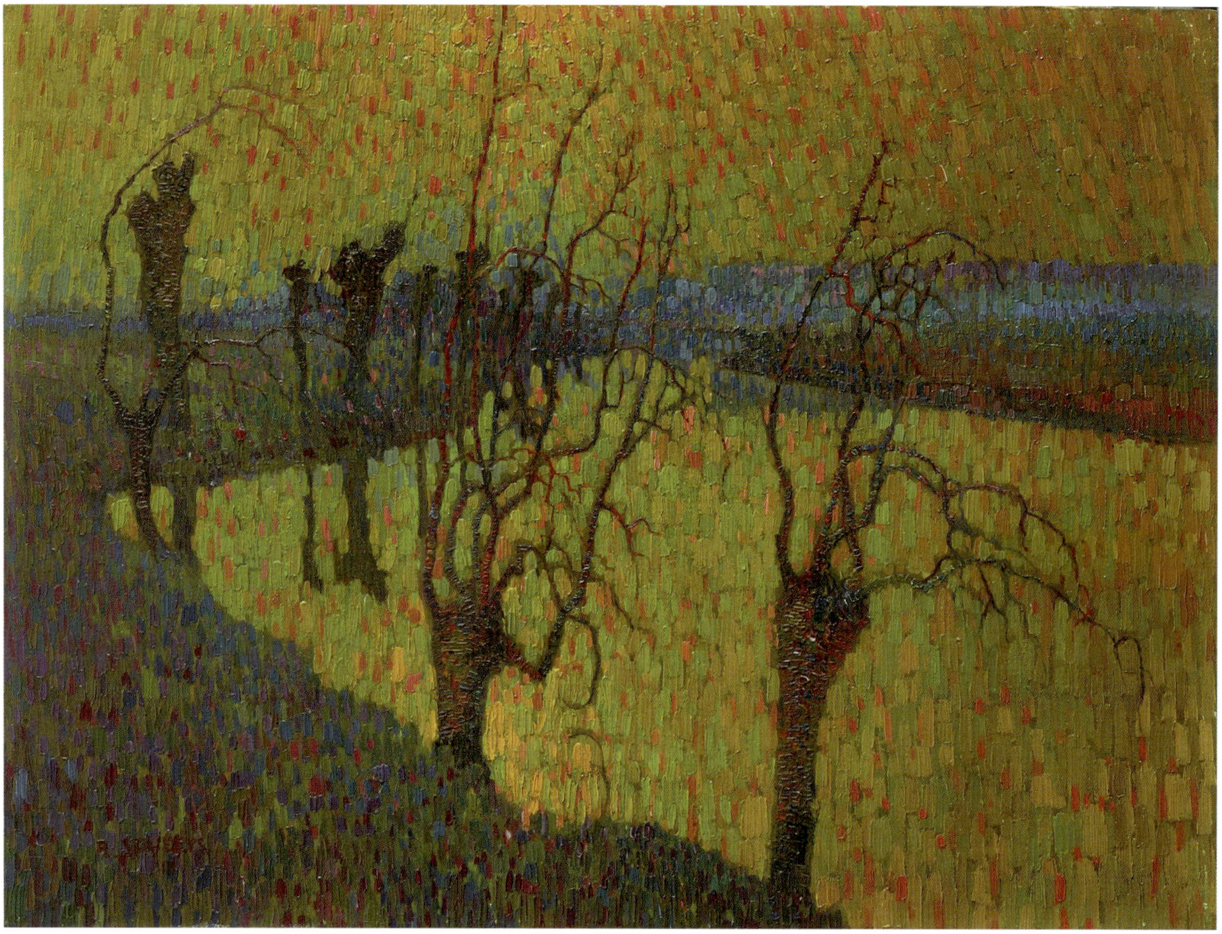

10. Albert Saverys (1886-1964)
The River Lys, 1918
Oil on canvas, 51.5 x 66.5 cm

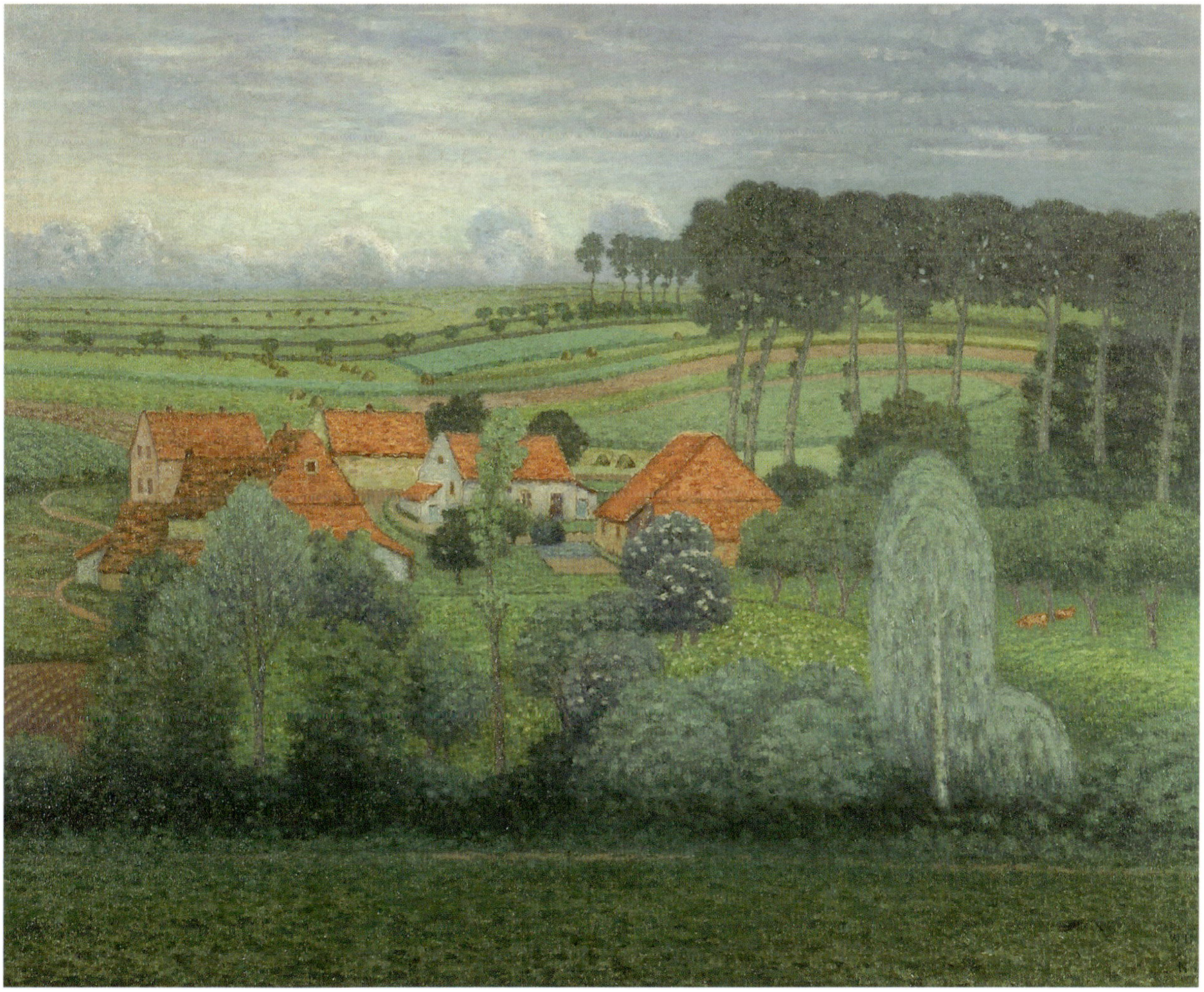

11. William Degouve de Nuncques (1867-1935)
Le Caillou-qui-Bique, 1909
Oil on canvas, 99 x 118 cm

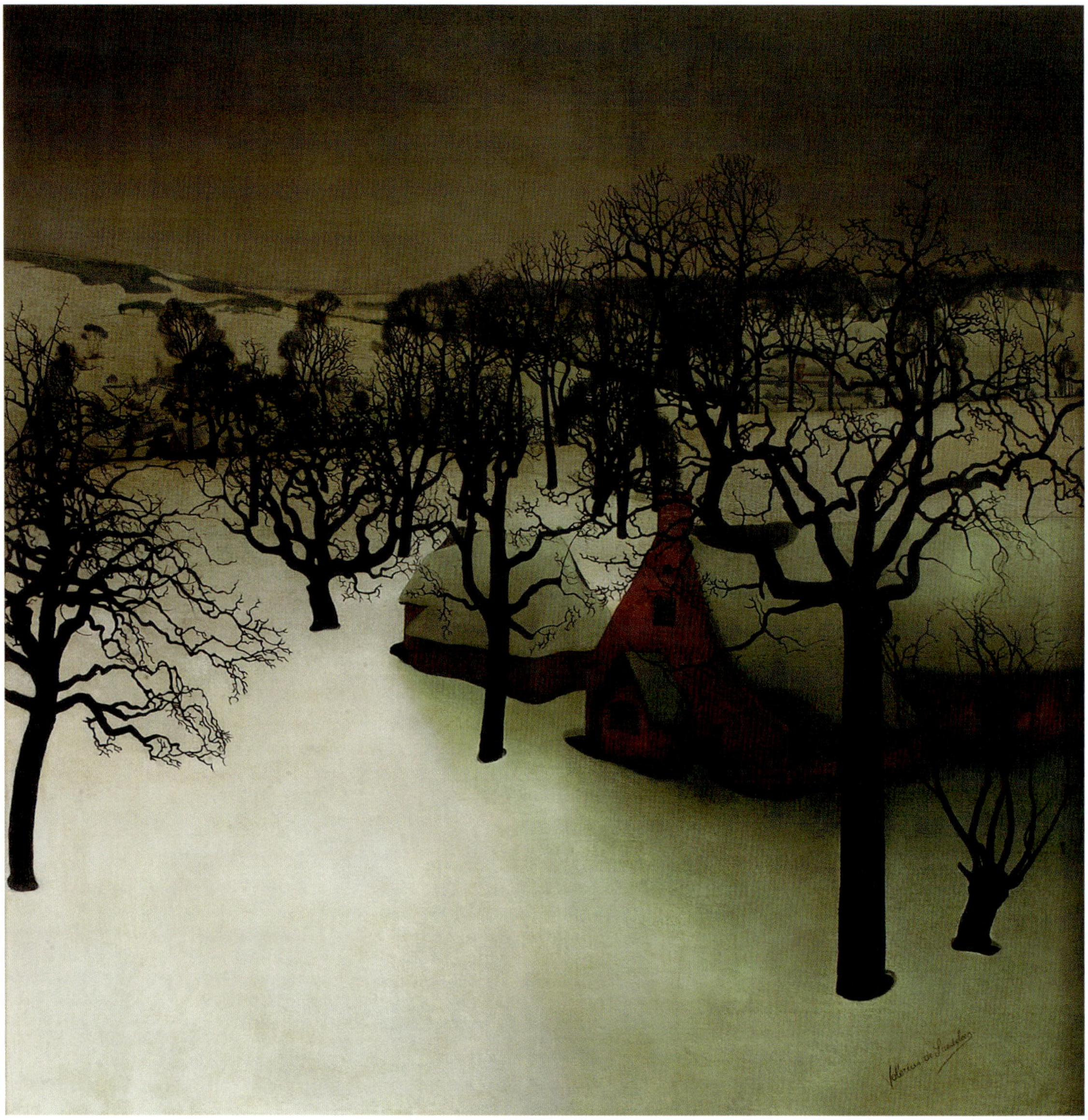

12. Valerius de Saedeleer (1876-1946)
Old Orchard in Winter, 1925
Oil on canvas, mounted on panel, 132 x 127 cm

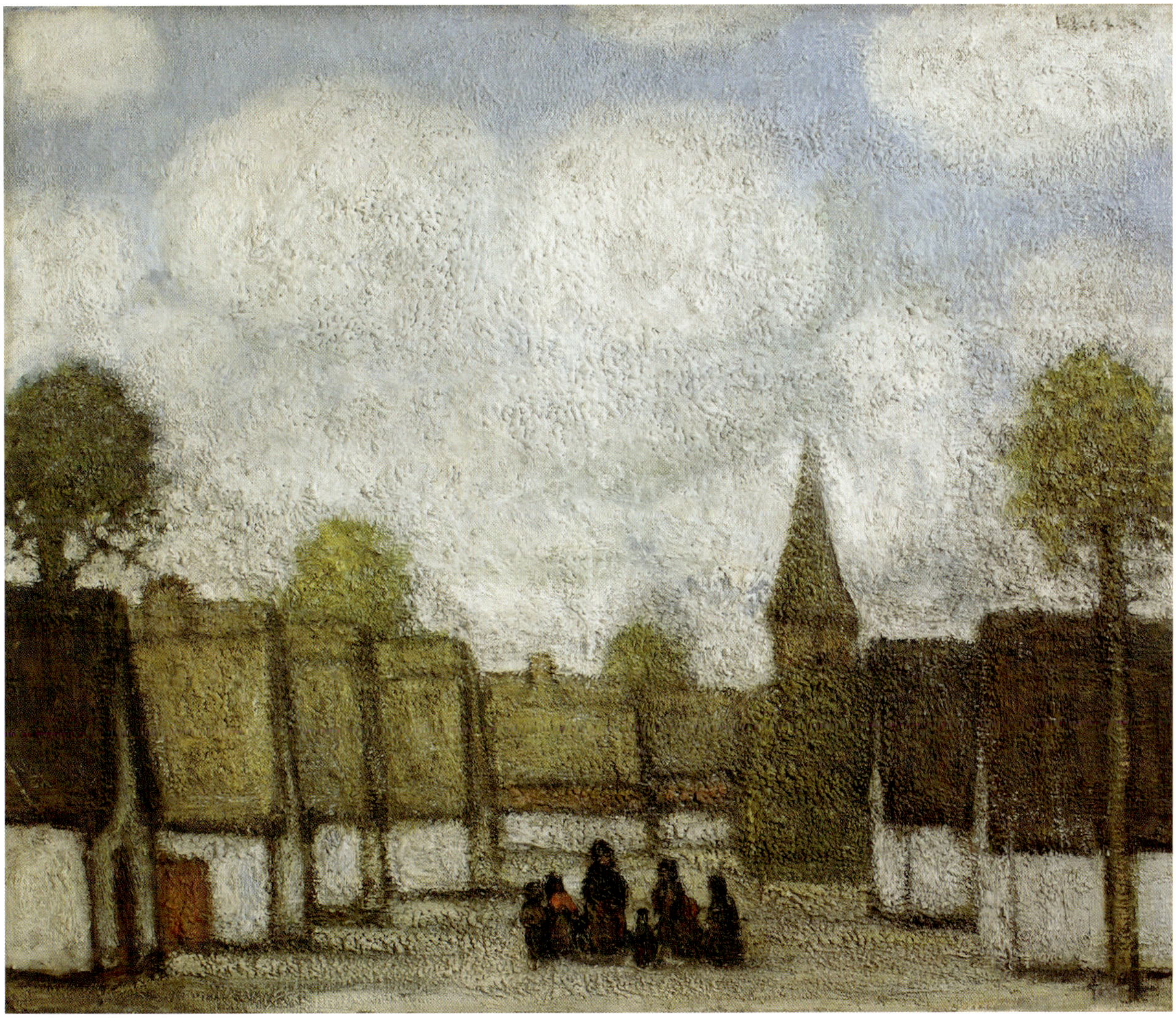

13. Jakob Smits (1855-1928)
The Village, 1903
Oil on canvas, 121 x 142 cm

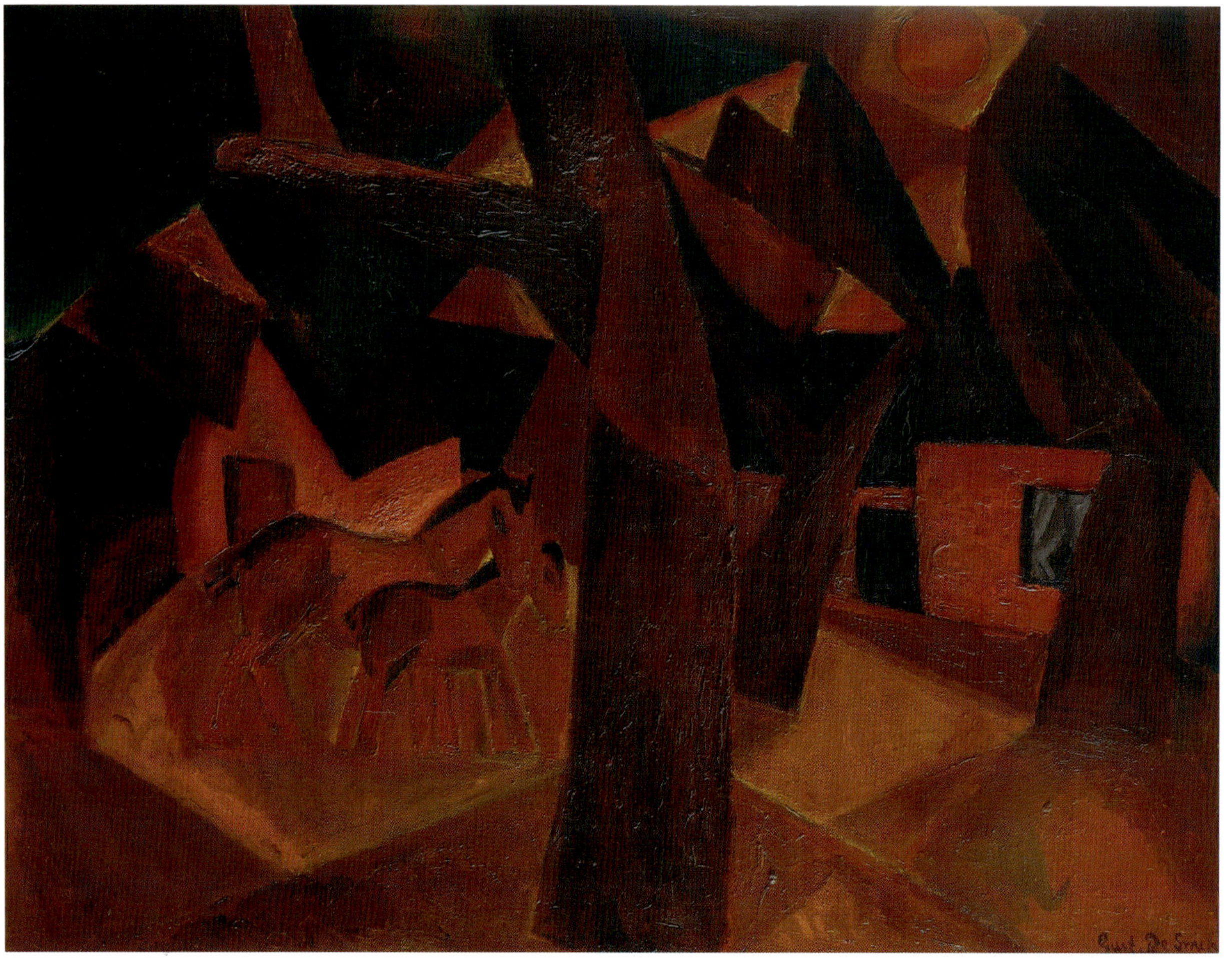

14. Gustave de Smet (1877-1943)
Horses in an Orchard, 1920
Oil on canvas, 80 x 100 cm

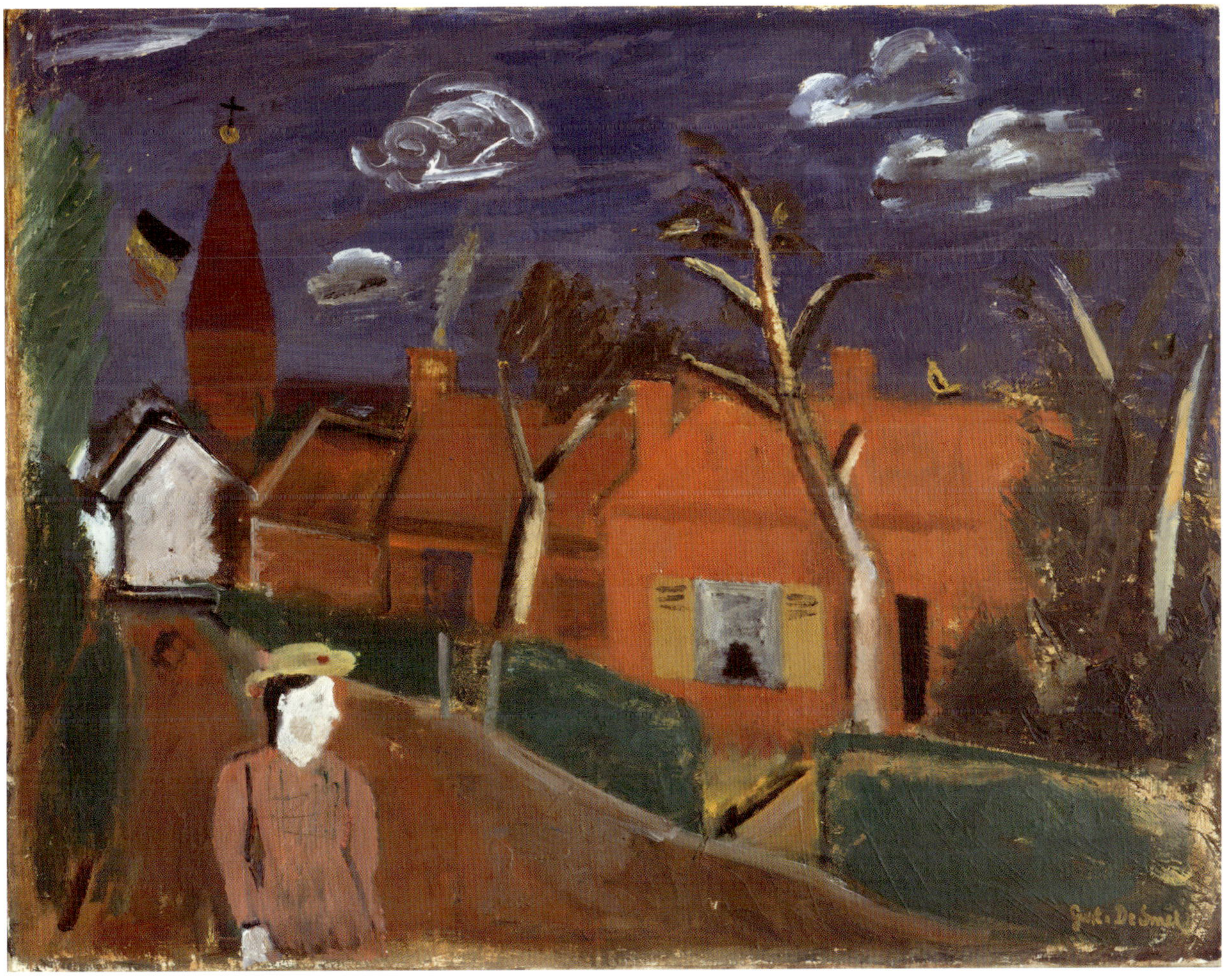

15. Gustave de Smet (1877-1943)
View at Laethem-Saint-Martin, 1936
Oil on canvas, 82 x 100 cm

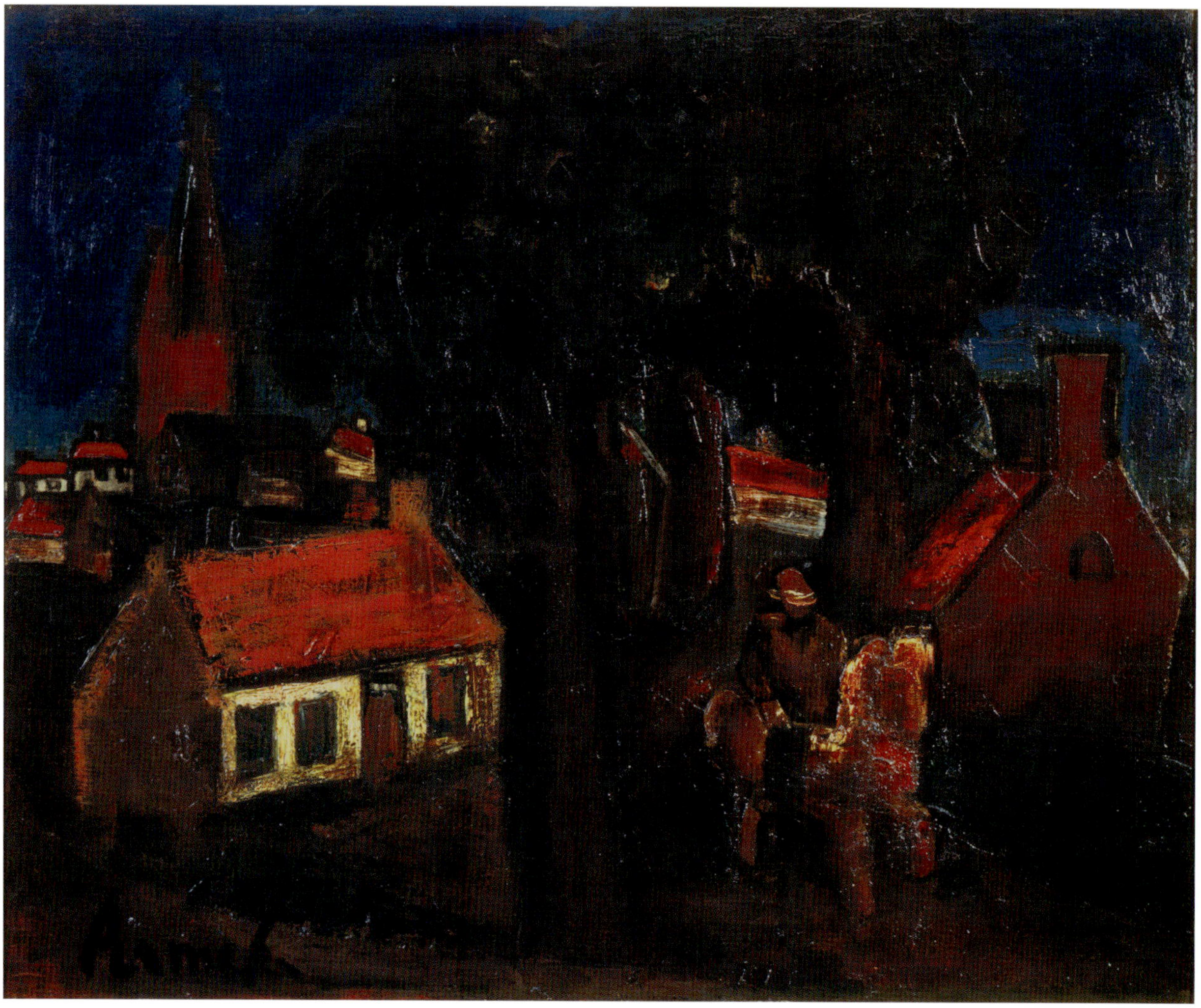

16. Constant Permeke (1886-1952)
The Village Rider, 1936
Oil on canvas, 100 x 120 cm

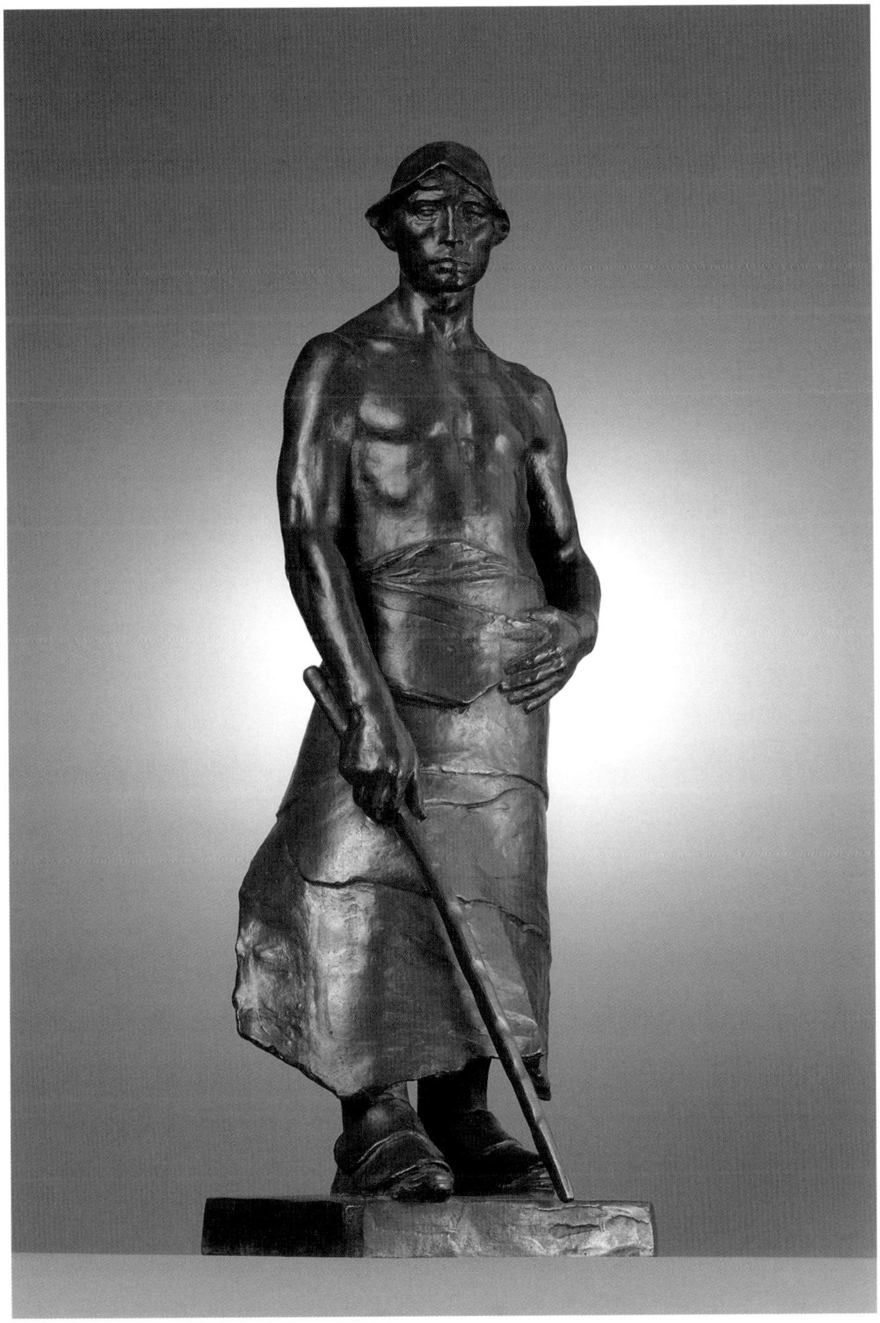

17. Constantin Meunier (1831-1905)
The Rolling Mill Worker, 1900
Bronze, 68.5 x 28 x 22.5 cm

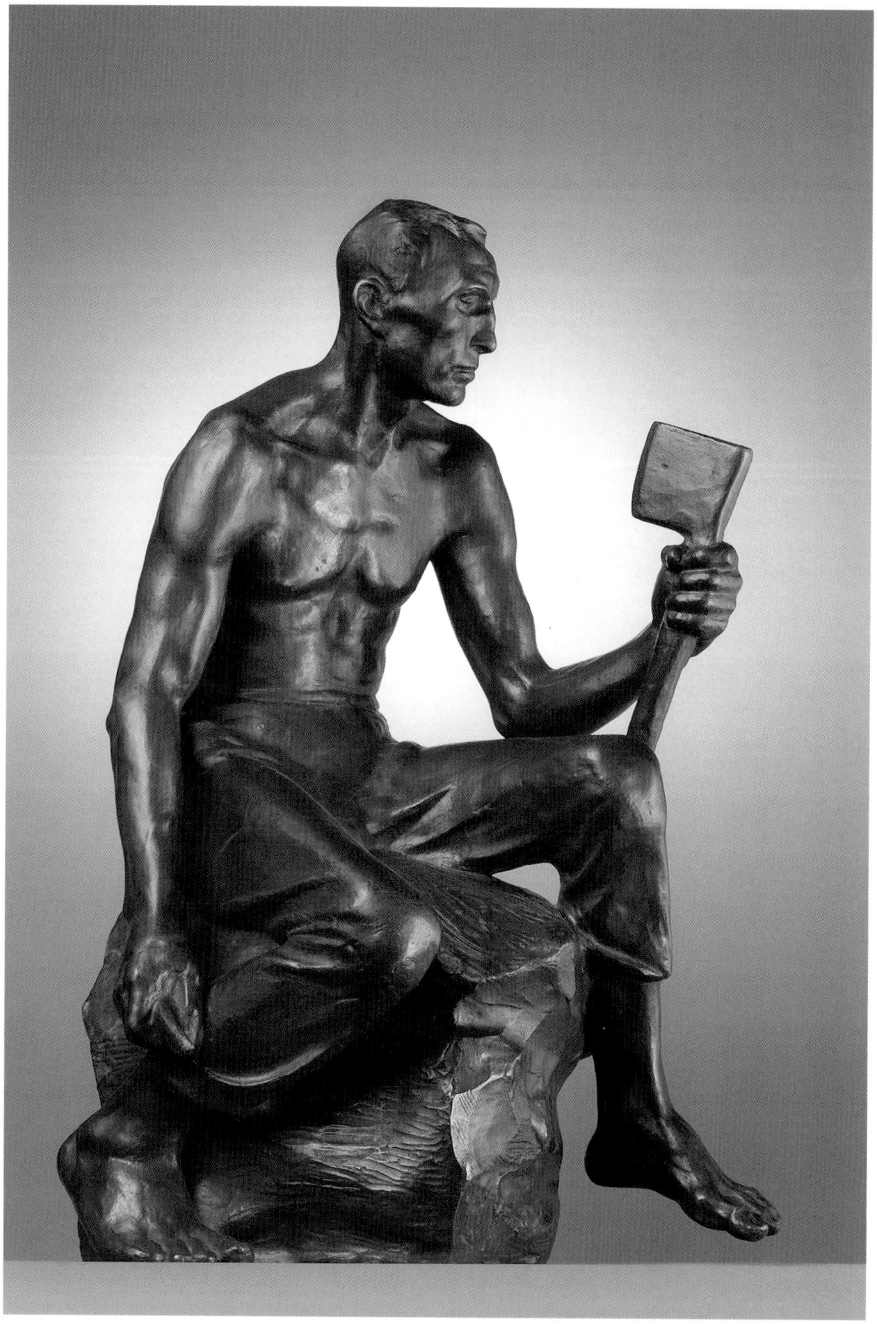

18. Constantin Meunier (1831-1905)
The *Woodcutter*, 1898
Bronze, 51.6 x 28 x 29 cm

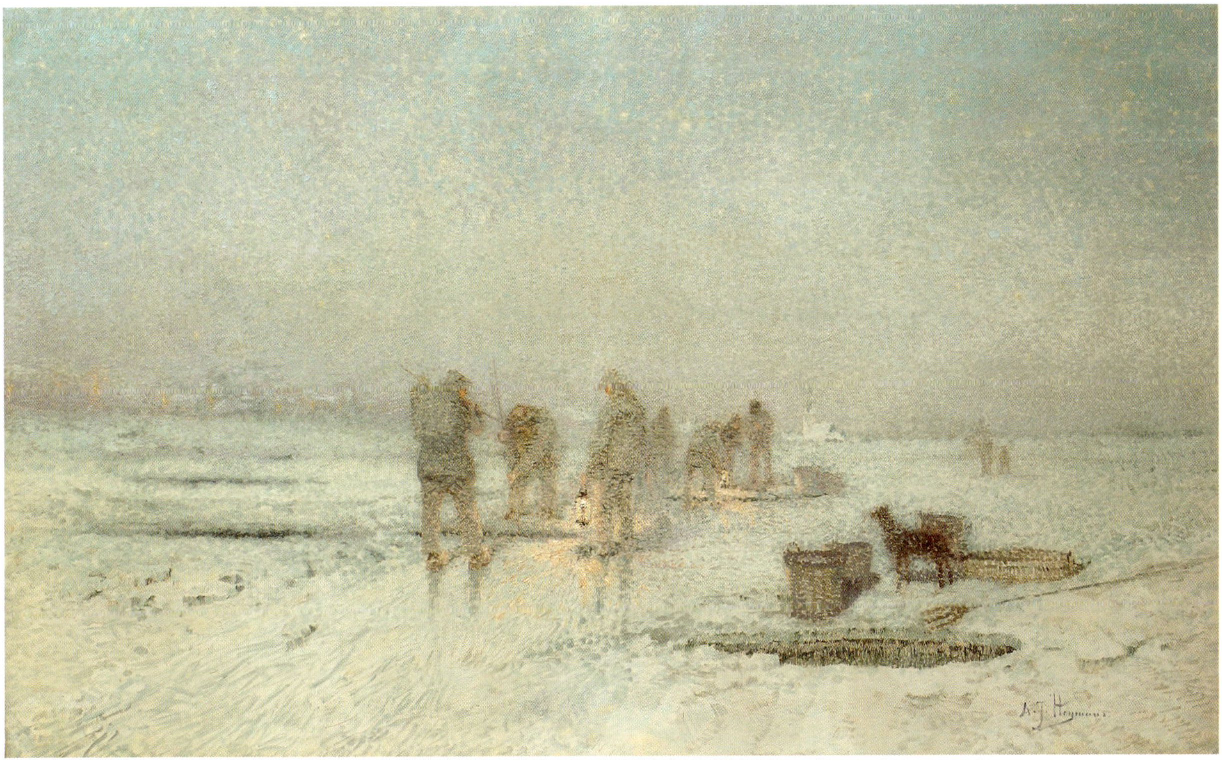

19. Adrien-Joseph Heymans (1839-1921)
The Eel Catchers, c. 1893
Oil on canvas, 105 x 166 cm

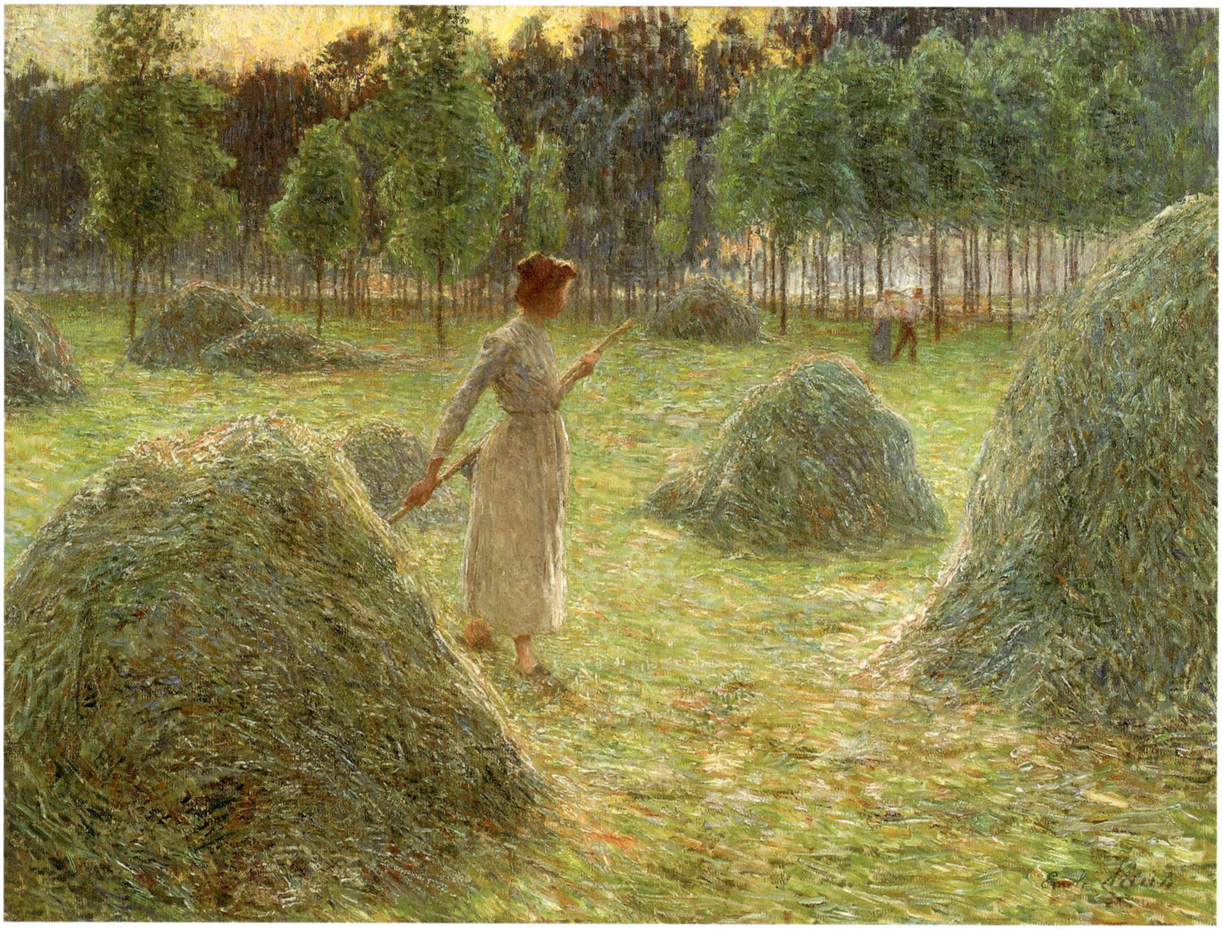

20. Emile Claus (1849-1924)
The Mower, 1905
Oil on canvas, 90.5 x 117.5 cm

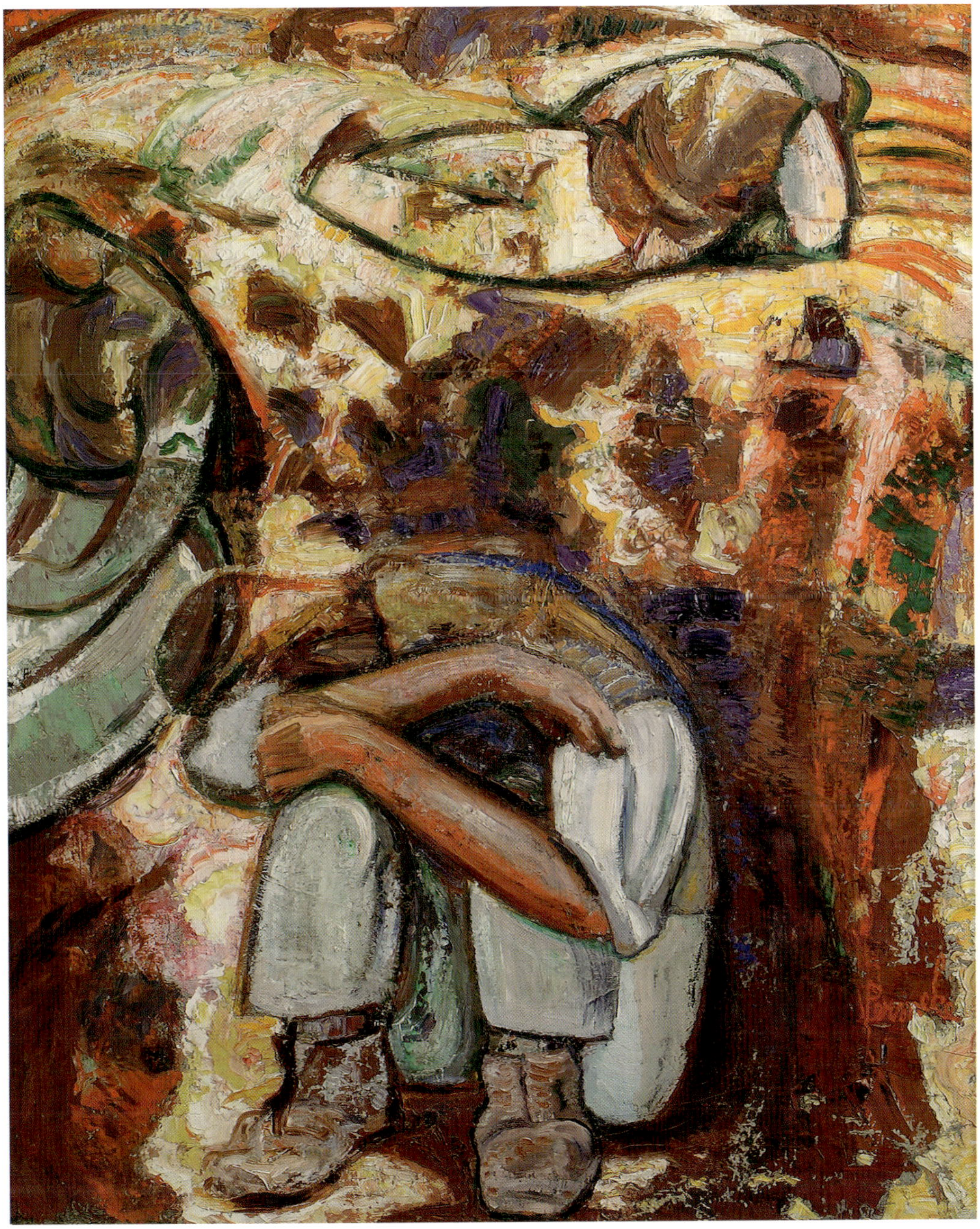

21. Constant Permeke (1886-1952)
Harvesters Sleeping in the Sun, 1917
Oil on canvas, 128 x 102 cm

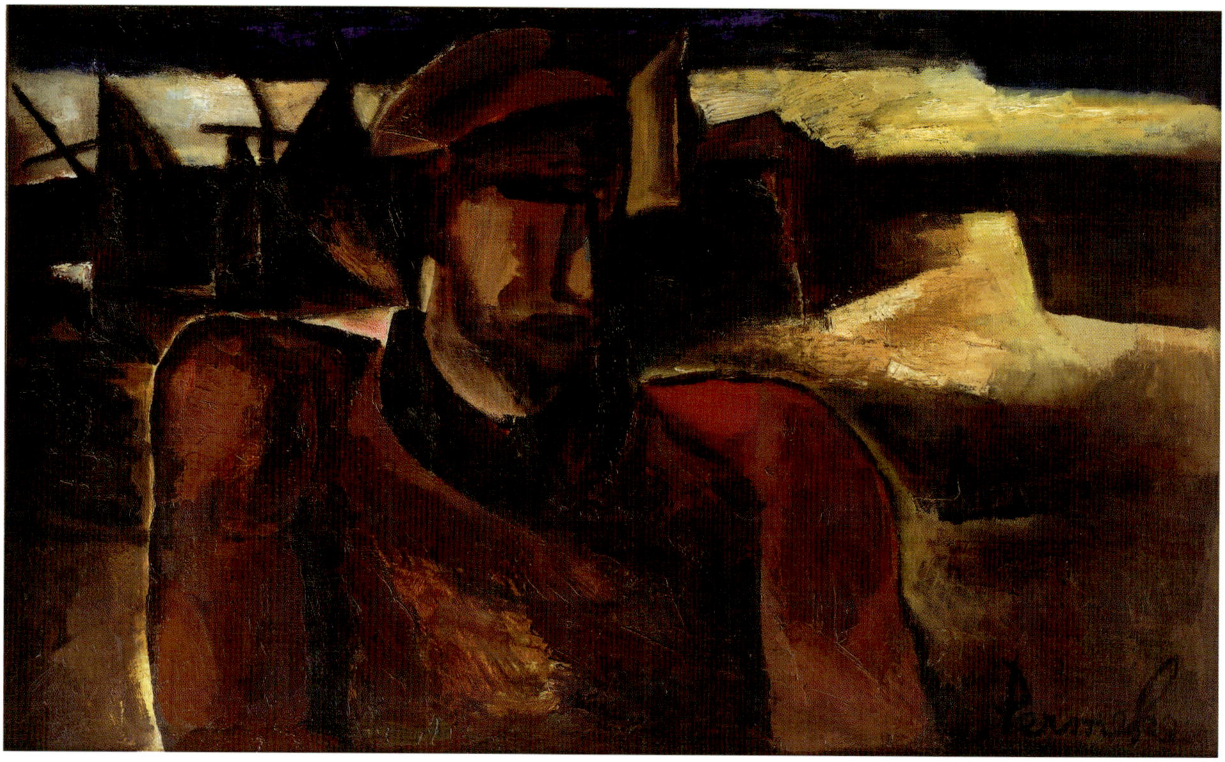

22. Constant Permeke (1886-1952)
Fisherman in Ostend, 1923
Oil on canvas, 82 x 129 cm

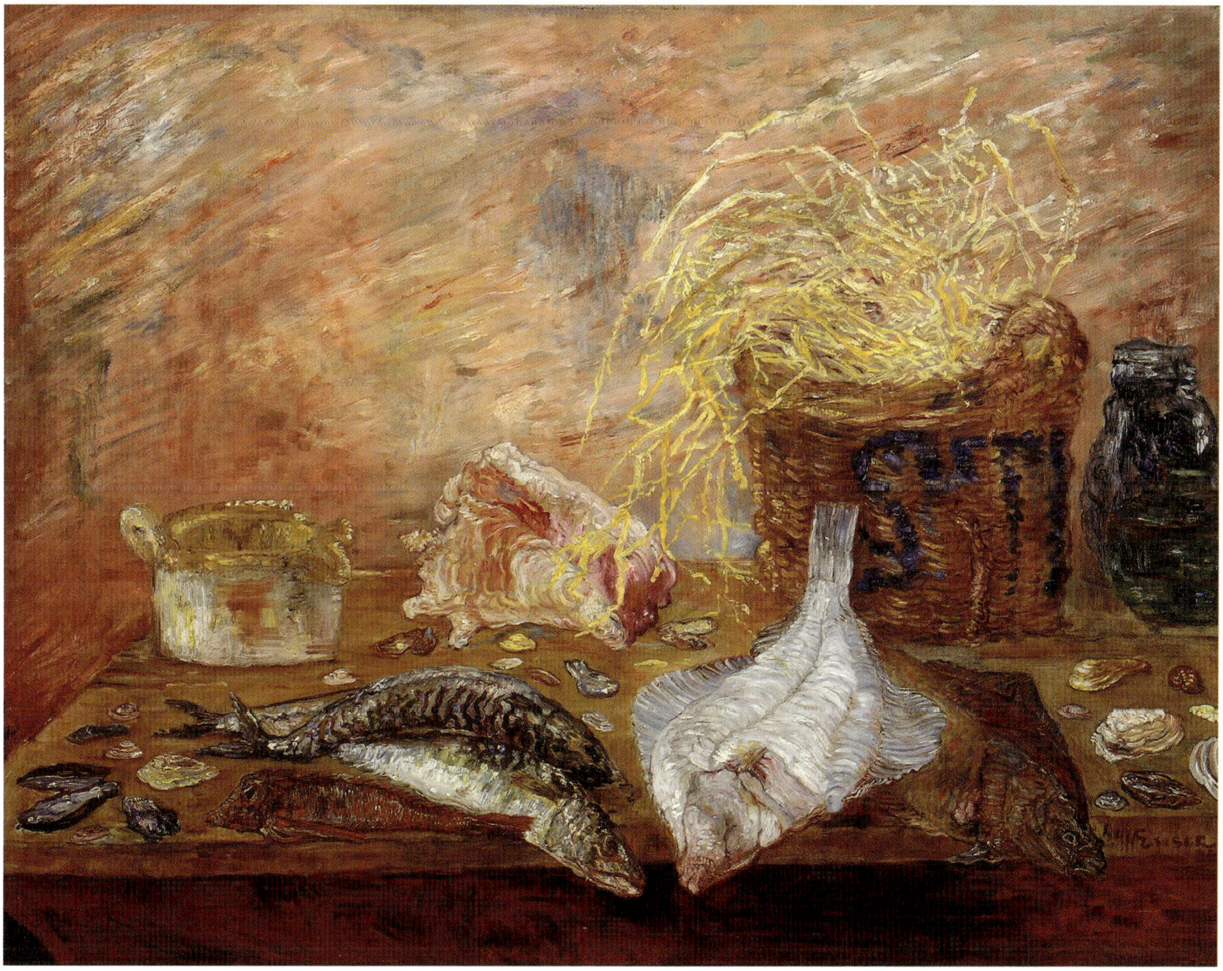

23. James Ensor (1860-1949)
Still life with Fish and Shellfish, 1895
Oil on canvas, 80 x 100 cm

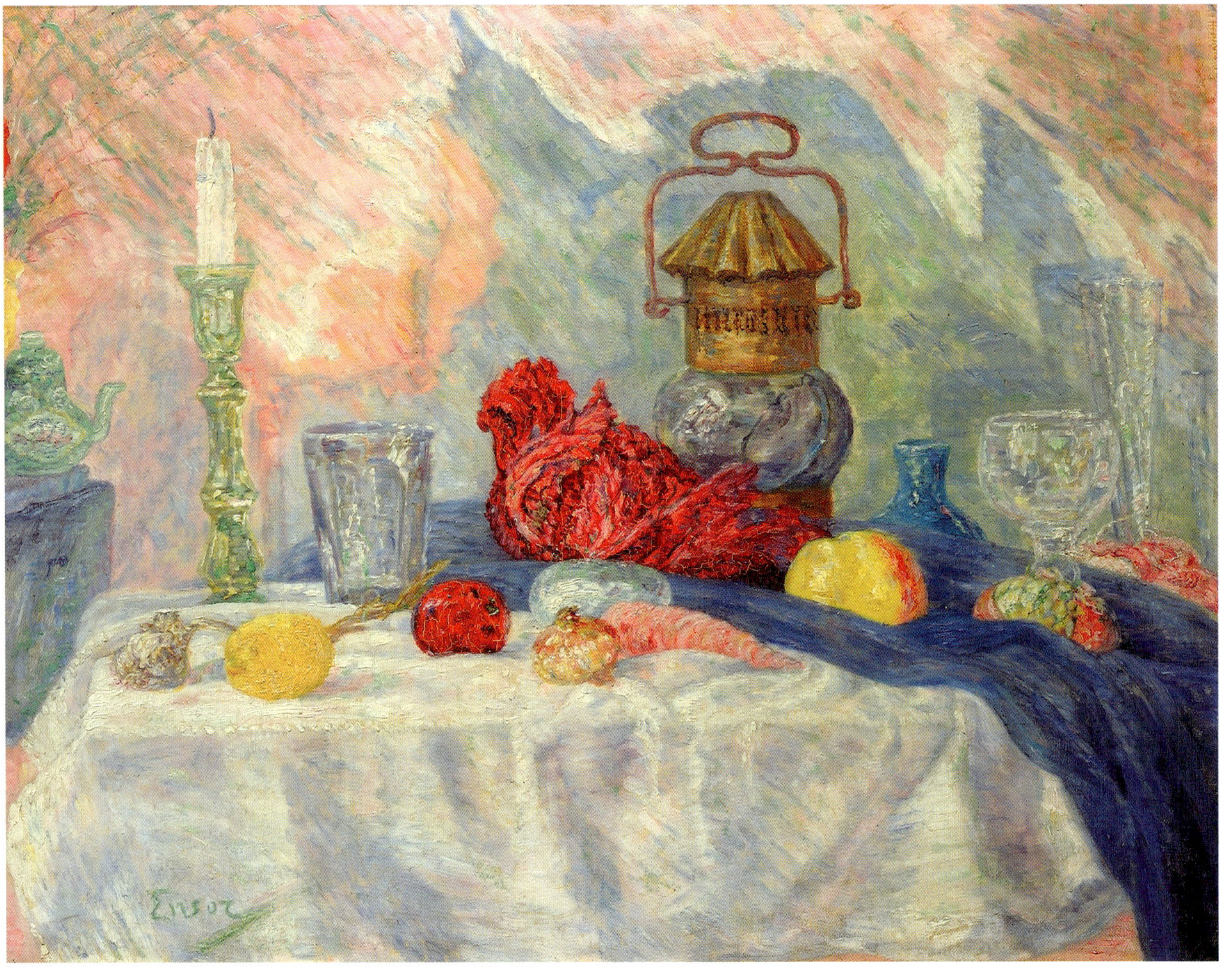

24. James Ensor (1860-1949)
Still life with Vegetables and Lamp, 1908
Oil on canvas, 55 x 65 cm

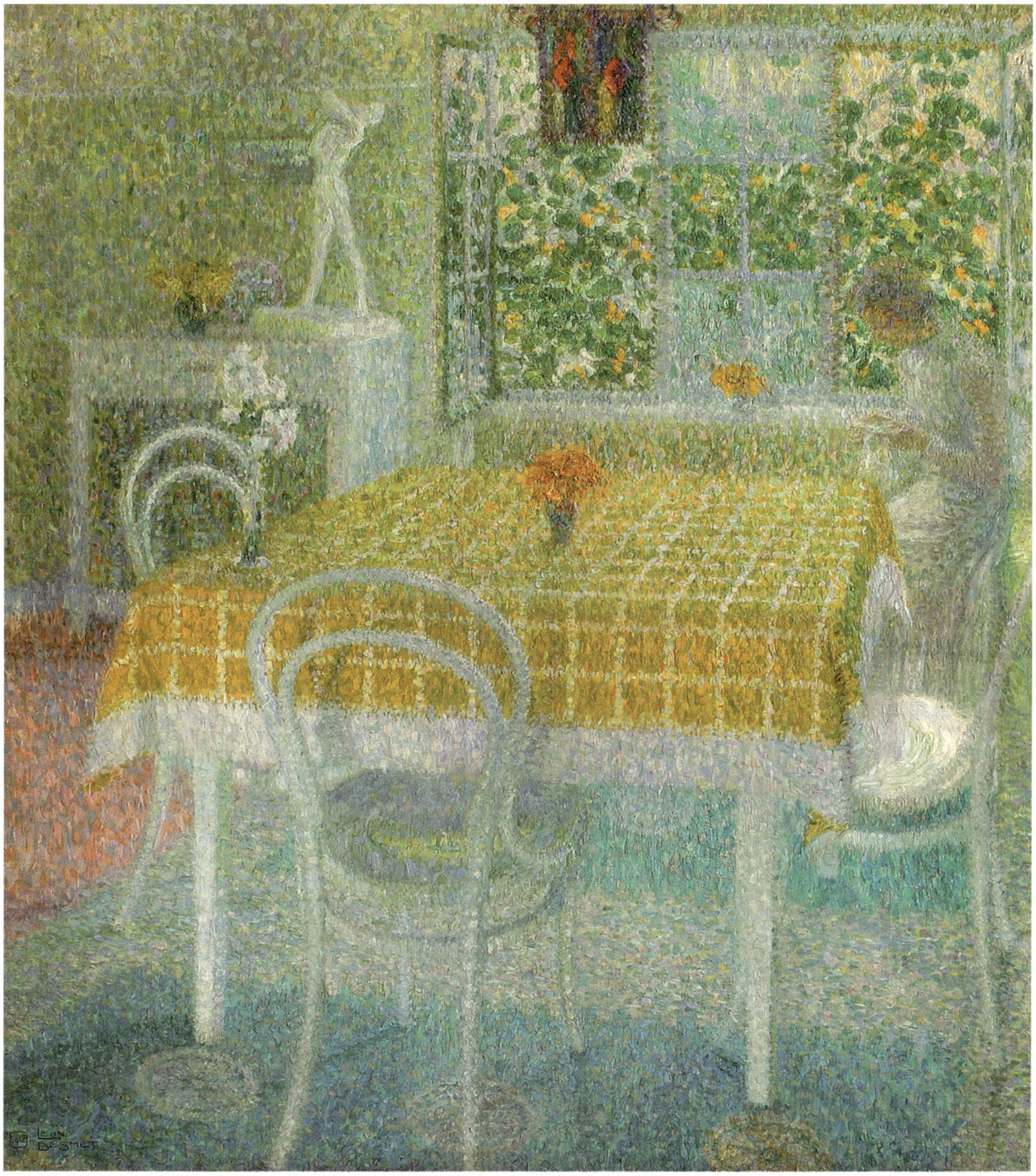

25. Léon de Smet (1881-1966)
The Table, 1910
Oil on canvas, 130 x 115 cm

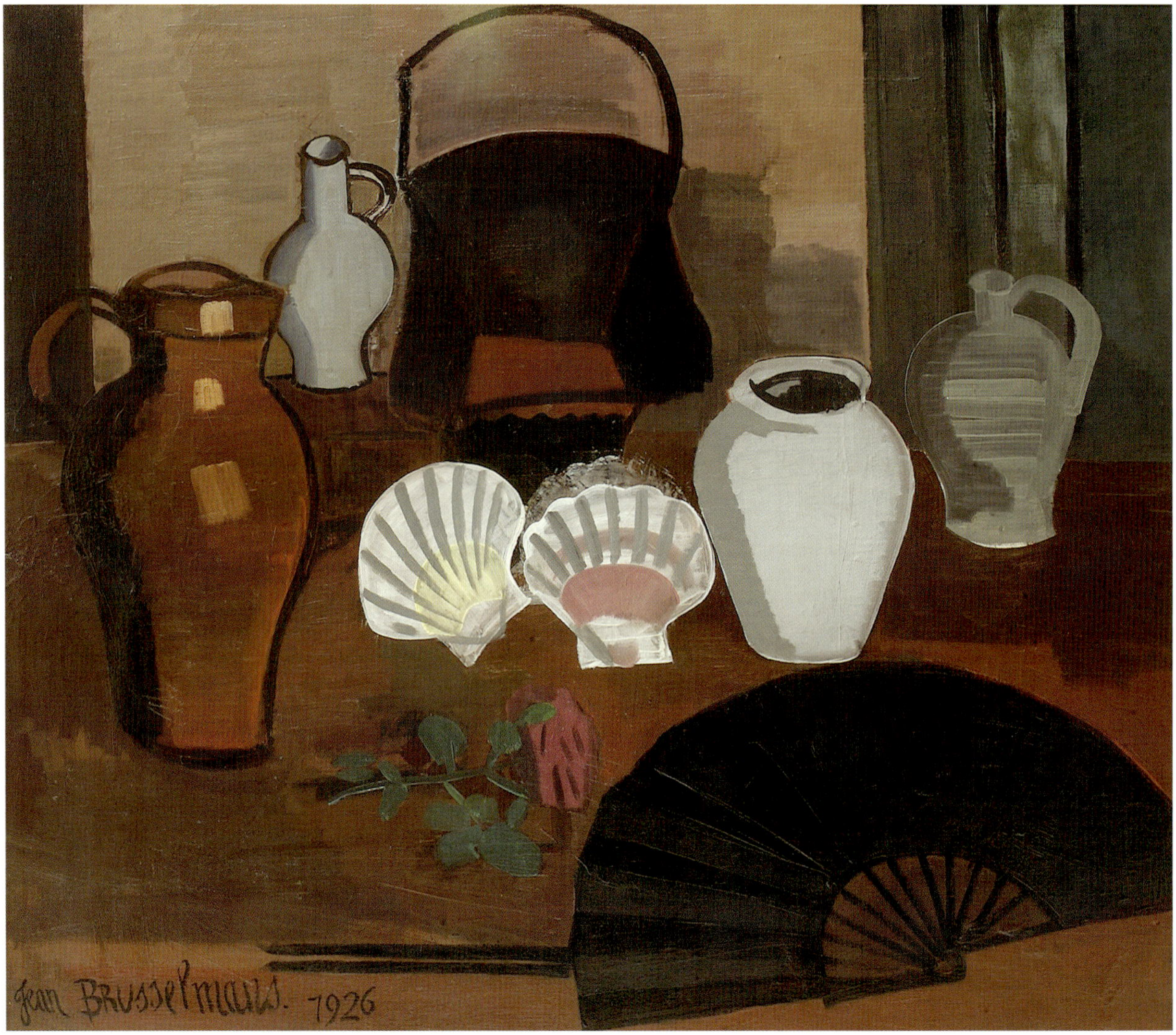

26. Jean Brusselmans (1884-1953)
Still Life with Two Shells, 1926
Oil on canvas, 99 x 111 cm

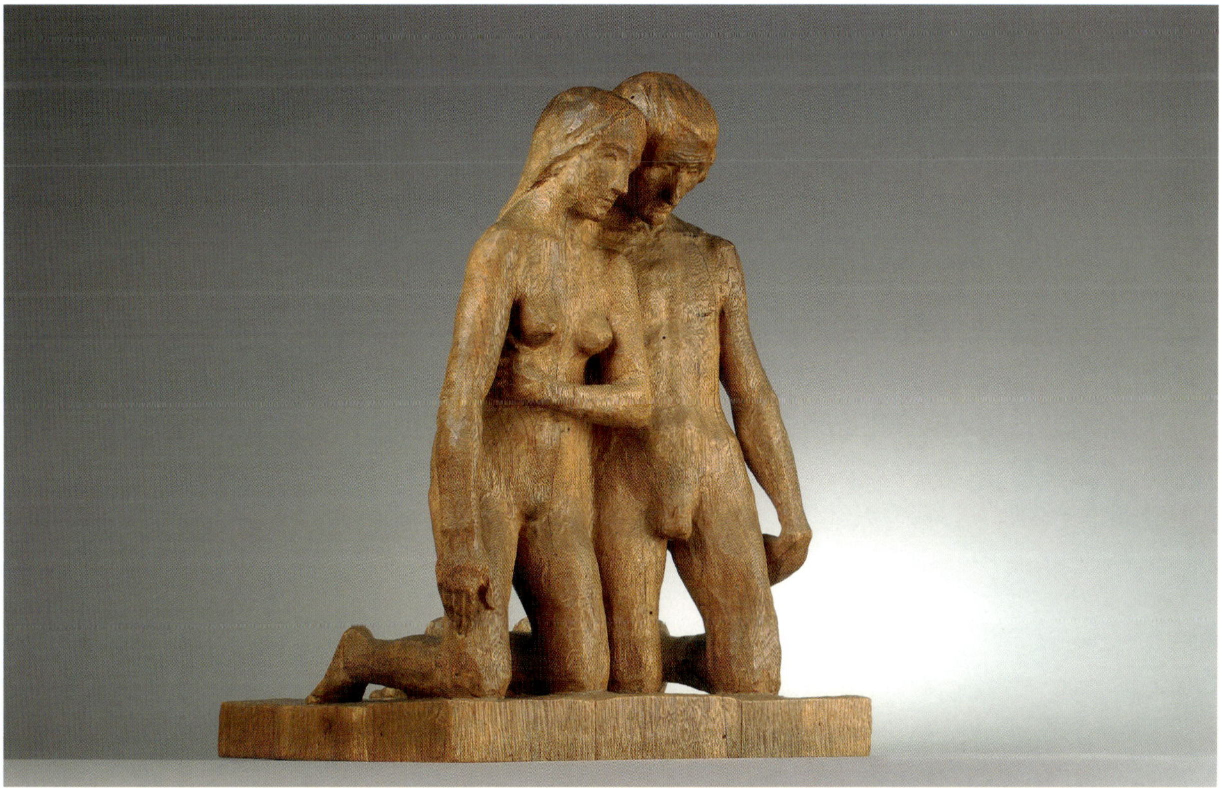

27. George Minne (1866-1941)
The Kneeling Pair, or *Adam and Eve*, 1889
Oak, 44 x 30 x 33 cm

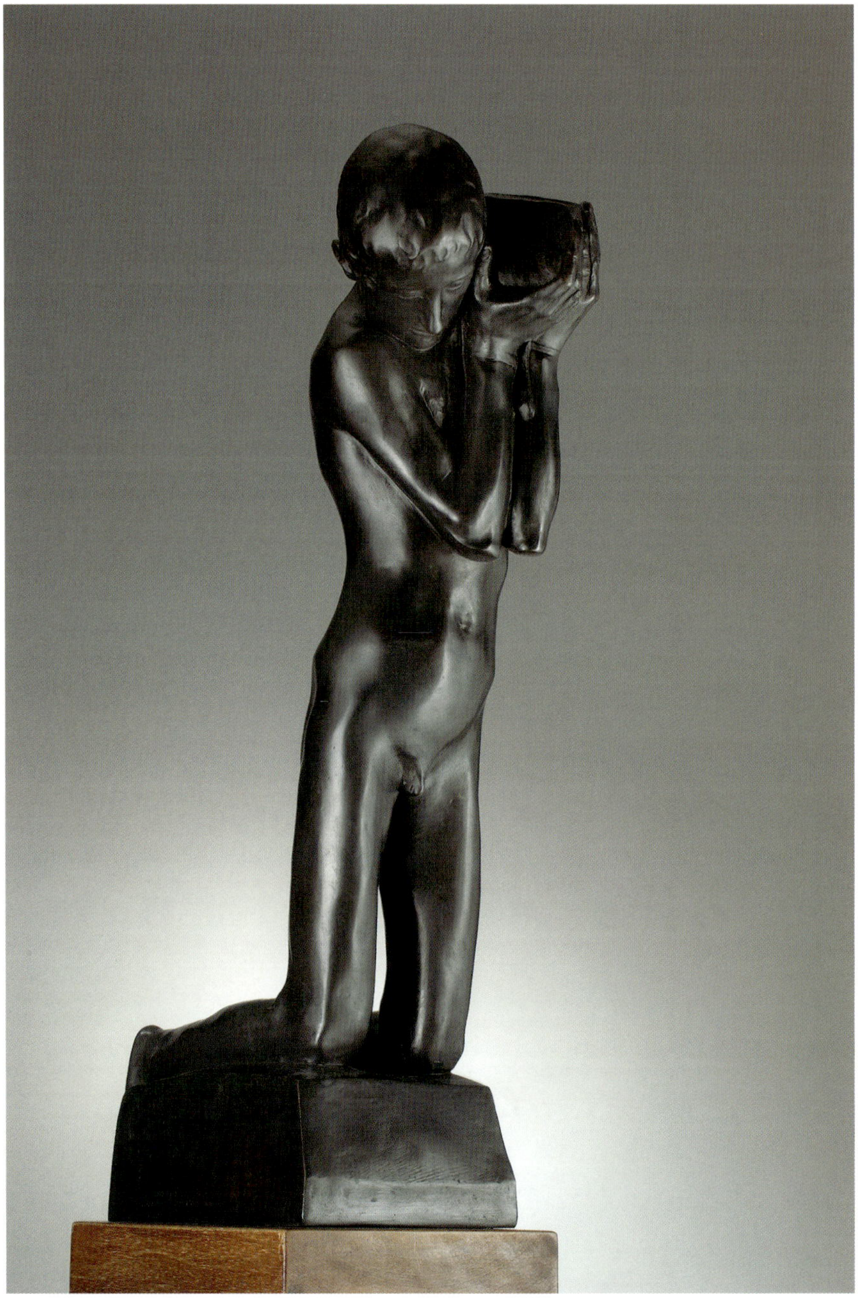

28. George Minne (1866-1941)
The Small Relic Bearer, 1897
Bronze, 64 x 17 x 42 cm

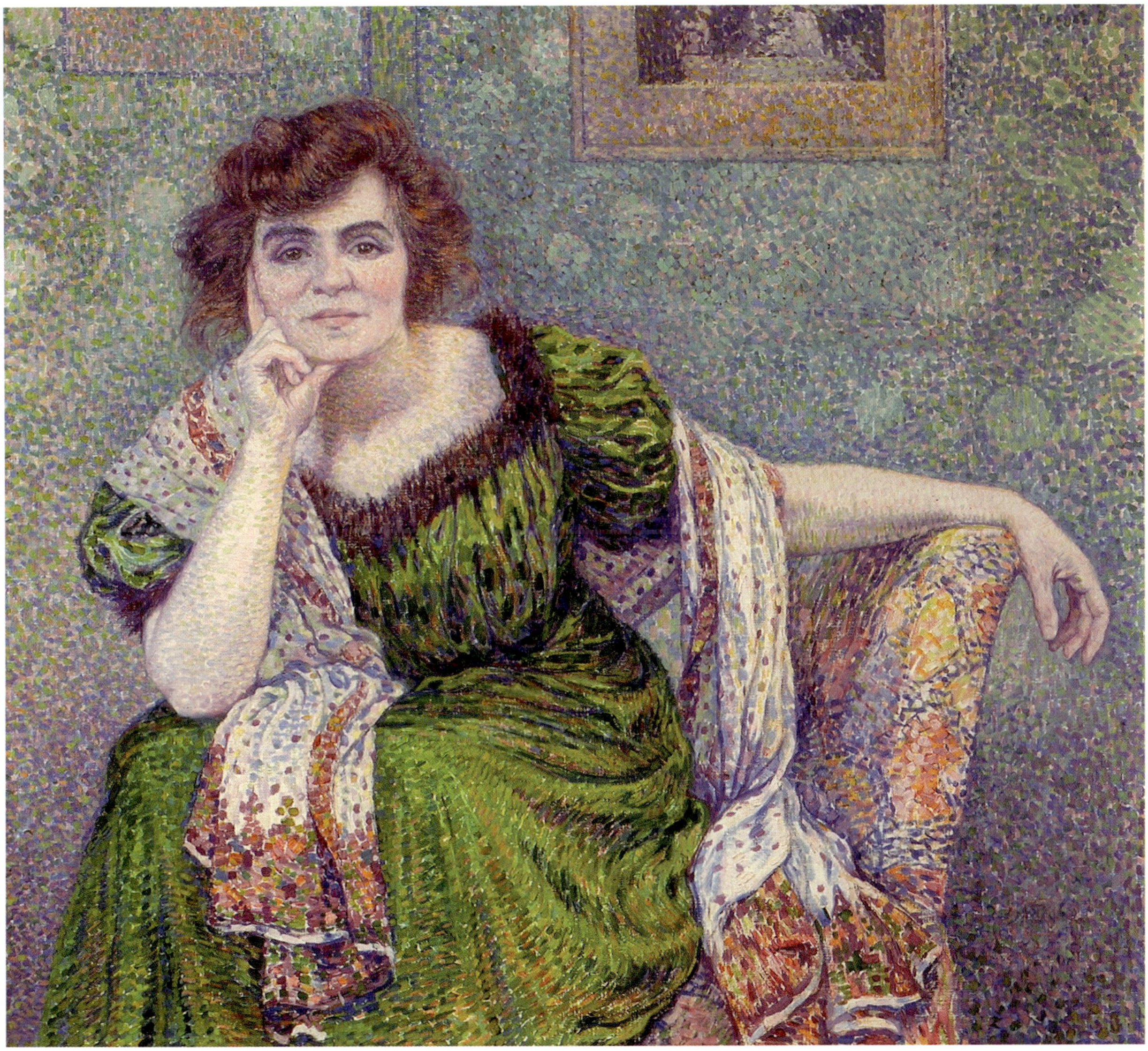

29. Théo van Rysselberghe (1861-1926)
Portrait of Claire Demolder, 1902
Oil on canvas, 97 x 104 cm

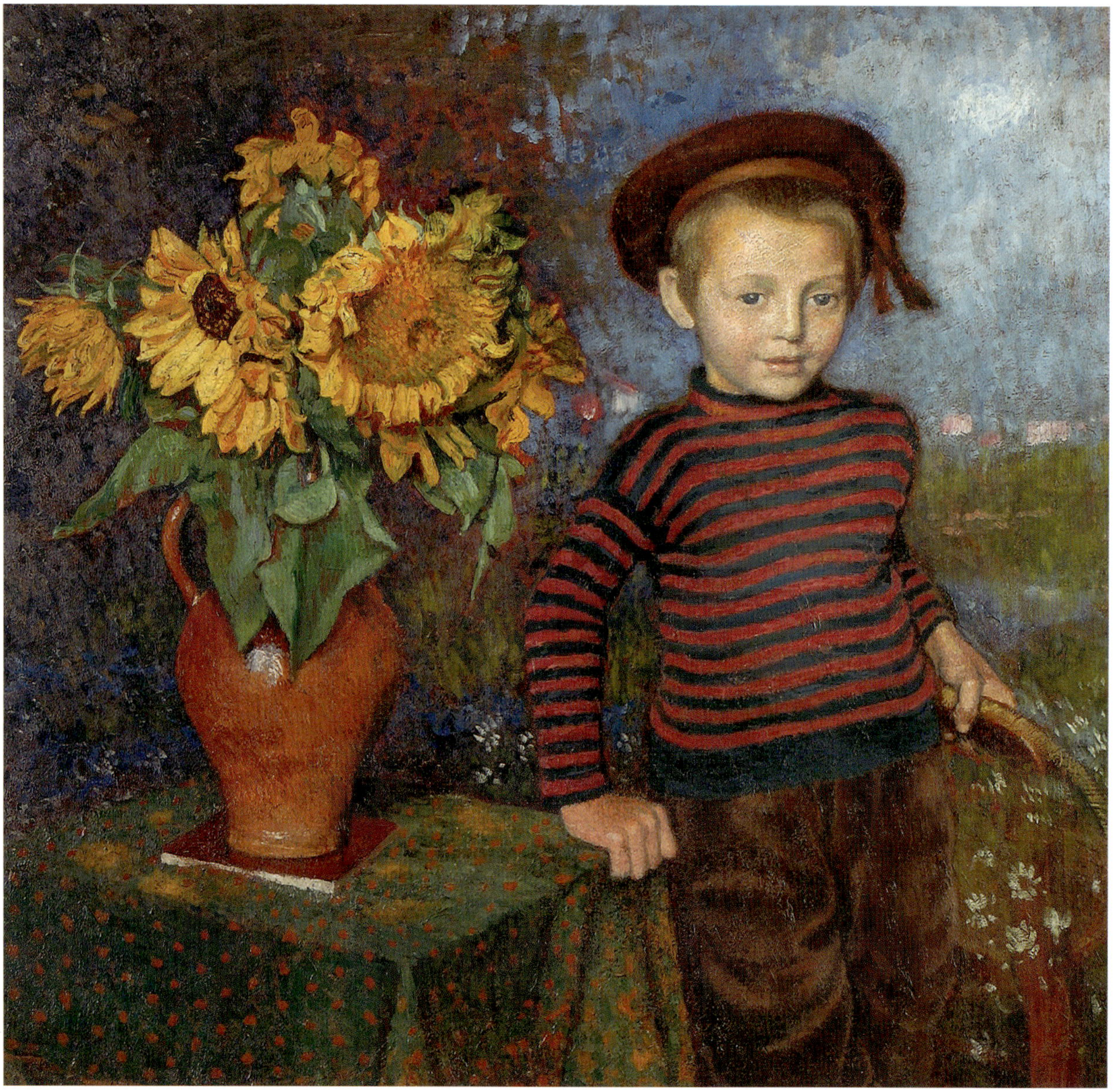

30. Georges Lemmen (1865-1916)
Little Pierre, c. 1901
Oil on canvas, 95 x 95 cm

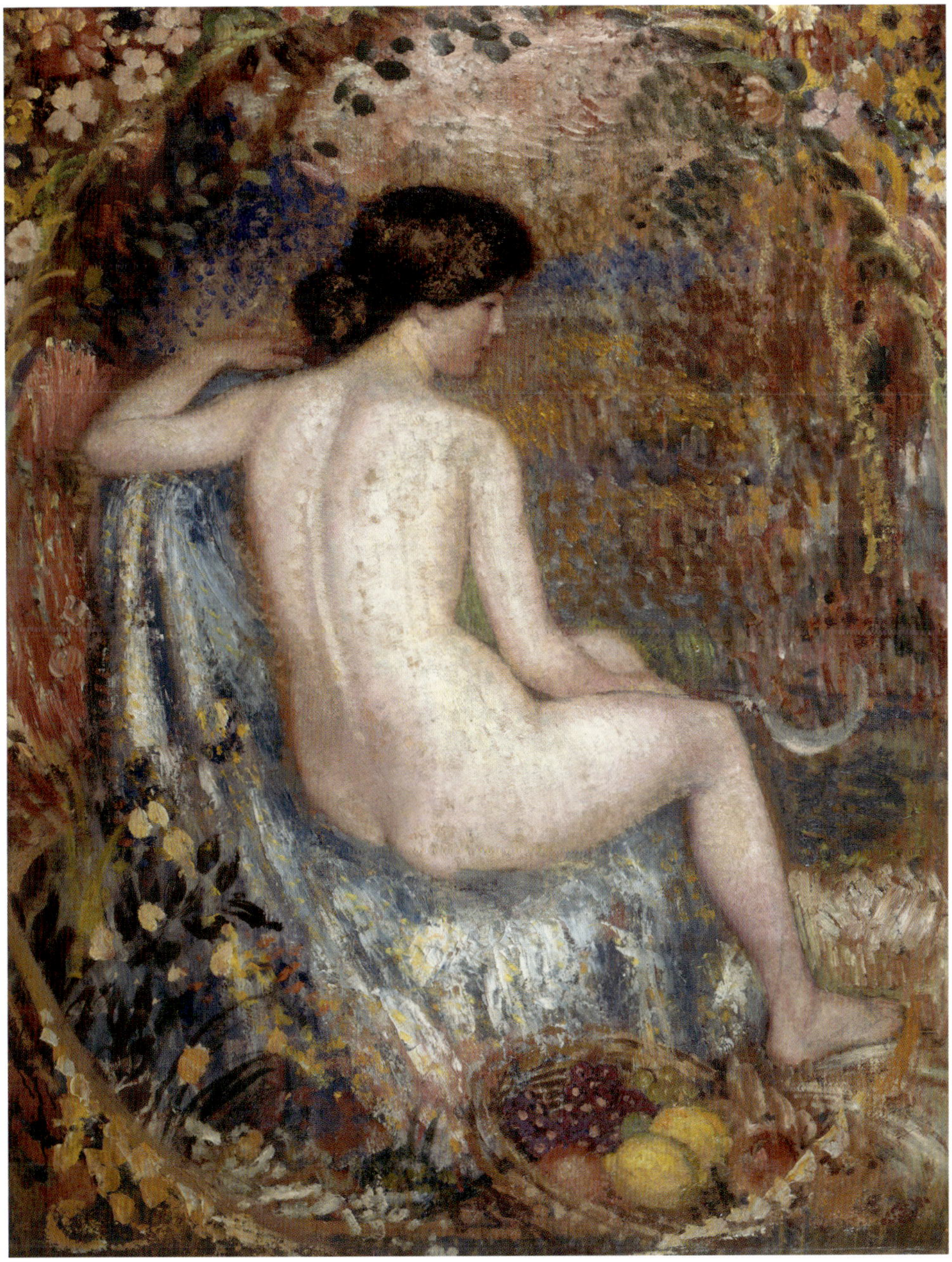

31. Georges Lemmen (1865-1916)
Nude, 1908
Oil, 94 x 70 cm

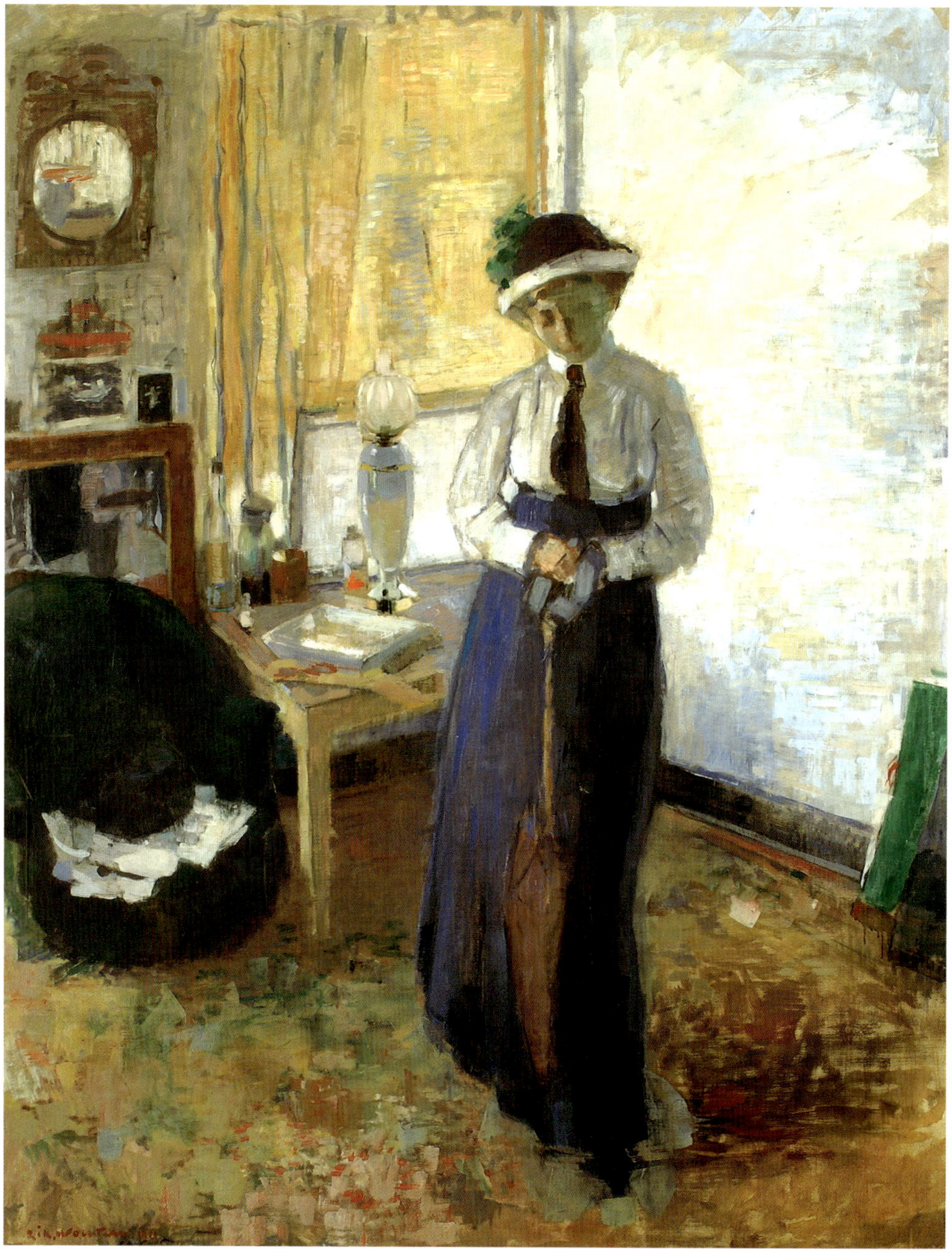

32. Rik Wouters (1882-1916)
Woman with Gray Gloves, 1911
Oil on canvas, 165.5 x 126 cm

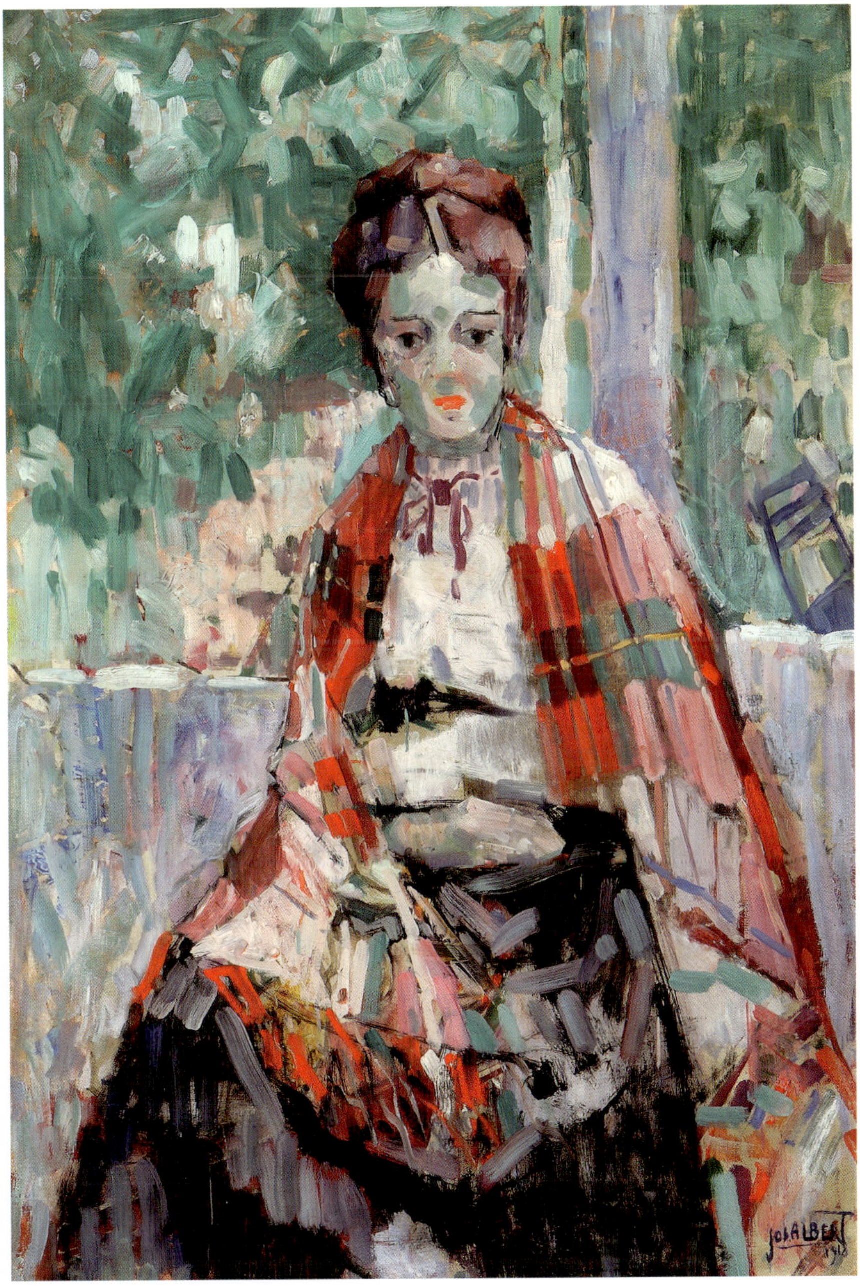

33. Jos Albert (1886-1981)
Portrait of the Artist's Wife with a Scottish Shawl, 1918
Oil on canvas, 103 x 67 cm

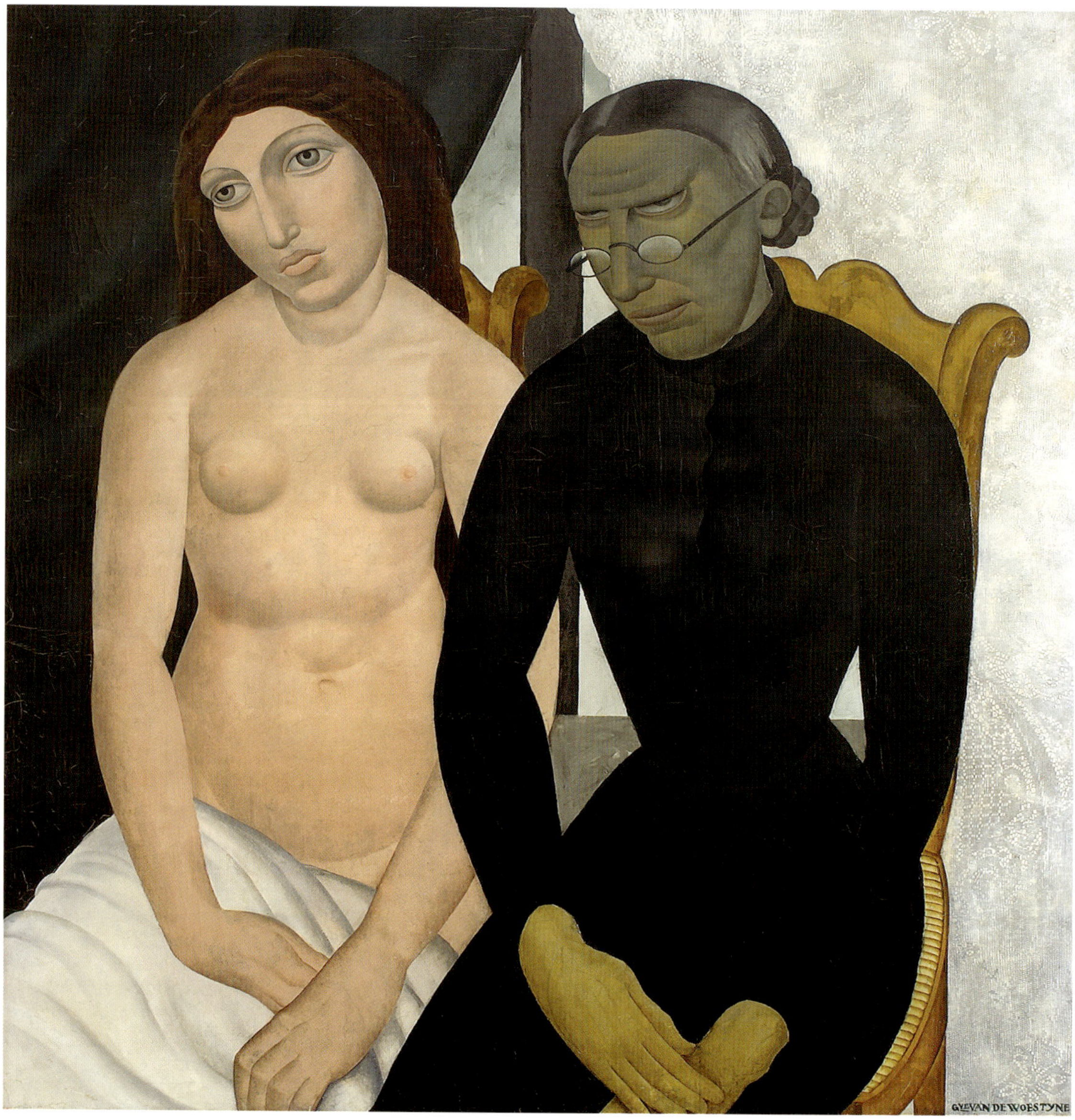

34. Gustave van de Woestyne (1881-1947)
Two Women, 1926
Oil on canvas, 150 x 145 cm

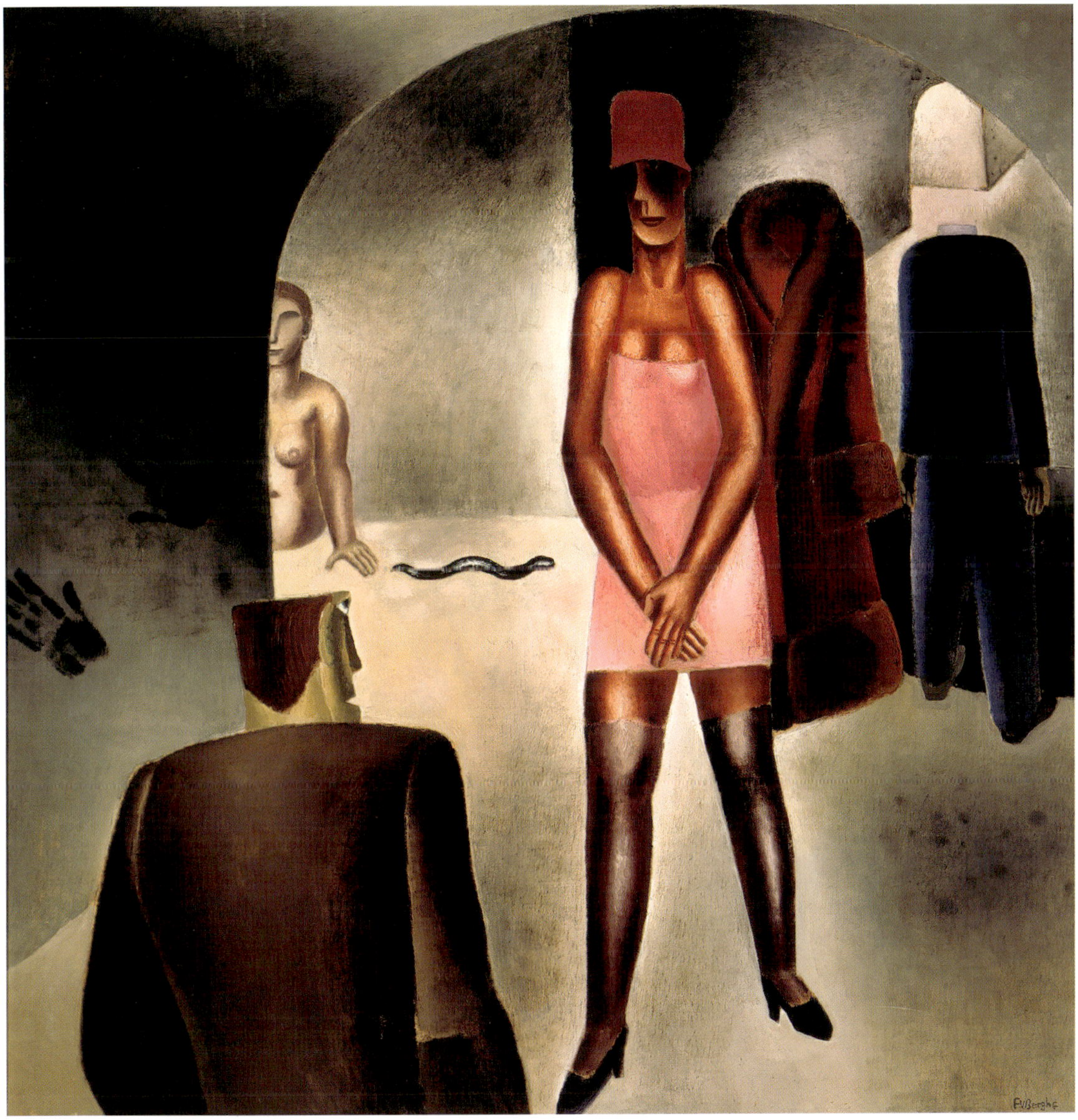

35. Frits van den Berghe (1883-1939)
Corridors, 1927
Oil on canvas, 116 x 111 cm

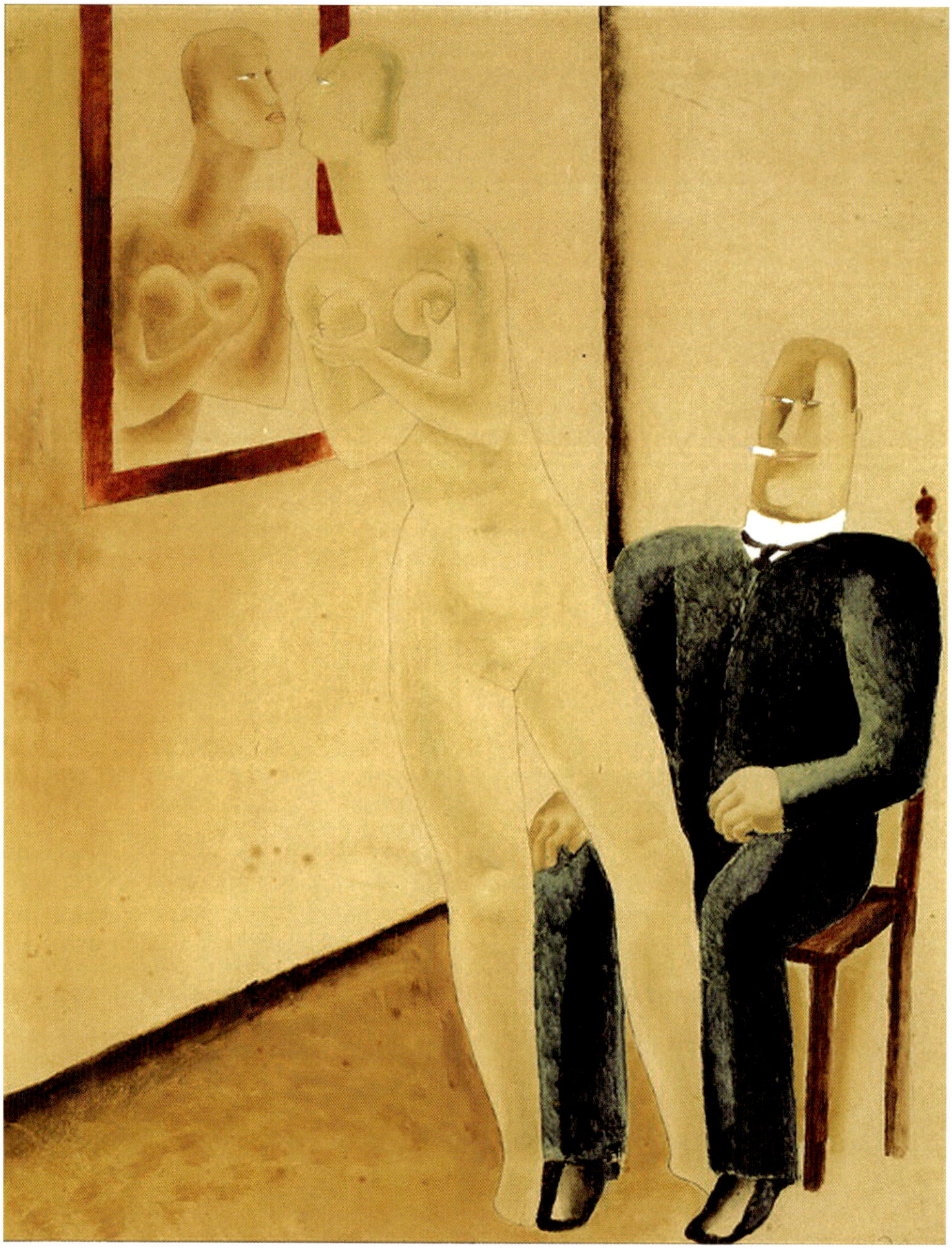

36. Frits van den Berghe (1883-1939)
The Mirror, 1924-25
Pencil, watercolor, and gouache on paper, 57 x 44 cm

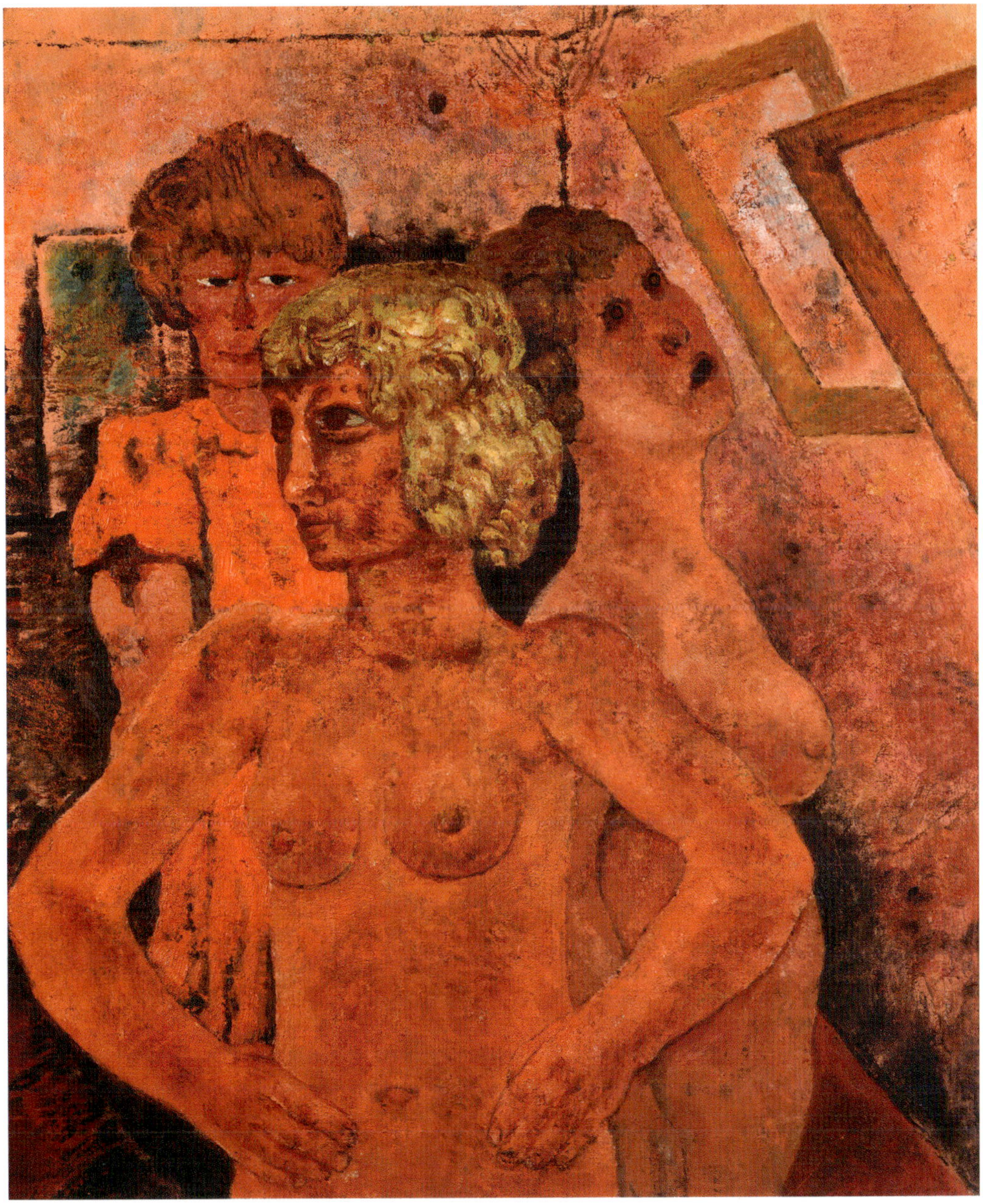

37. Frits van den Berghe (1883-1939)
Filles d'eau douce, 1931
Oil on canvas, 87 x 72 cm

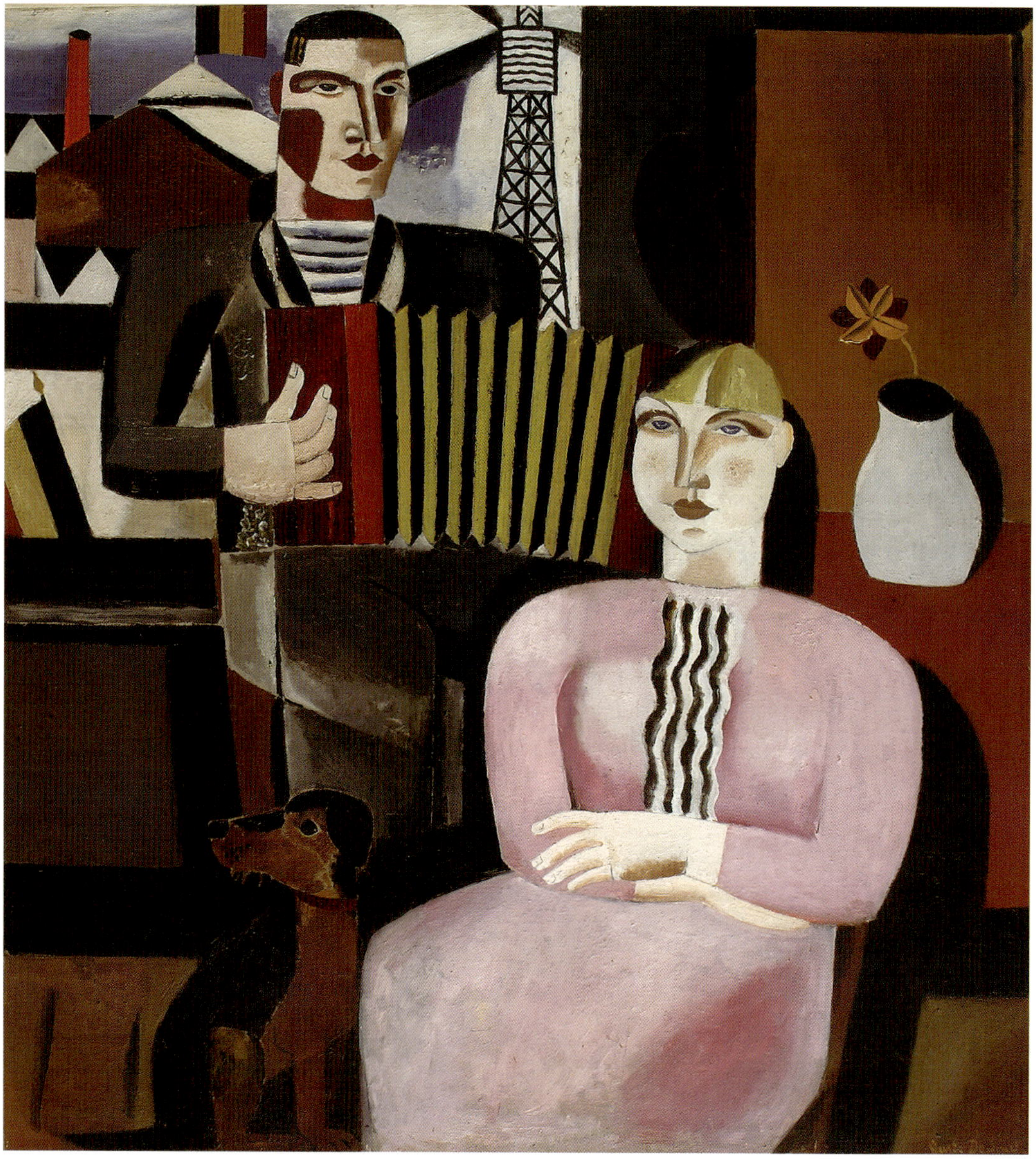

38. Gustave de Smet (1877-1943)
The Accordion Player, 1926
Oil on canvas, 135 x 120 cm

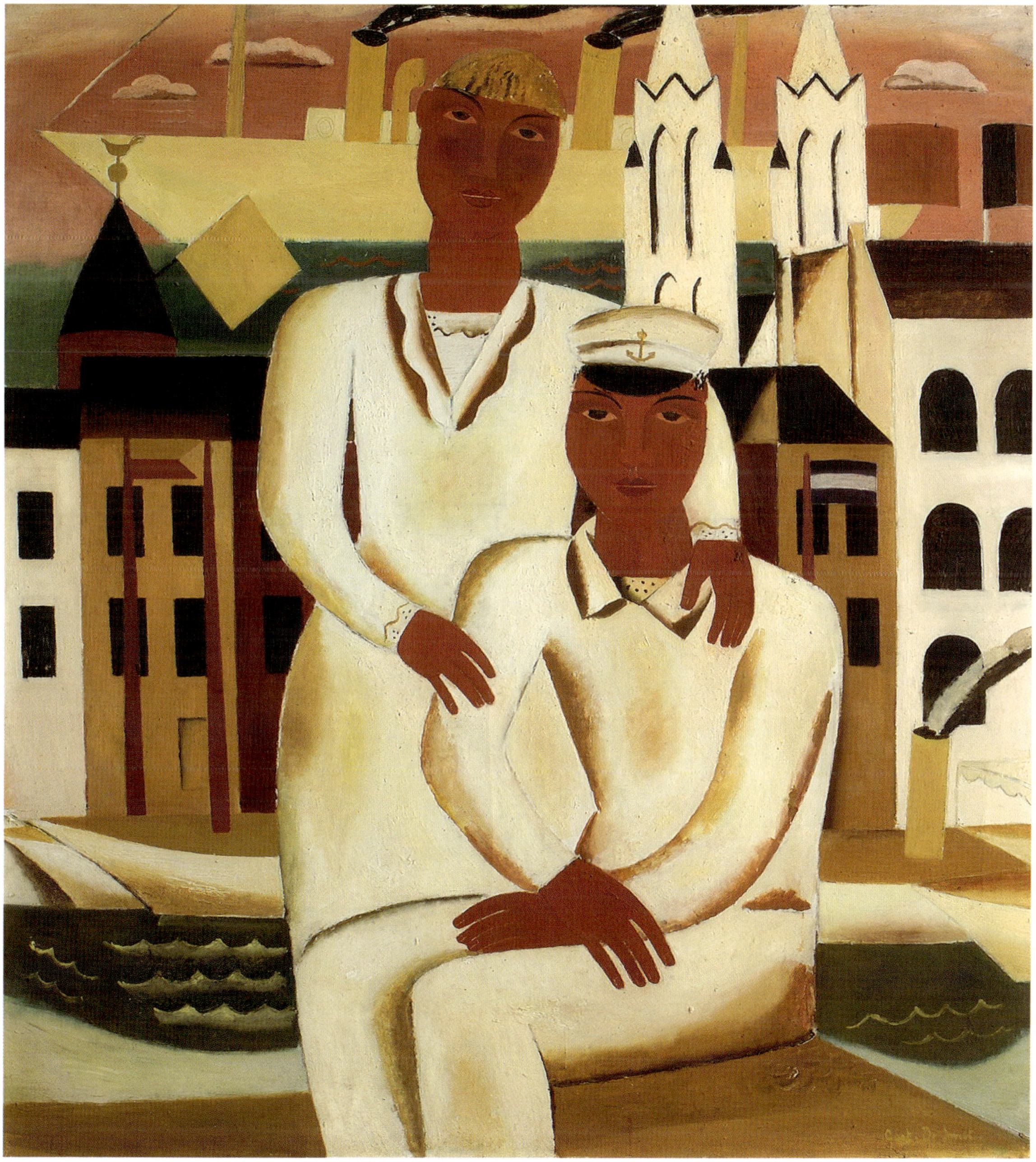

39. Gustave de Smet (1877-1943)
De Jonge Kapitein (The Young Captain), 1927
Oil on canvas, 135 x 120 cm

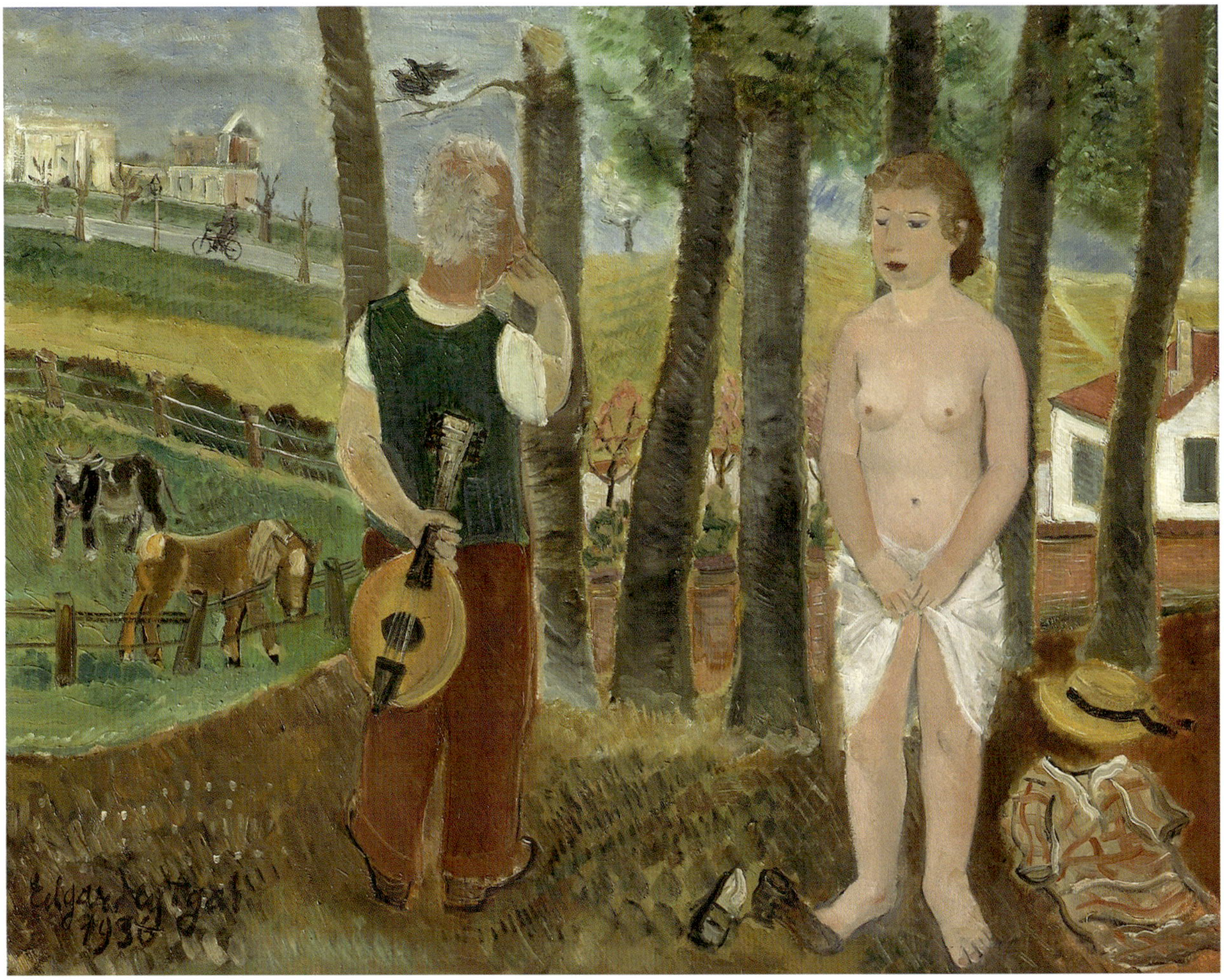

40. Edgard Tytgat (1879-1957)
The Interrupted Walk, 1936
Oil on canvas, 81 x 100 cm

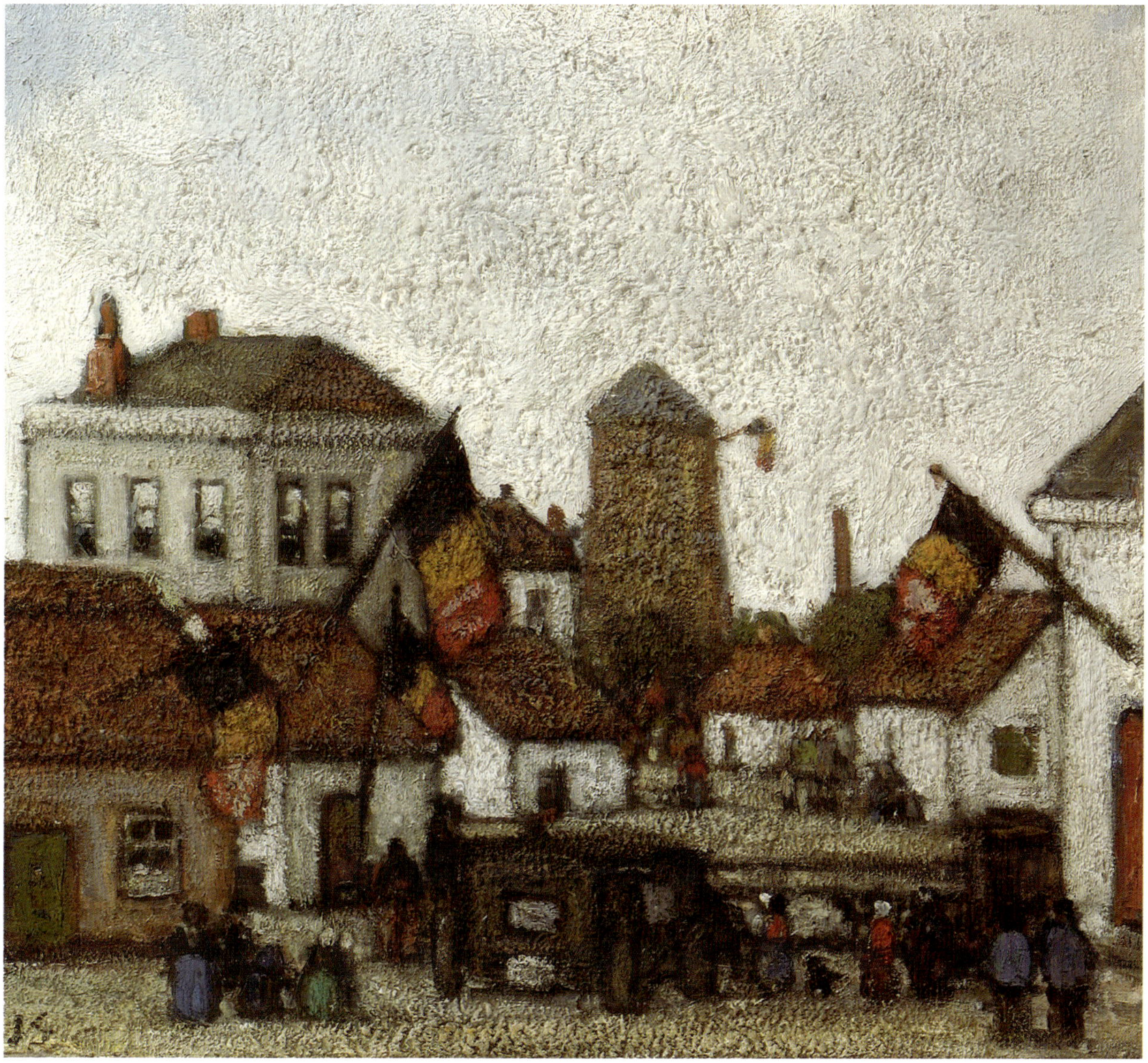

41. Jakob Smits (1855-1928)
The Armistice, 1919
Oil on canvas, 80 x 85 cm

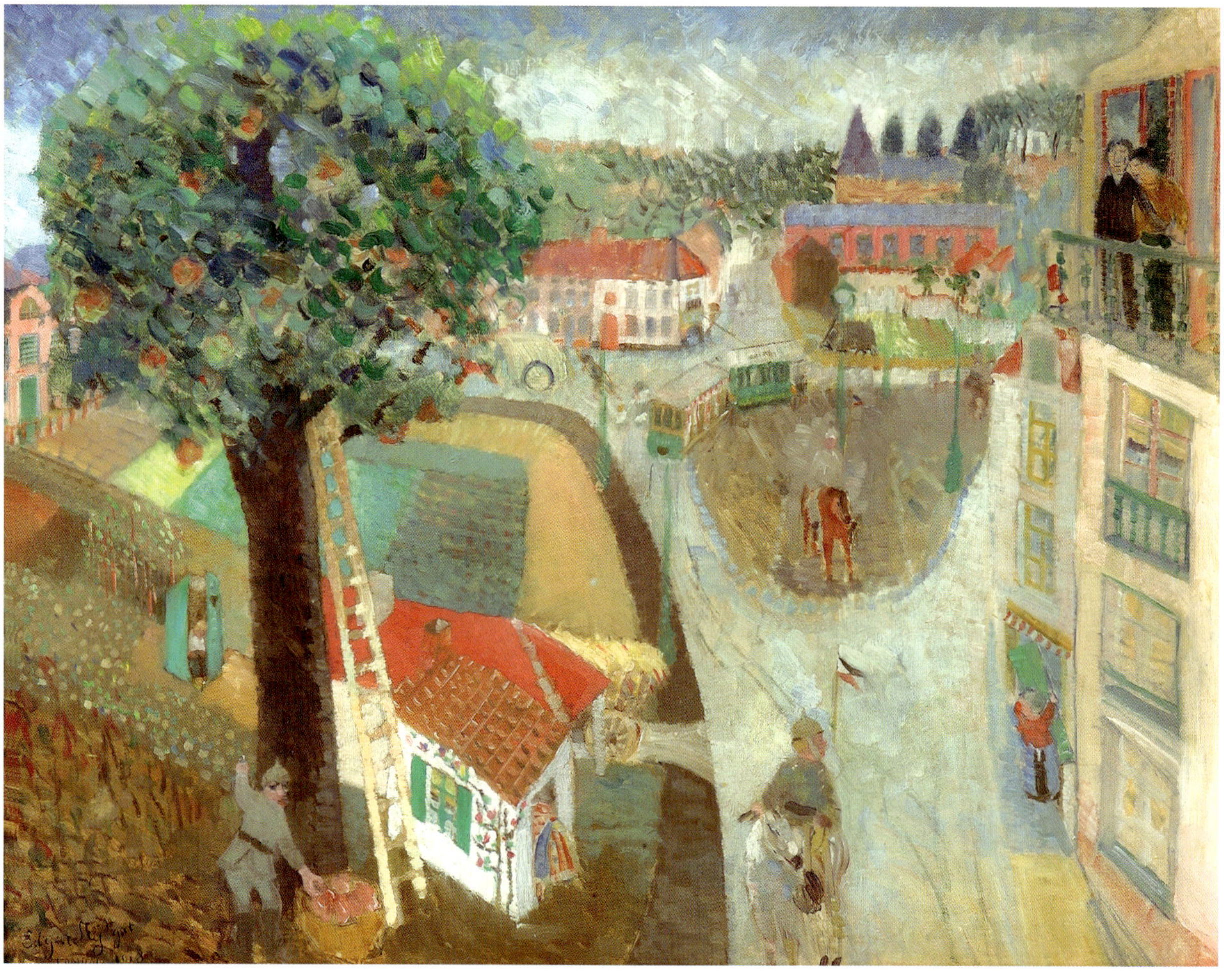

42. Edgard Tytgat (1879-1957)
The First Invaders at Watermael, 1918
Oil on canvas, 64 x 76 cm

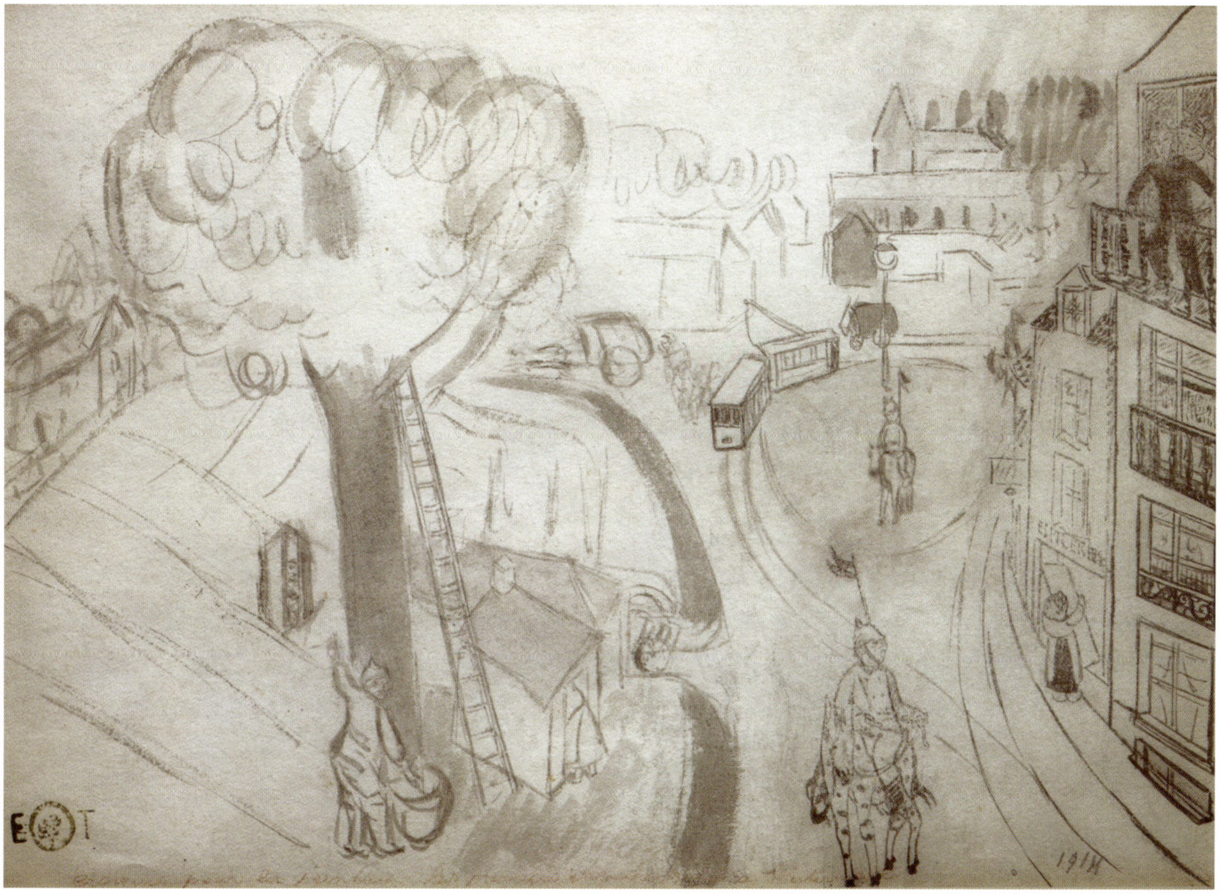

43. Edgard Tytgat (1879-1957)
The First Invaders at Watermael, 1914
Ink wash on paper, 24 x 33 cm

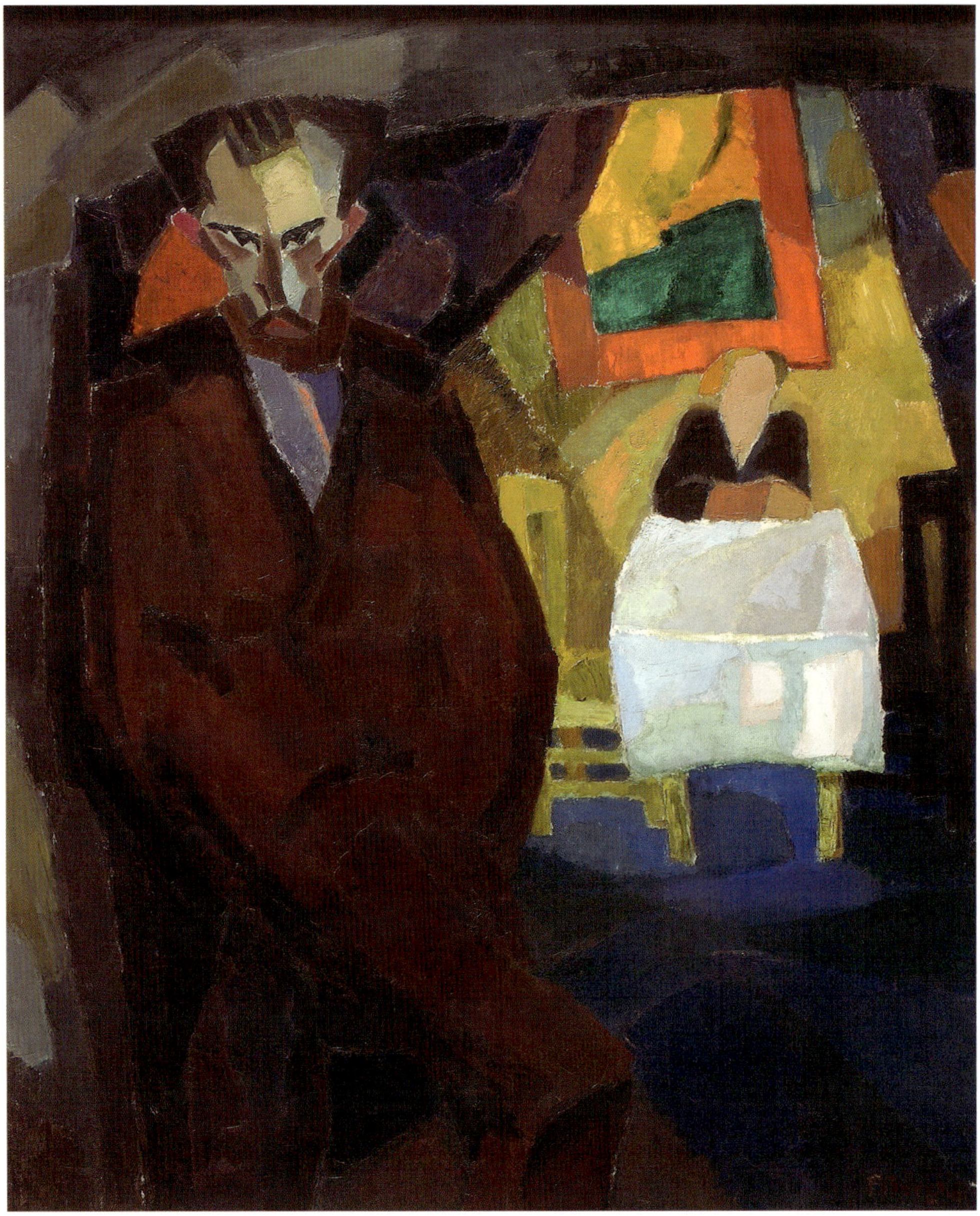

44. Frits van den Berghe (1883-1939)
Obsession III, 1919
Oil on canvas, 141 x 112 cm

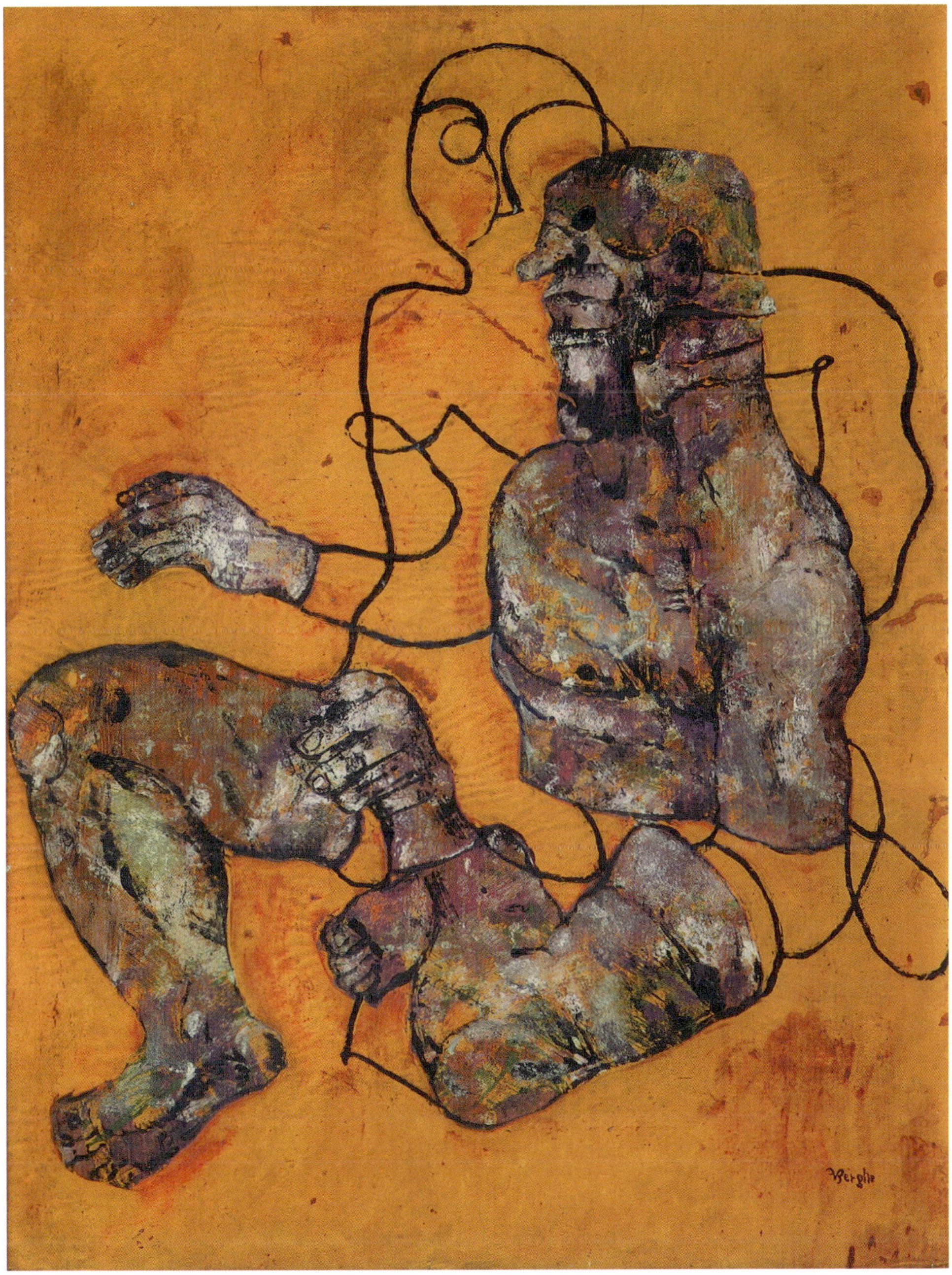

45. Frits van den Berghe (1883-1939)
The Last Gunner, 1929
Papier marouflé, 63 x 46 cm

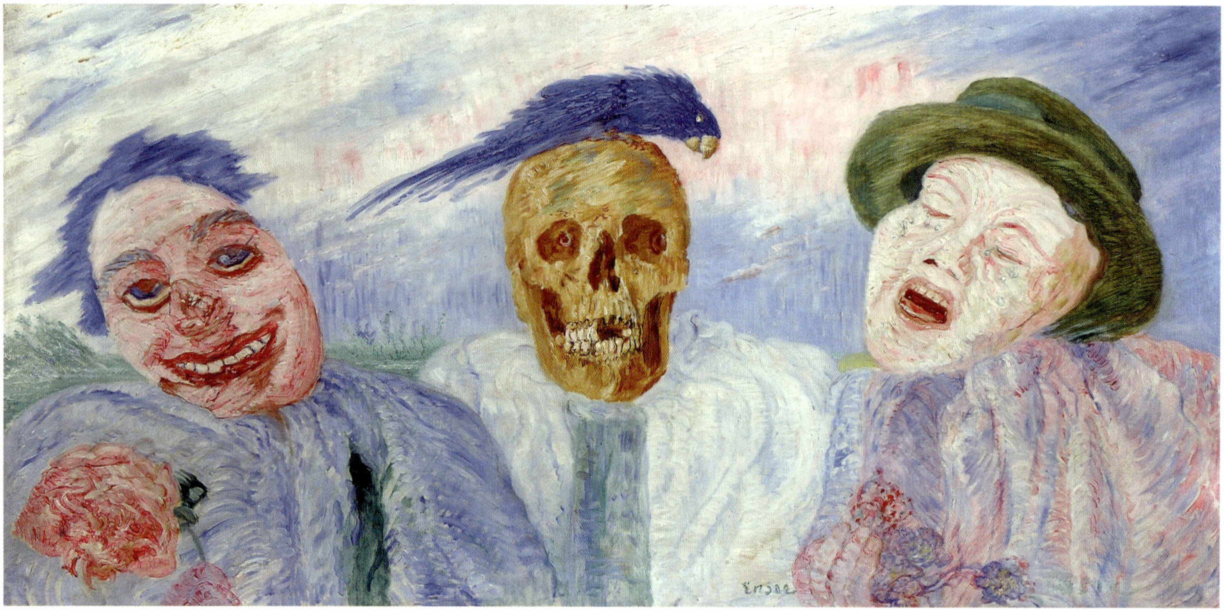

46. James Ensor (1860-1949)
From Laughter to Tears, 1908
Oil on canvas, 50.5 x 100 cm

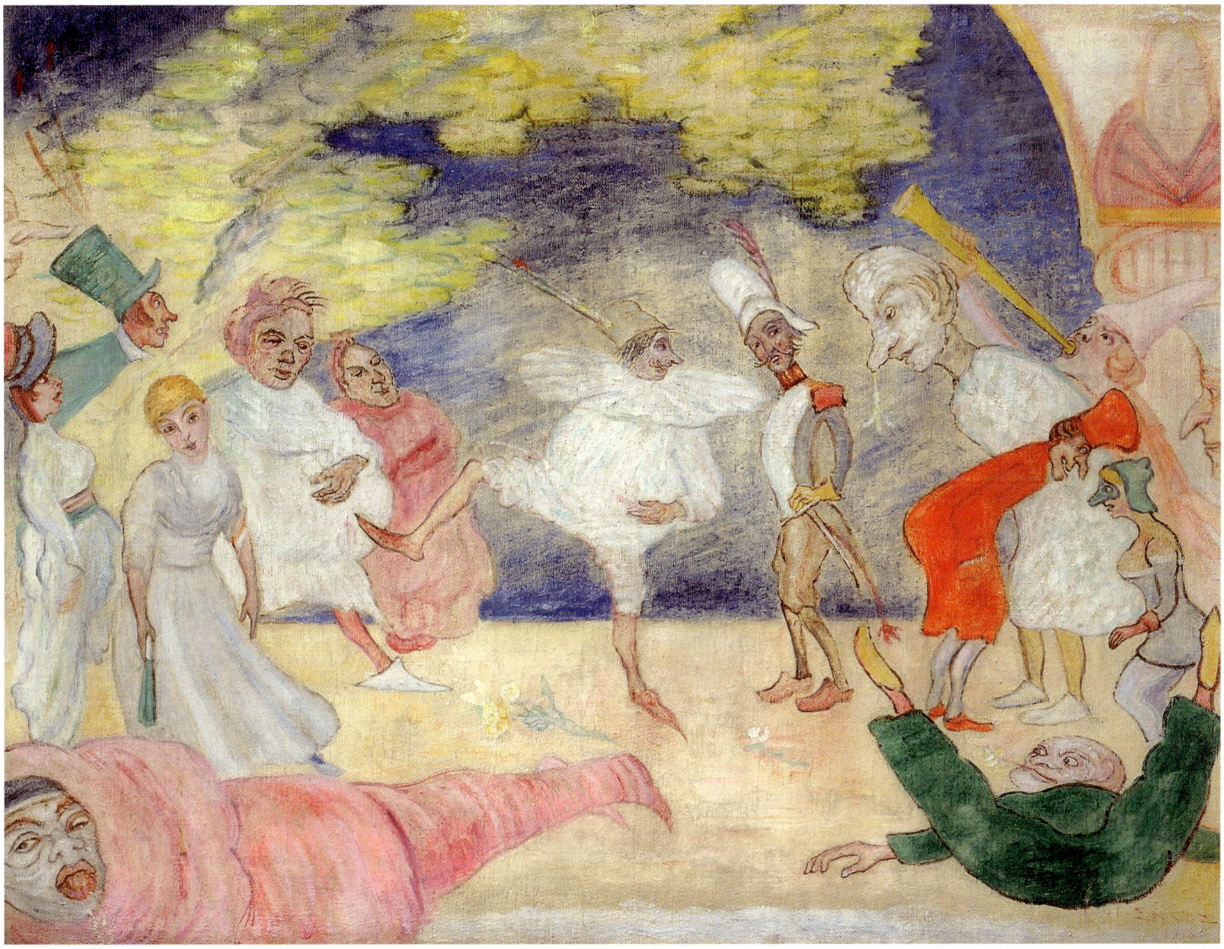

47. James Ensor (1860-1949)
The Fantastic Ballet, 1918
Oil on canvas, 81 x 100.5 cm

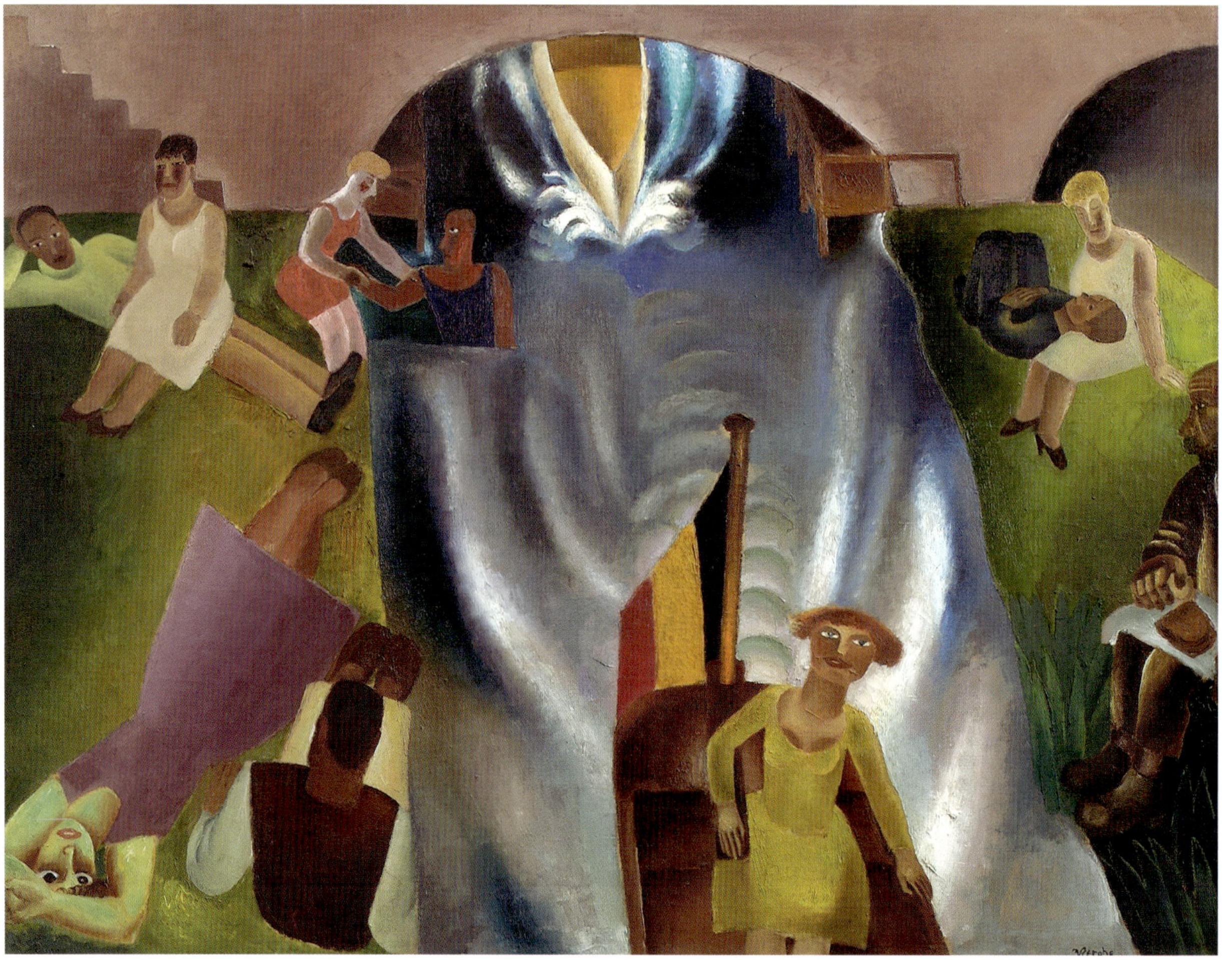

48. Frits van den Berghe (1883-1939)
The Riverbanks, 1926
Oil on canvas, 94.5 X 121 cm

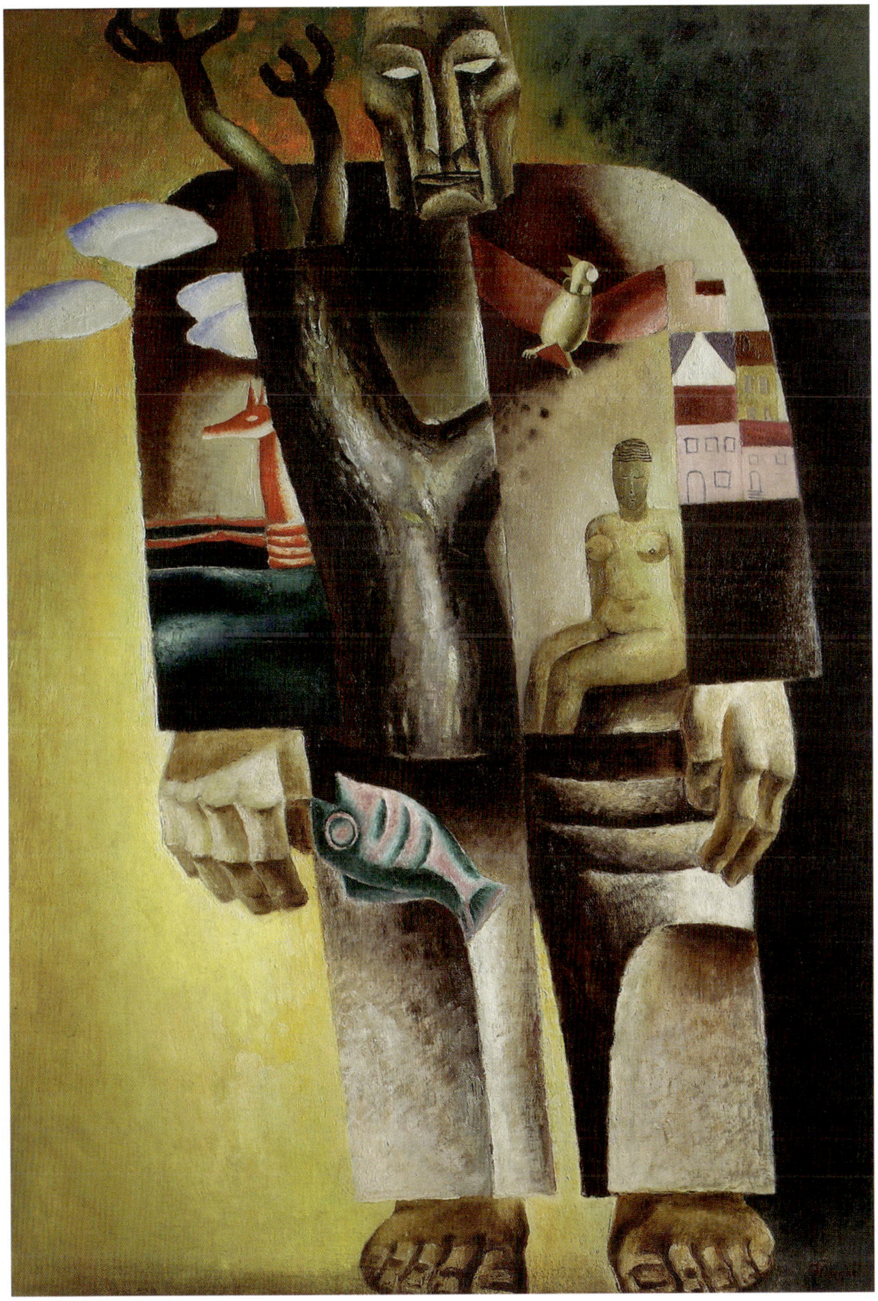

49. Frits van den Berghe (1883-1939)
The Geographic Man, 1927
Oil on canvas, 168 x 112 cm

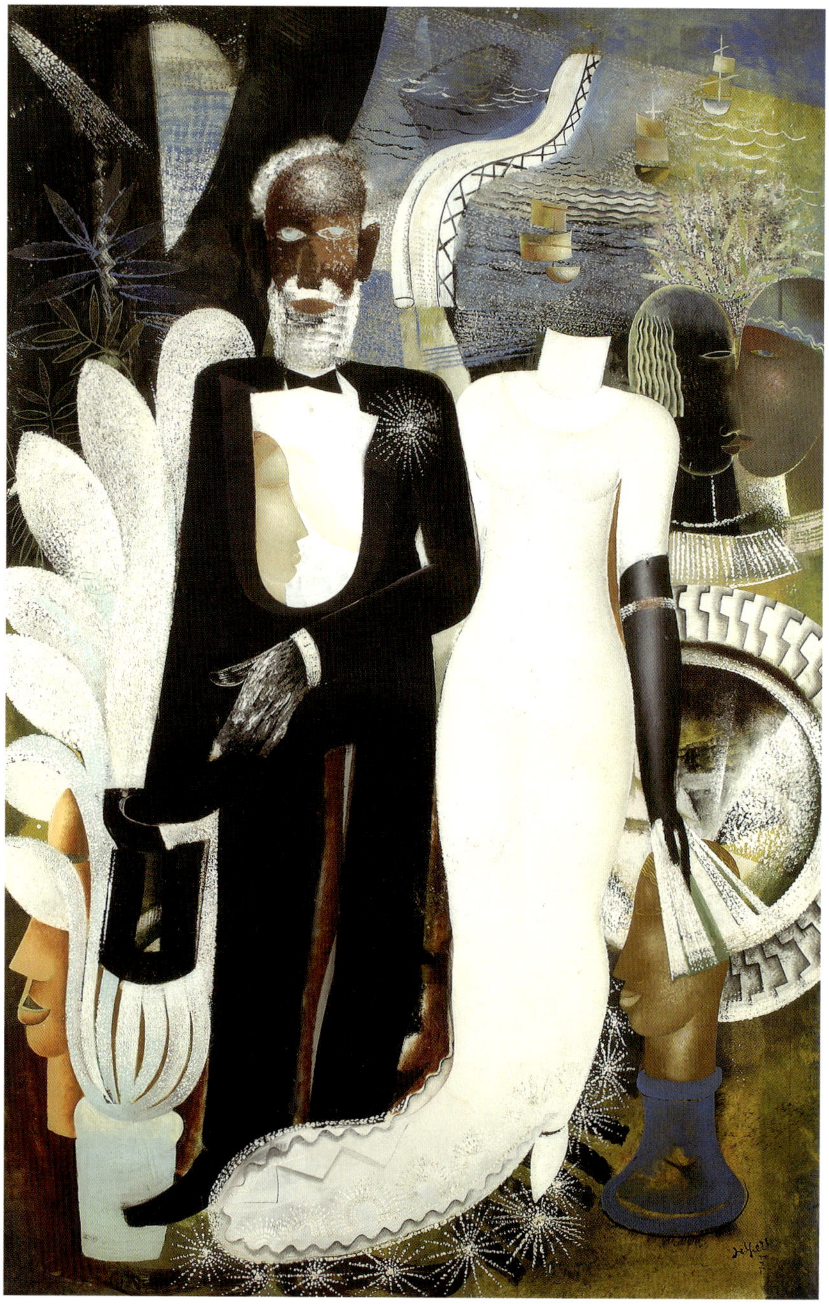

50. Floris Jespers (1889-1965)
Marriage of Convenience, 1927
Oil on canvas, 203 x 128 cm

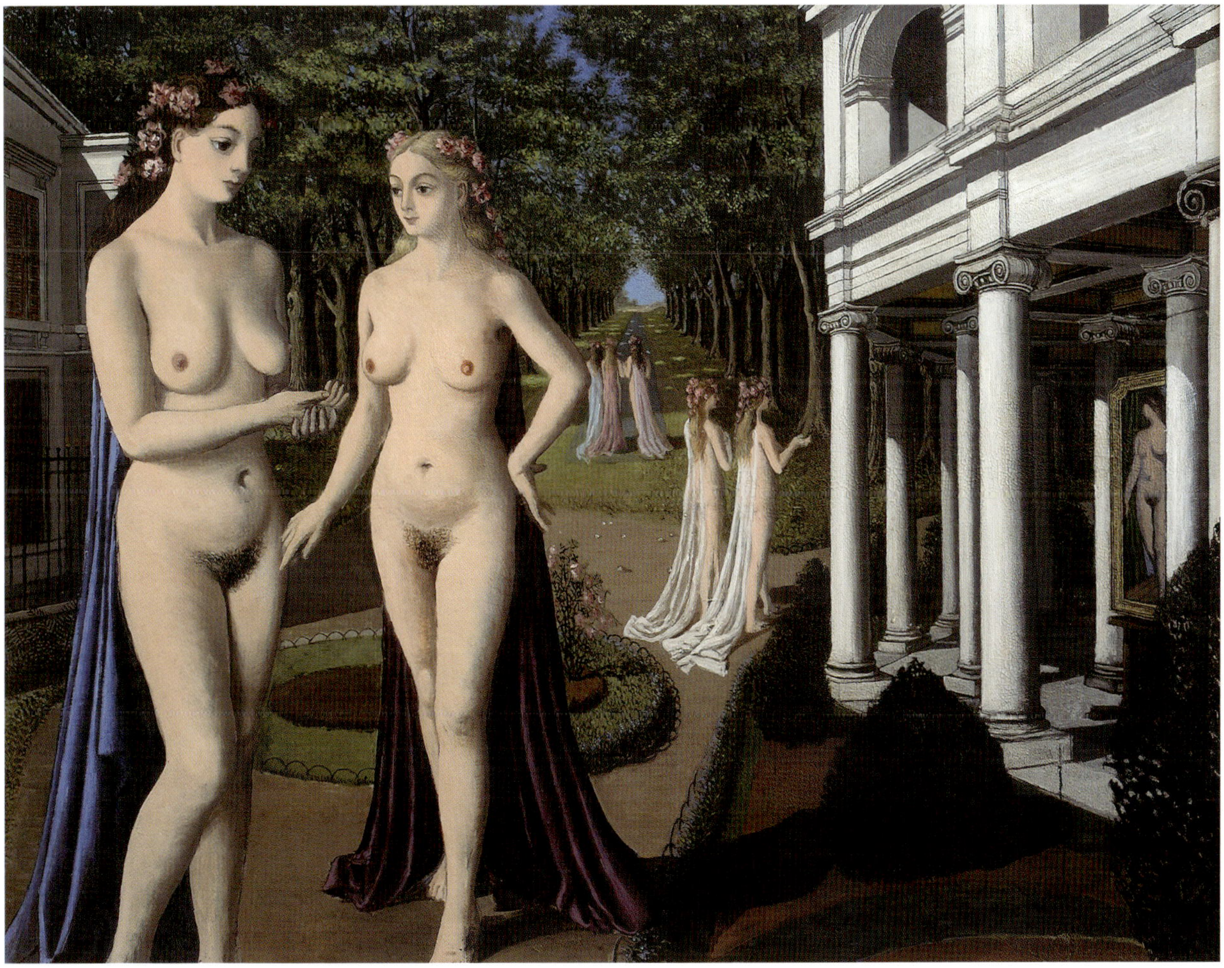

51. Paul Delvaux (1897-1994)
The Riddle, 1946
Oil on panel, 90 x 120 cm

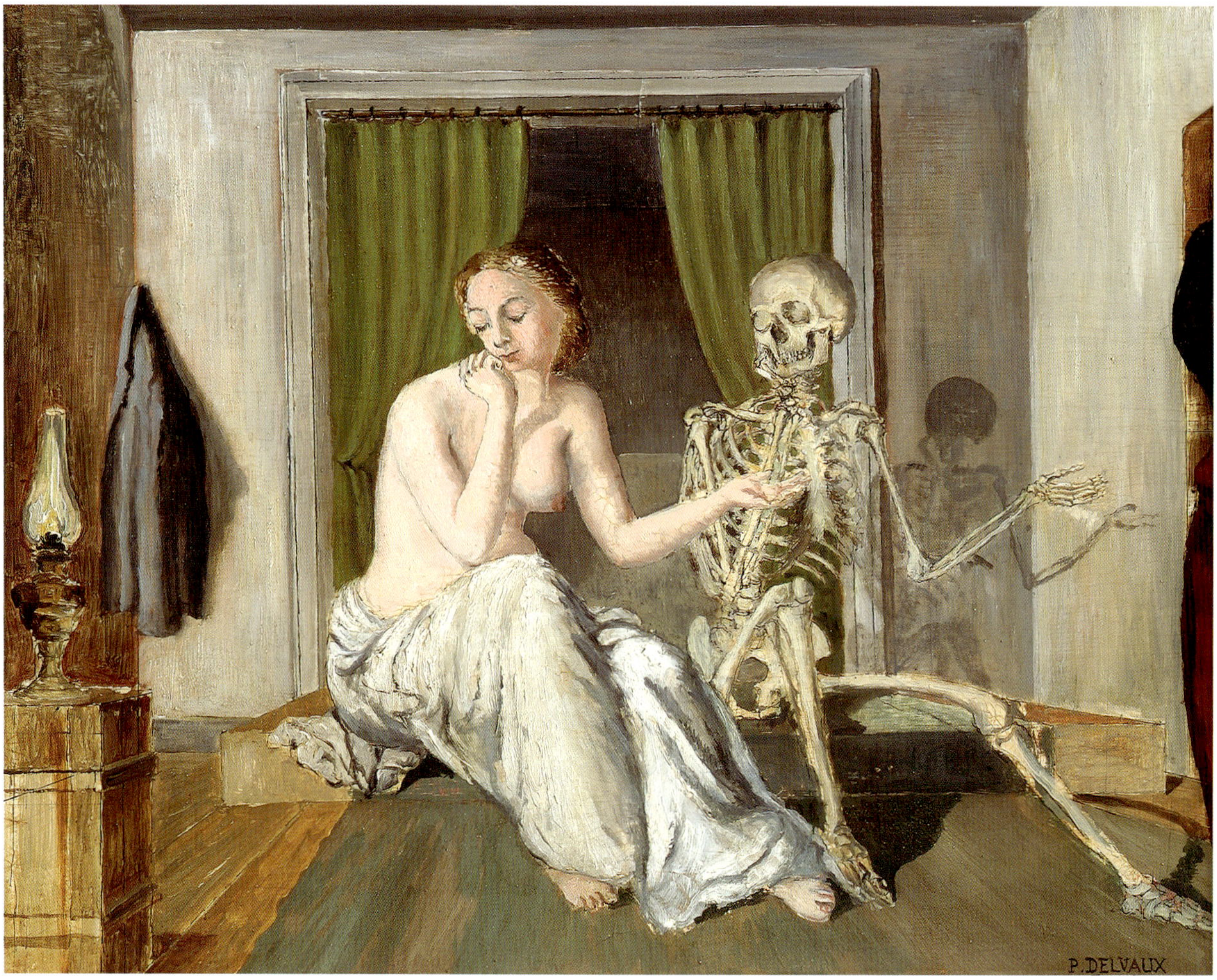

52. Paul Delvaux (1897-1994)
The Conversation, 1944
Oil on cardboard, 50 x 61 cm

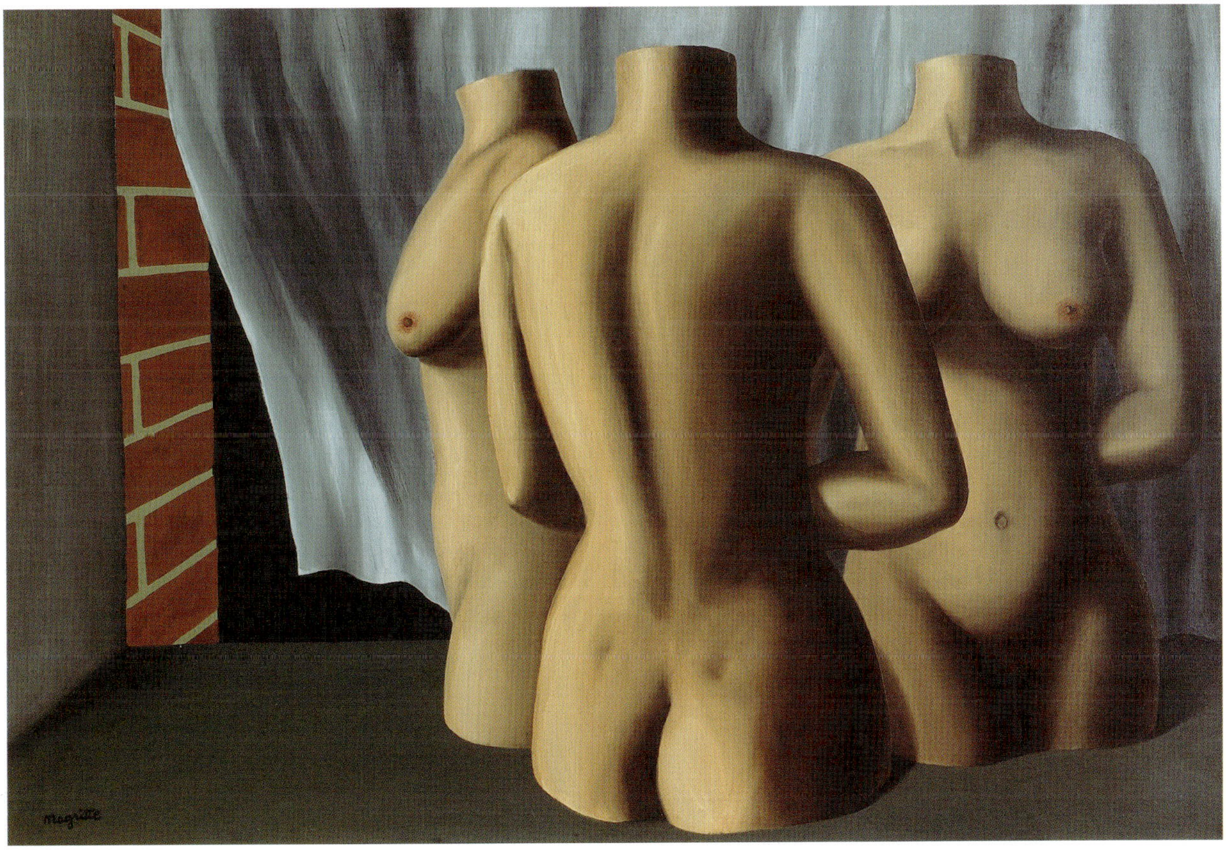

53. René Magritte (1878-1967)
Dialogue Raveled by the Wind, 1928
Oil on canvas, 81 x 116 cm